Educating the Gendered Citizen

Globalisation and global human rights are the two major forces in the twenty-first century which are likely to shape the sort of learner citizen created by the educational system. Schools will be expected to prepare young men and women for global as well as national citizenship. Male and female citizens will need to adapt to new social conditions, only some of which will encourage gender equality.

This book offers a unique introduction to the contribution that sociological research on the education of the citizen can make to these national and global debates. It brings together, for the first time, a selection of influential new and previously published papers by Madeleine Arnot and her colleagues on the theme of gender, education and citizenship. It describes feminist challenges to liberal democracy, the gendered construction of the 'good citizen' and citizenship education; it explores the implications of social change for the learner citizen and offers alternative gender-sensitive models of global citizenship education.

Reaching right to the heart of current debates, the chapters focus on:

- feminist democratic values in education
- teachers' constructions of the gendered citizen in Europe
- the inclusion of women's rights into English citizenship textbooks
- gender struggles for equality in school pedagogy and curriculum
- the implications of personalised learning for the individualised learner citizen
- globalisation and gender controversies in global citizenship education.

It is an invaluable text for all those interested in citizenship education, gender studies, sociology of education, educational policy studies, critical pedagogy and curriculum studies and international or comparative education.

Madeleine Arnot is Professor in Sociology of Education at the University of Cambridge, UK.

This book critically synthesises the best of the debates in feminist theory over several decades. I do not know of any book that covers in such depth such a gamut of topics, both at the domestic and international level, establishing the importance of researching the gendered citizen. Madeleine Arnot has offered us a remarkable research agenda, and insightful research findings, that will guide the debate and thinking on the gendered citizen for years to come. This is the kind of book that is a real tour de force in educational theory.

Professor Carlos Alberto Torres, University of California, Los Angeles, USA.

This is a wide-ranging book which is unique in the bringing together of gender and critiques of notions of citizenship and citizenship education in a sustained way. It is also timely: the debates on citizenship and global citizenship have indeed taken hold of the political imagination, but urgently need a gender lens. From a basis of sustained scholarship over many years and across many sites of research and analysis, Madeleine Arnot provides a majestic sweep across this complex and contradictory field.

Professor Lyn Davies, University of Birmingham, UK.

Madeleine Arnot is one of the world's best researchers on gender and education. This book collects her studies on citizenship, exploring a wide range of issues from personal identity to neoliberal globalisation. The chapters show her characteristic blend of precise intellectual analysis and original empirical research. The book finishes with a superb synthesis of ideas about gender, education and citizenship on a world scale.

Professor Raewyn Connell, University of Sydney, Australia.

Educating the Gendered Citizen

Sociological engagements with national and global agendas

Madeleine Arnot

LONDON AND NEW YORK

For Robin, Kathryn and Adam

First published 2009
by Routledge
2 Park Square, Milton Park, Abingdon, Oxon, OX14 4RN

Simultaneously published in the USA and Canada
by Routledge
29 West 35th Street, New York, NY 10001

Routledge is an imprint of the Taylor & Francis Group, an informa business

© 2009 Madeleine Arnot

Typeset in Times New Roman by Pindar NZ (Egan Reid) Ltd, Auckland
Printed and bound in Great Britain by TJ International Ltd, Padstow, Cornwall

All rights reserved. No part of this book may be reprinted or reproduced or utilised in any form or by any electronic, mechanical, or other means, now known or hereafter invented, including photocopying and recording, or in any information storage or retrieval system, without permission in writing from the publishers.

British Library Cataloguing in Publication Data
A catalogue record for this book is available from the British Library

Library of Congress Cataloging-in-Publication Data
  Educating the gendered citizen : sociological engagements with national and global political agendas / Madeleine Arnot.
  p. cm.
  1. Sex differences in education. 2. Education and globalization.
  3. Citizenship—Study and teaching. I. Title.
  LC212.9.A756 2008
  370.15'1—dc22
  2008014923

ISBN 10: 0-415-40805-9 (hbk)
ISBN 10: 0-415-40806-7 (pbk)
ISBN 10: 0-203-88992-4 (ebk)

ISBN 13: 978-0-415-40805-9 (hbk)
ISBN 13: 978-0-415-40806-6 (pbk)
ISBN 13: 978-0-203-88992-3 (ebk)

Contents

List of Illustrations vii
Sources viii
Acknowledgements x

PART I
Introducing gender education politics into citizenship debates 1

1 Sociological perspectives on the education of the gendered citizen: an introduction 3

2 Feminist politics and democratic values in education 29
   WITH JO-ANNE DILLABOUGH

PART II
Teachers' constructions of the gendered citizen 61

3 Teachers, gender and the discourses of citizenship 63
   WITH HELENA ARAÚJO, KIKI DELIYANNI, GABRIELLE IVINSON
   AND AMPARO TOMÉ

4 Changing femininity, changing concepts of citizenship in public and private spheres 95
   WITH HELENA ARAÚJO, KIKI DELIYANNI AND GABRIELLE IVINSON

PART III
Gendered pedagogies and citizenship curricula 113

5 'England expects every man to do his duty': the gendering of the citizenship textbook (1940–1966) 115
   WITH PATRICK BRINDLE

6　Gender and 'race' equality: affirmative and transformative pedagogies of citizenship (1970–2000)　138

7　Addressing the gender agenda: the limits and possibilities of national and global citizenship education　167
WITH HARRIET MARSHALL

PART IV
Individualised learning and global citizenship education　195

8　'Freedom's children'? Gender, individualisation and the neo-liberal learner citizen　197

9　Educating the global citizen: the gender challenges of the twenty-first century　223

Index　252

Illustrations

Figures

5.1 W.E. Williams's 'Women's Place' (*Current Affairs*, 11 January 1947).   126
5.2 The frontispiece to W.E. Williams's 'Women's Place'
    (*Current Affairs*, 11 January 1947).   128
5.3 'To whom is it "unfair" if a married woman works?'
    (W.E. Williams, 'Women's Place', *Current Affairs*, 11 January 1947).   131
5.4 'Women's place was everywhere'
    (W.E. Williams, 'Women's Place', *Current Affairs*, 11 January 1947).   133

Tables

1.1 Gendered discourses of citizenship   14
4.1 Student teachers' images of men and women in public life   99
5.1 Categorisation of sample texts   122
6.1 Male and female citizenship characteristics   140
6.2 Gender remedies and pedagogic strategies (1970s to 1980s)   143
6.3 Gender remedies and pedagogic strategies (1990s to 2000s)   146
6.4 Minority ethnic remedies and pedagogies strategies (1970s to 2000s)   155
8.1 Reduction of social rights and the radicalisation of social differences   216

Sources

Note: permission has been granted from the co-authors and publishers to reproduce extracts from the following publications.

Chapter	Source
1	Extracts from Arnot, M. 'Gender, citizenry and new feminist perspectives on education and citizenship', *British Education Research Journal*, 24(3): 275–95, 1997.
2	Original: Arnot, M. and Dillabough, J. 'Feminist Politics and Democratic Values in Education', *Curriculum Inquiry*, 29(2): 159–90, 1999. Reprinted as Arnot, M. and Dillabough, J. (2000) 'Feminist politics and democratic values in education', in S. Ball (ed.) *Sociology of Education: Major Themes* Vol. IV, London: RoutledgeFalmer, pp. 2178–221, 2000. Also reprinted in H. Lauder, P. Brown, J. Dillabough, and A.H. Halsey (eds) *Education, Globalisation and Social Change*, Oxford: Oxford University Press, pp. 161–78, 2006.
3	Original: Arnot, M., Araújo, H., Deliyanni, K., Rowe, G. and Tomé, A. 'Teachers, gender and the discourses of citizenship,' *International Studies in Sociology of Education*, 6(1): 3–35, 1996. Reprinted as: Arnot, M., Araújo, H., Deliyanni-Kouimtzis, K., Ivinson, G., and Tomé, A. 'The good citizen: cultural understandings of citizenship and gender amongst a new generation of teachers', in M. Leicester, C. Modgil and S. Modgil (eds) *Politics, Education and Citizenship*, Vol. 6, *Education, Culture and Values*, London: Falmer Press, pp. 217–52, 2000.
4	Original: Arnot, M., Araújo, H., Deliyanni, K., and Ivinson, G. 'Changing femininity, changing concepts of citizenship in public and private spheres', *The European Journal of Women's Studies*, 7(2): 149–68, 2000.
5	Original: Brindle, P. and Arnot, M. '"England expects every man to do his duty": the gendering of the citizenship textbook (1940–1966)', *Oxford Review of Education*, 25(1 and 2): 103–23, 1999.

6   This is an updated and extended version of Arnot, M. 'Gender equality, pedagogy and citizenship: affirmative and transformative approaches in the UK', *Theory and Research in Education*, *4*(2): 131–50, 2006.

7   This is an updated and extended version of Marshall, H. and Arnot, M. 'The gender agenda: the limits and possibilities of national and global education', *World Studies in Education*, *7*(1): 81–106, 2006. With extracts from Arnot, M. 'Citizenship Education and Gender', in A. Lockyer, B. Crick and J. Annette (eds) *Education for Democratic Citizenship: issues of theory and practice.* Aldershot: Avebury, 2004.

8   This is an updated and extended version of Arnot, M. '"Freedom's children"? Gender, individualisation and the learner citizen', *International Review of Education*, *52*(1): 67–87: 1–21, 2005

Acknowledgements

I first started getting interested in the education of the citizen when in the early 1990s the then Prime Minister Mrs Thatcher started to talk about an 'active citizenship'. The Hansard Society had been called upon to investigate the concept of citizenship and had taken on board a wide range of different political approaches, not least those of participatory citizenship. At the time, the school system was being marketised and all the known variables to do with social justice, including those of gender equality, were being rapidly replaced by the demands of a performance-led educational system. When my colleagues Kiki Deliyanni and Roula Zougou, from the Aristotle University in Thessaloniki, visited me from Greece seeking collaboration, we discussed the fact that, although the egalitarianism of the 1980s had made an impact in our two countries, we did not know what teachers in this new era thought about gender equality. These two strands of change became the focus of our EU-funded project on *Promoting Equality Awareness: women as citizens*. Amparo Tomé from the University of Barcelona and Helen Araújo in the University of Porto and Gabrielle Ivinson joined the three of us in what became a superb collaboration. Together we worked up the theme of gender, education and citizenship, and since that time have joined together our research agendas, participated in many joint conferences, and established Master's programmes which focused on politics, democracy and education in each of our countries. Over the last ten years, I have regularly visited Thessaloniki and Porto, and together we have discussed new forms of citizenship, new models of democratic education and new research on gender. This is what European integration means for me, and I have benefitted in so many ways from that experience.

The network of scholars working on this theme of gender, education and citizenship has expanded over the years. I am very grateful for colleagues Tuula Gordon and Elena Lahelma (Finland), Gloria Bonder (Argentina), Halleli Pinson and Hannan Alexander (Israel), Penny Enslin and Shirley Pendlebury (South Africa), Kathleen Weiler (US), Jane Kenway (Australia), Kathleen Lynch (Ireland), Janet Holland and Lyn Davies (UK) and many others for the conversations we have had, and for the lessons I have learnt from their work. I am sorry not to be able to name everyone. Many colleagues published their research on citizenship in the book that Jo-Anne Dillabough and I co-edited, titled *Challenging Democracy: international perspectives on gender, education and citizenship*. Jo-Anne began an intellectual journey which took us deep into feminist thought and its challenge to liberal democratic citizenship. I want to thank her for pulling me into the postmodern world by engaging with North American research and encouraging me to hold a more complex notion of citizenship identity. My thanks also go to Christopher Colclough, Elaine Unterhalter and Shailaja Fennell who have brought my study of citizenship into the study of development – a theme that defines my new project.

I owe a great debt to the doctoral students with whom I worked on issues relating to citizenship. I have learnt from Harriet Marshall and James Lee about global education and citizenship education in the UK respectively; from Daniel Faas, Avril Keating and Stravoula Phillipou about European citizenship; from Shu Ching Lee, Alison Phipps and Sunny Wang about gender, ethnicity and education in a global context, from Halleli Pinson and Antonina Tereschenko about political identities; and from Patrick Brindle about English citizenship education when he worked on the Leverhulme project on post-war English civic textbooks. My thanks also go to the many colleagues in a wide range of countries (for example, in Cuba, Iceland, Israel, Ireland, India, Japan, South Africa, Sweden, Taiwan and Trinidad) who invited me to discuss issues of gender, citizenship and education with them at various international conferences and on lecture tours. I am personally grateful to Philip Gardner, Len Barton, Michael Apple, Raewyn Connell, Carlos Alberto Torres, and to my dear friend, the late Terry McLaughlin, for their interest in my work and for the considerable personal support they have offered me. This field has huge potential to link a wide range of countries, colleagues and areas of research. Finally, I owe a debt of gratitude to Anna Clarkson at Routledge for always standing by me, in each of the many publishing ventures we undertake together.

Finally, I have dedicated this book to my wonderfully supportive husband Robin and our remarkably resilient daughter and son, Kathryn and Adam, who have put up with my lack of attention, my excessive travel and my doggedness in pursuing these interests.

Part I
Introducing gender education politics into citizenship debates

1 Sociological perspectives on the education of the gendered citizen

An introduction

The aim of this book is to engage with contemporary debates about citizenship education, democratisation and globalisation. The purpose is to encourage debate about how citizens are educated in ways that contribute to an international sociological field of citizenship education studies. The book cannot claim to cover the wealth of literature now available on citizenship and citizenship education, nor to explore in depth the philosophical basis of these concepts. However, by bringing together this collection of new and previously published papers (some of which I have updated and amended), I hope to show that there is an important line of sociological research on citizenship and citizenship education that complements and engages with the study of contemporary educational reforms. The education of citizens is now a global debate and brings us directly back to Durkheim's (1956) concerns about the relationship between education and society

The critical perspective I develop in this book is that of gender – what Yuval Davies and Stoetzler (2002) call the 'gender gaze'. A gender perspective never claims to be comprehensive, nor exclusive, but it does aim to be productive in assessing the social significance of education. Gender relations in Western European philosophy are central to the definition of the social contract between individuals and government and are deeply implicated in the distribution of power and control within society. Gender relations are also embedded within other sets of social relations including religious, ethnic, community relations and social class cultures that affect men's and women's differential access to citizenship rights and entitlements.

The educational system is the institution historically that shapes relations between citizens and, as these chapters show, which constructs the relationship of male and female citizens to the state. The extent to which the study of gender education is marginalised in current discussions of citizenship education is therefore really quite shameful. The aim of this collection of papers is therefore to establish clearly the importance of researching the schooling of the gendered citizen and of recognising the political significance of current gender struggles over education. Politically it is also important to define the terrain within which schools can contribute to a form of democracy that offers women and men equal status, whatever their social class, ethnic, or religious background.

The chapters of this book represent academic research I have been engaged with

4 *Sociological perspectives on the education of the gendered citizen*

since the early 1990s. In 1992, I began a programme of research on the gendering of citizenship and citizenship education, which has led me along a variety of different empirical and theoretical paths. This book collects some of the work I have published over the last fifteen years, much of which has been developed with others either in funded projects or through the supervision of post-doctoral and doctoral research. I have had the advantage and the pleasure of working closely with a number of colleagues – together we conceptualised, worked on and wrote various articles on our research and presented these at international conferences. For example, I learnt a good deal from my colleagues Helena Araújo in Portugal, Amparo Tomé in Spain, Kiki Deliyanni and Roula Zougou in Greece and Gabrielle Ivinson (then Rowe) in the UK about different discourses and social representations of citizenship and the impact of gender on citizenship in very different cultures and countries with strong political histories. Such comparative research on citizenship education is invaluable in my experience, not least because it highlights the exceptional nature of Anglo-Saxon traditions. Jo-Anne Dillabough and I also combined forces to engage with the political dimensions of feminist education theory. We have written many articles together in which we developed a critique of liberal democracy. I have included in this collection of papers our first major publication here, in which we revisited feminist educational theory in order to see what sort of democratic schooling was called for in the name of gender equality. After writing this article, we co-edited *Challenging Democracy: international perspectives on gender, education and citizenship* (Arnot and Dillabough, 2000) in which we published a range of new international research. I also worked with Patrick Brindle and Harriet Marshall, both of whom were doctoral students at the time. I am very grateful to them for allowing me to publish our work here, and for the lessons I have learnt from them about the history of English citizenship education and about global education respectively. I am greatly indebted to all these colleagues for allowing me to reprint our co-authored chapters in this collection.

The analysis of citizenship in this collection is informed largely by the British, American and Australian literature. The advantage of locating research on the education of the English citizen within this tradition is that I have been able to consider, with the help of my colleagues, an understanding of Anglophone versions of liberal democracy with their particular concepts of 'freedom'. The history of English citizenship education, it must be said, has to some degree been the history of English exceptionalism. England has had a long-term and deep-seated antipathy towards teaching about political issues and citizenship in schools (Heater, 1990). This absence was not for want of effort on the part of educational reformers throughout the twentieth century who campaigned for civics, citizenship, politics and social studies to be central aspects of a modern education. The two decades following the end of the war in 1945 was a period in which the language of equality of opportunity, both in education and in society, was at its height. After much debate, in 1990, Education for Citizenship was introduced as a cross-curricular theme, but it was only in 2002 that the subject was made a statutory part of the National Curriculum for schools in England and Wales. In the last two decades, however, it has become important to relate to the

European agendas that frame citizenship and more recent work on globalisation and global citizenship education. The global context has impinged on national citizenship education and has challenged its assumptions. These international interfaces are reshaping the education of the English citizen. The organisation and sequencing of the chapters reflect these various approaches to the education of the citizen, concluding as it were with a chapter on the most important gender debates that are likely to affect discussions about global citizenship education in the twenty-first century.

The organisation of the book

The book is divided into four sections – the first section focuses on the ways in which feminist theory addressed issues of democratic values and democratic schooling. The second section focuses particularly on the languages/discourses of citizenship that helped male and female student teachers in various European countries make sense of the notion of citizenship, their construction of male and female citizenships and their personal engagement with changes in male-female relations in society.

The third section takes the sociology of gender and citizenship studies into an analysis of the English citizenship pedagogy and curriculum historically and in the present. The three chapters in this section are very different but they indicate the possibilities of historical analyses of textbooks, the theoretical analysis of shifting politics within gender education reform movements and a critical analysis of the assumptions underlying the English citizenship and global education curricula.

The final section of the book moves out from the national context to consider how the neo-liberal notions of 'freedom' have started to shape the processes with which the school constructs the learner citizen. The tensions between, on the one hand, individualisation and, on the other, global citizenship education represent challenges to the education of the citizen that are likely to frame educational debates in the twenty-first century.

Below I describe how current concerns about the nature of social change in the twentieth and twenty-first centuries have been addressed by sociologists and where the study of gender, education and citizenship might be placed within that agenda.

Sociological engagements with education for citizenship

Sociological studies describe the twin processes of democratisation and globalisation as the leitmotif of the twenty-first century. These two epoch forces which simultaneously shape contemporary society and national educational systems are also mostly in conflict. Paradoxically, both speak the language of freedom and promise greater participation for all. Often those who wish to promote laissez-faire market economies and a rolling back of the nation state argue that their strategy is for egalitarian or even democratic purposes. In this context, support for neo-liberal discourses can be used to mask the increasing polarisation of wealthy and poor nations, and national inequalities with a veneer of respectability. At the same time, the revitalisation of human rights represents the strongest contemporary critique of such polarisations, the massive differences in wealth and opportunity of privileged and underprivileged communities within and across national boundaries. Human rights activists and theorists draw attention to the global migration of millions of people who are 'non-citizens' and thus denied the normal rights of citizenship. The realities of global poverty, war and terrorism have also created an image of the twenty-first century as one filled with conflict and dissonance rather than security. The concept of citizenship, therefore, has taken hold of the political imagination as one of the means by which such global complexity can be addressed. It has become the focus not just of social and political theorists, but also of educationalists keen to show that educational systems can engage with such extraordinary levels of ideological conflict and social change.

At the centre of the tension between globalisation and human rights are liberal democratic notions of the social contract that defines the relationship between individuals within a polity and the relationship of individuals to government. Brysk (2002) points out that human rights are seen as 'the highest stage of liberalism' where the ideal is that freely chosen governments protect the individual's rights. However, the more the nation state is threatened by global forces, the harder it is to see how such human rights can be protected. Today there is a 'citizenship gap' – 'a lack of political mechanisms to ensure individual membership, power holders' accountability, and respect for human rights in a globalising world' (Brysk, 2002: 246). Globalisation has led to increased opportunities for 'transnational investment, commodity networks and export dependency' but it has also increased the chance of greater threats to social rights, security rights and the abuse of labour rights.

A second key debate within contemporary social and political thought focuses on the tension between citizenship as a construct and human rights discourse. Citizenship is essentially about the individual's relationship to the nation-state, whilst the notion of human rights draws on universal concepts of a common humanity, without reference to any state. The focus of much contemporary political debate is on contemporary forms of national citizenship. From an historical point of view, there is interest in how definitions of citizenship have been shaped by, for example, civic republican, liberal, social democratic, neo-liberal or nationalistic, post-communist, communitarian or cosmopolitan ideals. These political ideals have different consequences for a range of social groups such as working classes and professional middle classes, the low paid and the unemployed, religious and minority ethnic communities, children, the aged and the disabled. Such ideals, whilst often appearing to be gender neutral, also construct male and female citizens in particular ways within and across such groups.

Much of the social scientific writing on citizenship, globalisation, human rights and democracy in the UK has been framed by the models of citizenship rights described by T.H. Marshall (1950) in *Citizenship and Social Class* in the post-war period. In this ground-breaking work, Marshall established the political, economic and social rights that would form the welfare state. Social regeneration after the Second World War was through the new concept of social citizenship which complemented the civil element and the political element of citizenship that had developed over the previous century. Citizens were to have:

> [The] whole range from the right to a modicum of economic welfare and security to the right to share to the full in the social heritage and to live the life of a civilised being according to the standards prevailing in the society. (Marshall, 1950: 10 quoted in House of Commons, 1990: 5)

The concept of social citizenship drew attention to the inequalities of citizenship created by a hierarchical and stratified society and questioned which of these inequalities could be redressed by the nation state – a theme that, as Bulmer and Rees (1996) point out, became the task of sociologists to investigate.

By the 1960s, this definition of social citizenship had been transformed by new social movements such as the women's and black civil rights movements. What was demanded was a 'floor of entitlements' – the rights of all individuals to have their basic needs met by the state (e.g. housing, nutrition and education). Today, there is strong sociological interest in how different types of citizens are positioned within the polity and what they receive from government in terms of support, provision and protection. However, contemporary social scientific interest now also wants to know what it feels like to be a citizen and what the emotional aspects of belonging and not-belonging within the civic community are. The state in advanced industrial societies extended the rights, responsibilities and duties of the citizen into the personal domain, family life and sexual spheres. The politics of inclusion therefore has created new yardsticks with which to assess contemporary models of citizenship.

Sociologists of education have contributed to this analysis of social citizenship by investigating the contribution of educational institutions. The last four decades have seen many empirical studies of the impact of education on social inequality and the role which different political philosophies have attributed to the educational system. Liberalism as the dominant philosophy of the post-war period, for example, defined the role of schooling as one of helping citizens develop their individual talents. Educational institutions were meant to give individuals a chance to better their lives, normally through social mobility and meritocratic institutions. Educational qualifications offered forms of social and cultural capital (Bourdieu, 1997) which could be converted into economic capital in the labour market. Schooling, under this regime, was meant to create a balanced society in which all could make a positive contribution, even though differently placed within the social strata.

However, by the mid-twentieth century, the post-war education system was shown by sociologists of education to be undemocratic. It sustained a wide gap between the maximum education of the professional classes and the minimum offered to working-class youth. Young working-class citizens had little chance of becoming involved in the decisions which affected their schooling. Even child-centred education, with its promises of development of individual talents, masked social differentiation and inequality. Also, the impetus for reform of the schooling of citizens in the UK increasingly came from economically driven agendas rather than liberal notions of providing a broad and balanced liberal education for all. By the 1990s, school curricula, school cultures and classroom learning were meant to help prepare young people for a neo-liberal, market-led economic order. Schools encouraged young people to fit the demands of globalising economies through vocationally oriented education or through the individualising and personalising of their learning careers. By the turn of the twenty-first century, most commentators agree that learning and the learning process, rather than the transmission of knowledge content per se, had become key to the education of young citizens. Young people are to be educated to become life-long learners, to be able to cope with a much riskier, less protected commodified world where there are no certainties, only fluidities, and where the conditions for an Enlightenment-based concept of citizenship, some argue,[1] are not only reduced but perhaps even lost (Wexler, 1991).

Critical sociological studies also addressed the formation of citizenship through policy research. Attention turned to the political significance of the rise of the neo-liberalism and neo-conservatism which shaped the New Right and Mrs Thatcher's government reforms of education in the late 1980s. These reforms resonated with similar neo-liberal marketisations of educational systems in Anglophone countries such as the United States, Canada, Australia and New Zealand, as well as in other European nations. The new agenda aimed at raising the quality of schooling through the decentralisation of school governance, the introduction of new standardised regimes of assessment and testing of pupils, an overall emphasis on competitive individualised learning and performance indicators for school success. Critical sociological analyses understood such neo-liberal agendas as antithetical to the social democratic ethos – representing more extreme versions of liberal models of possessive individualism. In effect, critical sociological research questioned whether social citizenship has in fact been delivered under social democracy – or whether, if delivered, it was then destroyed under the market-led neo-liberal reforms.

Whilst such studies tracked the impact of these political shifts on the governance of education and its organisation, on the whole, citizenship education received little critical attention. This neglect may reflect the decline of sociological studies of the curriculum since the late 1980s, or the greater interest in the effects of neo-liberalism and economic globalisation over the political and philosophical aspects of citizenship. We cannot rule out the possibility that initially the sociological field, concerned as it was with discursive deconstruction, with the politics of identity, culture, performance and language, saw citizenship education, human rights and the nature of democracy as a modernist project, and to engage with it would be to sustain the now displaced grand narratives of modernity, rather than work with the fluidities of the postmodern. Having said that, contemporary examples of post-structuralist analysis have provided fascinating deconstructions of 'the citizen' and its modelling through education (see Rose, 1990; Donald, 1996; Dillabough, 2000). Giroux (1988) recognised the significance of this curriculum subject when he argued that, unfortunately, because critical theorists were so engrossed in their mission of challenging liberal democratic processes and politics they

... failed to develop a programmatic discourse for reclaiming citizenship education as an important battleground around which to advance emancipatory democratic interests. (Giroux, 1988: 8)

The feminist study of citizenship education

There was, however, one sociological field that precisely did not take the education of citizens and citizenship education for granted. Indeed, rather than declining interest in the politics of the curriculum and schooling, feminist sociologists have taken an increasing and rather buoyant interest in defining the themes, boundaries and questions needed, on the one hand, to constitute this new research theme and, on the other, to sustain the theme of democracy and democratic education even within neo-liberal times. Jo-Anne Dillabough and I (Arnot and Dillabough, 2000:1) described this new field as 'the feminist study of citizenship education. Feminist research by the late 1990s had gradually started focusing on the relationship between gender studies and citizenship studies – drawing critically and constructively on the latter field to understand the nature of political philosophy, the construction of political identities and subjectivities, and the political consequences of the moral ethical formations of schooling.

Our synopsis of international gender research on the schooling of the citizen identified different levels of analyses which were not cumulative – rather they signalled different problematics, theoretical trajectories and empirical approaches to the study of gender, education and citizenship. First, there was a growing interest in the definitions of the male and female citizenship in national citizenship education programmes (their curricular goals, texts and pedagogies). Gender researchers had begun the process of identifying the ways in which male and female citizenships were framed in social time and place. Secondly, a number of leading gender authors had become interested in the ways in which everyday practices and experiences shaped young men and women's access to citizenship rights, their citizenship identities, sense of agency and political positioning. This more ethnographic approach suggested that the schooling of citizens created both the conditions for exclusionary civic practices and inclusionary civic virtues. Such new 'political landscapes' moved the discussion of gender relations and schooling cultures, organisation and structures into a closer relationship with democratic political theory. There was a shift from a concept of reproduction of the economic citizen to the political. In a context where the politics of education had been transformed through decentralisation and the marketisation of schooling, the notion of educating citizens for a liberal democracy looked that much more challenging. Key questions could be asked about the relationship between markets and morality, the link between a gendered citizenry negatively affected by neo-liberal reforms, and a gendered citizenry educated in late twentieth century notions of social inclusion and egalitarianism (see Arnot and Gordon, 1996 for a discussion of these tensions).

What made the marriage between feminist critique of political philosophy and feminist critiques of education so compatible was their joint interest in uncovering the gender assumptions that were embedded within liberal democratic notions of citizenship. Both emphasised the key separation of public-private spheres, their association with masculinity and femininity, and the consequent marginalisation and subordination of women as citizens. But there was also a common link in their critical analysis of the role of the nation state in the formation of male and female citizenships, the deconstruction of the shaping of political categories such as the 'woman' and the construction of national narratives (Arnot and Dillabough, 2000).

In 2002, Dillabough and I highlighted three problematics which had begun to shape research and theoretical writing in this emergent field of gender and citizenship studies (Dillabough and Arnot 2002: 64). Our most developed version of the three problematics distinguished between:

- sexual contract theory (following Carol Pateman's theory of the 'fraternal pact') and the resulting 'erasure of women from politics' implied by liberal democratic political philosophy;
- the ways in which the status of women as political actors/agents is shaped by the nation state and the 'nation space' and the contemporary understandings of the gendered polity that are reproduced through national educational politics and practice;
- the ways in which citizenship is understood as a symbolic identity within specific discursive framings, that can lead to differentiated notions of the 'I', the 'we' and the 'Other'. This analysis taps notions of identity, belonging, and difference, as well as social exclusion and marginalisation within and across gender boundaries.

These problematics overlap since they all address the construction of citizens – both the education of the citizen and education for citizenship (Beck, 1996). But the themes of location, time, space, identity and subjectivity in the construction of gendered citizen are hard to unpack empirically. Far more empirical research is needed to bring such theoretical axis to bear on curriculum provision and content, teachers' identities, knowledge and teaching styles – let alone young people's engagement and negotiation of such political socialisation. The sequence of research papers in this collection makes a modest start in relation to the three agendas. The chapters move between: an analysis of the interface between education feminism, feminist theories of the 'fraternal pact' and democratic values; the languages of citizenship especially in light of national shifts towards greater gender equality; gendered pedagogies and curricular change in English citizenship education; and finally, today's notion of individualisation and the ethical conscience associated with global citizenship education. Below I describe the contribution of the various papers to each of these themes.

Education feminism and the 'fraternal pact'

The natural starting point for the development of a sociological study of gender and citizenship education is feminist political theory, whose strong critique of liberal democracy resonates closely with feminist educational critiques of liberal democratic schooling. Carole Pateman's (1980, 1988, 1992) work offered a way into thinking through the gendered assumptions of Western European political philosophy. Her critique explored the masculinised/patriarchal basis of the concept of citizenship, in particular the gendered nature of the 'abstracted citizen' that lies at the heart of liberal democratic thought, and the dilemmas it poses for women wishing to participate more fully within democratic societies. Her analysis of the 'fraternal pact' that lies embedded within liberal democratic thought is a challenging critique of the ways in which women have been constructed both 'inside' and 'outside' Western European versions of democracy and citizenship.

The 'fraternal pact' ensured the separation of male public spheres and female private spheres, and supported the notion of a social contract in which it was taken for granted that men governed in the former and controlled women's sexuality and reproduction in the latter. The justifications for such a gendered polity were to be found in representations of women as having 'debasing self interests' (Kant), and an inability to generate an ethical consciousness (Hegel) (both cited in Lloyd, 1986). Women were symbols of emotion, natural feeling, caring for those closely related to them. Women were not seen to be capable of the objectivity and the principled behaviour which characterises precisely the worker, the soldier and the citizen. As a result, liberal democratic philosophy construed women as that which had *'to be transcended to be a citizen'* (Lloyd, 1986). Women's political disorder meant that they could justifiably be excluded from the original social contract, or in effect, the fraternal pact would be threatened.

Pateman's discussion of the social contract underlying liberal democratic citizenship resonated with the growth of education feminism which had developed major challenges to state schooling, not least the education of girls for one sphere and boys for the other. The contribution of feminist thought to understanding democratic values has been considerable. Feminist educational theories illustrate a history of engagement and counter-engagement between liberal, socialist, maternal, and post-structuralist positions. **Chapter 2** highlights, for example, the dominance of liberal feminism which, according to Connell, turned the concepts of rights 'against the patriarchal model of citizenship' (Connell, 1990), offering a 'powerful and sharp edged analysis of male dominance in most government institutions'. Liberal feminists rejected the second class education given to girls. They rejected the subordinated status of women within the public sphere – most noticeably within political and economic arenas – by arguing for the rights of women as individuals to achieve their full potential within such societies. They had the right to be educated to take their place within the public and private domains simultaneously.

Liberal feminism, however, had many critics, particularly within feminist educational thought. Chapter 2 investigates the contradictions that arose in relation to the other feminist strands of thought that drew inspiration from radical feminism, Marxism/socialist feminism and black feminism. These approaches were also strongly critical of the gender neutrality of liberal democracy with its promises of equality because of continuing social inequality and exploitation, particularly of female white and minority ethnic working-class youth. In some instances, as we show, some feminist perspectives argued for the privileging of the private sphere, women's lives and maternalism. In other cases, the focus was upon removing economic exploitation and oppression by dominant social classes and ethnic/racial groups.

A shift in thinking, away from Pateman's political analysis, was associated with the development of Foucauldian deconstructionist, post-Enlightenment feminisms (particularly post-structuralism and postmodernism), which rejected modernist grand narratives that sought explanations for the positioning of women in the dualisms of public and private. These new theories of gender and citizenship drew attention to the normalisation and surveillance of the 'female child', the 'female teacher', the associations of women with nationhood and nationalism, and the construction of a 'female citizen' that was in line with rational discourses of citizenship (Dillabough and Arnot, 2002, 2004). The value of such work, we argue, is that the notions of gender, gender relations and, indeed, citizenship were now seen to be discursively framed in particular historically specific periods. The construction of the female citizen and male citizen was now seen as less of a status and more of an identity and a set of social relations. Donald (1996) summed up this view thus:

> To become a citizen is [...] to become a subject within the symbolic order and to be subjected to it. (Donald, 1996: 175)

Chapter 2 concludes that feminist educationalists needed to revisit the social and political dimensions of their work in order to engage more critically with their 'epistemic' concerns as they emerge in relation to the study of gender and democratic schooling. Educationalists interested in working in this field of citizenship studies are encouraged to think through the levels and location of their research. With that in mind, Jo-Anne Dillabough and I identified three levels of political analysis: (a) the study of civic spheres; (b) the study of national narratives of education; (c) the analysis of political identities, differences and subjectivities. These highlighted, in the first case, the importance of discovering whether education contributed to the 'fraternal pact'. In the second case, research suggested that there was much that needed to be investigated in relation to the construction of the national imaginary and the relations within. The third level relates to a methodological deconstruction of the representation of 'woman' or 'man' that would shape, if not determine, teachers' abilities to shift their political thinking in line with contemporary gender change. Chantal Mouffe (1992) took the view that what feminists had shown was that liberal democratic versions of citizenship had become an obstacle to making democracy work for women in a more genuinely inclusive way. It was time to construct new definitions of citizenship that were based on the needs of contemporary women and men. The concept of what constituted democratic education had not only been problematised through such intellectual and political work, but had been shown to be both complex and contentious.

The languages of citizenship and gender change

The second sociological strand on gender and citizenship focuses on the languages of citizenship in the context of gender change. It is clear from the development of feminist thought, and from evidence of the changing position of women, that major gender transformations had taken place in Western Europe. A powerful relationship was forged between democratic movements and equality movements such that democracy itself was 'on the agenda'. Women campaigned publicly and forcefully to ensure their full participation in public life, to be involved in the democratic processes at international, national, regional, local and community levels. For a country to claim to be a democracy in the fullest sense of the term, it became clear that women would need to achieve the same capacity as men in terms of taking part in economic, political and cultural decisions. In response to the women's movement, a range of social policies and strategies were developed by governments to ensure women's greater participation and entitlements as citizens. These strategies included ensuring a better, more equitable distribution of women across a range of occupations; offering more support for women's role in the family, in childcare and in maternity provision; affirmative action to increase women's access to education, training and employment; and a push to increase women's participation in politics and public positions.

By the end of the 1990s, Europe also experienced rising alienation and disaffection amongst its youth. There appeared to be a form of social malaise, with the re-emergence of public expressions of racist and xenophobic attitudes and the rise of terrorism. In response to this mood, the European Union focused on improving social inclusion. Its 3rd Term Medium Action Programme aimed to increase the participation of women in democratic structures. Funding was available to improve the position of women within education, employment and the public sphere, so long as it linked across a variety of member states. In response to this call, my colleagues Helena Araújo, Kiki Deliyanni,[2] Amparo Tomé, Roula Ziogou and I bid for a project on *Promoting Equality Awareness: Women as Citizens*. We were joined by Gabrielle Ivinson. Our aim was to discover to what extent the new generation of secondary-school teachers sustained particular notions of male and female citizenship, especially in light of the levels of gender change experienced in each of our countries. It was clear from the start of the project that the English/Welsh framing of democracy with its strong liberal traditions and assumptions about the importance of the individual was different from that of the Mediterranean countries of Greece, Spain and Portugal, where civic republican concepts of *liberté*, *fraternité* and *egalité* were taught in schools. (At that point English schools did not teach citizenship education as a school subject.)[3]

Chapter 3 describes some of the findings of the project – in particular, it reveals different male and female discursive framings of citizenship. It was significant that all three Mediterranean countries had had experience of fascist governments as well as of democratic reform movements within the last fifty years. Yet despite these different political histories, student teachers all struggled to make sense of the concept of citizenship (a term that was not part of everyday speech in any of the five countries). Out of the *bricolage* came systems of representations about the relations between individual and the state, society and the 'common good'. The chapter reveals how student teachers drew on various religious and philosophical European traditions discourses to talk about citizenship. These were:

14 *Sociological perspectives on the education of the gendered citizen*

- *political discourses* drawing upon Graeco-Roman traditions of political life and the duties of the state in relation to civil society and to the individual, and the duties of the individual in relation to the state;
- *moral discourses* using the vocabulary and metaphors of Judaeo-Christian philosophies, especially those to do with core ethical values/virtues, social conformity and 'the common good'; and
- *egalitarian discourses* deriving from the humanistic traditions around the rights of individuals to freedom from oppression, from poverty, from violence (and more recently, to a range of social entitlements).

Significantly, each of the three discourses of citizenship privileged men and marginalised women as 'other'. None of the three discourses of citizenship privileged female over male spheres and, even more importantly, female student teachers (especially in the Mediterranean) expressed their distance from, rather than their empowerment by, these three discourses.

Chapter 3 also reveals the strong gendered imagery that came through concepts of 'the good citizen' constructed in relation to each of the discourses. Whilst strong male public roles were used by male teachers, there were far fewer roles for women. The data we collected from this comparative project indicated the dominance of what Connell (1990) referred to as the European equation between authority and a dominating masculinity. Men in Greece, for example, spoke of the political importance of the 'critical citizen' fighting for democracy, or the moral role of 'productive worker', contributing to economic growth; in contrast, Greek female student teachers preferred to discuss the duty to become a 'protesting citizen', fighting for rights promised yet still denied to women. In the UK, awareness of the impact of social class values in relation to social conformity triggered strongly gendered images of the good/moral citizen. Indeed, women's role as mothers and as carers was highlighted and appeared to be celebrated by women as an alternative source of critical, civic action. These findings are summarised in Table 1.1 below.

Chapter 4 describes precisely what sort of upheaval the demands for full female citizenship creates in the lives and understandings of the student teachers we interviewed. It explores the ways in which feminism and gender change impacted on student teachers' concept of citizenship and, in particular, on their understanding of the relevance of such an egalitarian/democratic movement for their personal and family lives.[4] Pateman's (1988) notion of the 'sexual contract' – the control of men

Table 1.1 Gendered discourses of citizenship

Political discourses of duty	The critical citizen The sceptical citizen	Graeco-Roman traditions
Discourses of morality, caring and common values	The caring citizen The classed citizen The mother as reformer	Judaeo-Christian traditions
Egalitarian discourses and social rights	The protesting citizen	Civil rights, social rights and welfare

over women's bodies as part of the right to govern – also appeared to be still intact. In Greece, female student teachers sustained maternalism as a political stance, while seeking more choice in their lives; male student teachers were alarmed at shifts in the family order. In Portugal, women's anxieties about egalitarian principles focused upon male domestic violence and control of women's sexuality. The English/Welsh student teachers in our study represented family life as a site for negotiation and compromise. Despite the continuing dominance of men within political discourses and the public sphere, some sources of female power were described, such as the power of women as mothers and heads of households; female sexual power; and feminism as power when challenging male dominance.

Giroux (1989) argued that:

> Citizenship is a form of cultural production ... the making of citizens must be understood as an ideological process through which we experience ourselves as well as our relations to others and the *world within a complex and often contradictory system of representations and images.* (Giroux, 1989, p. 16, my emphasis)

In a later paper, the research team explored the social representation of male and female citizenship. We argued that at the heart of the concept of male public civic sphere lay the tensions between power and sexuality, which was expressed in terms of anxieties about the 'bimbo' effect (sexually attractive women supporting male power) or 'the Thatcher effect' (the danger of losing femininity with power) (Ivinson *et al.*, 2000). Deep male anxiety about their loss of control over the public sphere meant that male teachers used the distinction between reproduction and sexuality to categorise women in public domains as either 'Mothers' and 'Madonnas' or as whores/sluts/bimbos. Women were not represented as legitimately successful and autonomous in public life.

Male student teachers in different European countries appeared to collude with differentiated gender roles and expressed little personal commitment to challenge masculine associations surrounding the public realm. We therefore concluded that degendering citizenship in the cause of democracy needed to engage with very deep connections between gender and citizenship. The analysis demonstrated that Pateman's 'civic freedom' in public life has to be counterbalanced by concerns about the 'natural subjection' of women in the private realm.

The two chapters in this section demonstrate the value of comparative research. It revealed the centrality of Western European traditions in teacher thought, and how new generation of teachers in the late 1990s in five different countries worked with highly gendered notions of public and private spheres. Gender transformations in such societies had not yet disturbed gendered citizenship.

Gendered pedagogies and citizenship curricula

In *Challenging Democracy* Jo-Anne Dillabough and I argued for the value of socio-historical explorations of nationhood and national narratives framing citizenship, not least because they encourage the exploration of the specificities of citizenship categorisations, relations and identities, located through time, place and space. However, few such socio-historical studies of citizenship are available, especially in so far as curriculum analyses are concerned. The three chapters in this section of the collection explore particular periods in the history of English citizenship education.

The first such period begins with the Second World War, a time when the country needed to address that fact that women had been released from family duties in order to contribute to the national war effort. The second period explores the last thirty years of the twentieth century when education feminists, discussed in Chapter 2, made strategic demands on school pedagogy and the curriculum at the same time as increasing demands for educational responses to multiculturalism, racism and difference. The third chapter in this section addresses the ways in which, by the turn of the twentieth century, a new citizenship education curriculum was introduced into English and Welsh secondary schools at a time when global education was increasingly defining a broader civic agenda. The chapter explores the political territory and pedagogic approach, and the potential for gender equality in both these new curricula.

Chapter 5, entitled '"England expects every man to do his duty": the gendering of the citizenship textbook 1940–1966' describes a small-scale historical project which Patrick Brindle and I undertook after the European study discussed earlier had been completed. This chapter focuses on the tentative way in which civic educators were prepared to engage with gender issues in the textbooks for citizenship education published just after the Second World War. In this period, education for citizenship had to contend with the deregulated nature of the English school curriculum. As a result, there were a number of different pedagogic approaches to gender and citizenship. We found that most of the 26 citizenship education textbooks from 1940 to 1960 we analysed took a *minimalist*, or *exclusionary* approach to female citizenship. In contrast, those civics texts published for girls in this period explored the notion of *women's rights* and the extent of women's access to and exclusion from the public sphere and the exercise of power. These textbooks offered a form of *critical engagement with gender relations*, considering what it would mean to have equal partnerships between men and women, equal pay, and a concept of male duty in relation to domestic work. Curiously, such progressive texts were produced by the Army Board of Current Affairs in the 1940s for schools and adult community groups. They aimed to achieve what McLaughlin (1992) called 'maximal models of citizenship' expecting participants to subject every opinion 'regardless how conventional and seemingly axiomatic' to critical questioning through group discussion.

Chapter 6 offers a different type of socio-historical analysis since it explores the ways in which gender equality reformers have addressed the key problematic of equality and difference within citizenship in the four decades since the 1970s. The pedagogic route 'from pupil to citizen', as Gordon *et al.* (2000) pointed out, lies in the physical, formal and informal levels of schooling – not just in the curriculum. All these levels have been the focus of gender reform politics since the 1970s and all of them have been challenged by education feminism. Although there are many critical analyses of this period (not least Arnot, David and Weiner 1999), most have not explored the connection between feminist struggles within the school system and the politics of citizenship. Pedagogical struggles in particular are not often seen as citizenship struggles even though they are representative of the political disarray over notions of equality and difference, particularism and universalism, and individual and group rights. Also getting to grips with the contradictory elements within such social reform movements is not easy. I found however that Nancy Fraser's analytic framework around notions of social justice and the redistribution and recognition politics of citizenship in the late twentieth century was useful in thinking through the contradictions between the affirmative and transformatory challenges to the school system. Fraser describes both 'race' and gender politics as 'bivalent collectivities' – a collectivity in which there is a conflict and a contradiction between the goals of universalism and the celebration of difference. Chapter 6 argues for 'a critical pedagogy of difference' that allows more explicit addressing of difference but within an egalitarian framework which also gives recognition to what Bernstein (2000) called pedagogic democratic rights.

The gendering of citizenship education

The third chapter in the section focuses on another major pedagogic initiative in relation to citizenship – the establishment of Citizenship Education in English and Welsh secondary schools in 2002. Citizenship education as a curriculum subject (with its related practices such as volunteer community work, school councils and pupil consultation) carried many different political goals. It was first introduced into the English school curriculum as one of five cross-curricular themes[5] in 1990. Schools were offered *Curriculum Guidance 8* (National Curriculum Council [NCC], 1990) – a document that was variously described as coy, inconsistent, ambiguous, or naïve in relation to egalitarian values[6] (see Beck, 1996; Inman and Buck, 1995). On the one hand, critics claimed that it reflected the political concerns of the New Right in the 1980s, with its emphasis on a form of possessive individualism balanced by 'a depoliticised' notion of community (cf. Beck, 1996); on the other hand, it represented 'old wine in new bottles' (Brown, 1991), drawing upon early twentieth-century concerns about providing 'a communal basis for political life' – a project supported by religious and other socially concerned bodies to counteract the excessive materialism of the 1980s.

The political compromises reached in *Curriculum Guidance 8* signalled the new politically functional role that the concept of citizenship was to play in official educational discourse. Conservative ministers promoted a model of 'active citizenship' that was associated with the 'rolling back' of the state by reducing state expenditure and welfare provision, with an even greater reliance on voluntary and privatised services (House of Commons Commission on Citizenship, 1990). As a result, reference to equal opportunities lacked 'the critical edge', and 'the rigour' that would be needed in order to achieve 'equal citizenship for all' (Inman and Buck, 1995: 93).[7]

In the event, the pressure from the subject-based National Curriculum prevented any easy transfer of such centrally orchestrated cross-curricular interventions. Whitty *et al.* (1994) discovered that any attempt to permeate such 'horizontal' integrative themes across the hierarchical discourses of specialist subjects was treated with suspicion and was faced with low levels of time and/or a lack of teacher commitment.[8] Having orchestrated a public panic about the dangers and indeed 'evil' of the 'moral relativism' (often seen as synonymous with the 'soft' egalitarianism and multiculturalism) of teachers and pupils, the government sought agreement on a set of *core* values and codes of moral conduct for schools (see School Curriculum and Assessment Authority, 1995). 'Citizenship' was brought alongside concerns about spiritual, moral and personal and social education, and thus distracted attention away from the many social problems confronting the country, from the severe political disenfranchisement of individuals in the UK, particularly in relation to local democracy, the quango state, and from the bureaucratisation of power.

In 2002, the Citizenship Order generated by the Advisory Group chaired by Bernard Crick established citizenship education as a compulsory subject in all secondary schools in England and Wales. At the time, a number of NGOs, working particularly in global education and development education, took the opportunity to promote a more global approach to the national focus of this subject. My experience of being involved in many of the early interest groups[9] on citizenship education led me to appreciate just how marginal were equality concerns – especially gender equality. By combining forces, Harriet Marshall and I were able to consider the limitations and possibilities for the promotion of gender and 'race' equality agenda in these two citizenship education programmes.

Chapter 7 discusses the significance for gender equality of, for example, the compromise reached between civic republicanism and liberal political philosophies in the so-called Crick Report. Such a compromise, as Osler and Starkey (2001) note, avoided a full-blown nationalistic perspective promoting Britishness and patriotism – yet it also resulted in a weakened egalitarianism. Although the Crick Report expected all pupils to be able to challenge prejudice and discrimination, citizenship education as conceived did not encourage a collective response to institutional sexism or racism.[10] The notion of common values was particularly problematic in the context of a pluralist multi-faith and ethnically diverse society. Also, although Harriet Marshall and I argued that the concept of global citizenship education offered new possibilities for a gender-sensitive form that would link gender to ethnicity, the focus at the time of writing was more on economic development than the concerns about difference, multi-positionalities and multiple citizenships.

Other differences between national and global education are noted by Davies *et al.* (1999). They argue that national citizenship education, with its more academic background, had a coherent base that emphasised community-based involvement and/or classroom-based cognitive reflection. In contrast, global education tends (although not exclusively) towards the affective (a point I discuss more fully in Chapter 9). Global education emphasises political activity, identifying issues that require 'immediate and perhaps radical attention' and, unlike national citizenship education, its broad agenda is not yet legitimated by inclusion in the statutory curriculum. From our point of view, it is significant that far more emphasis was given to gender equality and cultural difference within the less legitimate curriculum sphere than in the officially legitimated citizenship curriculum.

Some educationalists argue that the new English citizenship curriculum was sufficient in itself without bothering with the complexity of egalitarian concerns. For example, Davies *et al.* (2005: 124) suggest that:

> …a programme inspired by the ideals of liberal, pluralistic democracy is only what it is: it is not something else. A liberal programme of citizenship is not a feminist programme of education for citizenship, is not a programme of civic education actuated by a concern for citizenship in the postmodern world.

These authors' argument is that there is a danger if citizenship education has too many aspirations; it would only create disappointment (Davies *et al.*, 2005: 124). It would be better to have limited goals that were more appropriate to a liberal pluralistic democratic society. The aim should be to ensure that young people could play a better part in democracy rather than attempt to enforce a common identity, or indeed any identity.

However, when citizenship education only minimally addresses egalitarian concerns, the consequences are to be found in limited understanding of the importance of gender. When the IEA study researched the impact on student opinion of national citizenship education in some 28 countries, it found that there was strong support for women's political and economic rights amongst the 90,000 fourteen-year-old student respondents (Torney-Purta *et al.*, 2001:108). Some, however, believed that men had stronger rights over women when unemployed, and women should not expect equal chances to hold elected positions. And although the statistical evidence suggested that support for women in politics was increasing among young people, equality between the sexes was seen as the least important cause for which to 'take risks and make sacrifices'. The strongest support for women's rights came from countries such as Scandinavia where women were highly represented in the national legislature. Despite national citizenship education programmes, therefore, support for women's rights represented the largest difference in opinion between men and women. 'Females are more likely than males to support social movement involvements as important for adult citizens and to be willing to collect money for social causes.' Social class differences between men and women were also important. The data from such attitudinal research touches only the surface of young people's sense of themselves as citizens. Arguably 'engendering citizenship' involves a deeper understanding of patriarchal and gender relations in society and how they interconnect with governance, democracy and the role of the state.

Starkey *et al.* (2006) argue that there is a 'romantic view of citizenship' which links it to democracy (resonating with the 1789 French Revolution) – in these instances, the concept of citizenship is about inclusion. However, when citizenship is linked to nationality, there is a tension with the democratic values of inclusion – citizenship is about exclusion. This suggests that it is important in the context of promoting social inclusion to move *beyond* the notion of the national (Osler and Starkey, 2005); i.e. educating for a form of global citizenship based on human rights discourse (for example the recognises United Nations Convention of the Rights of the Child, which sees children as citizens).

The next set of papers in this collection precisely moves outside the national frame by focusing on the impact of individualisation and globalisation on the education of the learner citizen. As Demaine (2004) argues, children are already global citizens – they don't have to become this. The question is in what ways the school system has recognised that fact.

The power of individual freedom and global conscience collective

The final part of the book opens up the debate to a consideration of the social significance of individualisation and globalisation, and its probable relevance to gender relations. Two chapters explore the pressures on schools to adapt the ways they educate learner citizens for the twenty-first century. Studies of the relationship between globalisation and democratisation are characterised by the extremes of pessimism and idealism, particularly as far as gender equality is concerned. Globalisation as a political, cultural, economic epoch force is not just 'fuzzy', vague and complex. It is also seen as one of the most dangerous forces of social change this century is likely to see, creating ever-greater polarisation of countries, regions, social groupings and citizens. The movement of global capital is associated with the destruction of welfare states (through neo-liberal laissez-faire economics), the marketisation of state institutions, and the reframing of individuals' identities, biographies and lives.

At the same time, other commentators see the possibility of a new global order that could potentially address a radical global democracy (Held, 1996). Globalisation is therefore now associated with demands for 'an education for peace, democracy and human rights and the development of a global ethic' (Osler and Starkey, 2005: 21) – the creation therefore of a new normative 'global culture' (Delanty, 2000: 68). A new concept of citizenship based on the concept of human rights (as an ethical and legal concept) will encourage the notion of humanity and autonomous human beings, uncoupled from the nation state. This revitalisation of human rights in the late twentieth century arguably is already reshaping national citizenship models, and the 'abstract' citizen associated with liberal democracy will, it seems, be replaced by the concept of collective rights, a decontextualised and decentred self and a new form of personhood (Delanty, 2000).[11]

Chapter 8 takes up the theme by exploring the implications for education of what Beck and Beck-Gernsheim (2002) call *Freedom's Children* and its relevence for gender equality. Rather than encourage the reduction of gender, social class and ethnic inequalities, it seems likely that there will be spiralling differences between men and women's lives in this century. However, the language of freedom is embedded in new notions of personalised learning and individualised identities. Late modernity winners in a risk society will be those who are most able to take advantage of the fluidities, the opportunities and alliances that detraditionalisation brings. On the evidence so far, particular groups of female and male students will benefit whilst, at the same time, social class inequalities in educational institutions will experience aggravated polarisations (Bauman, 2000). Although women are assumed to be the 'postmodernity winners' the evidence presented in Chapter 8 indicates that there are likely to be greater inequalities between women in different social classes and the marginalisation of working-class male citizens in the twenty-first century.

In Chapter 8, I outline Bauman and Beck's view about the dangers of increasing individualisation. If the reduction of social rights is accompanied by a new emphasis on political rights (for example, through citizenship education) the effect, according to Beck, is likely to be the rise of 'the ugly citizen' with the possessive and egotistical individualism of the sort associated with 1990s neo-liberalism (cf. Thatcher, Reagan, Bush). An education that encourages the right to, and a consciousness of, freedom, at a time when there is a reduction of fundamental rights and fear of the future, will provide the conditions for the creation of this sort of citizen.

If educational systems are to adopt this language and practice of 'freedom' within the context of unequally stratified and hierarchically organised societies, then it is unclear what the moral basis of the new social order is. **Chapter 9** concludes the book with a discussion of the challenges facing those wishing to establish what I call a *new global conscience collective* (following Durkheim) to counter such individualisation and atomisation of society. Educationalists committed to such an emancipatory project promote the idea of developing a humane and humanitarian form of global citizenship education that will educate the next generation to experience 'outrage' at global injustices. This ambition marks a new stage in the education of citizens. The moral purposes of education are being drawn into the global revitalisation of human rights. The new drive is to ensure that young people are aware of global injustices and atrocities but are able to find their own form of political agency in relation to such phenomena.

Chapter 9 identifies five themes which have come to the fore in sociological studies of gender and globalisation that arguably should form the core of such a new gender-sensitive model of citizenship education. This emergent gender agenda which focuses on the recognition of diversity, sustainable development, sexual and reproductive citizenships, gender violence and peace education, women's global agency and activism, is challenging not least because it raises questions about the forms which patriarchal relations take within different cultural settings, the shaping of female lives in conditions often of subordination, exploitation and 'gender othering'. The implication here is that a gender-sensitive, global citizenship education could provide a space for addressing global and national gender-related inequities and the relationship between the two, whilst embracing a pedagogical philosophy that empowers students to find ways of engaging politically with contemporary global gender concerns. The themes of equality, diversity and difference across and within gender categories and relations, across nations and within nations, are assumed to be best served by this form of cosmopolitan citizenship education.

The concept of a global civil society (if democratically governed) is 'the "great white hope" of international relations, and a counterbalance to state, market, and organisational threats' (Brysk, 2002: 243). *Cosmopolitanism* in this context means ...

> ... the exchange of power across borders occurs increasingly through individuals and transnational entities. In this sense, human rights opportunities flow from the growing number of organisations above, below, and beside the state than can conceivably check human rights abuses ... These include not just the international human rights regime and movement but a broader range of international and nongovernmental organisations which monitor states, empower citizens, and aid victims ... (Brysk, 2002: 244)

Closing the 'citizenship gap' referred to at the beginning of this chapter therefore involves setting up a form of democratic global governance in which 'norms and identities must be transformed to foster universal members' reconstructions of sovereignty and evolving concepts of human dignity' (Brysk, 2002: 249). Cosmopolitan citizens would need to be active, to be able to conceptualise and 'to promote democracy, development and human rights' (Osler and Vincent, 2002: 111). However, focusing global citizenship education on the task of gender equality, I argue in Chapter 9, makes it that much more controversial.

Conclusion

Many countries are now considering the role of education in the creation of citizens for the twenty-first century (Cogan and Derricott, 2000). New centres for civic education have been set up; there is, for example, an Asian network of civic education, Commonwealth countries are being encouraged to consider citizenship education and the Council of Europe suggests it is time to consider what values and skills individuals will require in the twenty-first century (Cogan and Derricott, 2000). The movement to rethink development studies, environmental education, global and human rights education, multicultural education, peace education and world studies reflects concerns about the complexity of global economics and government; the vulnerability of societies and individuals; the multitude of citizenship identities; and the need to create greater social cohesion, stability and order in the world. Traditional distinctions between public and private activities, between national and international governments, are blurring. Global developments suggest that civil society needs to be reinforced in order to cope with the increased levels of risk, instability, and the speed of social change.

Considerable political will will be needed if a new citizenship education curriculum is to be developed that addresses the gender concerns raised in this book. The discourse of human rights – of which gender rights are now part – has become a major force within the global context. This gendered discourse has been used extensively in international development contexts but is now reaching into the forms of national citizenship education found in schools. The demand now is for a gender-sensitive global citizenship education.

However, the gendered citizen is still currently created by the educational actions of the state. This collection of sociological papers demonstrates some of the ways in which the education of young female and male citizens has been shaped by post-war welfare ideologies, by the new social movements in the late twentieth century, and by globalising pressures in the twenty-first century. The English model that privileged individualism and the autonomy of the rational (male) abstracted citizen now appears to be reshaped in the context of globalisation and the pressures to uncouple young citizens from their social basis in order to help them adjust to the demands of late modernity. Uncoupling citizenship education from traditional gender relations and structures may well benefit girls who are able particularly to engage with the individualising processes now encouraged in schools. For those who cannot benefit from the new era, gender could become a form of resistance and denial, strengthened by the knowledge that traditional gender cultures are anchors in an unstable world.

Until recently, as Bulmer and Rees (1996) pointed out, much of the discussion about citizenship in England has drawn upon T.H. Marshall's models of three sorts of citizen rights. Marshall combined citizenship and society in such a way that one could not be studied without the other. Arguably, this partnership of citizenship with society held up until the late 1980s when the New Right downplayed the relationship in favour of a form of civic citizenship (defined by the Citizen's Charter) that was uncoupled from society. Bulmer and Rees argue that, by the late 1980s and early 1990s, 'Marshall's Englishness' had had its time and place and new citizenship agendas appeared to be coming through that had more to do with the development of a postmodern risk society than with the continuing development of social citizenship. The role of the state in relation to the formation of citizens is now, therefore, a major concern.

The post-war welfare state and its educational provisions, according to Nikolas Rose (1990), were also well aware that the child was a 'citizen in potentia'. As Rose points out, the framing of post-war welfare states aimed to extend citizenship to the child by giving them education. He writes: 'Universal education, for Marshall, was a decisive step in the re-establishment of social rights of citizenship in the twentieth century, for it was an attempt to stimulate the growth of *citizens in the making*' (Rose, 1990: 122, my emphasis). Although in the nineteenth and twentieth centuries children were not

> citizens in the sense of having political rights to participate in the exercise of political power, and perhaps were only beginning to gain civil rights necessary for individual freedom such as liberty of the person and the right to justice, they had gained social rights. (Rose, 1990: 122)

Education was presented as the personal right of the child, but it also imposed, according to Marshall, a social and collective right; 'a duty of each individual to improve and civilize themselves for the benefit of the social health of the community'. Marshall saw this as a 'profoundly progressive recognition of a principle of inequality that lay at the heart of capitalist economic systems'.

However, as Rose points out, the politics and practices of welfare, far from extending citizenship in this benign sense, in fact functioned to maintain inequality, to legitimate existing relations of power, and to extend social control over potentially troublesome sectors of society. By the late twentieth century, 'The soul of the young citizen had become the object of government through expertise' (Rose, 1990: 131). Schooling as the modernist institution responsible for the formation of new generations of citizens was joined by all the other technologies of government, but at a time crucially when the discourse of free will, a laissez-faire ethos and self-promotion became the mechanisms of control. Schooling of citizens was only one such regulatory project, incorporating, shaping, channelling and enhancing subjectivity 'so that they are intrinsic to the operations of government' (Rose, 1990: 213). Rose argued:

> Universal and compulsory schooling catches up the lives of all young citizens into a pedagogic machine that operates not only to impart knowledge but to instruct in conduct and supervise, evaluate and rectify childhood pathologies (Rose, 1990: 122).

Today, the tension between disciplining the young citizen and the discourse of freedom, individualism, and free will/choice, may well not be resolved. As Chapter 9 argues, educational systems will increasingly promote greater freedom through neo-liberal discourses of performativity, individualisation and personalised learning, and counter-movements will encourage a global conscience collective. The 'soul of the global citizen' is likely in the future to be the new disciplinary and emancipatory focus.

Acknowledgements

This chapter draws upon a range of talks and articles. Examples are: material for the 'Rethinking Education' conference held at the Fundación Paideia, La Coruna in 1993, and developed for the 'Education and Equality of Opportunity' conference held by the Ministry to the Presidency in Athens, Greece in 1994; material for the VI 'Tornadoes Internationals de Coeducation' conference in Valencia, Spain (1994); the opening address for the 'Teachers, Gender and School Practice' conference at Aristotle University in Thessaloniki, Greece (1996); material for the conference on 'State Regulation, Citizenship and Democracy' in Turku, Finland (1996) and presented at the University of Oporto (1997). I am grateful to Kiki Deliyanni and Helen Araújo for these opportunities to share ideas.

References

Advisory Group on Citizenship (The Crick Report) (1998) *Education for Citizenship and the Teaching of Democracy in Schools. Final Report.* London: Qualifications and Curriculum Authority.

Arnot, M. (1991) '"Equality and democracy" a decade of struggle over education', *British Journal of Sociology of Education, 12*(4): 447–66.

Arnot, M. (1997) '"Gendered citizenry": new feminist perspectives on education and citizenship', *British Education Research Journal*, *23*(3): 275–95.
Arnot, M., David, M. and Weiner, G. (1999) *Closing the Gender Gap: postwar education and social change*. Cambridge: Polity Press.
Arnot, M. and Dillabough, J.A. (eds) (2000) *Challenging Democracy: international perspectives on gender, education and citizenship*. London: RoutledgeFalmer.
Arnot, M. and Gordon, T. (1996) 'A dialogue on gender, citizenship and marketisation', *Discourse: studies in the cultural politics of education*, 17, 3, pp 377-388
Bauman, Z. (2000) *Globalisation: the human consequences*. Cambridge: Polity Press.
Beck, J. (1996) 'Citizenship education: problems and possibilities', *Curriculum Studies*, *4*: 349–66.
Beck, U. (2001) 'Der hässliche Bürger', in A. Brosziewski, T.S. Eberle, C. Maeder (eds) *Moderne, Lonstanz: UVK Verlagsgesellschaft* (translated by D. Faas) pp. 57–68.
Beck, U. and Beck-Gernsheim, E. (2002) *Individualisation: institutionalised individualism and its social and political consequences*. London: Sage.
Bernstein, B. (2000) *Pedagogy, Symbolic Control and Identity: theory, research, critique Basil Bernstein*, rev. ed. London: Rowman and Littlefield.
Bourdieu, P. (1997) 'The forms of capital', in A.H. Halsey, H. Lauder, P. Brown, and A. Stuart Wells (eds) *Education, Culture, Economy, Society*. Oxford: Oxford University Press, pp. 46–58.
Bourdieu, P. and Passeron, J-C. (1977) *Reproduction in Education, Society and Culture*. (Published in association with Theory, Culture & Society) London: Sage.
Brown, C. (1991) 'Education for citizenship – old wine in new bottles?' *Citizenship*, *1*: 6–9.
Brysk, A. (2002) 'Conclusion: from rights to realities', in A. Brysk (ed.) and Demos *Globalisation and Human Rights*, California: University of California Press.
Bulmer, M. and Rees, A.M. (1996) 'Conclusion: citizenship in the twenty-first century', in M. Bulmer and A.M. Rees (eds) *Citizenship Today*. London: UCL Press.
Cogan, J.J. and Derricott, R. (2000) *Citizenship for the 21st Century*. London: Kogan Page.
Connell, R.W. (1987) *Gender and Power: society, the person and sexual politics*. London: Allen and Unwin.
Connell, R.W. (1990) 'The state, gender and sexual politics', *Theory and Society*, *19*: 507–44.
Davies, I., Evans, M. and Reid, A. (2005) 'Globalising citizenship education? A critique of "global education" and "citizenship education"', *British Journal of Educational Studies*, *53*(1): 66–89.
Davies, I., Gregory I. and Riley, S.C. (1999) *Good Citizenship and Educational Provision*. London: Falmer Press.
Delanty, D. (2000) 'Human rights and citizenship: the emergence of the embodied self', in G. Delanty (ed.) *Citizenship in a Global Age*. Buckingham: Open University Press.
Demaine, J. (2004) 'Citizenship and globalisation' in J. Demaine (ed.) *Citizenship and Political Education Today*. London: Palgrave.
Dillabough, J. (2000) 'Women in teacher education: their struggles for inclusion as "citizen-workers" in late modernity', in M. Arnot and J. Dillabough (eds) *Challenging Democracy: international perspectives on gender, education and citizenship*. London: RoutledgeFalmer.
Dillabough J. and Arnot, M. (2000) 'Feminist political frameworks: new approaches to the study of gender, citizenship and education', in M. Arnot and J.A. Dillabough (eds) *Challenging Democracy: international perspectives on gender, education and citizenship*. London: RoutledgeFalmer.
Dillabough, J. and Arnot, M. (2001) 'Feminist sociology of education: dynamics, debates and directions', in J. Demaine (ed.) *Sociology of Education Today*. London: Palgrave, pp. 30–47.

26 Sociological perspectives on the education of the gendered citizen

Dillabough, J. and Arnot, M. (2002) 'Recasting educational debates about female citizenship, agency and identity', *The School Field*, *13*(3/4): 61–89.

Dillabough, J. and Arnot, M. (2004) 'A magnified image of female citizenship in education: illusions of democracy or liberal challenges to symbolic domination', in J. Demaine (eds) *Citizenship and Political Education Today*. London: Palgrave MacMillan.

Donald, J. (1996) 'The citizen and the man about town', in S. Hall and P. du Gay (eds) *Questions about Cultural Identity*. London: Sage.

Durkheim, E. (1956) *Education and Sociology*. New York: Free Press.

Fraser, N. (1997) *Justice Interruptus: critical reflections on the 'post-socialist' condition*. London: Routledge.

Gilbert, R (1992) 'Citizenship, education and postmodernity', *British Journal of Sociology of Education*, *13*: 51–68.

Giroux, H. (1988) *Schooling for Democracy*. London, Routledge.

Gordon, T., Holland, J. and Lahelma, E. (2000) *Making Spaces: citizenship and difference in school*. London: MacMillan.

Heater, D. (1990) *Citizenship: a civic ideal in world history, politics and education*. London: Longman.

Heater, D. (2004) *A History of Education for Citizenship*. London: RoutledgeFalmer.

Held, D. (1996) *Models of Democracy*. Cambridge: Polity Press.

House of Commons Commission on Citizenship (1990) *Encouraging Citizenship*. London, HMSO.

Inman, W. and Buck, M. (eds) (1995) *Adding Value? Schools' responsibilities for the development of pupils*. Stoke-on-Trent: Trentham Books.

Ivinson, G. with Arnot, M., Araújo, H., Deliyanni-Kouimtzi, K., Rowe, G. and Tomé, A. (2000) 'Student teachers' representations of citizenship: a comparative perspective', in M. Arnot and J. Dillabough (eds) *Challenging Democracy: feminist perspectives on gender, education and citizenship*. London: RoutledgeFalmer.

Lloyd, G. (1986) 'Selfhood, war and masculinity', in C. Pateman and E. Gross (eds) *Feminist Challenges: social and political theory*. London: Allen and Unwin.

Lynch, J. (1992) *Education for Citizenship in a Multi-cultural Society*. London: Cassell.

Lyotard J.F. (1984) *The Postmodern Condition: a report on knowledge*. Manchester: Manchester University Press.

Marshall, H. (2005). 'Constructing global education in England'. Unpublished doctoral thesis, University of Cambridge.

Marshall, T.H. (1950) *Citizenship and Social Class*. Cambridge: Cambridge University Press.

McLaughlin, T.H. (1992) 'Citizenship, diversity and education: a philosophical perspective', *Journal of Moral Education*, *21*: 235–50.

Mouffe, C. (1992) 'Feminism, citizenship and radical democratic politics', in J. Butler and J.W. Scott (eds) *Feminists Theorise the Political*. New York: Routledge.

National Curriculum Council (1990) *Education for Citizenship,* Curriculum Guidance 8. York: NCC.

Osler, A. and Starkey, H. (2001) 'Citizenship education and national identities in France and England: inclusive or exclusive', *Oxford Review of Education*, *27*(2): 287–303.

Osler, A. and Starkey, H. (2005) 'Education for democratic citizenship: a review of research, policy and practice 1995–2005', Paper prepared for BERA Annual Review, November 2005, www.bera.ac.uk.

Osler, A. and Vincent, K. (2002) *Citizenship and the Challenge of Global Education*, Stoke-on-Trent: Trentham Books.

Pateman, C. (1980) *The Disorder of Women*. Cambridge, Polity Press.

Pateman, C. (1988) *The Sexual Contract*. Cambridge, Polity Press.

Pateman, C. (1992) 'Equality, difference, subordination: the politics of motherhood and women's citizenship', in G. Bock and B. James (eds) *Beyond Equality and Difference: citizenship, feminist politics and female subjectivity*. London: Routledge.

Rose, N. (1990) *Governing the Soul: the shaping of the private self.* London: Routledge.
School Curriculum and Assessment Authority (1995) *Consultation Document on Values.* London: SCAA.
Starkey, H., Hayward, J. and Turner, K. (2006) 'Education for citizenship' editorial for *Reflecting Education 2*(2): 1–7, http://reflectingeducation.net.
Torney-Purta, R.H., Lehmann, O. and Schulz, W. (2001) *Citizenship and Education in 28 Countries: civic knowledge and engagement at age fourteen.* Netherlands: IEA Secretariat.
Walby, S. (1994) 'Is citizenship gendered?', *Sociology*, 28(2): 379–95.
Wexler, P. (1991) 'Citizenship in the semiotic society', in B. Turner (ed.) *Theory of Modernity and Postmodernity.* London: Sage.
Whitty, G., Rowe, G. and Aggleton, P. (1994) 'Discourse in cross-curricular contexts: limits to empowerment', *International Studies in Sociology of Education*, 4: 25–42.
Yuval-Davis, N. and Stoetzler, M. (2002) 'Imagined boundaries and borders: a gendered gaze', *The European Journal of Women's Studies*, 9(3): 329–44.

Notes

1 Wexler (1991) argued that commodification has killed the Enlightenment concept of the citizen.
2 Her original surname was Deliyanni Kouimtzi but she now publishes under the surname Deliyanni.
3 Using a sociological perspective, this project explored the ways in which the citizenship was constructed in four different spheres: the public (political) sphere, employment, domestic, and private/intimate spheres. It uncovered the ways in which new male and female teachers addressed gender relations in each sphere and whether our sample of student teachers had (a) an accurate knowledge about gender and citizenship (gender literacy); (b) which discourses or languages of citizenship they used; and (c) what they aimed to achieve through education for citizenship.
4 Davies *et al.* (1999) found that English teachers were positive about citizenship education; concerned about the welfare of others, and about moral and ethical behaviour, and tolerant of diversity. Good citizenship meant knowledge of government and current affairs, the ability to question received ideas, uncritical patriotism, and obedience to authority. Osler and Starkey (2005) report that, on the whole, English teachers supported women's political rights.
5 Other cross-curricular themes were Environmental Education, Economic Awareness, Health Education and Careers Education.
6 There are eight components – community; a pluralist society; being a citizen; the family; democracy in action; the citizen and the law; work, employment and leisure; and public services.
7 For example, whilst professing the importance of equal opportunities as a cross-curricular dimension and recognising the violation of human rights represented by sexism or racism, the proposed syllabus was superficial and descriptive (Inman and Buck, 1995).
8 Also, little incentive to develop such cross-curricular policies and practices was given by Dearing's Report (1994) on the National Curriculum, with only the Office for Standards in Education (OFSTED) left holding onto the idea of a cross-curriculum theme.

9 I participated in the development of citizenship education at national level as an invited member of the: DfEE Working Group on Citizenship and Initial Teacher Education (2000); Citizenship Consultative Group (DFEE) (1998); SCAA National Forum on Values (1996) and Working Group on Initial Teacher Education (1996). Member of Citizenship Coalition Group (1996/8); Citizenship Alliance (1997/8); and, Citizenship 2000 (1998).
10 Notably, minority communities did not appear to have been involved in formulation of citizenship education.
11 Delanty describes three different critiques of human rights around post-colonial, transcultural and Habermasian perspectives.

2 Feminist politics and democratic values in education

with Jo-Anne Dillabough

> In our age, the contemporary women's movement has forged a particularly powerful connection and, with its determined critique of hierarchy and sustained anti-authoritarianism, turned itself into a virtual testing ground for democracy's most radical ideals. (Phillips, 1991a: 2)

Feminism and democracy, although apparently having a good deal in common, did not develop in tandem. In fact, it was only by the nineteenth century that the normative ideals of 'equality' united feminist and democratic movements in Western Europe and North America. One should not assume, therefore, that concerns about 'gender equality' are synonymous with the concept of democracy. Nor can it be legitimately argued that each and any form of democratic education would fulfil feminist educational ideals. Clearly, much depends on how democratic education and questions of equality are defined, conceptualised, and expressed in relation to gender politics and the authentic concerns of feminists. More significantly, some feminist theorising suggests that *gender equality*, as a goal, serves to obscure more complex explanations about the relationship of women to democratic social formations. Indeed, on such a view far more attention needs to be paid to a consideration of how, theoretically, we might unravel the contradictions which currently manifest the relationship between gender, education, and democracy.

The tensions between democracy and feminism are no more clearly expressed than in feminist critiques of liberal democratic theories, structures, and processes. One can identify important differences, for example, between feminist theories and the empirical tasks they have set for themselves – that is, critical distinctions that might explain the complexity of the relationship of women to liberal democratic politics, and the ways in which women's connection to the economy and family is circumscribed. Feminist political theorists have thus been inclined to examine the sources of, and complexity surrounding, female oppression and its manifestation in the language and practices of political liberalism. They also have exposed the illusions of 'political neutrality' central to many of the male-centred versions of traditional liberal democratic thought. These claims suggest that a major transformation of the concept of democracy, as we understand it, is required before women can achieve full status as citizens, on a par with that of men.

This kind of theoretical agenda offers us the possibility of re-assessing the contribution of *feminist educational thought* to our understanding of the political role of education in democratic societies. Therefore, in this exploratory chapter, we draw upon the insights of feminist political theorists to evaluate the ways in which feminist educational theorising in the last two decades has tackled the problem of a 'gendered' democracy. What contributions have been made to, and what theoretical insights are proffered on, the relationship between democracy and the gendering of values in schooling? Is there a need, for example, for a more systematic and structured approach to the study of democratic educational values through feminist theory? If so, what analytical framework and conceptual tools are required to undertake such a task?

We begin by describing the key feminist debates that address the gendering of liberal democracy. In the first section, feminist critiques of liberal democracy, the gendered construction of the *nation* and *nationality*, and the notion of 'woman' as a political category are discussed. What is interesting about these debates is precisely what they expose about the complex nature of gender politics within the 'democratic state'. They also provide novel insights into the ways in which feminist educational theorists might reconsider the links between gender and democracy.

In the second section, we revisit major but contrasting traditions of thought – that of liberal feminism, maternal feminism and socialist feminist educational theorising – to illustrate shifts in thinking about democracy and democratic education. We then go on to discuss the rise of new feminisms and their contribution to our understanding of democratic relations in education. In the final section of this chapter, we describe the key levels of political analyses which have been drawn upon by feminists to examine the 'gendered' foundations of democratic education.

Feminist political theory

Feminist educational thought and its relevance to questions of democracy are scrutinised more effectively when considered against the work of feminist political and social theorists. Three themes emerge from a survey of recent writing in feminist political theory that provide some understanding of the relationship between gender and democracy.

Order and disorder: the basis of a fraternal pact

The work of Carol Pateman, a feminist political theorist, signals for many a new theoretical agenda. Her influential set of texts, such as *The Sexual Contract* (1988) and *The Disorder of Women* (1989), indicates the ways in which social concepts of order, disorder, civic society and the citizen have been constructed historically as gender dualisms – that is, the binary male and female divide – and offers an understanding of associated male power over women. Pateman argues that the concept of liberal democratic citizenship developed by English philosophers was, in effect, what Marx called a 'political lion's skin' worn only occasionally and somewhat reluctantly by women.

Pateman's central concern lies with the legitimacy of liberal theory, particularly because all concepts derived from the liberal tradition privilege the ontology of maleness and the 'epistemic' dominance of masculinity in liberal political thought. She argues that concepts such as the 'political [or social] order' are, by definition, gendered. For example, mainstream political philosophy has equated the concept of *social order* with a rational, autonomous selfhood in which individuals act according to universal and objective moral principles, thus transcending private interests. Yet at the source of such notions of the individual, Pateman (1989, 1992) argues, is a Western European version of *masculinity*. Men, for the predominantly male European political philosophers, exemplified the potential of humans to create a social order that is based on 'rationality' and 'truth'. 'Rational' thought and male versions of political autonomy are thus seen as central to the functioning of a pure democracy.

On the other side of the equation, that of *disorder*, we find women characteristically portrayed as psychologically unbalanced and therefore unable to articulate a political consciousness (Lloyd, 1986). Pateman (1992) states,

> Women, our bodies and distinctive capacities, represented all that citizenship was not. 'Citizenship' has gained its meaning through the exclusion of women, that is to say (sexual) 'difference'. (p. 19)

Thus, the 'lethal' combination of women's psychological 'disabilities' and sexual characteristics implied that they be excluded from the original social contract or, in effect, *the fraternal pact* (cf. Pateman, 1989). In constructing this civic brotherhood, however, men have legitimated their autonomic right to that power in public life, and at the same time, their sexual rights over women:

> The brothers *make a sexual contract*. They establish a law which confirms masculine sex-right and ensures that there is an orderly access by each man to a woman. (Pateman, 1988: 109)

The 'sexual contract' is established through, for example, the separation of public and private spheres. This separation is representative of the historical distinction between 'male' and 'female' as antagonistic universalising categories. Women become symbols of emotion, natural feeling and caring for those related to them. Women *qua* women are not capable, it would seem, of the 'objectivity' and principled behaviour that characterises the soldier and the citizen.

This separation of public and private spheres has serious consequences for both men and women as 'citizens'. Men, by transcending the private domain, become social and public, whereas women, who are constructed as symbolic of the private domain, are excluded by definition from the social (civilised) order. Thus, while women are included within the liberal democratic project as symbols of morality and femininity (Yuval-Davis, 1997a), they are *excluded* from possessing political power and, as it naturally follows, from the realm of citizenship. Consequently, the greatest weakness of the liberal model is the very premise upon which women's citizenship has been constructed; that is, a reliance on the gendered nature of the public/private split or what Phillips (1991a, 1991b, 1992) calls the 'political settlement'. In this 'settlement', gender inequality is embedded in the political principles and social relations which are legitimated by a theory of liberal democracy.

In short, feminist political theorists have raised questions that challenge the core of our understanding of citizenship and the civic sphere. Their analyses can be used to consider, for example, the challenge to the 'fraternal pact' put forward by social movements such as the international women's movement, the ways in which women have been inserted into the public sphere, and the shifting boundaries between public and private domains. Moreover, many questions too are raised about the role of education in relation to this political project – to what extent, for example, did the development of educational systems mirror and institutionalise the fraternal pact? We might also ask, just how is democracy taught to the young? Is it through a reassertion of a gendered notion of citizenship – a privileging of male public spheres – that redefines democracy as a neutral and *degendered* entity (Phillips, 1991a)?

The gendering of nationhood and nation-states

In recent years, both feminist political and social theorists have turned their attention to the study of state practices in response to questions of 'citizenship' and 'national identity'. Their primary concerns have centred on debunking myths about the egalitarian nature of democratic citizenship in the nation-state and exposing diverse forms of marginalisation associated with, for example, civic nationalism. In this model of analysis, feminist political theorists do not simply view citizenship as a masculine entity, as it appears in the work of Carole Pateman. Rather, the goal is to examine how questions of nationhood and the 'civil society' impact on the very nature and constitutive elements of women's marginalisation in an era of increasing globalisation and advanced modernisation. Of particular significance within this tradition is the study of the ambivalent manifestation of gender and male domination in nationalist and political rhetoric; in particular, those discourses which persistently function to marginalise women already defined as 'Other' in the state. Therefore, the aim in much of this work is to explore the gendered dynamics of national politics and its impact on the political and social identities of culturally oppressed and differently positioned women.

Some of the most interesting work in this area has been conducted by Nira Yuval-Davis (1997a, 1997b), Yuval-Davis and Anthias (1989), and Pieterse and Parekh (1995). Yuval-Davis (1997a, 1997b), for example, suggests that women are represented in nationalist discourses as romantic symbols of cultural morality who do not possess political agency, but who instead function as maternal catalysts of national identity in the broadest sense. She writes:

> women are 'required to carry this burden of representation' – the symbolic bearers of the collectivity's identity and honour, both personally and

collectively. (…). Girls did not need to act; they had to become the national embodiment. (Yuval-Davis, 1997a: 45)

In this 'identity' representation, there is no explicit conflict between gender and nation. In fact, as Yuval-Davis (1997a) describes it, it seems very clear; women are not given any formal role in the development of the nation. They instead are seen as keepers, cultivators, and symbols of it. This implies a certain responsibility that is placed upon women to reproduce and cultivate in democratic subjects those dominant cultural values which are endorsed by those who dominate the political machinery (and indeed political memory) of the state. This 'reproductive' process leads to a cultural privileging that exalts not only the state's position on national identity, but women's position within it. In doing so, however, nationalist rhetoric not only privileges the dominance of male super-ordinance in state hierarchies but represses, both epistemically and politically, the many cultural and national understandings of gender which reside on the margins of the state.

This legitimised practice of privileging also means that women who oppose or resist the dominant view of culture and nationhood[1] are viewed as 'non-persons' or 'non-citizens'. The 'non-citizen' is not only viewed as 'deviant', but is prevented from contributing to the *formal* development of the nation. The 'non-citizen', then, is that which signifies 'difference'. Yuval-Davis (1997b) writes:

> the study of citizenship should consider the issue of women's citizenship not only by contrast to that of men, but also in relation to women's affiliation to dominant or subordinate groups, their ethnicity, origin, and urban or rural residence. It also should take into consideration global and transnational positionings of these citizenships. (Yuval-Davis, 1997b: 4–5)

In summary, the work of Yuval-Davis and related feminist work (see Pieterse and Parekh, 1995) has raised key questions about the role of national rhetoric and symbolism in the formation of gender identities. Yuval-Davis's (1997a, 1997b) work can be used to consider, for example, the ways in which civic nationalism or neo-colonialism simultaneously conditions and undermines the cultural identities and political representation of women (and girls and boys) in diverse educational contexts. It also sheds light on the ways in which national activity, as part of political socialisation in education, is implicated in reproductive and sometimes traditional patterns of gender identity-formation.

Such work also exposes a link between the liberal democratic schooling project, globalisation, and gender in the broadest sense. It raises questions, for example, about the relationship between the social exclusion of women and girls in education and school restructuring as a response to modernisation and globalisation. It might also help us to question how national narratives concerning such issues as 'boys' and girls' achievement', 'standards' or 'school choice' (as liberal democratic practice) might lead to school exclusions when gender identities do not conform to a broader cultural narrative on identity and citizenship. Many questions, too, are raised about feminist theory and education outside 'Western' nations and the role of feminist politics there.

'Woman' as a political category

A third conceptualisation which has emerged in response to feminist critiques of liberal democracy is a concern with the ways in which women's roles and social practices have been represented as political categories in the polity, especially those associated with the democratic state. Does the state support a formal view of women as political agents, or do women have historically determined apolitical roles in a democracy? Are women still seen, as they were at the early stages of the suffragist movement, as 'benevolent philanthropists,'[2] or are they political actors who possess agency in their own right?

Such questions are addressed by feminist political theorists and philosophers who are concerned with the epistemological significance of women's representation in both political theory and the state. For example, the feminist political philosopher Roland Martin (1994) argues that the category 'woman' has been erased from politics and political theory:

> ... women, children, and the family dwell in the 'ontological basement,' outside and underneath the political structure. This apolitical status is due not to historical accident or necessity but to arbitrary definition (...). Since the subject matter of political theory is politics and since reproductive processes have been traditionally assigned to women and have taken place within the family, it follows that women and the family are excluded from the very subject matter of the discipline. (Roland Martin, 1994: 107–8)

Roland Martin's description of women's 'apolitical status' in the state leads to a historically determined and socially constructed vision of womanhood – that of *benevolent actor* and *virtuous being*. In this context, women, as mothers and caregivers, are constructed against the grain of formal political action and are consequently seen as outsiders to the political process.

By contrast, the category 'woman,' as described by Iris Marion Young (1995), not only illuminates a vision of women as political in the formal sense, but also points to women's collective resistance to more conventional definitions of political participation. To put this another way, women are seen as motivated political actors in their own right. Young writes:

> One reason to conceptualise women as a collective, I think, is to maintain a point of view outside of liberal individualism (...). Without conceptualising women as a group in some sense, it is not possible to conceptualise oppression in a systematic, structured institutional process. (Young, 1995: 192)

Women are thus placed at the centre of democratic politics as a form of gendered resistance to masculine conceptions of the state. This oppositional practice is designed to challenge those liberal assumptions which view women as the 'victim', conflate the categories 'women' and 'domesticity', and ultimately function to exclude women from full political participation.

In such polarised representations, we find binary images of the category 'women': on the one hand, a daughter of the nation-state thought to instil a moral 'ethics of care' (Gilligan, 1982, 1986) in society through her connection to the private sphere; and, on the other, an active *social* agent with membership in a political collectivity. At first glance, such contemporary visions appear irreconcilable and indeed contradictory. Nevertheless, they bear some relevance to current understandings of democracy. For example, the notion of women as daughters of the nation-state invokes symbolic images of care in the maintenance of democratic relations. At the same time, Young's description of the feminist collectivity points to an image of women as agents who actively participate in the reconstruction of a democracy.

Both modern and postmodern (and indeed post-structural) feminist political theorists have justifiably exposed both these images as problematic because they essentialise women in unacceptable ways. However, a feminist political and social analysis (rather than simply deconstructive analysis) of the varied and conflicting categories of 'womanhood' provides an alternative lens through which to examine the relationship between gender and democracy. It also implies a necessity for unravelling the complex web of relationships which underpin questions about women's inclusion and participation in a democracy.

In confronting these issues, one must go beyond a simple examination of 'woman' as a gender category in order to address Iris Young's (1995) interest in *women's relation to the 'political'*. The simplest and arguably most powerful mechanism for achieving this end is to examine the potential links between the *feminist project* and *democratic principles*. In so doing, one learns that democratic concepts, such as equality, do not necessarily converge at the centre of all feminist projects and do not apply to the history of all women's struggles. Wilson (1995) writes:

> It is not (…) possible to say that (feminism) is a commitment to equality, since some feminists have argued, both in the past and today, for separate spheres of influence, emphasising difference and complementarity rather than equality. (Wilson, 1995: 8; (feminism), our addition)

In short, feminist political theorists have raised questions about the suspected and elusive character of 'equality' and its contradictory role in the 'emancipation' of women. They also have exposed the gendered classifications which manifest the male-oriented trajectory of liberal democratic thought. Indeed, such efforts have called into question the very structures of liberal democratic thinking and its role in the formation of gender identities. In our view, such insights can be used, for example, to critique state education and its regulation of women and girls' (and men and boys') identities. We might also ask how a critical analysis of gender categories might force us to question the precepts of democratic educational practice and the manner in which feminists have examined 'gender and democracy' in education over time.

Feminist analyses of gender and democracy in education

The feminist critiques described thus far provide some insight into the ways in which gender and democracy have been examined in the social sciences. We now draw indirectly upon these arguments to reassess a range of contemporary feminist perspectives in education. We demonstrate how each theoretical stance provides some insight into the relation between education and the liberal democratic project, although not always making this agenda explicit or central, nor necessarily building upon each other's work.

Feminist research originally achieved its status by demonstrating that state politics and institutions rested upon a patriarchal notion of civil society.[3] An assumption about the reality of women's oppression has always applied across feminist research, although sometimes reference is made to a normative concept of masculine control (i.e. the patriarchal state), and at other times a non-normative notion of female oppression is identified (e.g. contradictory state discourses, local power relations). Such discrepancies in feminist thought have led to educational research which draws upon different 'objects and subjects' of study and operates at different levels of political analysis. Some studies are more highly focused on the ways in which the macro-structures of schooling (whether political or economic) shape the distribution of educational opportunities and privileges among male and female pupils, whereas others concentrate more upon the particularity of gendered experiences in education. Similarly, the epistemological and methodological standpoints of writers on gender and education are varied and even, on occasion, incompatible. Such standpoints range, for example, from the structuring of gender regimes and codes to analyses of the discursive framing of the educational project and its construction of particular subjects (e.g. 'the girl', 'the pupil', 'the teacher'). Often there is a tension between analyses which might highlight modes of social control, regulation, and governance of educational 'subjects' or the disciplining of the body, or studies of youth cultures, rebellions, and diverse coping strategies.

Other types of feminist research make claims about the potential for gender reform inherent in the liberal democratic project using the spaces and possibilities available in the educational system. Such possibilities may involve the deconstruction of educational texts and practices or the promotion of critical pedagogies (see Luke and Gore, 1989). Still other research has promoted the development of feminist values (e.g. caring) and female modes of authority (see Gilligan, 1986). Feminist pedagogies have also been described, as have the strategies for the politicisation of young people's experiential knowledge. Such a diverse field represents precisely the contradiction of the liberal democratic educational project. It allows itself to become the subject of its own critique at the same time as obscuring its connections with political and economic conditions. In keeping with this concern, we begin therefore with a critique of liberal democratic theory and its relationship to feminist models of democratic education.

Feminist theory and liberal democratic education

In many national contexts, the state has had to respond to increasingly confident feminist campaigns, many of which have drawn extensively from the discourse of liberal democracy (Heater, 1990). In the twentieth century, such campaigns intensified, using the language of liberalism to struggle for women's equality. Some of the key assumptions which underlie liberal feminism are described below.

i. The 'principle of political neutrality'[4] is viewed as sacrosanct in the liberal democratic state. Such neutrality serves to constrain the actions of government and individuals (see Whelehan, 1995), both of which may otherwise restrict women's potential for political agency in the state.
ii. Female autonomy is central to women's 'self-improvement and basic livelihood' in the liberal state because, as Whelehan (1995: 29) argues, 'men hold such rights naturally'.
iii. Political equality between the sexes must be examined through the lens of opportunity, access, and self-determination. These female entitlements are to be achieved through various procedural forms of competition in a free society.
iv. Women are capable of rational thought (Wollstonecraft, 1992, original publication, 1792). These rational capacities must be drawn upon to challenge the assumption that women are inferior to men in their ability to engage politically (see also Whelehan, 1995).

Each of these assumptions, in different ways, supports the notion of a free public society (with inherent liberties) open to women. Under liberalism, the long-term goal of feminism is to empower women to take up their rightful place in this 'open' society through the development of *female autonomy*. A second goal is to *degender*, as far as possible, the public sphere through the legal recognition of women's right to equality on par with that of men. Liberal feminist analysis has thus highlighted the *importance of bringing women into the male public sphere, while still retaining the social functioning of the female private sphere.* Paradoxically, however, it is the separation of public and private spheres that has protected the 'privacy' of the home and celebrated individualism and individual rights in the public domain. Unfortunately, this rather unnatural separation has meant that ideological concerns about the masculine dimensions of democratic life have yet to be applied by liberal feminists to a serious critique of women's positioning in the private domain. Nevertheless, the exposure by feminist political theorists of the divisions between such gendered spaces has made possible the liberal feminist critique of the public sphere.

The educational assumptions which are manifest in liberal feminist thought revolve around the notion of *opportunity*; that is, schooling, as the first point of entry into the economy, provides one of many opportunities through which men and women can achieve political equality in the public realm. According to the liberal feminist, then, the opportunity structure of schools must accommodate the needs of women who wish to take up a place within a competitive economic sphere.

38 Feminist politics and democratic values in education

As a consequence, liberal feminists have made numerous contributions toward the development of a particular form of democratic discourse (e.g. rights, equal opportunity) in schools, and at the same time, incurred some difficulties.

One such contribution emerged as a result of women's struggle to gain access to male forms of high-status education. For example, liberal feminists provided statistical data that highlighted women's under-employment and under-representation in the public sphere. Such work exposed the failure of liberal democratic societies to give women anything other than secondary and marginal status and revealed the extent to which education was successful in ensuring the reproduction of a sex-segregated labour force. Liberal feminists also revealed how the state and the state education system, both of which should have been neutral arbiters, had been captured by men. Education was indeed, as Carole Pateman had suggested, a *fraternity*, with men dominating the machineries by which social justice was defined.

Another target of analysis within liberal feminist critiques was the assessment of official school knowledge and its representation of women. For example, several textbook and curriculum studies demonstrated how official knowledge was aligned with hegemonic male structures in society, thus legitimising male-dominated public spheres and masculine forms of citizenship. The curricular traditions regulating women defined a female role that privileged the domestic and emphasised a vocational education that was service-oriented rather than subject-centred. Women were to be educated as daughters of the nation, imbued with an ethos of duty and service to both society and to their menfolk (Brindle and Arnot, 1999; Dyehouse, 1976; Davin, 1978). Whereas boys were differentiated along lines of social inequality (class differences), women were reduced to biological and/or psychological characteristics.

Women, despite their differences in social status and life experiences, were categorised in such educational discourses as more homogeneous than heterogeneous. Therefore, liberal feminists, albeit unintentionally, exposed the 'gender essentialisms' (see Roman, 1992) of schooling. Significantly then, liberal democratic feminists turned the concept of rights 'against the patriarchal model of citizenship' and produced a 'powerful and sharp edged'(Connell, 1990) analysis of male dominance in education.

Although this model of education is worthy of some admiration, a number of key political issues concerning women's oppression have been either undermined or ignored. First, liberal feminism has tended to accept the political, civic, and economic sphere as unproblematic. For example, in merely accepting and thus defending 'equality' as the centrepoint of liberal feminist thinking, the ideological premises upon which liberal democratic theory was structured went unchallenged. We also learned little about how liberal ideals function as part of a discourse of modern Western capitalism. Indeed, we failed to understand precisely how democratic schooling, as a political discourse, became a regulating force linked to the establishment, state agendas, and the construction of gender identities.

Second, at this macro-contextual level, little attention was given to women's positioning in the domestic sphere. As a consequence, liberal feminism could not easily address the key constraints which have restricted women's participation in political, civic, economic, and cultural decision making – the role, for example, of domestic labour; the lack of childcare; the control of women and girls by 'husbands' and fathers, and the political regulation of sexuality. Democratic education therefore meant urging women to participate more fully in the public sphere, and to pursue non-traditional subjects and vocational courses. It also meant releasing the intellectual potential of women into the economy. Much liberal feminist research has therefore focused on the 'presumed deficits' of girls, relying on hopes of improving their achievement status rather than confronting the gendered nature of school structures.

Sexism within the curriculum, the classroom, the playground and indeed in the teaching profession[5] could be left relatively unaffected, once more formal discriminatory practices had been removed. Freedom of subject choice, movement, play, expression and action, although allegedly liberating, later proved to be deeply problematic. In such 'spaces' could be found precisely those practices and gender conventions that shaped traditional male and female identities and constrained the possibility of real equality between the sexes. Ironically, liberal feminists eventually found themselves arguing for the closure of options and of freedoms, such as 'freedom of choice' (Arnot, 1991, 1993), so that formal equality could be achieved (e.g. affirmative action).

The notion of female citizenship was also deeply problematic in the liberal feminist model of education. Women were to be educated toward greater autonomy and encouraged to work toward their own self-determination through education. Female citizenship therefore implied equal membership in masculinised subjects, more or less regulated by the sexist ethos of school subjects themselves. Seen in this light, democratic schooling was best understood as the 'training ground for the *female* entrepreneur' (see Dietz, 1985, emphasis added), and the institutional form capable of granting women an equal chance in the race towards individual achievement.

In short, liberal feminists focused on the most overt contradictions of capitalist democracy – the gap between, for example, equal opportunity as a principle and the reality of differential treatment. However, they failed to identify far deeper obstacles to gender equality. As a result, liberal goals for women's rights (now thought to have been achieved) were embedded in a neo-liberal agenda that focused on creating more competitive and rationalised performances in the market. The representation of the democratic school, from a strong liberal view, is an institutional form that touts its competencies, excellence, marketability, and technical skills, all of which (at least in theory) are thought to be equally applicable to men and women.

Women, maternalism and democratic education

We turn now to the second set of responses to the historical construction of female education and its link to democratic principles. Much of mainstream feminist educational theory is persuaded by the notion of *gender difference*. Difference, in

40 Feminist politics and democratic values in education

the maternal frame, however, has substantially different meaning from that which is expressed by, for example, feminist post-structuralists. It is most concerned with biological (and psychological) variations between men and women and their impact on the formation of gender roles in society. As Elshtain (1981, 1992) argues, women are different by the very nature of their positioning within the private sphere. Recognition of the 'private' as a valid sphere of political activity therefore implies the inclusion of women's voices in the reconstruction of democratic practice. Political theorists who defend this position can be identified, broadly speaking, as *maternal feminists*.

Maternal feminist analyses – the empirical study of those aspects of a woman's life that are qualitatively different from a man's life – have exposed the limits of democratic 'rights' which refer only to the public sphere. As Anne Phillips (1991a: 30) argues, 'for feminists, failure to explore the nature of most of the private sphere is a failure in democratic debate'. Maternal feminists therefore argue that liberation lies not with concepts of equality and equal rights, nor with democratic freedoms drawn from liberal democratic discourses, but with an explicit recognition of the role of the 'nurturer' as central to the reconstruction of the public sphere. Key to this new form of the social order is not the 'brotherhood of man' but relations between mother and child. The social and emotional relations which necessitate the restructuring of the 'fraternal' political consciousness are thus central to defining the foundations of a 'women-centred' democracy.

Within this tradition, and of increasing significance in fields beyond political theory, are the writings of feminist philosophers and psychologists (e.g. Gilligan, 1986; Belenky *et al.*, 1986). In particular, the work of Carol Gilligan focuses quite explicitly on the feminist values of motherhood and caring and indicates how such ideals challenge masculine understandings of justice and morality in the democratic state. Perhaps Dietz (1985), in critiquing this viewpoint, best characterises how such values might influence the nature of the political sphere when she writes:[6]

> public discourse and citizenship should be informed by the values of mothering – love, attentiveness, compassion, care and 'engrossment' – in short, by all the virtues the liberal, statist, public realm disdains. (Dietz, 1985: 33)

Such virtue, whether a result of women's physiological difference or their gendered experiences since childhood, is thought to reflect different ways of knowing and evaluating the world (see Gilligan, 1986; Belenky *et al.*, 1986). If such values are reflected in formal political spheres, then the possibility exists of constructing an alternative political framework to that of liberal democracy – one that has a *caring ethos* at its centre.

Within this position, the educational strategy has been one of privileging female notions of humanity, caring, and mothering. Noddings (1988) refers to such practices as a *relational ethics* of care:

> A relational ethic is rooted in and dependent on natural caring. Instead of striving away from affection and towards behaving always out of duty as Kant

has prescribed, one acting from a perspective of caring moves consciously in the other direction; that is, he or she calls on a sense of obligation in order to stimulate natural caring. (...) Because natural caring is both the source and the terminus of ethical caring, it is reasonable to use the mother-child relation as its prototype (...). Caring as a rational moral orientation and maternal thinking with its (...) interests are richly applicable to teaching. (Noddings, 1988: 219–20)

The consequences of this argument for democratising education are extensive and have been realised, at least in part, in some American and British women's studies programmes and teacher education faculties. Emphasis in such programmes has been on the social and moral aspects of education. Such a model implies, for example, 'woman-centred' courses that embrace values such as *connectedness*, co-operation, and mutual support (Belenky *et al.*, 1986). It also implies the elimination of the specialisation and fragmentation of knowledge and a male-dominated elite structure of disciplines in higher education (see Noddings, 1997). Instead, knowledge is acquired in an open and non-threatening educational environment; teaching is dialogical, students are empowered and women contribute their own versions of the 'truth'.

Women's lived experience and the status of women as 'knowers' thus takes centre stage in a more inclusive, gender-specific version of *woman-centred democratic practice*. The process of inclusion is not individual but collective, using common experiences as the means by which such liberation is encouraged. Education is seen, therefore, to represent a more humane and less disaffected context in which the 'feminine subject' becomes the axis upon which educational strategies pivot. As a consequence, the category 'woman' not only remains intact but is celebrated for its anti-elitist and less hierarchical forms of moral authority (i.e. the mother-child bond).

It is only in exceptional circumstances that educational policy makers have applied such arguments to the development of a women-centred democratic school. One could argue, however, that our understandings of democracy and democratic schooling have been widened considerably by such efforts. Women's concerns about, for example, men's limited role in the private sphere or male violence have created a new terrain for the reconstruction of democratic life and a new focus for the democratisation of education. Indeed, domestic inequality, questions about masculinity and control over sexuality have all been implicated in the new 'democratising' of human relations and the gendered recontextualisation of knowledge in schools and higher education.

Maternalism in question

Democratising education might have been a relatively simple affair if it were only about inserting an identifiable women's culture into our understanding of democracy. Clearly, however, such simplicity masks a certain complexity about gender relations. For example, while maternal feminism takes up the challenge of the public/private distinctions, it fails to either treat as problematic the political category of 'women' or, on the other hand, to address the differentiation of women's experiences and their multiple positionings by the state. In other words, maternal feminists universalise the importance of the private sphere in ways which may function, albeit unintentionally, to demean 'the "feminine" identities they construct.'[7] Therefore, while liberal feminism fails to question female subordination in the private sphere, maternal feminists essentialise the woman as 'mother'. However, as Butler (1995: 49) writes: 'all women are not mothers; some cannot be, some are too young or too old to be, some choose not to be, and for some who are mothers, that is not necessarily the rallying point of their politicization in feminism'.

Butler's (1995) concerns speak to the tensions which arise in response to questions about 'gender essentialisms in feminist theory itself'. And she is right to expose and confront these tensions. Nevertheless, maternal feminists have also quite justifiably argued that women's knowledge must shape educational practice and should do so even more if we wish to transform the current state of gender politics in educational institutions. Questions still remain, however, about how a maternal feminist might reconstruct a new version of democracy and democratic education, fashioned upon a premise which contradicts itself – that is, that one 'sex', with its set of accompanying values, is morally superior to the other.

Democracy and difference

Socialist and Black feminists sought to address gender politics in terms of the *differences* between and among women rather than in terms of the differences between men and women. They achieved this by demonstrating significant differences in the relationship between working-class and middle-class women, and of the culturally oppressed to capitalist economies (see Barrett, 1980; Weis, 1983). These early interests in diversity and difference led to a critique of liberal feminist theories and called into question a degendered 'neutral' education system. In short, socialist and black feminists' efforts to politicise women's differences challenged the very possibility of a degendered liberal polity and led to an analysis of modern forms of male-directed economic power. Clearly, an increasing awareness of the extent of social inequalities between women of diverse backgrounds (and across national boundaries) belied the simplicity of both liberal and maternal feminist arguments.

Even though this recognition of 'difference' has challenged much feminist thinking, it is more difficult to examine the particular relationship between socialist feminist initiatives and democratic values in education. One could argue, for example, that socialist feminism never really engaged with the concept of democracy or democratic school movements (e.g. free schooling, open schooling). It instead concerned itself with a critique of our rather naive views of modern education and its links to capitalist social formations. This concern led to the exposure of schools as hegemonic state institutions, which behind their illusions of neutrality (Bourdieu and Passeron, 1977; Bernstein, 1977) and their liberal guise

(Bowles and Gintis, 1976), reproduced a highly diversified and stratified work force (e.g. Althusser, 1971). Socialist feminist initiatives thus focused on developing politicised cultures of resistance to ensure a more democratic school environment. For example, Gramscian models of feminist education centred primarily on challenging male dominance and masculine *gender codes* (Arnot, 1980) through counter-hegemonic educational practices (see also Weiler, 1988).

This image of educational practice has implied the celebration of a radical consciousness through alternative curricular forms and critical pedagogy. Unfortunately, much of this work stopped short of challenging male dominance in the private sphere and failed to prevent the celebration, by the male left, of the assertion of hegemonic masculinity in counter-school cultures (e.g. Arnot, 1984). It therefore seemed unlikely that the dominance of a masculinised bourgeois culture identified by French theorists such as Bourdieu and Passeron (1977) would be challenged in the classroom, and neither were the forms of male authority which supported such a culture necessarily challenged by a Marxist 'feminist pedagogy' (Luke and Gore, 1989). Instead, socialist feminism tended to reinforce the distinction between public and private spheres and failed to define what democratic participation would mean in the home. As Jagger (1983) argued, a more equal division of domestic labour and women's control over biological reproduction should be essential to the achievement of democracy. Many, however, argued for community control over biological reproduction in the name of the common good as a radical ideal. Deeply problematic issues such as public coercion versus private rights and the role of the state in relation to domestic relations were therefore never fully resolved.

The rising importance of black feminism enriched the debate by introducing different 'knowledge claims' about gender relations and new political spheres of action. Black feminists took exception to the constraints of rationalist theorising in education (Carby, 1982; hooks, 1989; Mirza 1993). Many of the new critiques analysed the relationship of black families and black women to capitalism and imperialism (Phoenix, 1987; Hill-Collins, 1990), set the agenda for new conceptualisations of black women's experiences of the educational system and urged the political recognition of gendered discourses of racism in schools (see for example, Blair 1995; Blair and Holland, 1995). Liberal and socialist discourses on gender were exposed as Eurocentric, ethnocentric and colonialist in both form and content (Mirza 1992). Black women were shown to inhabit 'other worlds'; their experiences of education, and indeed, of political struggle were fundamentally structured around the community (a 'third space' according to Mirza and Reay 2000). Individual social mobility in this context was framed by a 'desire for inclusion that is strategic, subversive and ultimately far more transformative than subcultural reproduction suggests'. Black women's political agency as a result was shown to bear a fundamentally different relationship to structure than that accounted for in rationalistic models (Brah and Minhas, 1985). Black feminists ignited an interest in postcolonial accounts which were more relational in approach (Mirza, 1993).[8]

In retrospect, socialist feminists scrutinised all analyses that presumed a unitary category of 'woman' and attempted to demarcate the lines of social exclusion, particularly for those at the economic periphery. Their work, together with related black feminist and lesbian feminist critiques (e.g. Brah and Minhas, 1985; Weis, 1983), began to expose other systems of identification (e.g. race, class, sexuality) as central elements at work in the production of female subordination. Consequently, this work had much to offer in its early focus on difference and its recognition of the socially constructed nature of gender categories. Increasingly, therefore, academics became aware of the need to address difference. Questions about difference, by the beginning of the 1980s, were clearly on the agenda.

New feminism(s) and the 'deconstruction' of democracy

In the period between 1980 and 1985, the debate among liberal, maternal and socialist feminism(s) escalated and its locus changed substantially. Increasingly, modern feminist perspectives were seen as historical responses to the inadequacies of totalising discourse(s). A concern also arose that all feminism(s) in the modern period were defined, at least in part, by liberal discourse since many feminist advancements had taken place in national contexts in which liberalism had substantial political credibility. Such perspectives were challenged by diverse feminist communities (e.g. lesbian feminists) who argued that their identities could not be found in a liberal democratic discourse nor in alternative radical and social frameworks. Liberal feminism, in particular, not only had failed to represent the diverse political interests of women, but had addressed women who had benefited primarily from membership in white, middle-class culture. Such concerns suggested that the category 'woman' was not only 'illusory' (see Butler, 1990), but repressed women's differences. Similar criticisms were directed at socialist feminism, because class and political economy were central to its edifice as a modern political theory.

These 'master narrative(s)' had constructed a version of the social order that found causal explanations for women's inequality. Women's social positioning was the result of, for example, gender socialisation patterns, capitalist exploitation, or men's oppression of women. Women's subjective experiences, in the case of liberal feminism or maternal feminism, had been largely ignored or universalised. In the case of socialist feminism, women's experiences were put down to class determination. Such explanations, it seemed, bore little relation to the complexity of women's identities and experiences.

Post-structural feminism

In the mid-1980s, a variety of new feminism(s) emerged which can be subsumed, albeit loosely, under the banner of post-structuralism. The terrain of post-structuralism within political theory is vast. Two theoretical and empirical issues, however, now manifest the realm of post-structural feminist work in relation to questions about liberal democratic practice. These are: (1) the links between modern forms of governance in democratic states ('govermentality') and the regulation of gendered identities; and (2) the local expression of male dominance and its link to the production and regulation of the gendered citizen. We restrict our discussion here to the identification of features which have distinguished the *political* perspectives of feminist post-structuralists from other brands of feminism in their understanding of gender and democracy.

Over the last two decades, many post-structural (and, in some cases, postmodern) feminists have argued that the main task for feminism is to embrace three issues which are currently debated about theories of liberal democracy:

i. there is a false dichotomy between 'conceptual devices' thought to explain incontestable human experiences in liberal democratic discourse (e.g. state vs. individual, man vs. woman, subject vs. object, private vs. public);
ii. subjective, diverse and contradictory human experiences shape and thus reconstitute shifting gender relations and our understandings of the liberal state; and
iii. societies depend upon both fluid and contradictory social forces, both of which are unstable elements in the development of democratic society and the gender relations that prefigure it.

In keeping with these assumptions, democracy cannot be seen as something which is generated solely by state apparatuses or characterised as purely conceptual, because its very foundations are thought to shift in line with context and its local manifestations of power. Instead, one must view *democracy as one of many local sites where political power is both exercised over, and expressed by, individuals who are positioned differently within the polity.* This expression of power in language can only be understood as 'relational' or in dynamic tension. Such dynamic tensions lead to particular notions of gender, which are historically constructed and contextually bound – hence, Foucault's (1979) emphasis on 'the history of the present'. The 'conceptual devices' most commonly drawn upon by feminist post-structuralists in deconstructing democracy and democratic schools are 'identity', 'performativity', 'difference' and 'subjectivity'. Such terms provide analytical devices for assessing women's relationship to, or embeddedness within, democratic society.

Although feminist post-structuralism appears incommensurate with the concrete goals of democratic schooling, some provocative research has emerged within this tradition. This research suggests that schools, as local sites, play a significant role in reconstituting the nature of gender politics in society (see Walkerdine and Lucey, 1989) and what we understand democracy to be. It has also challenged the normative and universalistic assumptions which characterise 'democratic' schooling and its apparent role in women's/girls' emancipation. In that sense, it is responding precisely to the problematic which emerges in endorsing either a unitary category of womanhood (e.g. maternal feminism) or feminist positions that are more deterministic in their explanations about women's marginal status in the state (e.g. socialist feminism). In this section, then, we focus on what we believe to be the most exemplary post-structural analysis of democratic schooling – the work of Valerie Walkerdine and her colleague Helen Lucey.

In *Democracy in the Kitchen*, Valerie Walkerdine and Helen Lucey (1989) illustrate how modern education regulates women's and girls' identities, and, ultimately, democratic citizenship. They suggest, for example, that primary-school teachers are positioned within liberal discourses that not only construct, but control, the 'good female teacher' and the 'pupil'. Using Foucault, they also describe the female teacher as one who must monitor the development of male-centred democratic concepts such as 'free-will' through gendered educational discourse, thus cultivating support for the democratic order drawing upon 'non-coercive strategies'. According to Walkerdine and Lucey (1989), the promotion and circulation of this discourse is a 'management technique', in which students come to accept as 'normal' modern forms of liberal democratic governance and the ideal of the 'bourgeois individual'. Such discourses develop as part of a history of educational ideas and are concerned with issues of gender and sexuality:

> It is women, whose sexuality itself is regulated to produce 'normal femininity', who become the central prop of the new form of pedagogy. Teachers trained in psychology were to assume the entire responsibility for the 'freedom' of children, and for the continuous maintenance of the bourgeois democratic order. I want, therefore, to demonstrate that women, positioned as teachers, mothers, carers and caring professionals (…) are held absolutely necessary for the moral order. (…) It places them as responsible for ensuring the possibility of democracy, and yet as deeply conservative. (…) My argument is that (…) women of all classes have been placed as guardians of an order which is too difficult to escape. If you are told you are totally responsible for the nature of the child and with it, therefore, the possibility of freedom, of democracy – how much guilt and pain is involved in resisting such a notion? (Walkerdine, 1986: 177)

In our view, the work of Walkerdine and her colleagues signalled a new theoretical agenda for many feminists in education. It suggested, for example, that liberal democratic ideals (e.g. freedom) in schools positioned women teachers within a discourse of 'correct mothering' which ultimately served to reconstitute subordinate gender identities in schools, only one (the male) of which was 'the right citizen'. It thus became clear that the construction of democratic relations in schools was closely related to issues of sexuality, most notably the reproduction of women's marginalised sexuality through educational practices.

In this model of democratic education, women teachers are 'used' to implement liberal ideals such as 'autonomy', 'freedom', and 'choice', even when they themselves are constrained by such discourses; that is, the liberal initiative offers only 'an illusion of choice'. According to Walkerdine and Lucey (1989), it is therefore within the particularity of gender struggles, as configured within democratic discourse, that women's constructed sexualities, social identities and political status can be found.

Critical pedagogy and the democratic school

An additional strand of work within the post-structural tradition is more explicitly concerned with pedagogy as a form of deconstructive practice. This work has developed primarily as a reaction to other radical forms of critical pedagogy which draw upon the language of liberal democracy to critique the role of schooling in the development of modern societies. Perhaps the best example of this work is a collection of feminist pedagogy edited by Carmen Luke and Jennifer Gore, entitled *Feminisms and Critical Pedagogy*. In this collection, Luke and Gore (1989) argue that a post-structuralist feminist pedagogy is needed to challenge those who draw upon the male-centred language of democracy as a so-called 'neutral' method of achieving gender equity in schools. Their greatest concerns are with male sociologists of education who merely advocate a commitment to critical pedagogy (as a form of democratic rationality) in the public sphere rather than addressing the statist divisions between the public and the private.

Feminists working along these lines tend to confront issues that male sociologists of education or other feminists have ignored or inadequately addressed, such as: teaching and its role in the shaping of gendered subjectivities (Davies, 1989); pedagogical tools which can be used to 'deconstruct' the dominant heterosexual discourses of schooling (see Lather, 1992; Middleton, 1993, 1998); the regulating and gendered functions of contemporary educational reform (see Blackmore, 1996; Delhi, 1996; Kenway and Epstein, 1996); the gendered and racialised discourses of schooling (e.g. Davies, 1989); and histories of sexuality, the body and discipline in schools (see Ellsworth, 1997; Middleton, 1998).

According to the post-structuralist, such issues should be continually addressed in order to 'keep things in process, to disrupt, to keep the system in play, to set up procedures which continuously demystify the realities we create, and to fight the tendency for our categories to congeal' (Caputo, 1987: 286, cited in Lather, 1992: 7). Deconstructing concepts such as democracy must therefore serve as a 'safeguard against dogmatism' (Lather, 1992: 7) and as a mechanism for rejecting the normalisation of liberal democracy itself.

Making alliances

Another strand of work which rests on the margins of post-structural/postmodern theorising is the culturalist theory of schooling developed by Cameron McCarthy and Michael Apple (1988) and McCarthy (1990), which theorises the *dynamic relation between race, class, and gender* and its link to democratic practices in education. The main premise of this work is that schools, as sites of struggles over the meaning of democracy, take on a mediational role in both the construction and articulation of diverse political issues (such as gender) in the polity. Gender is therefore positioned within a complex matrix of social forces (e.g. 'race' and class)[9] which shape democratic relations in schools. This work is known as the *non-synchronous* model of schooling (McCarthy, 1990). McCarthy writes:

> *The concept of non-synchrony* (…) raises questions about the nature, exercise and multiple determination of power within that middle ground of everyday practices in schooling (…). The fact is that, as Hicks (1981) suggests (…), dynamic relations of race, class and gender do not unproblematically reproduce

each other. These relations are complex and often have contradictory effects in institutional settings. (McCarthy, 1990: 85; italics, our addition)

McCarthy's work on 'race' informs the gender and democracy debate in two ways. First, it speaks to the significance of 'building alliances' across diverse political communities to understand the nature of democracy and democratic relations in schools.[10] Second, it points to the part played by 'difference' in 'opening up a kind of epistemological space' (see Robinson, 1998: 1) for rethinking the democratic educational project and its characterisation of marginalised political identities. For example, McCarthy suggests that any attempt to characterise the experience of marginality through recourse to a single social formation such as 'race' or 'gender' misrepresents the experience of marginality in a democracy; that is, questions about 'race' cannot be abstracted from their context while other social forces, such as gender, are kept in place. Democratic school relations and the struggle for equality must therefore be seen as a complex set of political acts which are linked to diverse forms of identification in the nation-state.

Although controversial, Giroux's work on the politics of pedagogy and its implications for feminist practice should not be overlooked. His book, *Postmodernism, Feminism and Cultural Politics* (Giroux, 1991), intervened in the gender and democracy debate by suggesting that educators engage with women's identities, voice, and experience rather than focus solely on organised knowledge in schools; that is, the 'everyday' and the 'particular' of female experience should be the premise of democratic schooling since such an approach acts to counter the traditional narratives of 'abstract' and objective forms of rationalized knowledge.[11] He writes:

> Central to the notion of critical pedagogy is a politics of *voice* that combines a post-modern notion of difference with a feminist emphasis on the primacy of the political. (Giroux, 1991: 54; italics, our addition)

By contrast, Connell's (1987, 1995), Mac an Ghaill's (1994, 1996) and Epstein and Johnson's (1998) work extends the feminist analysis by suggesting that 'heterosexual masculinities'[12] inform the construction of the so-called democratic schooling project. The central goal of this work has been to extend our understanding of how gender relations and, ultimately, how sexual identities are socially constructed in relation to both state and social formations (e.g. race, class, sexuality). It also demonstrates how the democratic schooling project has sought recourse to 'heterosexuality' in shaping both students' and teachers' gender identities and gender hierarchies in the state.

Levels of feminist political analysis

In this section, we attempt, albeit experimentally, to bring together the various feminist analyses to construct a more systematic base for theory development. Insofar as each feminist tradition has worked on, and with, particular gender problematics, they have offered their own descriptions of how power and politics operate, at which level such forces become significant and the key issues that educational research should address. We now attempt to make sense of this extraordinary diversity by describing such problematics in terms of different *levels of feminist political analysis*. In so doing, we hope to offer some insight into those empirical/theoretical connections which still need to be made across feminist theories, and those issues that still remain underdeveloped in feminist educational research. We also attempt to illustrate how our earlier descriptions of key feminist debates in political theory bear some relevance to current questions still remaining in feminist educational thought.

In our view, one of the dangers which underlies the development of feminist thought thus far is precisely its non-cumulative line of development. For example, feminist thought is often based on critique, rather than any systematic set of investigations, or indeed on any theory of gender. In addressing this concern, we suggest that feminists begin to develop theories which link both modern ideals of social justice and political agency with postmodern questions of difference and particularity. For example, theorists such as Fraser and Nicholson (1995) and Weir (1997) argue that we must counter the 'false antithesis' expressed about the distinctions between modern feminist thought (e.g. equality) and postmodern feminist thought (e.g. difference), and even more significantly, the fragmentation of the field. Therefore, not unlike feminist political and social theorists, we, too, must reconcile modernist questions of feminist solidarity and social structure with postmodern concerns about hierarchies of identification and difference (see Dillabough, 1997, 1999).

Drawing upon the three theoretical traditions of feminist political theory described earlier in this chapter, we suggest that feminists in education have been working primarily at three levels of political analysis. We identify these levels as follows.

1 Civic Spheres.
2 Education and National Narratives.
3 Political Identities, Differences and Subjectivities.

Within these levels of political analyses, we identify how feminists in education might draw upon arguments made by feminist political theorists to develop a more coherent feminist theory of democratic schooling.

Level 1: Civic spheres

As we have seen, feminists in education, particularly since the late 1960s, have been working predominantly on what might be called the civic sphere. Broadly speaking, a feminist emphasis on the civic sphere has implied a commitment to the study of women's social positioning in the public sphere. Such work has been instrumental in exposing women's uneasy relationship to public decision making, to patriarchal machineries of education and forms of regulation, and, for example, male public discourses in schools. The organising principle in this domain is the notion that equal representation and participation in the public sphere is key to full citizenship. Women, as second-class members of the polity, have therefore made considerable efforts to 'assimilate' into the public sphere through liberal democratic initiatives in education. Such assimilation mainly takes the form of educational reforms (e.g. curricular initiatives, affirmative action), but it also can involve political activism, particularly around education (promoting concepts of the glass ceiling, for example).

While this kind of liberal focus has led to a gendered restructuring of the public sphere, privileging the public dimensions of civil society poses a number of limitations for the study of gender and education. For example, a key tension currently identified at this level by feminist political theorists and still inadequately addressed in education is the conflict between, on the one hand, the increased presence of women in the male public sphere and, on the other, male/gender dominance in the 'female' private sphere. In fact, much liberal feminist research still remains solely concerned with women's, girls', and boys' positions in state education.[13] Liberal feminists have also been particularly interested in the gendered nature of public achievement and success rather than the preparation of men for private life or a critique of the role that domestic discourses play in reconfiguring gender relations in the polity. As many feminist political theorists have argued (cf. Pateman, 1992), this obsession with gendered successes or failures is flawed precisely because participation in the public sphere is still premised upon a patriarchal notion of civil society.

By contrast, maternal feminists have chosen to celebrate the private 'female' sphere over and above public patriarchy. The danger here, as feminist political theorists have suggested, is that maternal feminists may increase private patriarchy by *essentialising* femininity itself (see Dillabough and Arnot, 2000; Acker and Feuerverger, 1997; Dillabough, 1999). Unlike maternal feminists, socialist feminists recognised the exploitative nature of the public/private distinction, exposing its associations and functions within capitalist social formations. They nevertheless worked with the concept of the 'public' in education, failing on some level to investigate the political and social significance of the 'private'.

In seeking to address these limitations, one could argue that a creative association of public and private is to be found in the use of Foucault's concept of discourse, in which political categories no longer represent true or necessary conceptual distinctions, and language, knowledge and power are seen as linked (Walkerdine and Lucey, 1989). However, while the categories of 'public' and 'private' are seen as constituted through discursive practices and the construction of 'subjects' – whether 'mother', 'teacher', or 'child' – the danger here is that women and girls (in fact, all political subjects) are denied their political agency and the cultural, economic and structural basis of identity-formation in particular sites (the home, the school) remain under-theorised.

A novel way of addressing these concerns is to question how feminists might consider weakening the *strong* boundaries between the public and private spheres in order to uncouple the fraternal social contract (i.e. the male public sphere) with the framing of the sexual contract (i.e. men's control of female sexuality). For example, liberal democracy's shaping of privacy, sexuality, and the marriage contract are as significant to the analysis of modern educational systems as the framing, through state and local discourses, of the public citizen. Addressing this issue might reveal the limitations of over-emphasising women's positioning in the civic sphere at the expense of understanding gender relations in the private sphere and their role in shaping democratic subjects, processes, and actions.

Level 2: Education and national narratives

As feminist political theorists argue, an analysis of the public sphere cannot but make some reference to the nation and nation-state (cf. Yuval-Davis, 1997a, 1997b) and the gendered nature of citizenship and civic communities. Therefore, at this level of theoretical analysis, particular attention is given to the ways in which economic structures, nationalist rhetoric, and cultural politics shape unequal relations between women of diverse social classes and ethnicities. Related work also has been concerned with the impact of neo-liberalism (e.g. demise of the welfare state, token forms of democracy) and globalisation on the gendered formation of national identities in late twentieth-century democracies (see Brah, 1996).

Clearly, attention to such issues not only is necessary, but is a timely step forward in attempting to understand the relationship between contemporary feminist thought and democratic education. To date, however, related work in education has failed to resolve questions about the impact of nationalism on gender identity-formation and gendered notions of democratic citizenship in schools. As a consequence, the question of human rights, diverse forms of feminist activism, 'racial'/cultural struggles and movements, and identity politics (as civic activism) are often divorced from an analysis of educational inequalities, the shaping of gendered subjectivities in schools, or the politics of difference. Educational inequality or the study of *individual* subjectivity thus becomes the focus of feminist analysis. Consequently, serious concerns about 'identity' and 'difference,' which are relevant to questions of justice and citizenship, still lurk on the margins of feminist educational research.[14]

The two key sites for the national education of the 'citizen' are teacher training and the school, the key principles being those that shape the structure of teacher training and the curriculum. For example, the educational discourses and pedagogic devices (cf. Bernstein, 1977) which shape the curriculum have privileged particular concepts of democracy (i.e. the liberal individual), and constructed the child as an educational subject and the teacher as its professional agent (cf. Walkerdine and Lucey, 1989). This privileging within curriculum theory is a mechanism drawn upon by the state to secure particular notions of national identity and political participation. It is through the practice of liberal democracy that such ideals are legitimised, at least in part. As a consequence, questions about the contested nature of national/cultural identities and their impact on the construction of a gendered 'citizenry' in schools still remain largely unexplored. In fact, educational studies are only now beginning to address how identity, difference and differentiation;

how social values, and the construction of outsiders or the 'other,' are gendered processes which concern the shaping of the 'citizen' (Holland *et al.*, 2000).

Some current feminist work, for example, is examining the nature of the 'ideal' citizen, particularly in relation to contemporary politics in schools and higher education (see Arnot *et al.*, 1996; Dillabough, 1999). International and comparative work that examines the ways in which young people construct 'the citizen' and view themselves within the context of a gendered civic sphere (Bonder, 1997; Holland *et al.*, 1997) is also in its inception. Such research attempts to capture the contested nature of 'citizenship' as it has been expressed in different political and economic phases, and through continuously transforming gender relations.

Despite this work, more comparative efforts are needed to examine how gender relations and gender politics evolve within dynamic educational cultures in the nation-state, especially those national contexts associated with rapid social and political change.[15] This could be achieved by focusing on the political concepts (and everyday assertions) any nation employs in relation to questions of gender and how such concepts (e.g. citizenship) are situated within a broader nationalist discourse of power relations. In our view, such an approach would contribute to the development of a novel analytic framework for assessing the relationship between cultural identity-formation and the shaping of the male and female 'citizen' in schools and higher education.

Level 3: Political identities, differences, and subjectivities

School and classroom structures and experiences are central sites for research. It is here that feminists have developed their critique of male hegemony, seeing its operation in the interaction of teacher and pupil, and the gender conflicts between pupils. Perhaps more importantly, it is a site that can be reshaped along democratic lines. Therefore, understanding the political dimensions of classroom life is one that many have described as essential to the teaching of democracy, and inclusive education. At the same time, it is also in everyday interactions that pupils' identities and subjectivities are shaped and interpreted in ways which reinforce distinctions between masculinity and femininity, as well as those of, for example, sexuality, ethnicity and class.

Much post-structural and postmodern educational research has highlighted, through individualised narratives, the processes of social exclusion, particularly in relation to those constructed as 'other'. At the same time, such research has resisted using the categorisation of public/private, or classifications such as male and female, preferring to report them as discursive entities, which permanently shift and are reconstituted. Therefore, for many feminist post-modernists and post-structuralists in education, to claim an identity, to lay the foundations of a new democratic project for women, or to even engage in identity politics as part of democratic practice, may be to engage in an act of *domination*: 'the subject is an instance of mastery, of narrative closure, of the freezing of a process of difference/difference' (see Weir, 1997: 25). Identities must therefore be seen as discursively constructed within the language of democracy itself. They also must be seen as sites of 'open political contest' (see Butler, 1995) and as a struggle to identify with political hierarchies that are framed by democratic discourse in school spaces. These ideas are useful reminders of the none too simple relationship between the official *discourses* which underlie the democratic education project and the local construction of gender identities.

Despite post-structuralist scepticism about the modernist project of democratic schooling, problems still remain. For example, many critics of feminist post-structuralism argue that in endorsing 'illusory' conceptions of 'womanhood' and 'democracy', the potential for women to possess political agency is lost (see Dillabough, 1999; see also Weir, 1997). We may therefore be collapsing the original democratic project and the notion of women as political actors into the realm of the unknown and conflating contemporary feminist politics with some of the worst excesses of neo-liberal individualism.

It may also be the case that feminist post-structuralists, by focusing almost exclusively upon individual experiences in the study of gender identities, have inadvertently positioned themselves in the very discourse they wish to deconstruct (i.e. liberal democratic discourse about the importance of the 'self' and 'identity' over community). What still remains problematic, then, is the desire to take the study of the specificity of women's and girls' subjectivity to an extreme with less room for a rigorous analysis of education and its role in undermining women's potential for political agency.

Conclusions

What we demonstrate in this chapter is that it is no longer possible to take for granted definitions of democracy based upon liberal principles, nor can we base democratic politics on the interests of women *as* women in the simplest of senses. As Chantal Mouffe (1992b) argues, old versions of citizenship have become an obstacle to making democracy work for women in a more genuinely inclusive way. It is time to change the ways in which we struggle for democracy in education – to abandon the 'lion's skin' and construct new and more flexible definitions of citizenship that are not only inclusive at a social level, but are based upon the needs and concerns of contemporary women worldwide. If this is to be accomplished, feminist work must go beyond an engagement with questions of voice, subjectivity, and difference. It must also remain committed to the idea that women, as agents of knowledge (not foundationalist knowledge!), need to make claims about their identity in order to effect broad social and political change. These agents are not uniform in character; they take multiple, dynamic positions that often are in tension. However, they must be viewed as members of a heterogeneous community who are concerned with how new social and political formations (e.g. neo-liberalism) structure the relationship between gender and democratic education. In our view, then, the difficult task for feminists is to problematise the gendered premises of democratic education, while still defending a notion of 'radical democracy' (Fraser, 1996) which accords women's political agency without repressing difference (see Dillabough, 1999).

The nature of democratic life for women thus remains a key issue in the United Kingdom, North America and elsewhere. As Weiler (1993, 1994) suggests, we are now engaged in a battle over the meaning of education and democracy. The warring factions reside between those who wish to extend our understanding of democracy and those who would restrict access to knowledge and power to the elites. In these circumstances, neither 'equality' nor 'difference', as isolated theoretical concepts, can meet the challenges of contemporary gender oppression in the state. As Phillips (1991a) argues, democracy and democratic education need to be 'engendered'.

In short, we have argued that the current state of education feminism and the study of democratic education would be greatly improved by drawing upon the work of feminist political theorists. This focus may provide us with novel conceptual tools for rethinking the role of feminist theory in the development of democratic education. It may also allow us to confront questions about gender which remain, as they have done since the beginning, as questions which are necessarily political in nature.

Acknowledgements

I am grateful for the support given to Jo-Anne Dillabough by the Social Sciences and Humanities Research Council of Canada, and to the Leverhulme Trust for the research fellowship I was granted for this work. Jane Gaskell, Phil Gardner and Wendy Luttrell kindly gave helpful comments on an earlier draft of this article. I would like to thank Jo-Anne Dillabough for permission to include this article in the collection.

The ideas in this chapter also were later developed by Jo-Anne Dillabough and I in: *Challenging Democracy: international perspectives on gender, education and citizenship* (RoutledgeFalmer, 2000); 'Recasting educational debates about female citizenship, agency and identity' in *School Field*, 2003, vol. XIII, pp 81–107; and 'A magnified image of female citizenship in education: illusions of democracy or liberal challenges to symbolic domination' in J. Demaine (ed.) *Citizenship and Political Education* (Palgrave, 2004).

References

Acker, S. and Feuerveger, G. (1997) 'Doing good and feeling bad: The work of women university teachers', *Cambridge Journal of Education*, 26(3): 401–22.
Althusser, L. (1971) 'Ideology and ideological state apparatus', in L. Althusser (ed.) *Lenin and philosophy and other essays*. London: New Left.
Arnot, M. (1980) 'Socio-cultural reproduction and women's education', in R. Deem (ed.) *Schooling for women's work*. London: Routledge.
Arnot, M. (1982) 'Male hegemony, social class and women's education', *Journal of Education*, 164(1): 64–89.
Arnot, M. (1984) 'A feminist perspective on the relationship between family life and school life', *Journal of Education*, 166(1): 5–24.
Arnot, M. (1991) 'Equality and democracy: a decade of struggle over education', *British Journal of Sociology of Education*, 12(3): 447–66.
Arnot, M. (1993) 'A crisis in patriarchy? British feminist educational politics and state

regulation of gender', in M. Arnot and K. Weiler (eds) *Feminism and Social Justice in Education.* London: Falmer Press.

Arnot, M., Araújo, H., Deliyanni-Kouimtzi, K., Rowe, G. and Tomé, A. (1996) 'Teachers, gender and the discourses of citizenship', *International Studies in Sociology of Education,* 6(1): 3–35.

Barrett, M. (1980) *Women's Oppression Today: problems in marxist feminist analysis.* London: Verso.

Belenky, M.F., Clinchy, B.M., Goldberger, N.R. and Tarule, J.M. (1986) *Women's ways of knowing.* New York: Basic Books.

Benhabib, S. (1995) 'Feminism and postmodernism', in S. Benhabib, J. Butler, D. Cornell, and N. Fraser (eds) *Feminist Contentions: a philosophical exchange.* New York: Routledge, pp. 17–57.

Bernstein, B. (1977) *Class, Codes and Control, Vol 3*, 3rd ed. London: Routledge and Kegan Paul.

Blackmore, J. (1996) 'Doing "emotional labour" in the education market place: Stories from the field of women in management', *Discourse, 17*(3): 337–51.

Blair, M. (1995) 'Race, class and gender in school research' in J. Holland, M. Blair and S. Sheldon (eds) *Debates and Issues in Feminist Research and Pedagogy,* Clevedon: Multilingual Matters/Open University.

Blair, M. and Holland, J. with S. Sheldon (eds) (1995) *Identity and Diversity: gender and the experience of education,* Clevedon: Multilingual Matters/Open University.

Bonder, G. (1997) 'Young girls' construction of the citizen in Argentina', Paper presented to the Gender and Education Conference, Warwick, England.

Bourdieu, P. and Passeron, J-C. (1977) *Reproduction in Education, Society and Culture.* (Published in association with Theory, Culture & Society) London: Sage.

Bowles, S. and Gintis, H. (1976) *Schooling in capitalist America. Reform and the contradiction of economic life.* London: Routledge.

Brah, A. (1996) *Cartographies of diaspora: Contesting identities,* London: Routledge.

Brah, A. and Minhas, R. (1985) 'Structural racism or cultural difference: Schooling for Asian girls', in G. Weiner (ed.) *Just a Bunch of Girls: feminist approaches to schooling.* Milton Keynes: Open University.

Brindle, P. and Arnot, M. (1999) '"England expects every man to do his duty": the gendering of the citizenship textbook (1940–1966)', *The Oxford Review of Education, 25*(1 and 2), 103–23.

Butler, J. (1990) *Gender trouble: feminism and the subversion of identity.* New York: Routledge.

Butler, J. (1991) 'Contingent foundations: feminism and the question of "postmodernism"', in J. Butler and J.W. Scott. (eds) *Feminists theorize the political.* London and New York: Routledge.

Butler, J. (1995) 'Contingent foundations', in S. Benhabib, J. Butler, D. Cornell, and N. Fraser (eds) *Feminist Contentions: a philosophical exchange.* New York: Routledge.

Carby, H. (1982) 'Schooling in Babylon' in Centre for Contemporary Cultural Studies, *The Empire Strikes Back; race and racism in 70s Britain*, London: Hutchinson. Davis 1983.

Casey, K. (1989) *I answer with my life.* New York: Routledge.

Connell, R.W. (1987) *Gender and Power.* Cambridge: Polity Press.

Connell, R.W. (1990) 'The state, gender and sexual politics', *Theory and Society, 19*: 507–44.

Connell, R.W. (1995) *Masculinities.* Cambridge, Polity Press.

Coole, D. (1993) *Women in Political Theory: from ancient misogyny to contemporary feminism.* New York: Harvester, Wheatsheaf.

Davies, B. (1989) *Frogs and Snails and Feminist Tales.* Sydney, Australia: Allen and Unwin.

Davin, A. (1978) 'Imperialism and motherhood', *History Workshop Journal,* 5: 9–65.

56 *Feminist politics and democratic values in education*

Delhi, K. (1996) 'Between "market" and "State": engendering education change in the 1990s', *Discourse*, *17*(3), 363–76.

Dietz, M.G. (1985) 'Citizenship with a feminist pace: the problem with maternal thinking', *Political Theory*, *13*: 19–37.

Dillabough, J. (1997) 'Degrees of freedom and deliberations of 'self': the gendering of professional identity in teacher education', Paper presented to the Women Studies Network Conference, London Institute of Education, London, England.

Dillabough, J. (1999) 'Gender politics and conceptions of the modern teacher: women, identity, and professionalism', *British Journal of Sociology of Education*, *20*(3): 373–94.

Dillabough, J. and Arnot, M. (2000) 'Feminist perspectives in the Sociology of Education', in D. Levinson, R. Sadovnik and P. Cookson (eds) *Sociology of Education: An Encyclopaedia*. New York: Garland.

Dillabough, J. and Arnot, M. (2001) 'Feminist sociology of education' in J. Demaine (ed) *Sociology of Education Today*, London, Palgrave.

Dyehouse, C. (1976) 'Social darwinistic ideas and the development of women's education in England 1880–1920', *History of Education*, *5*(1): 41–58.

Ellsworth, E. (1997) *Teaching positions: Difference, pedagogy and the power of address*. New York: Teachers College Press.

Elshtain, J.B. (1981) *Public Man, Private Woman: women in social and political thought*. Princeton, NJ: Princeton University Press.

Elshtain, J.B. (1992) 'The power and powerlessness of women', in G. Bock and S. James (eds) *Beyond Equality and Difference: citizenship, feminist politics, and female subjectivity*. London: Routledge.

Epstein, D. and Johnson, R. (1998) *Schooling Sexualities*. Buckingham: Open University Press.

Foucault, M. (1979) *Discipline and Punishment: the birth of the prison*. Harmondsworth: Penguin.

Fraser, N. (1996) 'Equality, difference and radical democracy', in D. Trend (ed.) *Radical Democracy: identity, citizenship and the state*. New York: Routledge.

Fraser, N. and Nicholson, L. (1995) 'Social criticism without philosophy: An encounter between feminism and post-modernism', in S. Siedman (ed.) *The Postmodern Turn: new perspectives on social theory*. Cambridge: Cambridge University Press.

Gilligan, C. (1982) *In a Different Voice: psychological theory and women's development*. Cambridge, MA: Harvard University Press.

Gilligan, C. (1986) 'Moral orientation and moral development', in E. Kitty and D. Meyers (eds) *Women and Moral Theory*. New Jersey: Rowman and Littlefield.

Giroux, H. (1991) *Postmodernism, Feminism and Cultural Politics*. New York: State University of New York Press.

Haywood, C. and Mac an Ghaill, M. (1996) 'Schooling masculinities', in M. Mac an Ghaill (ed.) *Understanding Masculinities*. Buckingham: Open University Press.

Heater, D. (1990) *Citizenship: the civic ideal in world history, politics and evaluation*. London: Longman.

Hill-Collins, P. (1990) *Black Feminist Thought: Knowledge, Consciousness and the Politics of Empowerment*, Boston: Unwin and Hyman.

Holland, J., Lahelma, E. and Gordon, T. (2000) 'The abstract individual and school processes', in M. Arnot and J. Dillabough (eds) *Education, Democracy and Citizenship: emerging international feminist perspectives*. London: Routledge.

hooks, B. (1989) *Talking Back, Thinking Feminism, Thinking Black*, Boston, Massachusetts: Southend Press.

Jagger, A.M. (1983) *Feminist Politics and Human Nature*. Rowman and Allanheld; Sussex: Harvester Press.

Kenway, J. (1995) 'Masculinities in schools: under siege, on the defensive and under reconstruction', *Discourse*, *16*(1): 59–81.

Kenway, J. and Epstein, D. (1996) 'The marketisation of school education: feminist studies and perspectives', *Discourse*, *17*(3): 301–314.

Lather, P. (1992) *Getting Smart*. New York: Routledge.

Lloyd, G. (1986) 'Selfhood, war and masculinity', in C. Pateman and E. Gross (eds) *Feminist Challenges: social and political theory*. London: Allen and Unwin.

Luke, C. and Gore, J. (eds) (1989) *Feminisms and Critical Pedagogy*. New York: Routledge.

Mac an Ghaill, M. (1994) *The Making of Men: masculinities, sexualities and schooling*. Buckingham: Open University Press.

Mac an Ghaill, M. (ed.) (1996) *Understanding Masculinities: social relations and cultural arenas*. Buckingham: Open University.

McCarthy, C. (1990) *Race and Curriculum: social inequality and the theories and politics of difference in contemporary research on schooling*. London: Falmer Press.

McCarthy, C. and Apple, M.W. (1988) 'Race, class and gender in American educational research: Toward a nonsynchronous parallelist position', in L. Weiss (ed.) *Class, race and gender in American education*. Albany, NY: State University of New York Press, pp. 9–39.

Middleton, S. (1993) 'A post-modern pedagogy for the sociology of women's education', in M. Arnot and K. Weiler (eds) *Feminism and Social Justice in Education*. London: Falmer Press.

Middleton, S. (1998) *Disciplining Sexuality: Foucault, life histories, and education*. New York: Teachers College Press.

Mirza, H. (1992) *Young, Female and Black*, London: Routledge.

Mirza, H. (1993) 'The social construction of black womanhood in British educational research: towards a new understanding' in M. Arnot and Weiler, K (eds) *Feminism and Social Justice in Education: international perspectives*, London: Falmer Press.

Mirza, H. and Reay, D. (2000) 'Redefining citizenship: black women educators and 'the third space' in M. Arnot and J. Dillabough (eds) *Challenging Democracy: feminist perspectives on gender, education and citizenship*, London: Routledge.

Mouffe, C. (1992a) 'Feminism, citizenship and radical democratic politics', in J. Butler and J.W. Scott (eds) *Feminists Theorise the Political*. New York: Routledge.

Mouffe, C. (ed.) (1992b) *Dimensions of Radical Democracy*. London: Verso.

Noddings, N. (1988) 'An ethic of caring and its implication for instructional arrangements', *American Journal of Education*, 96(2): 215–30.

Noddings, N. (1997) 'Stories and affect in teacher education', *Cambridge Journal of Education*, *26*(3): 435–48.

Pateman, C. (1988) *The Sexual Contract*. Cambridge, Polity Press.

Pateman, C. (1989) *The Disorder of Women*. Cambridge: Polity Press.

Pateman, C. (1992) 'Equality, difference, subordination: the politics of motherhood and women's citizenship', in G. Bock and B. James (eds) *Beyond equality and difference: Citizenship, feminist politics, female subjectivity*. New York: Routledge.

Phillips, A. (1991a) *Engendering democracy*. Cambridge: Polity Press.

Phillips, A. (1991b) 'Citizenship and feminist theory', in G. Andrews (ed.) *Citizenship*. London: Lawrence and Wisehart.

Phillips, A. (1992) *Democracy and difference*. Cambridge: Polity Press.

Phoenix, A. (1987) 'Theories of gender and black families' in G. Weiner and M. Arnot (eds) *Gender Under Scrutiny: New Inquires in Education*, London, Hutchinson.

Pieterse, J.N. and Parekh, B. (eds) (1995) *The Decolonialisation of Imagination: culture, knowledge and power*. London: Zed Books.

Robinson, S. (1998) 'Individualism, identity and community in globalising society', Symposium paper presented to the Learned Societies, Ottawa, Canada.

Roland Martin, J. (1994, first published 1982) 'Excluding women from the educational realm', in L. Stone (ed.) *The education feminism reader*. New York: Routledge.

Roman, L. (1992) 'The political significance of other ways of narrating ethnography. A feminist materialist approach', in M.D. Lecompte, W. Milroy and J. Priessle (eds) *The Handbook of Qualitative Research in Educational Theory*. San Diego, CA: Academic Press.

Ryan, B. (1992) *Feminism and the Women's Movement: dynamics of change in social movement ideology and activism*. New York: Routledge.

Stone, L. (ed.) (1994) *The Education Feminism Reader*. New York: Routledge.

Walkerdine, V. (1986) 'Post-structuralist theory and everyday social practices', in V. Walkerdine (ed.) *Feminist Social Psychology*. Milton Keynes: Open University Press.

Walkerdine, V. and Lucey, H. (1989) *Democracy in the Kitchen*. London: Virago.

Weiler, K. (1988) *Women Teaching for Change*. The Critical Educational Series. Massachusetts: Bergin and Harvey.

Weiler, K. (1993) 'Feminism and the struggle for democratic education: a view from the United States', in M. Arnot and K. Weiler (eds) *Feminism and Social Justice in Education*. London: Falmer Press.

Weiler, K. (1994) 'Freire and a feminist pedagogy of difference', in P. McLaren and C. Lankshear (eds) *Politics of Liberation: paths from Freire*. New York: Routledge.

Weir, A. (1997) *Sacrificial Logics: feminist theory and the critique of identity*. New York: Routledge.

Weis, L. (1983) 'Schooling and cultural production: a comparison of black and white lived culture', in M. Apple and L. Weis (eds) *Ideology and Practice in Schooling*. Philadelphia: Temple University Press.

Whelehan, I. (1995) *Modern Feminist Thought*. Edinburgh: Edinburgh University Press.

Wilson, E. (1995, first published 1986) *Hidden Agendas: theory, politics, and experience in the women's movement*. London: Tavistock Publications.

Wollstonecraft, M. (1992 [1792]) *Vindication of the Rights of Women*. London: Penguin.

Young, I.M. (1995) 'Gender as seriality: thinking about women as a social collective', in L. Nicholson and S. Seidman (eds) *Social Postmodernism*. Cambridge: Cambridge University Press.

Yuval-Davis, N. (1997a) *Gender and nation*. London: Sage.

Yuval-Davis, N. (1997b) 'Women, citizenship and difference', *Feminist Review*, 57: 4–27.

Yuval-Davis, N. and Anthias, F. (1989) *Woman-Nation-State*. London: Macmillan.

Notes

1 In the liberal democratic state, the dominant view of women is one that endorses white, middle-class notions of female citizenship.
2 See Ryan (1992) on the subject of 'benevolent philanthropy'.
3 This comment may come across as a naive view of the history of feminist research. Indeed, feminist research has a much longer history than the type we refer to here. We refer here only to second-wave feminist research.
4 See Whelehan (1995) on the question of liberal feminism.
5 See Acker and Feuerverger's (1997) research on the experiences of female academics and their working conditions.
6 Noteworthy is the fact that Dietz (1985) is merely describing, rather than supporting, the maternal position.
7 See Butler's (1991 and 1995) argument on this point.
8 These points were raised and developed in Dillabough and Arnot (2001)
9 It is important to note that 'race,' rather than gender, is the central element in this work.
10 We are not suggesting that other female scholars in education do not make such alliances. Clearly, scholars such as Elizabeth Ellsworth, Michelle Foster, Avtah Brah,

Heida Safia Mirza and Anne Phoenix have all made links between race and gender in their efforts to understand social relations in schooling and the state. We refer here to Cameron McCarthy, Michael Apple and Henry Giroux's work simply to highlight efforts made by male theorists in America to align with the work of feminists concerned with democratic education.

11 Interestingly, Giroux's now dated view appears to resonate with the maternal view on the development of a women-centred epistemology.
12 See, for example, Haywood and Mac an Ghaill's (1996) work on 'Schooling Masculinities.'
13 There is now a concern with boys' achievement and masculinity in the media and educational research (see Kenway, 1995).
14 We do not wish to suggest that questions of identity and difference in educational research are not addressed. In the present theoretical climate, however, such questions tend not to be addressed in relation to the *political* concerns of feminists.
15 Particularly interesting sites for this examination are those national contexts which are thought to be in the process of democratisation (so-called developing countries), those countries with less capital wealth than Western states, or states which have taken a neo-liberal stance on contemporary politics.

Part II
Teachers' constructions of the gendered citizen

3 Teachers, gender and the discourses of citizenship

with Helena Araújo, Kiki Deliyanni[1], Gabrielle Ivinson[1] and Amparo Tomé

Current debates about the role of the educational system in relation to the formation of citizens focus on the failure in 'partial' or immature democracies (as some have called Western European nations) to ensure that all citizens are equal (Arnot, 1995). In the context of theories about ethnicity and citizenship, there is much concern about the ways in which minority ethnic groups are constructed as the 'Other', especially in relation to national and European citizenship (Gillborn, 1992; Coulby and Jones, 1995). In terms of gender relations the debate focuses on the contradictions between, on the one hand, the modernising of gender relations through cultural discourses and, on the other, the continued failure to improve women's participation in the labour market and in economic and political decision making. Democratic structures within advanced industrial economies have only conceded limited political gains to women, most notably in relation to access to education and elite professions (Arnot, 1995).

The policy of the Equal Opportunities Unit of the European Commission to promote greater equality awareness, particularly in relation to women's participation and representation in public life, encouraged an interest in the level of knowledge and understanding about citizenship and the role which gender relations play. This exploratory paper addresses those concerns. It analyses some of the findings of a sociological research project (funded by the EC) entitled *Promoting Equality Awareness: women as citizens*, which investigated the discourses of citizenship used by student teachers and their trainers in universities and colleges in Greece, Spain, Portugal, England and Wales. The overall aim of this project was to develop critical training materials to promote equality awareness amongst student teachers – materials which could be used in both teacher training courses and in secondary schools.

The first stage of the project set out to tap the levels of 'gender literacy' of student teachers at the point at which they finished their professional training, and secondly, to uncover the language/discourses of citizenship being used and the ways in which gender issues were addressed through such discourses. Detailed analysis of the levels of 'gender literacy' can be found in the final reports of the project (Arnot *et al.*, 1995; Tomé *et al.*, 1995), based on surveys of secondary student teachers in the five countries.[2] This chapter focuses specifically upon the second of the themes – the *discourses of citizenship* in relation to gender.

Qualitative data was collected from single-sex focus groups conducted with secondary student teachers in Greece, Spain and the United Kingdom; from semi-structured interviews with a sample of their trainers in all five countries; and from open-ended questions in the survey and interviews with student teachers and their trainers in Portugal.[3]

The intention here is to outline the analytic framework developed by the research team to understand both the common themes and the differences regarding citizenship that are emerging across national contexts. Such exploratory and rather tentative comparisons throw light on national traditions, distinctive historical phases and some of the factors which might affect teachers' values in relation to citizenship, gender relations and the goals of education. The first part of the paper begins by considering current theoretical debates in sociology of education concerning the nature of citizenship and its implications for citizens' identities. Two themes provide the focus of this overview: rationality and social justice; and unity and difference. These themes are then taken up in an exploratory manner when considering the ways in which student teachers describe how they might define citizenship, whether they could identify a role for themselves in relation to citizenship and how gender relations might be shaped by such definitions. Attention is also paid to what constitutes the ethical virtues of 'a good citizen'.

The results of this analysis suggest ways in which the new generation of teachers currently understands the relationship between individuals, the collective or 'common good', and the role of the state. They also suggest that particular discourses of citizenship are sustained by past legacies, by government strategies and the subtle ways in which they are continually being restructured, particularly by women. Our analysis of such data speculates about the possible implications of student teachers' views for women's position and participation in advanced industrial societies/postmodern societies.

Education and citizenship as a modern (male) narrative

Two themes can be found running through recent sociological and historical writing on citizenship and education for citizenship. The first concerns the relationship of citizenship to the economy and the use of education as a means of rational control; the second relates education to patriarchal relations which underlie liberal democratic Western European political philosophy. Although there is not the space to discuss these two strands in adequate depth, it is important, before looking at our data, to identify the criteria by which we can begin to understand teachers' conceptions of citizenship. The two themes are referred to here as (a) rationality and social justice and (b) unity and difference.

Rationality and social justice

In a well-argued review of theories of citizenship and education, Gilbert (1992) contrasts the claims of Derek Heater (1990) and Philip Wexler (1990), noticing that whilst Heater stresses the significance of the concept of citizenship in understanding modern societies, Wexler emphasises its irrelevance for postmodern society. Heater's seminal account of the concept of citizenship as a civic ideal in world history gives a new slant to our understanding of education as the 'modernist project par excellence' (Gilbert, 1992: 56). Citizenship education, in whatever form, is portrayed as buffeted by the impact of three major political doctrines: *nationalism* which requires a citizenry schooled to display enthusiastic loyalty; *liberal democracy* requiring a citizenry to cast its vote with understanding and due deference to their betters; and *socialism*, where citizens could potentially destabilise middle-class, capitalist establishments (Heater, 1990: 76–88).

Heater (1990) argues that nationalism is likely to favour civic education, raising mass consciousness of national identity with the aid of flags, patriotic songs and the celebration of national anniversaries. Central control over education combined with overt teaching strategies, particularly in history and languages, helps homogenise society and overcome differences. Socialism requires education systems to equip individuals with a basic understanding of political structures and some understanding of left-wing theoretical analyses, so as to encourage active political participation in the name of social justice.

Liberal democracy, on the other hand, requires a different agenda for the education of its citizens. Here, all citizens would be encouraged to develop their talents and to achieve individual autonomy through a broad and balanced education. In England, however, many industrialists and conservatives argued that the populace should be politically ignorant or passive. Political education was eschewed in favour of a particular role for the state education system, not dissimilar to that described in the United States by Giroux (1980). Whilst an overt patriotic spirit was being engendered by civic education, schools in America came to function as 'training grounds for character development and economic and social control' (Giroux, 1980: 329). Thus, despite its alleged commitment to the ancient Greek ideals of democracy, the American state education system came to be associated with 'social control, obedience and conformity' (Giroux, 1980: 330).

The philosophical basis for this shift, Giroux argues, is best described as a transition from the 'political' to the 'technical'. The new technological rationality, with its emphasis on efficiency, surveillance and control, organised schooling in ways that were far from the Greek ideal of educating the citizen 'for intelligent and active participation in the civic community' (Giroux, 1980: 329). Intelligence would have been viewed by the ancient Greeks 'as an extension of ethics, a manifestation and demonstration of the doctrine of the good and just life' (*ibid.*). As Giroux states:

> ... in this perspective, education was not meant to train. Its purpose was to cultivate the formation of virtuous character in the ongoing quest for freedom. Therefore, freedom was always something to be created, and the dynamic that informed the relationship between the individual and the society was based on a continuing struggle for a more just and decent political community. (Giroux, 1980: 329)

Such a transition from the political, in the sense of participatory democracy, to the technical, nevertheless could sustain its own mirage of freedom. European political discourses were powerfully reframed by the French Revolution around the themes of Liberty, Equality and Fraternity, even though the new modern social narrative on democracy, as Lyotard (1984) argues, had more to do with social control than freedom. The Enlightenment established humanity as 'the hero of liberty' and the subject of history in ways which constructed a legitimating consensus among 'the people' who are also abstractly defined (Lyotard, 1984, quoted in Gilbert, 1992: 54). The development of an educational system was seen as integral to such democratic discourses, but it had purposes that were far from the ideals of such 'freedom':

> The state resorts to the narrative of freedom every time it assumes direct control over the training of the 'people', under the name of the 'nation', in order to point them down the path of progress. (Lyotard, 1984: 32, quoted in Gilbert, 1992: 54)

If the Enlightenment was the 'best hour' (Wexler, 1990) for modern concepts of citizenship, citizenship was 'an emblem of modernity', of equal freedoms, of the bond between people in often hierarchically structured and ethnically diverse societies. The concept of citizenship offered liberal democracies 'a direct sense of community membership based on loyalty to a civilisation which is a common possession' (Marshall, 1965: 101).

With shifting economic and political conditions, such modernist narratives and such concepts of citizenship were contested again and again (cf. Heater, 1990). New forms of solidarity and 'rationalities' were formed and reformed, impinging more or less upon state educational systems. Yet, whatever the limits and the opportunities represented by this modernist project in the name of liberty, fraternity and equality, according to Lyotard and Wexler, the development of postmodern conditions spelt its death knell. Quoting Habermas' view that the quest for citizenship has failed, Wexler argues that:

> Contemporary society has killed the Enlightenment's modern individual, first by commodification, then by communication. The death of the individual is the cornerstone of the poststructuralist philosophy that superseded liberal humanism. (Wexler, 1990: 165)

Wexler argues that the individual/society relationship which underpinned the quest for autonomy, participation and influence has been replaced by the themes of 'no individual, no society'. Indeed, according to Margaret Thatcher, 'there is no such thing as society' (Heater, 1990). Instead, in the swirling chaos of postmodern society, Wexler notes the rise of an information society involving processes of commodification; the growth in consumerism; the role of culture in the production of knowledge, political life and the fragmentation of identities. In this new world, traditional institutions are declining, new organisational forms are being developed (for example, post-Fordism) which stress less formal means of control, decentralisation and the proliferation of communication networks. Old truths and moralities are challenged, as are old ethical 'virtues'.

In this world of multiple subjectivities, there is little chance of generating collective identities or coherent world views about the meaning of citizenship through education, especially among the youth of today, affected as they are by the new media-led cultural politics. Writing as an American, Wexler argues:

> In this society, citizenship is an archaic term. It is not part of the language of everyday life. Its value for understanding this life is not evident either. Of course, political scientists and educators write about citizenship and citizenship education. Does citizenship have meaning outside of such an expert culture? Or, is citizenship a linguistic residue of the modern era that has passed? (Wexler, 1990: 164)

These analyses emphasise the centrality of the concept of citizenship of the Enlightenment project and the contradictory role of education especially in relation to issues of social justice. They also raise questions about the centrality of the concept of citizenship to individual identity in the late twentieth century.

Unity and difference

Another important question when investigating the discourses of citizenship is the relationship between unity and difference. Below we discuss contemporary debates within the women's movement about equality and difference, especially in the context of Europe and of European political/philosophical traditions.

When considering women as citizens within Europe, Yuval-Davis (1992), like other feminist political theorists, challenges evolutionary theories of the development of rights. She argues that the processes of inclusion and exclusion are contained within national political histories. The 'community' in ancient Greek philosophy, used in the context of the United Kingdom by T.H. Marshall (1965), refers to civic community as a natural social unit implying 'organic wholeness'. Even though this concept of community is a social construct, community boundaries are assumed to be natural, internal diversions are rarely recognised and the only form of change that is represented is internal growth.

The politics of difference are subsumed into the notion of a 'given collectivity' and are not usually presented as an ideological or material construction. Yet boundaries, structures and norms are the result of a 'constant process of struggles, negotiation and general social developments' (Yuval-Davis, 1992). Of great importance, therefore, is an understanding of the processes by which such arbitrary notions of collectivity are constructed, especially insofar as they define membership, identities, cultural 'needs' and national self-determination. Yuval-Davis (1992) argues that, although citizenship rights are represented as 'universalistic', they are not 'universal discourses'.

The implications of the various social constructions of public/private spheres and male/female worlds for discourses of citizenship are important. Privacy, for example, is both publicly determined and gendered. Thus, the supposed 'femaleness' of private spheres does not have a natural basis. Similarly, in some countries, the concept of 'public life' does not exist. The dichotomy between public and private spheres is both culturally and historically specific and as Marshall and Anderson (1995) have pointed out, equal significance should be attached to the privatisation of the public sphere and the invasion of public values in private worlds.

> Perhaps the most important statement from feminist cultural studies is the recognition that the accepted notions about the appropriate public sphere are socially constructed notions … to provide advantages to those who had the power to construct them, usually white males. That people accept the dominant notions of the public sphere enhances its power. Other ways, alternative voices, and differently framed priorities are delegitimised as personal problems or fringe group interests. (Marshall and Anderson, 1995: 182)

The boundaries of community also define de facto those who are excluded from membership and many of the inequalities of those within. The construction of a new community in Europe provides examples of the different status being awarded to different groups of people. As Yuval-Davis points out, whilst some women gain the right of free movement, others (15 million minorities) have restricted movement. The concept of 'Fortress Europe' signifies the centrality of religion, but also of xenophobia and racism in the European context and the difficulties these represent for those who wish to construct a new concept of citizenship (Pearson, 1992). As Sultana (1995) argued in an excellent overview of 'a uniting Europe', the project itself is characterised as much by the tensions created by difference as it is by the goal of solidarity.

An alternative strand in current debates about unity and difference can be found amongst feminist political theorists.[4] Pateman (1992), who set in train feminist critiques of the gendered nature of European political/philosophical thought, focused both on the masculinised basis of citizenship in such traditions and the dilemmas it poses for women wishing to participate more equally in democratic societies. Pateman's analysis of the 'fraternal pact' which underlies liberal democratic thought, as well as her exposure of the gender assumptions which shape the citizen as male, are challenging critiques of the ways in which women have, by definition, been included as a negative reference point in theories of democracy and citizenship. At the same time, she recalls what she refers to as 'Wollstonecraft's dilemma' – whether women should fight for equal/identical rights with men or whether they should fight for recognition of women's particular contribution to citizenship and society. Should motherhood, for example, provide the basis of citizenship for women or should one sustain the notion that men and women deserve identical treatment? She has pointed out that all too often: 'Motherhood and citizenship are … set apart' (Pateman, 1992).

Key questions addressed in our research were the extent to which citizenship was still being applied to male public spheres; whether women were imagined transforming political life; whether women were attempting to construct alternative models for fulfilling citizen's responsibilities; or whether they were seeking a form of citizenship where gender difference might be irrelevant to the provision of equal rights. Below we explore further the meaning and relevance of citizenship to issues of social justice and the gendered aspects of citizenship as a concept, first at a general level and second in relation to three discourses (the political, the moral and the egalitarian) used by student teachers or their trainer.

The discourses of citizenship

Reading the responses of student teachers for the first time, one could be forgiven for thinking that Wexler had indeed captured the meaninglessness of citizenship as a basis for political identity. It seemed that the concept of citizenship meant little to student teachers and their trainers in all five countries. In Greek there is no word for 'citizenship'. Not surprisingly, it was hard to initiate discussions on this topic. Little success was had until, somewhat surprisingly, the English word 'citizenship' was used in the Greek discussion groups.

In England and Wales, despite having an appropriate word, student teachers initially appeared to have difficulty in defining and using the term. 'Citizenship' appeared to have few, if any, connotations or links to everyday life or identities. One male student teacher, who seemed to speak for many of the British student teachers, suggested that he had no idea what a citizen was. Typical responses were:

> I don't know. I think there is such a thing as citizenship. (English male student teacher)

> ... I think I'm a citizen but I mean I'd have to delve into a dictionary really. (English male student teacher)

A group of English female student teachers also struggled for meaning:

> Does it mean anything to you to say that I am a citizen?

> No.

> Nothing at all.

> From what people say, yes, I feel that way but I would feel nothing today... Oh, I am a citizen. That doesn't mean anything to me really.

> I can't really relate to the actual word citizen.

Yet discussions with student teachers revealed that, although citizenship had little currency in everyday discourse in all five countries, it was possible to identify the different metaphors, associations and values which they called into play in trying to make sense of the term. Student teachers articulated complex relations between their moral stances and their critical interpretations of modern society. Below, we attempt to unravel at least some of the common threads, distinctions and tensions which arose in the focus-group discussions.

The spatial dimension of citizenship

The spatial dimension of the concept of citizenship refers to the way it was used to signal membership of geographic, cultural or political communities. Citizenship can be brought into relation with localities of different size and scale, such as villages, regions, nation states, international orders, the European context and the global village (cf. Portugal). At times, it was possible to detect strong, individual, political identities in respondents' descriptions of the community boundaries and the criteria for membership.

In the United Kingdom alone, a range of geo-political communities was mentioned, including the United Kingdom, Great Britain, England, Scotland, Wales and Northern Ireland, Europe, the international community and the global community. A range of criteria for membership was also used, such as being resident, having been born in the country, having been educated in the country, cultural membership and membership of racial groups. As the following set of quotations suggest, the expression 'being part of' begged the question of what membership actually referred to in practice.

> Well, um, I'm a bit confused about this citizenship. Is it citizenship as in general or a community, … or is it citizenship as in part of a country? (English female student teacher)

> Well, as I see it, the word citizen to me means part of the country, in fact I suppose it means more part of the community, more European community. So the word citizen I would equate with being part of Europe. (English female student teacher)

> No, it's being part of a member of a town, somebody who lives in an urban community. (English female student teacher)

Citizenship as inclusive/exclusive

For some student teachers, membership of a regional or national community had more emotive than physical/residential connotations. Male student teachers, in particular, spoke of concepts such as pride in being part of a particular country/ nation or sharing a national cultural heritage.

> I think there is an element of pride that comes out for me, proud to be a citizen of this country. (English male student teacher)

> Yes, in a way, an era of pride, a country pride, I suppose. It goes along certain different levels, depending on who you'd be discussing citizenship with … You'd be proud of being Welsh, I suppose. (English male student teacher)

On the other hand, national pride can be constructed as a reaction to difference. The concept of citizenship could be the vehicle by means of which the individual is constructed in opposition to those who are excluded by the category of membership. The following quotation gives some hint of this dialectic between self and 'otherness'.

> … the only time you really think of citizenship is when you are introduced with another culture and you find yourself alienated, especially going abroad. I think in Britain when I meet people from other countries that come over here, I'm very conscious of just doing what is right so these people do have a good impression. I think that's the only time I'm aware of being a citizen. (English male student teacher)

Students also constructed citizenship as an abstract, but nevertheless inclusive category. They described a sense of belonging somewhere even if 'somewhere' was vaguely defined. We found rather abstract references to belonging to 'a group', 'a culture', or 'society'. These descriptions implied more than formal criteria of membership such as place of residence, place of work or place of birth. They appeared to stress the 'feeling of belonging' rather than any explicit political identity. One Portuguese science educator, for example, spoke of 'habits', 'principles' and 'visions', concepts closer perhaps to Bourdieu and Passeron's (1977) notion of *habitus*. He stated:

> We understand a citizen of a nation state as someone who belongs to a culture, who has certain habits, certain principles, certain visions of the world. (Portuguese teacher trainer)

A related critical tension identified in the discussions with student teachers was that between *ascribed* and *achieved* citizenship. The question of whether citizenship was something that could be earned touched on whether women, minority ethnic groups and those with disabilities could apply. If the concept of citizenship was seen as a 'cultural arbitrary', rather than a 'natural' category, then there was always the possibility that it could be restructured, or its membership redefined.

The citizen and the state

Student teachers in Greece, however, used other benchmarks in their discussions of citizenship – namely the relationship between the individual and society. They referred less to a cultural concept of citizenship or nation and more to a political entity represented by the state. Being a citizen offered this female teacher trainer:

> ... a sense that you belong somewhere, that you are a member of an organised society in which you have the right to act and which offers you an entity.

Greek student teachers showed particular awareness of the way in which organised society provided a framework of legally defined benefits for the individual. One student described citizenship as:

> a concept of living in the context of an organised state, according to the range of laws that have, as a precondition, the benefit of the citizen within the same organisation. (Greek male student teacher)

However, tensions between 'the benefits' of citizenship in these definitions and the potential loss of individual freedom were referred to frequently. In Greece, the contradictions between a protective organised state and the unprotected citizen were clearly at the forefront of student teachers' understanding of citizenship.

In the Portuguese and Greek groups, tensions were found between the need for respect for, and perhaps conformity to, the state and the need for civic activism and political reform. In some instances, what McLaughlin (1992: 236) has referred to as *minimal* views of citizenship were used to define the good citizen. Reference was made to citizenship which involved civil status and the associated rights based on the rule of law. In these discussions, stress was laid on conformity to core values, community-based voluntarism and limited political engagement. In other groups however, the 'thicker' *maximal* version of citizenship was found which McLaughlin described as, 'a richer thing than, say, the possession by a person of a passport, the right to vote and an unreflective "nationality"' (*ibid.*).

These maximal views of citizenship tend to define the citizen in social, cultural and psychological terms, somewhat in line with McLaughlin's description:

> ... the citizen must have a consciousness of him or herself as a member of a living community with a shared democratic culture involving obligations and responsibilities as well as rights, a sense of the common good, fraternity [sic] and so on. This latter maximal interpretation of the identity required by a citizen is dynamic rather than static in that it is seen as a matter of continuing debate and redefinition. It also gives rise to the question of the extent to which social disadvantage in its various forms can undermine citizenship, especially when a sense of effective personal agency is seen as a necessary ingredient of what is at stake. (McLaughlin, 1992)

As McLaughlin points out, maximal views of citizenship pre-suppose a considerable degree of explicit understanding of democratic principles, values and procedures and require individuals to have the necessary dispositions and capacities for the conceived level of democratic participation. It was possible to identify student teachers who did indeed expect critical engagement with, and participation in, political and social life. This suggests that unquestioning conformity per se was considered unacceptable by these student teachers and may also be a matter of concern in a democratic society.

These generic tensions in defining the boundaries of citizenship were differently expressed in the focus-group discussions in each country. In the next three subsections we present preliminary findings which explore these tensions further in the context of three discursive frameworks which, from our reading of our collective data, appear to have shaped the meanings attached to the word 'citizenship'. Such discursive frameworks suggest that not one but a number of different languages are drawn upon to make sense of contemporary citizenship – languages that each allow for maximal or minimal concepts, and which each have gendered dimensions. Within such discourses one can also glimpse, even from such a preliminary investigation, the tensions between identity and the ideals of social justice, unity and difference.

The three discursive frameworks we explore are what we choose to call:

(a) political discourses;
(b) moral discourses; and
(c) egalitarian discourses.

Political discourses

Political discourses appear to be active in countries which construct notions of political duty, both in relation to the individual and society, and of the state to the individual. All schools in Greece teach the traditions of ancient Greece and provide civic education on the *Principles of a Democratic Regime*. It would appear that lessons learned from the dictatorship of the colonels, which ended in the 1970s, have deeply influenced student teachers' understandings of citizenship. It was significant that they used the notion of the citizen as a vantage point from which to define membership of the *polis* used in its original sense as the city. In one group discussion, male student teachers mentioned:

> Citizenship is a person that is integrated into a 'city' with the ancient meaning.
>
> A democracy.
>
> Specific community with a specific legislature.
>
> I mean, in a political organisation.
>
> A citizen is one who participates in the election.

These notions of citizenship signalled a complex interaction between the rights of individuals to make political choices and the right to be informed about choices, opportunities, rights and responsibilities. They also involved the right to be elected and to elect those who would govern. Political representation and participation were presented as key symbols of the freedom enjoyed by all citizens.

Without the freedom to participate in 'every aspect of work relations, in every aspect of life, financial, cultural, social, everything' (Greek male student teacher), the citizen would not be able to exercise his/her rights and duty to control the direction of events in society. Citizenship was described as the need to make decisions to protect one's own life, choices (liberty and autonomy) and also to sustain solidarity with others. As one Greek male science education lecturer commented:

> The intervention of man in the polis, in the city (…) is the capacity of interfering in the life of the polis (…). It is the intervention of the subject on the city, he [sic] has the capacity to intervene, to take and share decisions. I have always thought that power must be shared by all. That capacity of people to feel that they have an obligation to intervene, that they have the right to intervene, to understand that citizenship will necessarily give them a set of rights and duties. (Greek male teacher trainer)

These kinds of view were elaborated further in some of the Portuguese discussion groups. One teacher trainer referred to 'collective edification' and described it as the need to seek improvement in the rights for others, their social benefits and the promotion of the social good.

The critical citizen

In the context of this political discourse, a good citizen was not necessarily constructed as one who obeys. Indeed, in countries that have experienced right-wing dictatorships such as Greece, Portugal and Spain, conformity may threaten the rights of citizens. In Greece, it was precisely the 'cultural arbitrariness' of the state which raised doubts about the desirability of conformity and justified the role of the good citizen as social critic. As one female student teacher commented:

> I don't agree with the term [i.e. a good citizen]. As things are today, I don't know what it means to discuss the good citizen. I mean, even if somebody is a good citizen, he becomes a bad one, the reality transforms him. (Greek female student teacher)

The good citizen, for some Greek student teachers, was someone who had a duty to act, and to change the established order, to mobilise and fight for rights. The comments which follow illustrate the way in which this 'maximal' view was discussed as positive but also as a potentially dangerous task:

> To be a good citizen does not mean you must always obey what the state lays

down because if so, the citizens would be considered a weak willed, undecided people. Citizens must be fighting, socialised, in order to be able, when the time comes, to overthrow everything that is going wrong in Greece, or even in the international order. (Greek male student teacher)

A good citizen is one who participates actively in society, contributes to the democracy, builds democratic regimes, is interested in good relations among citizens. Today, however, a good citizen takes care to protect himself. (Greek male student trainer)

Another student in the discussion group replied:

I agree that a good citizen has to protect himself but I imagine he should try to start structuring another better social life every time he has the possibility to do it. (Greek male student teacher)

This debate amongst predominantly male student teachers about self-protection, mobilisation and participation in decision making in political life presented an image of the citizen fighting to keep control of a potentially dangerous state. The memory and experience of dictatorship, particularly for the older student teachers, seemed to be present in their constructions of a politicised citizenry. As one male student teacher emphasised:

We should never, as citizens, stop caring about who is governing, about the methods, etc. We should try to intervene, to be politicised, to be active. This is the only way to control. This is the citizen's right. Otherwise, I mean if the citizens don't care, one day they realise that things have happened and they have not been informed. (Greek male student teacher)

There seemed to be a similar concern in the Portuguese student trainers' discourse about sustaining critical participation. They expressed a need for social commitment as well as a capacity to act and take decisions. They justified this with reference to over 50 years of right-wing dictatorship (Salazarism from the 1930s to the late 1960s). To them, individual participation implied critical collective participation and distancing one's self from the historical past of the 'New State', in which people's conformity to the government and its laws was not only expected, but also built into educational institutions. The new mission was variously described as 'additive amelioration' or 'collective edification'.

It is the capacity of participating in the life of the 'polis' in the city to which he [sic] belongs, the capacity to take and share decisions (...). It is the people's capacity to feel that it is their duty to intervene, that they have the right to participate, to understand that citizenship will necessarily give them a set of rights and a set of duties. (Portuguese teacher trainer)

76 Teachers, gender and the discourses of citizenship

In contrast, one Portuguese teacher trainer argued for ethical correctness in the following terms:

> The good citizen is the one who obeys the state, who keeps strictly to the constitution, who with his profession fulfils 100%, who does not in any way prevaricate. (Portuguese teacher trainer)

However, this latter emphasis on maintaining the political order of the constitution under all conditions appeared not to have been shared by Portuguese student teachers.

Despite a history of dictatorship under Franco, student teachers in Spain appeared less likely to articulate critical political discourses. Spanish male student teachers, in contrast with female colleagues, referred to a new democratic state and highlighted the ideals of the French Revolution and the role of the state:

> Citizenship means a group of people who live and relate to each other in an '*estado de derecho*' (constitutional state) and have the same duties and rights. (Spanish male student teacher)

> The idea of citizenship to me is related to the French Revolution, and since then, everyone has the right to be a citizen. (Spanish male student teacher)

However, their references to the political sphere appeared to be improvised and abstract, with few mentions of actual political roles *vis-à-vis* the state. Female student teachers tended to draw upon moral discourses to highlight the critical role of the 'caring citizen' (see below).

The sceptical citizen

In Britain, discussions with student teachers tended not to highlight the role of citizens in maintaining democratic regimes and their principles or practices. Interventionist and critical political discourse were rarely present. However, student teachers in Britain seemed aware of the arbitrariness of the state and were critical of the moral behaviour, intentions and actions of politicians. They did not, however, offer an equivalent image of the critical citizen. Some of their representations of the good citizen suggested a 'sceptical citizen', ever on the alert, but not necessarily active in promoting democracy. The European traditions of Greek political philosophy or the French Revolution appeared not to have shaped their understandings of the concept of citizenship. This may be a reflection of a different political history, incorporating the British monarchy and a recognition of the different status of a subject from that of a citizen. It may also be due to the lack of civic education in most schools. The following extracts demonstrate Welsh student teachers' sensitivity to the problems of defining citizenship as a status, as well as a recognition of the politically contested nature of the concept:

> If you look at it (citizenship) in a very modern way, some people would say

Teachers, gender and the discourses of citizenship 77

it is a bit funny to be a citizen in Britain because we have still got a queen, so that we're subjects rather than citizens. So it's a bit of a conflict there, calling yourself a citizen in a monarchy. (Welsh female student teacher)

You think of the word citizen as being part of citizen of what? The State. Whenever I hear the word citizenship I always think of the relevant stuff coming out of the … the Citizen's Charter, I can't separate the two. I think a Citizen Charter doesn't really seem to have much concrete meaning to me. (Welsh female student teacher)

The current government is seen to be 'promoting' citizenship for political reasons – as much as for social reasons, which isn't necessarily the best way to go about it. (Welsh female student teacher)

Descriptions of the role of the citizen in a multiracial metropolis revealed the importance of recognising difference. It may well be that social discrimination has affected British student teachers' political discourses. Their language suggested more about their 'politicisation' than their conceptualisation of polity. What follows is a typical discussion about the dilemmas involved in defining a political identity. The context of race, gender and class inequalities provide frameworks for those who appear to engage with more 'maximal' or 'empowering' definitions of political life. A group of English female student teachers training in a multiracial inner city area commented that citizenship meant:

Having a voice and a right to changing anything.

It's a lovely ideal, isn't it?

Because it doesn't happen. You don't all have an equal voice in society. I don't just mean colour or sex – the man in the street doesn't have the same…

I think to a certain extent it is a sense of belonging to something. That may be why I have no concept of it because I was born here, but I don't feel British.

But you've got a right to be here.

You could argue that I have the right to be here but that's by the by. I'm here till whatever happens but it doesn't mean that I'm happy to be here in some respects but I can see that there are certain things that are working against me, because I'm here and because I'm black.

… if you are a black person and you are a citizen here it means a totally different thing from someone who is white. (English female student teachers)

The references have more to do with the structuring of discrimination than the

78 *Teachers, gender and the discourses of citizenship*

power of the electorate. In politicised discourses such as this, student teachers appeared to be alert to the different experiences of particular groups and the inequalities they may face within a democracy. However, apart from 'having a voice', little emphasis was placed on sharing decision making or critical action at state level or in the public sphere. This is characteristic of the scepticism referred to earlier. Only one English female student teacher talked about the difficulty of having a 'political voice' or of taking an active role in a democratic crisis while being informed and free to say what she thought. Often the most that came across from student teachers' comments was a suspicion that all was not well.

> ... the thing is Britain is over-flooded with money basically, that they can afford for everybody to have a good standard of living. There is no reason why anyone in Britain can't have a good ... (life). (Welsh male student teacher)

> I think the country is in real trouble to be honest. (Welsh male student teacher)

> The non-Europeans have trouble, possibly with Western values ... Asians and that, they probably have less rights, whether they should have or whether they shouldn't ... (Welsh male student teacher)

This critical awareness amongst British student teachers appeared to have little to do with exercising rights and duties, especially in terms of intervening in the actions of the state. Although these comments demonstrate aspects of a 'maximal' view of citizenship, they appear to focus on the effects of state policies on people's lives rather than on the possibilities of 'civic action' described by their Greek and Portuguese counterparts.

Moral discourses

Moral discourses bring together concepts of culture, community and 'the common good'. The focus here was less on state membership described as a legal status and more on the 'feeling' of belonging to a community. Individuals were discussed in relation to shared values, especially those which relate to Judaeo-Christian traditions of 'good neighbourliness', moral behaviour and caring.

The caring citizen

These moral discourses are especially well articulated by women in Catholic countries such as Spain and Portugal. There appeared to be a great emphasis on conformity and respect for social values and rules. The person at the heart of this discourse would live in society without exceeding the limits of unsociable behaviour and would also sustain the virtues of loyalty, honesty and sensitivity to the problems faced by others. The good citizen could be summarised as:

Teachers, gender and the discourses of citizenship 79

> ... one who takes part in things ... who rules himself by moral and ethical principles. (Portuguese teacher trainer)

Social order and caring for others were valued because they provided a check to excessive individualism. Responsibilities to the community rather than to the state appeared to be valued above rights. Descriptions of solidarity connoted universal rather than culturally specific notions of the common interest. Fraternity rather than freedom was also central to the discourse.

Solidarity was associated with a range of groups which did not involve the state; for example, with neighbours, the community and within personal relations. When solidarity was mentioned in relation to a country or the global village, the references still tended to be made to an abstract concept of 'society'.

> I am a good citizen when I have the feeling that I must contribute as far as I can with love for the society and for my fatherland, with respect for the laws and to the governors and having always in mind that the common interest is much more important than my personal interest. (Greek male teacher trainer)

In Spain, female student teachers, in particular, drew upon the language of Christianity to construct the good citizen as caring and self-sacrificing. Descriptions of the need to respect, to tolerate difference and to serve were sometimes vocational in tone. A group of Spanish female student teachers commented:

> Citizenship means service to the community.

> Citizenship means respect for different cultures.

> Citizenship should mean to educate people for the good of the rest.

Service to the community and respect for others were mentioned more often than political principles. At the centre of moral discourse was the 'good person'.

> I never think of people as citizens, but I talk about people as good or bad. (Spanish female student teacher)

> Good people are good citizens. It is impossible to think of an example of a bad person being a good citizen. (Spanish female student teacher)

Moral discourses were used very differently by Spanish male and female student teachers. For men, the school had a duty to lead morally:

> We can't avoid it; if we suppress the idea of 'leadership' and if we don't lead people a little bit ... Because people don't show their ability to do anything on their own. However, we must study the ways of doing it without seeming authoritarian. (Spanish male student teacher)

Some were clear that the educational response should not amount to moral indoctrination:

> I think that the question is one of being a good professional, isn't it? Because subjectivity is always there. The good professional gives tools for the students' reflexivity. (Spanish male student teacher)

Female student teachers did not refer to professionalism in this way. They tended to describe an invisible ethical framework, a code of conduct or set of 'virtues' which were not necessarily sanctioned by formal regulations. At the same time, imposing such values was considered problematic by some, because of the dangers of moral relativism.

> She considers herself a good citizen, but from her own point of view. You know what I mean. You are biased in your own values and on your own rules. (Spanish female student teacher)

There are also other dangers, recognised, for example, by a female Portuguese teacher trainer. Traditional Christian moralities and 'mentalities' could be responsible for perpetuating gender differences:

> In the Portuguese context, there is still a traditional mentality, a separation of the place of men and women, due to our Christian mentality. Therefore, there's the idea of women as secondary to men, they are here to serve men. It's a process that will take a very long time, all this question of women's liberation in the 1960s and '70s, people think that the differences are already gone. (Portuguese female teacher trainer)

Christian principles were often described as a form of surveillance, used to inform and judge the behaviour of individuals within a community. In some of these descriptions the notion of rights was presented as a means of enforcing Christian values; Portuguese teacher trainers spoke of the rights to health as '*mens sana, in corpore sano*' (austerity, strength of mind), the rights to housing (in the sense of a home which was warm inside and gave a sense of community sharing) and the rights to education (a way of giving something of oneself to another, of teaching the poor and the weak).

However, even though the concept of 'the caring citizen' might mean being involved in charity work at the community level, in voluntary associations and in caring roles within the family, it was noticeable how difficult some student teachers found it to apply the term 'citizenship' to family life. For example, a male Portuguese lecturer commented:

> I never thought about the idea of a citizen within the family. Within the family, I tend to think more about a father, a husband, a son, a brother. There are concepts that I associate with family life and that of citizen is not one of them … (Portuguese male student teacher)

Some student teachers in Britain struggled to recognise the relationship of community spirit and community activism to citizenship. It would seem that the image of the good citizen was not equated with the caring professions or charity work. For one male student teacher, charity work represented 'a failure on the part of the state to do its job properly' and was therefore not considered to be the exercising of moral responsibility. In the following remarks, these two male student teachers appeared to be searching for a more meaningful definition of community activism than just 'good works'.

> You say what do you think is a good citizen, then instantly in your mind you get things like charity work and group work. There are a lot of people who are in very caring professions – that doesn't mean they are a good citizen. (English male student teacher)

> For me I can't think of something called citizenship, but things that make me feel, that's being a good citizen. For instance, there's all sorts of things such as charity work, that strike me as good citizenship but that's very tangible, people on committees, or running church fêtes and all sorts of things like that and it goes much further and deeper and people work a lot harder, but that must stem from something a little bit deeper in psychological terms. … Perhaps something like a sense of community. (English male student teacher)

Other English and Welsh students recognised the value of the suppression of individualism in relation to collective values. One described a citizen as:

> Someone who thinks a little bit beyond themselves – less selfish. (English male student teacher)

Although British politicians have emphasised individual advancement and materialism, these student teachers were at pains to stress the importance of maintaining concern for the community. The tension between individuals and the collectivity was a thread which ran through much of this particular discussion. Tolerance was high on their agenda:

> Being able to accept other people's views as well as your own. (Welsh female student teacher)

> Admitting that people are not always going to be same as you contributing to society. (Welsh female student teacher)

These student teachers' views appeared to value diversity rather than homogeneity of communities.

The good citizen and social class

Notions of 'goodness' and the 'good citizen' constructed within moral discourses again were not unproblematic, especially if they implied social and moral conformity. For those student teachers who seemed to be using a maximal version of citizenship (McLaughlin, 1992), the 'good citizens', by the very nature of their being 'good', were in danger of undermining the goal of creating challenging, inquiring citizens. In Portugal, conformity to dominant values signalled for some 'dangerous shades'. For some English student teachers, the 'good citizen' was presented as limited and thus 'exceptionally boring'. Indeed, if dominant cultures were perceived to be class dominated or oppressive, then the model of the caring and thus conforming citizen offered little that was positive.

> All the connotations to citizenship we have in society are very middle class … I'll be a good citizen and play cricket, that type of thing … it has no relevance to most people … the average man in the street. (English male student teacher)

Amongst the English and Welsh student teachers, the class imagery that was used to describe the 'good citizen' was particularly striking. We found a surprisingly dated image of the respectable 'bowler-hatted gentleman' of the 1950s. This image of male respectability in the public sphere provided a sharp contrast to the critical citizen described in political discourses.

> A middle aged balding fellow with a nice garden and semi-detached house. (Welsh male student teacher)

> The citizen is a necessarily nice man in a bowler hat who had got a job … in the city and then comes back to his nice semi-detached house with a wife and 2.5 kids. (Welsh male student teacher)

> The first thing that springs to my mind about a citizen is that I get an image of a man in a bowler hat and a suit. (Welsh male student teacher)

> A Percy Sugden type of person in neighbourhood watch who would have a very stereotyped idea really. (Welsh male student teacher)

> … [whose wife] would wear navy blue and cream and make jam. (Welsh female student teacher)

Concern about class, gender and ethnic biases amongst student teachers who described Britain as multicultural and pluralist suggested that any concept of 'the common good' was highly problematic. Some student teachers appeared to be affected by concerns about imposing social values which would limit rather than extend social justice. They were unwilling to support values which they suggested might limit the opportunities of children to express themselves freely and develop their abilities.

On the other hand, they were also concerned that imposing one set of values (even if they were egalitarian) might conflict with those of the children's families and their ways of life. Teaching values was not something they considered to be neutral and they were particularly concerned about being seen to indoctrinate.

These class-laden images of citizenship were described in terms which were not appealing, and student teachers were clearly struggling to find ways to imagine and articulate modern versions of citizenship which could accommodate cultural pluralism and economic change. For those who had already engaged in practice teaching in inner cities, and had witnessed at first hand conflictual community relations and diverse family structures and values, the framing of coherent and egalitarian-moral discourse, of a maximal kind, was a complex affair. The English and Welsh students reported that the likelihood of parental resistance to any one egalitarian-moral perspective provided an added anxiety.

In Greece, the good modern citizen was described as someone who overcomes self-interest and contributes to the common good, through economic rather than caring activities. The good citizen can be defined as the 'productive citizen', somebody who works for the good of society by contributing to the wealth of the nation. Fraternity in this context would mean working hard, paying taxes and encouraging greater national productivity. According to one Greek teacher trainer, a productive citizen:

> ... contributes with all his force to the modernisation of society. (Greek male teacher trainer)

The shift in the construction of the modern Greek citizen is away from the individual of ancient Greek and Christian cultures towards an economic role. The legacies of previous traditions are, however, evident in student teachers' concerns for the rights and dignity of others. What is not clear is how far the notion of the 'productive citizen' includes women's contribution to economic progress. Indeed, this kind of framework may well render domestic labour invisible, thus further damaging women's status.

Mother as reformer

In contrast, it would seem that by mobilising moral discourses, women student teachers in Catholic countries such as Portugal and Spain were able to focus on feminist political empowerment. They argued that if ethical virtues are the basis of good citizenship, then those with sensitive or caring dispositions, who are committed to solidarity and co-operation, will make good citizens. Here, a Portuguese teacher trainer highlights the way women may be constructed as effective citizens within such a discourse:

> A person who in principle is more sensitive to the problems of others, I think, women are more sensitive to what surrounds them. I think my grandmother

is a good citizen, she has those dispositions ... in men it is harder to find. (Portuguese female student teacher)

The theme of 'mother as reformer' also emerged in some Greek female student teachers' discussions. They described how women could potentially make up for a lack of public political power by mobilising power within the family. These women did not engage with abstract ideals of the 'critical citizen' but described women changing society by raising a new generation of politicised children. In this way, young Greek female student teachers were able to define a position for themselves within a moral discourse.

Alternative feminist models of citizenship could also be offered by female groups in Portugal, Spain, England and Wales. Some student teachers found ways to value female contributions to society by drawing on traditional gender roles. There was some suggestion that society could sustain complementary concepts of the good citizen. They suggested that women could be constructed as 'home citizens' and 'family builder citizens':

> Traditionally it is expected that men do it by working, building up power structures while women do it in a more nurturing sense within the family. So men do it organisationally and women do it at a more personal level. (English female student teacher)

> I think we are able to do everything a man does, considering specific situations, children ... All issues are masculine. I think few women know what they should or should not do as citizens ... women exercise more citizenship in the family, in private life, they are not yet accustomed to being citizens. (Portuguese female teacher trainer)

> Citizenship has to be dealt with within the family, parents, children and schools as a reflection on the family. (Spanish female student teacher)

Egalitarian discourses

The egalitarian discourses of the post-war period in the United Kingdom have been associated, on the whole, with the provision of what Marshall (1965) called social rights through state welfare provision. The predominant notion here is redistributive justice (cf. Rawls, 1972), where individuals are perceived to be entitled to basic human rights such as health care; education; housing; the right to work without discrimination; protection by legislation; social and family policies; and state provision of services. The extent to which these rights and services are provided and protected by the state will differ between countries. The extent to which rights are equally shared by all citizens, and over which range of public/private, male/female spheres, will be culturally and historically specific.

Thus, in Portugal and in Spain, discussion about rights in relation to full citizenship is a relatively new phenomenon in the new discourses of recent socialist governments. These egalitarian discourses tend to be superimposed on existing discourses and therefore do not entirely replace previous understandings of the social order and gender hierarchies. Alternatively, discourses become active at formal constitutional levels, without reference to everyday practice. Not surprisingly, a number of student teachers were aware of the formal provision of citizenship rights in relation to the state, but were not satisfied that all citizens had the same knowledge about such rights or how to claim them.

In Portugal, for example, men and women have only recently acquired rights under the new constitution established on 25 April 1976. The constitution was concerned with the creation of a 'social equilibrium', where particularly men and women would work in complementary fashion. The discursive logic of these egalitarian discourses tends to evoke the new constitution as consensual, and to evoke rights as if they have already been acquired.

In contrast, in Greece contemporary discussion about rights dates back to the early 1930s, before the first dictatorship, when the communist party was becoming stronger. Within the associated socialist discourses, attention was focused on the relation of individual rights to the organised state. The rights referred to in these discourses were not only those to justice, peace and equality, but also the rights to work, to be educated, to health provision as well as to corporal, psychological and intellectual rights.

The protesting citizen

Although the state was portrayed as the provider of benefits in the form of individual rights, it was also assumed that individuals would have to fight for them. We found that, in line with strong national political discourses, Greek female teachers constructed the notion of the Protesting Citizen. They voiced their concerns that the state might infringe individual rights and freedoms:

> The citizen often has the feeling that his [sic] rights are infringed by the laws. (Greek female teacher trainer)

> Citizens must be able to claim these rights – if you have been given them and are not able to see or claim them, it is not good. (Greek female teacher trainer)

There was a sense of Greek women's insecurity which might derive from feelings of exclusion and marginalisation from the political rights of citizenship. This led to a depiction of good citizens as those who struggle to achieve their rights.

> The term of citizen means to claim your rights, I believe we don't claim our rights enough. Take me, for example, in some cases, although I had the law with me, I was treated very badly. I could claim legally some things, but I didn't succeed. Maybe because I am a woman ... or maybe I was not able enough ... (Greek female student teacher)

> The notion of citizen makes me think of the insecurity I feel all the times I want to claim these. What are considered legal rights of the citizen, when as a citizen in the Greek state I tried to claim, I felt unprotected. (Greek female student teacher)

However, most Greek student teachers appeared to speak with indifference of the social rights and benefits provided by the state. For many years, welfare services were poor and many people had learned to supplement them with private initiatives (such as extra teaching help at home). To some extent, rights were more important in abstract than in relation to the implementation of legislation.

Greek political discourses, such as those detected in relation to the critical citizen described above, tend to be rooted in the language of civil rights which dealt with speech, movement, information and leisure. As one student teacher commented:

> It is a network of matters that secure individual independence, individual activism, political action, possibility of social action. (Greek female teacher trainer)

Individuals were seen to need such rights as a precondition for their full political participation. One female trainer considered the most important right to be the right to:

> … create within the society within which he (she) lives, according to his (her) personality and abilities. (Greek female teacher trainer)

The threat of an authoritarian government appears to have left a legacy of suspicion about the role of the state in Greece, and egalitarian developments could possibly be kept in check by this undercurrent. Concerns therefore were different from those expressed by English and Welsh student teachers. In Britain the lack of a written constitution and tradition of struggle over rights might have influenced student teachers' discourses.

> I think there is a cult of ignorance because we have never had them defined. In the absence of a Bill of Rights, freedom, proper Freedom of Information Acts, … The concept of us having rights is one, we had a revolution 400-odd years ago which fizzled out and we got the old regime back again and there has never been a strong democratic movement. It is something that has evolved so gradually over a period of years there has always [been] the same sort of people behind it, keeping things like the House of Lords. The idea of a right … I think is something that hit us rather suddenly – things like gay rights, women's rights, ethnic rights, all these sorts of things have happened very, very suddenly. There is a worrying lack of legal definition for them. We think we'd all like to say, 'Yes, I treat everyone equally,' and that's great and there are very few people who would probably say differently. I don't think there is sufficient reinforcement, such as a state fallback. (English male student teacher)

This student teacher described the British historical legacy as a slow evolution which tended to engender complacency and ignorance about individual rights but which has recently attracted renewed interest. Some English and Welsh student teachers date this new 'rights debate' to the 1980s, although discussion of children's rights were said to have been more recent. One of the main problems discussed was whether to use the law to ensure rights and to sustain, for example, freedom of speech in context of the scepticism referred to above. Some student teachers considered removing censorship at the same time as worrying about encouraging those such as the 'moral majority' in the United States. If freedom of speech is guaranteed for all, oppressive views might be promoted by those in power.

We considered it worth exploring whether student teachers found any meaning in the language of rights and if so, how they might apply to different contexts. We found differing degrees of awareness of rights amongst student teachers in different countries, and different perspectives about the most salient rights. The list from which to draw was extensive. Student teachers referred, for example, to those who did not receive full rights of citizenship. They mentioned ethnic groups, racial groups, migrants, immigrants, those who were poor, those who were ignorant, AIDS victims, language groups, social class groups, and particular age groups, amongst others. Even so, the language of rights in relation to the 'good citizen' was problematic. For some, if applied to the private sphere, it could be seen as oppressive and potentially destructive.

For some student teachers though, an air of optimism characterised their responses.

> What is not your right today, can become it tomorrow if you mobilise. (Greek male student teacher)

In Spain, society was represented as 'running a course', as if moving forward away from its historical past. There was a view that rights could be achieved without tension through positive intervention by the state or other agencies:

> Equality seems to grow … we are living in a transition, so we all will be equals in the near future. (Spanish male student teacher)

However, there were many who could not see equal opportunities or equality as a natural phenomenon that would be achieved without political intervention, particularly through educational reform. Spanish female student teachers appeared far more critical and more pessimistic about the new society. Women teachers did not see themselves as part of the 'transition' narrative set up by the socialist government. They did not position themselves as feminists, nor did they relate to the strong egalitarian discourses supported by men. Instead, as we have shown, they mobilised a moral discourse around femininity, caring and community-based cultures.

This struggle for women's rights is reminiscent of that found in Greece. As we have seen, some female student teachers also expressed insecurity about the assumption that all individuals would be included within the framework of citizenship and would achieve full rights. They too stated that women needed to fight for their rights.

Some Portuguese female education lecturers expressed concern about using the distinction between the public and private spheres. They pointed to the importance of linking the rights of citizenship to the private and not just the public sphere.

> If a woman is subject to violence within the family, within the strictly private, what can she do to stop this violence? She has to resort to the courts (…). She has to come out of the private sphere and come out to the public … there is a connection in my point of view. Citizenship has also to do with the private world of the family.

Portuguese student teachers also grappled with the difficult relationship between the discourse of rights and that of biological difference. Male and female student teachers' discussions suggested that they took the formal equality between the sexes, as written in the 1976 constitution, for granted. But, surprisingly, female student teachers used biological differences as the basis for arguing that women could play a different contributory role in contemporary society as mothers and carers. They suggested that if women were able to use biological differences constructively in public life, working in education and caring professions, they would be more likely to be valued themselves as citizens.

Student teachers and the language of citizenship

Discussions with student teachers have illustrated how different concepts of citizenship are constructed around political discourses, moral discourses and egalitarian discourses. Within each, gender relations were considered. Male and female student teachers in the different countries gave us insights into the complex ways in which gender difference shapes their representations of the citizen and, in particular, the 'good citizen'.

Two major concerns can be identified in the data. The first involves the gendering of different spheres in relation to notions of citizenship. The data indicates the continuing identification of gendered spheres, and especially the dominance of what Connell (1990) referred to as the European equation between authority and a dominating masculinity. The image and language of discourses associated with citizenship were largely male. Even concepts of community were associated more with male notions of responsibilities rather than female contributions within the family and neighbourhood. Political and egalitarian discourses, especially, appeared to apply to public spheres, and to assume both a relevance to men and a role for men in terms of 'civic action'.

In the five countries in our study in which under 15% of representatives in national assemblies were women, references to the rights and duties of citizens centred on the state or government. As male-dominated institutions, such references reinforced women's position outside the discourses of citizenship. Indeed, modes of civic action described within political or egalitarian discourses emphasised public rather than private action. We gained the impression in our discussions with student teachers in Spain and Greece that political struggles over rights and duties have been delegated to men. The more recent transition in Spain from a nationalist to socialist government and the new focus on rights seemed to have less relevance for women than for men.

Moral discourses, in contrast, were described in ways which appeared initially to override the distinction between public and private. This was achieved through references to the common good and common values. Yet such discourses, in the various national forms, were often premised on a concept of good public works. Citizenship in this context had little to do with parenting roles, caring for the aged or the sick within the home. Whilst male student teachers worried about the nature of social values, conformity or the possibility of encouraging a productive, law-abiding member of society, female student teachers indicated the importance of the family as a relevant site for discovering the 'good citizen'. Indeed, in some countries, women's roles as mothers and as carers were highlighted, and appeared to be celebrated as alternative sources of critical, civic action. The artificiality of the boundary between public and private was most apparent in the context of moral discourses.

In the first section of this chapter we referred to Heater's suggestion that within modernist narratives, concepts of citizenship can be contested again and again. New forms of solidarity and new 'rationalities' can be formed and reformed, impinging more or less upon state educational systems. This perspective makes it possible to understand the national tensions between political, moral and egalitarian discourses found amongst the new generation of student teachers, as well as the differences between national contexts. Student teachers today carry with them the legacies of nationalism, of liberal democracy and of socialism. For the older Greek student teachers, the legacies of the 1970s can be identified in their fears concerning the power of the 'organised state' and the need to forge ahead in what they referred to as a struggle for democracy. Their comments portrayed them as engaging in contemporary efforts to forge new political projects.

In contrast, Spanish teachers' representations of citizenship reflected the work of the Spanish central government, which has been trying for the past 12 years to define a new sense of national membership over and above regional and ethnic identities. After 40 years of dictatorship (1939–1975), Spain established a new constitution (1978). The struggle for democratic and human rights was described as a process of learning, and an understandable level of insecurity about the nature and exercise of rights and duties could be detected in discussions.

A new version of what it meant to 'be Spanish' was described by many groups and can be seen as a necessary prerequisite for a break from Francoist Nationalist discourses. Symbolic as well as economic and political strategies were being employed to disconnect the past. However, the transformation was not complete. Symbolic relics such as the colours of the flag and the national anthem remain, even if the anagram has changed. The royal emblem now replaces the fascist one; the green passport has been changed for the European. The military is not present, except occasionally, and the church is not visible, although it continues to retain strong economic and ideological power. Civic education in this new political context is being designed to promote a new system of values in an educational structure that is not truly democratic. The references we found to community values and the tentative egalitarian and political discourses therefore should not surprise us.

Within such national transformations also lie shifting definitions of political, economic, civil, social and reproductive rights. As Phillips (1991a, 1991b) points out, there is no necessary progression from, say, civic to political to social rights (cf. Marshall, 1965). Different nations construct the notion of rights differently and at different periods. In Britain the establishment of the welfare state in the 1940s laid the ground for a floor of entitlements, including social rights in housing, education and welfare, while such modern versions of social rights have only recently been introduced in the new egalitarianism of post-Salazar Portugal.

In sharp contrast, student teachers in Britain have been brought up as 'Thatcher's children' – a generation which was told that 'the age of egalitarianism is over' (quoted in Arnot, 1992). These relatively younger student teachers expressed concern over protecting individual freedom while at the same time valuing tolerance, suggesting a sensitivity to social diversity. Some have come through the period of their youth realising the emphasis on market philosophies and materialistic values. They expressed concern about the lack of 'belonging' to a community. Their benchmarks in terms of citizenship were not as clearly demarcated as those of their counterparts in the other countries. Working with concepts of diverse heterogeneous communities, they appear to be grappling both with egalitarian discourses and social movements of the past, as well as with current alienations from the present. There was little evidence from this small sample of the ability to articulate discourses of citizenship which were either personally meaningful or liberatory.

Without a programme of civic education similar to that provided in the other three countries studied, each new generation of student teachers in Britain is likely to come into the profession with insufficient training to articulate an intellectual, political framework for their social and moral concerns. The tensions between individual and collectivity were not easily articulated nor resolved. Our study revealed the weakness of political discursive frameworks amongst student teachers in Britain, suggesting that there might not be an adequate platform on which to build either a moral or an egalitarian project.

Our data portrayed the relationship between the individual and the state as a permanent dynamic which remains at the core of the concept of citizenship. As feminist political theorists are all too aware, the traditions of Western European political thought have constructed an abstract individual in relation to abstracted sets of social relations, in particular the state. Perhaps because of the illusion of universalism implied by civil, political and social rights, the gendered nature of the concept of the individual and the gendered basis of the state (Connell, 1990) are not generally exposed. For some female student teachers, such illusions are not sustained; for others, the abstraction allows them to ignore gender dynamics.

One of the key issues in the project was whether women could transform political life; whether women could offer alternative models for fulfilling the responsibilities of a citizen; or whether women should outline a role for themselves as citizens to ensure they achieve the rights owed to them. Our evidence suggests that feminist debates are still current and can be articulated in certain contexts. Some female student teachers attempted to extend the concept of citizenship to family life. The concept of a 'caring citizen' or a 'family builder' citizen was offered as the way forward. Yet, as we have seen, these concepts have tended to be sustained by a moral discourse which can fail to recognise exclusionary and oppressive practices in the state. Morality can emphasise the caring role of women, but without a transformation of the concept of citizenship within political or egalitarian discourses, women are unlikely to achieve equal status and equal levels of participation to men.

According to Walby (1994), modern forms of patriarchy have developed new modes of inclusion for women, particularly in the public sphere. Some elements of that process can be found in the changing position of women in public life. At the same time, the major shifts in private and domestic spheres appear to focus on the weakness of men's participation rather than a recognition of the forms of patriarchal control which affect women's lives. For some, the way forward is to extend the concept of democratic citizenship, either through feminising political and moral discourses or by reframing egalitarian discourses.

Whether male-ordered democratic discourses can be transformed by women successfully is a matter for debate. Certainly none of the discourses used by student teachers is unproblematic in its construction of what constitutes the citizen and the 'good citizen', and in its consequences, both for society generally, and for women in particular.

Conclusions

This project extends our knowledge of a new young generation of professionals who will take up key roles in the educational systems of each country studied. The knowledge and understandings they bring to bear on their practice in the school system will help shape, even if it will not determine, their approach to the education of male and female youth. The vision they bring to young people will draw on their concerns about political and social life, moral values, as well as representations of 'the community', the common good and the virtues of the good citizen.

In the context of recent national and European concerns about education for citizenship, this study supports Giroux's contention that:

> Teachers rather than students should represent a starting point for any theory of citizenship education. ... It is ... appropriate to begin with those educators who both mediate and define the educational process. ... This is not to deny that students represent an important concern in both the development and defects of such a theory; in fact, it is precisely this concern that demands that we construe a theoretical framework giving teachers and others involved in the educational process the possibility to think critically about the nature of

their beliefs and how these beliefs both influence and offset the day-to-day experiences they have with students. Similarly, it is important that teachers situate their own beliefs, values and practices within a wider context so that their latent meanings can be better understood. This 'dialectical situating' ... will help illuminate the social and political nature of the structural and ideological constraints that teachers face daily. (Giroux, 1980: 350)

What emerged from our analysis was how the themes of liberty, equality and fraternity constructed gender and gender relations in different nuanced ways. Ellis (1991) suggests in her article 'Sisters and Citizens' that the exclusion of women in male hierarchies of power is significant because it can lead to (a) the trivialisation of women's issues, (b) the alienation of women from participation in the body politic through the creation of masculine ethos and tradition, and (c) the failure of political life to provide the basis of female identities as citizens.

Our data suggests that from the student teachers' point of view, women are not easily characterised as part of the 'brotherhood of man' (Dietz, 1985) even when they act as community activists and carers. Women – even those committed to critical citizenship – are not necessarily 'freed' by political discourses, nor are they easily granted rights in all spheres of their lives. Perhaps Benton (1991) may be correct when she argues that:

> A politics of citizenship founded on liberty, equality and above all 'fraternity' offers little of value to members of the sorority. (Benton, 1991: 163)

Before answering that question, however, more work needs to be completed on how gendered discourses maintain the sexual division of labour in society.

Acknowledgements

The project was funded by the Human Resources, Education and Training Division of the European Commission (Stage 1 in 1994–1995 and Stage 2 in 1995–1996) as one of the projects put forward by its Equal Opportunities Unit. It was funded under the 3rd Medium-term Community Action Programme. The projects under this programme encouraged the development of measures designed to promote the participation of women in decision-making processes in economic and social life. We are grateful to the Equal Opportunities Unit and the EC for their financial support.

Each national project team had a number of members who worked on coordinating, or participating in, the data collection. We would like to thank, in particular, Amanda Coffrey, Pat Mahony, Sneh Shah, Daniella Tilbury, Xavier Ramblas, Xavier Bonal, Roula Ziogou, Christina Athanasiadou and Eleni Mavrogiorgou. Thanks are also due to Jo-Anne Dillabough and Debbie Mills for their assistance on this paper. The views represented here are entirely those of the authors. I am grateful to all four co-authors – Helen Araújo, Kiki Deliyanni, Gabrielle Ivinson and Amparo Tomé – for allowing me to include this article.

References

Arnot, M. (1992) 'Feminism, education and the new right', in M. Arnot and L. Barton (eds) *Voicing Concerns: sociological perspectives on educational reforms*. Wallingford: Triangle Books.
Arnot, M. (1995) 'Feminism and democratic education', in J. SanTomé Torés (ed.) *Rethinking Education*. Madrid: Murata Press.
Arnot, M., Deliyanni-Kouimtzis, K. and Ziogou, R. with Rowe, G. (1995) *Promoting Equality Awareness: women as citizens*, Final Report, June. Brussels: Equal Opportunities Unit, European Commission.
Benton, S. (1991) 'Gender, sexuality and citizenship', in G. Andrews (ed.) *Citizenship*. London: Lawrence and Wishart, pp. 153–63.
Bourdieu, P. and Passeron, J-C. (1977) *Reproduction in Education, Society and Culture*. London: Sage.
Connell, R.W. (1990) 'The state, gender and sexual politics', *Theory and Society*, 19: 507–44.
Coulby, D. and Jones, C. (1995) *Education and European Systems*. Stoke-on-Trent: Trentham Books.
Dietz, M.G. (1985) 'Citizenship with a feminist face: the problem of maternal thinking', *Political Theory*, 13: 19–37.
Ellis, C. (1991) 'Sisters and citizens', in G. Andrews (ed.) *Citizenship*. London: Lawrence and Wishart.
Foster, V. (1996) 'Space invaders: desire and threat in the schooling of girls', *Discourse: studies in the cultural politics of education*, 17: 43–63.
Gilbert, R. (1992) 'Citizenship, education and postmodernity', *British Journal of Sociology of Education*, 13: 51–68.
Gillborn, D. (1992) 'Citizenship, race and the hidden curriculum', *International Studies in Sociology in Education*, 2: 57–73.
Giroux, H. (1980) 'Critical theory and rationality in citizenship education', *Curriculum Inquiry*, 10: 329–36.
Gordon, T. (1992) 'Citizens and others: gender, democracy and education', *International Studies in Sociology of Education*, 2: 43–55.
Heater, D. (1990) *Citizenship: the civic ideal in world history, politics and education*. London: Longman.
Lyotard, J.F. (1984) *The Postmodern Condition; a report on knowledge*. Manchester: Manchester University Press.
Marshall, C. and Anderson, G.L. (1995) 'Rethinking the public and private spheres: feminist and cultural studies perspectives on the politics of education', in J. Scribner and D. Layton (eds) *The Study of Educational Politics*. London: Falmer Press.
Marshall, T.H. (1965) 'Citizenship and social class', in *Class, Citizenship and Social Development*. New York: Anchor Books.
McLaughlin, T.H. (1992) 'Citizenship, diversity and education; a philosophical perspective', *Journal of Moral Education*, 21: 235–50.
Pateman, C. (1992) 'Equality, difference, subordination: the Politics of motherhood and women's citizenship', in G. Bock and B. James (eds) *Beyond Equality and Difference: citizenship, feminist politics and female subjectivity*. London: Routledge.
Pearson, R. (1992) 'Looking both ways; extending the debate on women and citizenship in Europe', in A. Ward, J. Gregory and N. Yuval-Davis (eds) *Women and Citizenship in Europe*. Stoke-on-Trent: Trentham Books.
Phillips, A. (1991a) 'Citizenship and feminist theory', in G. Andrews (ed.) *Citizenship*. London: Lawrence and Wishart.
Phillips, A. (1991b) *Democracy and Difference*. Cambridge: Polity Press.
Rawls, J. (1972) *A Theory of Justice*. Oxford: Oxford University Press.
Rowbothan, S. (1986) 'Feminism and democracy', in D. Held and C. Pollitt (eds) *New Forms of Democracy*. London: Sage.

Sultana, R.G. (1995) 'A uniting Europe, a dividing education? Supranationalism, Eurocentrism and the curriculum', *International Studies in Sociology of Education*, 5: 3–23.
Tomé, A., Bonal, X. and Araújo, H. (1995) *Promoting Equality Awareness: women as citizens,* Final Report. Brussels: European Commission.
Walby, S. (1994) 'Is citizenship gendered?', *Sociology, 28*(2): 379–95.
Wexler, P. (1990) 'Citizenship in the semiotic society', in B. Turner (ed.) *Theories of Modernity and Postmodernity.* London: Sage.
Yuval-Davis, N. (1992) 'Women as citizens', in A. Ward, J. Gregory and N. Yuval-Davis (eds) *Women and Citizenship in Europe.* Stoke-on-Trent: Trentham Books.

Notes

1 Gabrielle Ivinson published the original version of the article under the name Rowe. Kiki Deliyanni-Kouimtzis in the original.
2 The research is based on questionnaires of approximately 300 secondary student teachers in Greece, 375 in England and Wales, 103 in Catalonia, Spain and 180 in Portugal. Interviews were conducted with 14 teacher trainers in Greece and 40 teacher trainers in England and Wales, and with 9 Spanish and 10 Portuguese teacher trainers. In this report, the English and Welsh are referred to as 'British', and the Catalan as 'Spanish'. The majority (75%) of Greek male student teachers were between 30 and 40 years old; the majority of female teachers were between 22 and 30 years old. English and Welsh student teachers' average age was 24 years.
3 The qualitative methodology is described in Arnot *et al.* (1995) and Tomé *et al.* (1995). Eight single-sex focus groups were conducted with male and female student teachers in England, five groups in Greece (two male, three female) and two groups in Spain. Each focus group had approximately five student teachers.
4 See Pateman (1992); Phillips (1991a, 1991b); Dietz (1985); Rowbothan (1986); Walby (1994); in education see Foster (1996); Gordon (1992).

4 Changing femininity, changing concepts of citizenship in public and private spheres

with Helena Araújo, Kiki Deliyanni and Gabrielle Ivinson

Carol Pateman (1988), in her influential writings on the nature of citizenship, argued that behind the notion of a *social contract*, which classic political theorists used to describe modern forms of civil society and modern forms of state regulation, lay a *sexual contract*. This other contract shaped the relations between men and women in different periods in society, providing the conditions for the operation of the social contract. Pateman points out that without an understanding of the relationship between, on the one hand, the processes of democratic development and, on the other hand, the historical legacy of women's subjection to men through *a sexual contract*, political theorists would be unable to describe the social order. Following a similar line, Sylvia Walby (1994) suggests that before citizenship can be properly understood, a dynamic theory of gender relations in both the public and private spheres is required.

Recently, when reflecting on the nature of the sexual contract today, Pateman (1997) argued that the heyday of modern patriarchal institutions was between the 1840s and the 1970s – a period in which the marriage contract played an important role in shaping male-female relations and female citizenship. Since then, although institutional cultures have left their legacies, there have been major changes in the social and sexual contracts. One of the most significant of these has been the changing relations between men and women in the family (Dench, 1997a). Catherine Hakim (1997), for example, reports on a complex situation. On the one hand, most European countries have social customs and public policies that favour directly or indirectly a single form of sexual control, either through what she calls an egalitarian symmetrical role model of the family or a clear division of labour between the sexes. The EU appears to be favouring the rapid adoption of the egalitarian symmetrical role model of the family developed, for example, in Sweden. However, there is no evidence that this model is to be found in practice. The majority of governments seem to prefer (to varying degrees) the continuation of a sexual division of labour in the family and separate sex roles, even though the evidence suggests that an 'increasing diversity of models of sexual contract' can be found in the various populations.

In this chapter, we report on more of the data collected as part of a European research project conducted in Greece, Portugal and the UK (England and Wales).[1] The aim of the project was to investigate how groups of young professional men and women considered gender relations in society, how they conceptualised citizenship in relation to gender and how they understood the processes of social change. We chose to study students who were completing their professional training in preparation for work in one of the most important institutions within modern society – that of schooling. By investigating how groups of student teachers talked about their own lives in relation to the gender order and in relation to processes of gender change, we aimed to discover how they engaged politically with the issue of gender equality – a theme that has had considerable influence on European educational systems in the last twenty years.

In previous publications related to the project, we explored the common discursive frameworks and languages of citizenship used by the sample of student teachers (Arnot *et al.*, 1996; chapter 3). Using cross-national comparisons, we then explored the different ways in which gender relations and change were interpreted as a disrupter of, and a threat to, representations of public/private boundaries in different countries (Ivinson *et al.*, 2000). What appeared to be at work here were nationally specific representations of citizenship. Perceived transformations in sexual relations (Pateman's sexual contract) were clearly important in the way student teachers talked about social change generally and also how they spoke about citizenship at a personal level. By re-examining cross-national differences, we extend our analysis here into the construction of the private sphere. Using the data collected from a survey of 855 student teachers and 13 focus groups (although not evenly distributed across the various countries) we explore first the masculinisation of the public sphere – before illustrating how, in three of the countries studied – Greece, Portugal and the UK – student teachers engaged with the private sphere. However, we begin with a brief discussion of the concept of the sexual contract and the ways in which it has been conceptualised theoretically in contemporary society.

The sexual contract

The concept of the sexual contract was first used and developed by Pateman (1988) seven years after Jean Bethke Elshtain published *Public Man, Private Woman*. Elshtain (1981: 3) argued that the public and private spheres were basic 'guides to our orientation of the world' even although some political theorists often took this distinction for granted and marginalised it from the citzenship debate. Key to the valuing of women's political agency, as citizens and also as women, has been the gendered relationship between the two spheres. The problem Elshtain posed was the extent to which women's difference from men (for example, in relation to mothering) could (or should) be related to mainstream concepts of citizenship within liberal democracy.

Pateman's concept of the sexual contract addressed the problem posed by Elshtain, adding a degree of scepticism about the flexibility of modern democratic thought to respond to women's needs as citizens. Classical political theory, she argued, with its interest in the social contract (the means by which individuals are governed by the state) had seriously neglected the *sexual contract* and, thus, social expectations about the nature of proper exchanges between men and women in society and in private life (Dench, 1997a). Pateman argued that modern civil society was, in actuality, a patriarchal social order. Counterposed to the story of 'freedom' associated with the social contract was the 'story of subjection' represented by the sexual contract. Accordingly, civil freedom is not universal, as classic liberal democratic theory would have us believe, but a masculine attribute, premised upon the right of what she called a *fraternal patriarchy*, to subordinate women to the needs of men. Women were subordinated not just to individual men through the marriage contract, but to all men through political and economic dominance. Thus, in constructing a civic brotherhood in the political realm, men legitimated their autonomic right to power in public life and, at the same time, their sex-right (or patriarchal right) over women.

> The brothers make a sexual contract. They establish a law which confirms masculine sex-right and ensures that there is an orderly access by each man to a woman. Patriarchal sex-right ceases to be the right of one man, the father, and becomes a 'universal' right. The law of the male sex-right extends to all men, to all members of the fraternity. (Pateman, 1988; 109–10)

Modern patriarchy, Pateman argues, is foremost about women's subjection in the family. The failure by those concerned with citizenship to recognise the sexual contract leads to the isolation of women and to the view that, as wives and as mothers, women are not political subjects (Arnot and Dillabough, 1999). The marriage contract is deemed to be politically irrelevant and motherhood is denied a political status. Pateman adds,

> The possibility that women's standing in marriage may reflect much deeper problems about women and the social contract or that the structure of the marriage contract is similar to the other contract is dismissed. (Pateman, 1988: 7)

Of central importance to Pateman's analysis is the separation and opposition of the categories *natural* and *civil.* By positioning the family (and, by association, women) within the natural world, the private and the female are both represented as outside civil society. Classifications of private/public, natural/civil and female/male, therefore, become the means by which men acquire legitimate power over women. Ascribed natural differences between men and women (in terms of their distinctive capacities and attributes) allow women to be incorporated into citizenship *as women*, but not on the same terms as men. The study of the ways in which such classifications (indeed antinomies) work will reveal, therefore, what it means to be an individual/human being in liberal democracy.

The extent to which the gendered political discourses identified by Pateman have shaped modern life is debatable. Clearly, much social policy has been premised on a separation between public and private spheres (Pateman, 1997). However, as far as we are aware, very little empirical research has been carried out on how these two forms of social contract are represented and combined by individuals or by groups (such as professionals) and in what ways explicit and implicit forms of political regulation have been understood in different countries. We also have to bear in mind, as Dench and his colleagues emphasise in *Rewriting the Sexual Contract* (Dench, 1997b), that late modernity has witnessed major changes in how men and women relate to each other. Moving away from the notion of a contract as formal rights and statuses, Dench (1997a) argues that there are now numerous sexual divisions of labour in the public and family spheres. Women's structured inequality is now contrasted with evidence of major changes in personal relationships and gender expectations. Wilkinson (1997), drawing on data from young people's attitudes in the UK, suggests that 'old paradigms of sex relations are rapidly becoming obsolete' (Wilkinson, 1997: 238) and that the so-called 'genderquake' (Wilkinson, 1994) has created major instabilities in relationships, family life and in the workplace, and more subtle transformations in the balance of power between the sexes.

> But perhaps most important of all, the influence of feminist ideas has so permeated our culture that the very legitimacy of the old style sexual contract has come under unprecedented challenge from the majority of women who now reject the idea that a man's place is at work and a woman's place is at home. (Wilkinson, 1997: 239)

By focusing on the concepts of citizenship used by groups of student teachers in different European countries, we begin to discover how far the distinction between the sexual and social contracts (and the private and public spheres) was sustained. We investigated how student teachers in European countries understood public and private spheres and the possibilities for women's participation in civic life. We asked: was there any evidence that feminism had impacted on their concept of citizenship? In what ways was the private sphere being reconstructed in student teachers' views? In the rest of the chapter we explore these questions. We begin with a theme found in common in three European countries – the separating of the public sphere – a feature that reflects, but is also facilitated by, its association with masculinity.

The separation of the public sphere

The association of masculinity with public life was found to be most simply expressed in our survey when we asked student teachers to indicate who had most control over decision making in various areas of policy and in public appointments (Arnot *et al.*, 1995). Women's influence was reported to be weak in Greece, Portugal and the UK, especially in relation to the economy. This view was confirmed in responses to a question in which the respondents were asked to choose three words, from a wordbank of 33 in Greece and the UK, and 49 in Portugal, to describe men and women in public and working life. A high level of agreement between male and female student teachers was revealed. Strong consensus was reached – more than 40 per cent of the sample in each country chose words such as 'competitive' and 'powerful' to describe men in public life.[2] (See Table 4.1.) There was no equivalent consensus over women in public or working life, although 'active', 'struggling', 'efficient' and 'competent' were chosen more frequently than other words to describe women in these spheres. The findings signal a perceived lack of threat to male dominance in civic life.

Single-sex focus-group discussions, with a small sample of student teachers in each country, illuminated similarities and differences between national contexts in terms of the ways in which historically constituted discourses associated with European cultures were drawn upon (Arnot *et al.*, 1996). In terms of political discourses,[3] it was noticeable that both male and female student teachers in each country associated public life with masculinity. Yet male and female student teachers did not seem to share the same discursive frameworks. Preliminary analysis[4] of focus-group data (Arnot *et al.*, 1996) suggested that male student teachers, particularly in the Mediterranean countries, drew upon formal and legalistic frameworks (such as Graeco-Roman classical tradition or French civic republicanism). They worked with notions of the *polis*, an 'organised society' and the 'state'. They identified with the concept of the 'critical citizen' who would fight for 'collective edification' and social justice over and above the actions of the state,[5] even though they appeared ambivalent about their own role in relation to such ideals (Ivinson *et al.*, 2000). In contrast, public life, especially in the sense of a participatory democracy, was a concept that few female student teachers in our research related to. The only exception was talk about the right to vote, arguably the most basic political right and one long denied to women. Their political discourse was framed around the notion of being represented rather than representing political positions. This finding in itself is a matter for concern because it signals women's disenfranchisement from key spheres of political decision making.

Exploring this theme further, the public sphere was found to be counterposed to femininity, and female student teachers spoke of it as threatening. Representations

Table 4.1 Student teachers' images of men and women in public life

	Greece N=298	Portugal N=180	UK N=374
Men in public life	**competitive**	**competitive**	**powerful**
Women in public life		struggling	efficient
Men in working life	**competitive**	**competitive**	**competitive**
Women in working life	*effective*	*active*	*conscientious efficient competent*

Source: Arnot *et al.* (1995)

Note
The words selected by more than 40 per cent of the respondents in each country are printed in bold type. The italicised words in each column are the words selected by 30–40 per cent of each national sample.

of public and private life that vary across cultures and through time are threatened by changes in representations of gender (Ivinson *et al.*, 2000). However, a noticeable consensus emerged between men and women across nations: that traditional concepts of femininity, especially female sexuality, were incompatible with the forms of power associated with the public sphere. The price women had to pay for participation in public life was most often expressed in terms of the need to imitate male styles of behaviour. As one Greek female student argued:

> I am saying that there is a way of behaving we, women, take it as read and then we get a public position and we reproduce the same models.

Similarly, it was argued if women wanted to become successful within male career structures, they had to become more like men:

> ... to get through these career structures, [which] were made by men and defined by men, to get through male career structures to the top, you will have to be more like men because men made those structures. (Greek male)

This dilemma was articulated more fully by British female students who, as they spoke, found ways to distance themselves from key public figures such Margaret Thatcher, who was described as an atypical woman. She was said to have followed a masculine career route:

> No, thinking about, going back to Margaret Thatcher, what she'd done before she went into parliament, it was actually the sort of route that a man would follow. She was a chemist, then she trained to be a lawyer, to practise as a lawyer and then went into parliament, so she followed a traditional male route. (UK female)

The fact that Margaret Thatcher was also the mother of two children was not mentioned. In the most extreme examples, descriptions of assertive, public women carried negative connotations explained in terms of greed or inadmissible egotism. One female student teacher commented: 'I think, who would want to be like Margaret Thatcher, to be honest.' Similarly, in the male focus groups in the UK, the opposition between the conventional representations of femininity and traits such as autonomy, assertiveness and unattractiveness was articulated at length. The following reference to Margaret Thatcher revealed the uncoupling of power and femininity:

> ... when you think of Margaret Thatcher, you don't normally associate femininity with her, at least I don't. (UK male)

There was an underlying assumption that women's access to political power was not acceptable and, in this respect, we can detect an example of what Connell (1987) has called gender 'cathexis'. The emotional energy attached to an object, here the category of the person in public space, was clearly gendered. Portuguese female student teachers described how, in these circumstances, female sexuality was defined as 'frivolous' – the opposite to the 'seriousness' of political life (Araújo, 1999). The accessibility of women to men, while legitimate within the sexual contract of marriage, was illegitimate in the corridors of power. Two young women commented that men still retained their 'hero' status (masculine sexuality) within this public realm; in contrast women were denigrated. Thus gender differences were 'exaggerated'.

> ... men are still considered to be heroes, when they have intimate relations with women, and women are seen as frivolous. This is still very present, this is one of the most difficult things to change. (Portuguese female)

When associated with public life, women's sexuality was impugned (comparable with the spinster rather than the whore). Alternatively, their status as good mothers, and thus a key attribute of 'traditional' femininity, was called into question, as this British student implies:

> In general, people seeing women in public life think: 'This woman must be a spinster or divorced or she must have someone to take care of her children because otherwise she would not be able to have this kind of job, would she?' (UK female)

Further, it was recognised that, in relation to public life, female physical attractiveness, clothes and hairstyles were legitimate targets of attention and public comment in a way that men's were not. The reference to the 'bimbo' in the following extract highlights a deep-rooted antipathy between autonomy and attractiveness in images of successful professional women.

> I think that even people who are in professions like acting and singing, they are always, women, I feel, are portrayed as being bimbos. You have to be gorgeous, you have to be skinny ... for a woman you have to be under 35, have long hair and be fantastically good-looking and you're just something on someone's arm. (UK female)

At the core of these representations of femininity within a masculine public life was the notion of a 'dedicated' female sexuality. By participating in male public life, women challenged an implicit sexual contract which restricts female sexuality to the private sphere and dedicates it to one man. Findings suggest that these student teachers recognised, albeit in rather negative ways, that the insertion of women into public life represents a disruption to the classification of public and private spheres and challenges the basis of fraternal democracy. There appeared to be little opportunity to apply concepts such as the 'protesting' or 'critical' citizen to women in public life and in all three countries the gendered notion of public and private space was taken for granted.

However, this is not the same as suggesting that male student teachers positioned themselves in the public sphere and female student teachers necessarily positioned themselves in the private sphere. Indeed, male student teachers spoke as if they themselves were distanced from the public sphere and represented it as a sphere for 'other men'. As we reported in Ivinson *et al.* (2000), male student teachers appeared to be as threatened by the power associated with public life as female student teachers. This may account, on the one hand, for men's greater use of political discourses, in comparison with women, when talking about public life and, on the other, for the projection of their anxieties onto representations of female sexuality. Thus women's success in public life was portrayed as having high risks for women themselves, explained in terms of 'femininity'.

In the next section, we show how these male and female student teachers recognised the shifts (and conflicts associated with these shifts) in gender relations occurring in family life and the private sphere, and the threat such changes might represent to the social order as they understood it.

Challenging the sexual contract: matriarchy, sexuality and domestic power

Discussions on family life showed that student teachers in the various European countries grappled in different ways with the consequences of changes in women's work patterns (for example, female entry into traditionally male spheres, high levels of female economic activity and the new economic independence of married women). Female student teachers in all four countries appeared to be engaging with egalitarian discourses around the notion of civil rights, social entitlements and personal respect associated with the women's movement and other civil rights campaigns (Arnot *et al.*, 1996). In most female discussion groups, the family was talked of as a pivotal arena of female liberation, at the same time, paradoxically, as the concept of femininity and female sexuality was represented as the source of the problems currently facing women and, on occasion, men.

In the following three sub-sections we compare how Greek, Portuguese and British male and female student teachers talked about challenges in private life in their national contexts.

Matriarchy and male dominance in Greece

In Greece, male and female respondents presented different images of family life. While both described the positioning of women at the centre of the family, male student teachers expressed their anxiety by referring to this as female power. Women's dominance over key areas of decision making, especially that of control over the organisation of domestic work and reproduction decisions (e.g. abortion, contraception), was represented as less of a threat than female sexual power (Arnot *et al.*, 1995; Deliyanni and Athanassiadis, 1997). Core masculine identities were at stake within the private sphere of family life, where women's sexual power (although recognised as natural) was described as potentially overwhelming for men.

> Women do what they want in the family. They are the heads in what concerns the organisation, the upbringing of the children, everything. Even in the emotional level, please tell me who can say no to the tears of a woman? (Greek male)

The image of Greek women conjured up by these male student teachers was one of cunning and an emotional force. In the following quote, women were described as 'grizzling' but also 'sly' – references to what could be considered an illegitimate use of femininity.

> A woman will do what she likes, sometimes grizzling, sometimes with complaints, she will manage to persuade you to do what she wants. She is much more sly or smarter in some cases. (Greek male)

By representing women as sexually and emotionally powerful in the family sphere, male student teachers were then threatened when that power was used outside the private sphere. Men described themselves as 'being in danger' in public life of being manipulated by women, precisely because of the sexual power granted to women through the sexual contract. Thus:

> Women today have a very important arm that they can use in the labour market and in social life if you like, their beauty. The fact that they are the beautiful sex. It is then much easier for a woman to find a job – she is able to mobilise the mechanisms. (Greek male)

Greek female student teachers represented women in a somewhat contradictory fashion. They created an image of Greek women fighting to change the conditions of Greek family life in order to ensure greater freedom, and yet they partly blamed themselves for these conditions. Many confronted this dilemma by talking of the lack of compassion and help women received from their partners in achieving change. When they spoke of their own domestic situations, they represented themselves as fundamentally alone and unsupported in their struggle for self-expression and autonomy. There seemed to be a general acceptance among these young women that equality between the sexes did not exist and that traditional discourses about womanhood gave recognisable advantages to men, not least because fathers and sons were presented as having choices in the domestic sphere. In contrast, they suggested that women still had to 'fight' for individual rights.

> … inside the family, the woman fights for her rights, whereas these same rights have been established for the man. (Greek female)

Despite representing good citizens as 'protesting citizens' (Arnot *et al.*, 1996) these young Greek women gave little credibility to the sources of female domestic or sexual power described by male colleagues and, as a result, male advantage in the family appeared incontestable. As two student teachers commented:

> And then how can they [women] ask the man they live with to contribute? How can you change a man aged 25, 30, 40 years and persuade him that you should both accomplish this task together? (Greek female)

> Why should men change? Change for them would mean losing all the advantages they have amassed up to now? (Greek female)

The implied sexual and social contracts were repeatedly legitimated by the stricture that gender inequality was women's fault. For example:

> It's our fault, we have to become conscious of our disadvantaged position, we have to claim. (Greek female)

> It's the fault of women, we bring up and socialise the new generation. We have to teach new roles to our children. (Greek female)

The struggle for sexual freedom in the Portuguese family

In contrast, the Portuguese female student teachers appeared to be much more aware of the hidden, more subtle sexual inequalities in domestic life. Here society rather than individuals was represented as 'in transition', and gender differences in public and private life were counterposed. Female respondents recognised that, although more Portuguese women had taken up public positions, individual rights were still being applied unequally to men and women, and traditions still dictated that there should be explicit gender differentiation in the home. The contradiction between transforming the social contract but not the sexual contract was most clearly exposed in the Portuguese female student teachers' discussions.

> In public life, people do not like to say that there are differences, but in contrast, at home, everybody does what they are interested in. Everything is hidden. (Portuguese female)

Female participants pointed to the inequalities experienced on a daily basis, for example, when working women came home and were expected to undertake domestic responsibilities while their husbands watched television and read. However, the insertion of egalitarian ethics into this domestic setting was understood to be subversive and one that demanded courage:

> There are many more women with jobs. Women had already got the courage to say 'I work for such and such hours and why should I be the person to do things in the house, I who arrive home tired?' This courage did not exist some years ago. (Portuguese female)

The egalitarian language of 'rights' and of individual entitlement made its appearance even more forcefully here than in discussions about the public domain. As two respondents commented:

> You have as much right to be seated on the sofa watching television as he does, and to not cook the lunch. (Portuguese female)

> I have the right to arrive home and say that I do not want to cook lunch. (Portuguese female)

Resistance to female domestic rights was said to come from individual men, whose lack of co-operation could develop into violence. Portuguese female students drew on many personal examples and insights to explain the forces preventing women's right to independence:

> It is socially accepted that the husband can beat his wife, that he slaps her face, this is quite acceptable in order that she behaves herself. (Portuguese female)

By demanding respect, the young women were questioning male dominance enshrined in the marital contract. On the other hand, they presented an image of the way fraternity worked to control women's sexuality. One of the most striking themes in the Portuguese discussions was the enforced dependency of young women on the men in their lives: fathers, brothers and husbands. Female adolescents were controlled through regulation of their movements, by parental disapproval of their sexual activity, but not that of their brothers, and by moral teachings around premarital sex and the importance of virgin marriages. 'Women,' explained one female student, 'should stay virgins until they marry' while 'men already have a master's degree in sex by that point'. While men were expected to be unfaithful, it was 'contra nature' if women were unfaithful in marriage. Codes of conduct ensured the continuation of inequalities between girls and their brothers in terms of personal freedom. For example, girls 'had to depend on their brothers' to take them outside the home, especially at night. Female Portuguese participants expressed an awareness of the various ways in which their movements and sexual activities were controlled. This might explain their use of the language of rights in relation to domestic roles and the way they spoke of a struggle for personal autonomy:

> I have the right to go out and return late, and my parents need to have confidence in me. I feel more independent ... I had to fight to win this right. (Portuguese female)

In contrast, Portuguese (like the Greek) male student teachers represented women as central to private life, even though some indicated that (in their experience) gender changes had taken place within the private domain. Others drew pictures of 'authoritarian fathers' as justifications for their own more egalitarian approaches, while recognising that changes had been brought about by forceful mothers. The rationale for women's rights was therefore not clearly identified but the recognition of sex differences was used by some to support feminising the public realm:

> ... women are more sensitive, more maternal – the majority of women – and

we need to see this at the political level, we need a less authoritarian politics, where there is a greater sensibility. ...They are more sensitive, like the State Secretary for Health, she is a highly competent woman. (Portuguese male)

Negotiating equality in the British family

Despite their different sources of anxiety about men and women's position in the family, both male and female participants represented the family as a protected, almost sacred domain. However, in contrast to their male colleagues, women projected themselves into family relations as potential or actual partners or wives. While the analysis of the gendering of the private sphere was similar, male and female student teachers displayed different levels of personal and hence political engagement in the issue. Egalitarian discourses were strongly represented in female discussions (Arnot *et al.*, 1996) in which young women talked about personal experiences of resistance and struggles for equality within their parental families:

> I might have shouted at my father, 'I have the right to state my opinion,' because I thought everyone had the right to say what they wanted. (UK female)

> I stopped doing the washing up. My brother didn't have to do it. Where did my mother get the idea that I should do it? (UK female)

Although there was a general consensus that equality in relation to family life was problematic (unlike their Portuguese and Greek counterparts) they did not want to use the language of rights and power in relation to family life. They tended to speak of themselves as potential partners rather than as daughters. They were eager to stress that family decisions about domestic work were a matter of *negotiation* (rather than a struggle), achieved by 'muddling through' and finding a 'natural course'.

> ... haven't felt it necessary in my personal life ... I think that a relationship between a man and a woman, or whatever set-up you have got, is an arrangement and you have so much compromise, but it's not a question of exerting your rights or power. (UK female)

British female student teachers spoke of legal rights only when family structures had broken down, for example, in cases of divorce.

British male student teachers, in comparison, had stronger views about differentiated gender roles. They spoke of women's pivotal role as the 'nucleus of the family' and stressed that women should continue to maintain family structures. Some related families to the wider social context describing them as the 'building blocks of society', sometimes alluding to their role in socialisation. Their discussions seemed to veer between a recognition that gender inequality existed and that power relations maintained family relations. Although they recognised the dilemmas experienced by mothers who attempted to retain careers, they also tended to deny that there was any gender inequality in their own relationships, and that domestic labour was something women actively chose. In comparison with British women, who spoke about negotiating relations in personal relationships in terms of 'compromise', and of 'muddling through', some men talked about the tensions arising in personal relationships as a 'battle of wills' and 'strength of personality'. They spoke of both femininity and masculinity within domestic life as powerful and active, and hence recognised gendered power conflicts within contemporary relationships.

> I think that when you get married there is always a battle of wills between two people and the more dominant one will take over and make the decision; and that person might well be female and not necessarily the man. I'm not sure it's based on gender. It may be based on strength of personality. (UK male)

Some male student teachers, but by no means all, referred to women's *reproductive* rather than their sexual capacity as the source of gender power. For example:

> In some ways I think that women might actually call the shots. Because if a male wants a family he has to totally abide by what his wife or girlfriend wants. If she doesn't want children, then that's it. He has to obey that. So childbearing, or making a family unit, then I think that women actually ... (UK male)

We wish to suggest rather tentatively at this stage that these men also associated 'feminism' as a movement with a particularly potent kind of power. This was most evident in comments about who should have custody over children in cases of divorce.

> Men do very badly in terms of getting children if there is a divorce. I think the child automatically goes to the women, unless there is a very good reason why it shouldn't, and I think that is highly unfair to the men. (UK male)

By emphasising the reproductive power of women, they gave the impression that decisions about whether or not to have children were out of their control, and yet they resented notions that men were considered to be no good at looking after children. Most of the men also rejected the idea of using the language of rights in the family, although some were inclined to talk about rights within the family in a non-legal sense, and one even used the term 'citizenship' to describe his relationship with his wife!

Conclusions

Our findings bear on both Pateman's and Hakim's arguments. On the one hand, we have tapped, in a limited way, the legacy of traditional gender roles and the desire to sustain a sexual division of labour in the family, in Greece, Portugal and in the UK.

At the same time, we have illustrated a diversity among nations, in the way public and private life was spoken about, that is likely to relate to specific cultural tensions.

Despite historical, discursive and material changes in the sexual contract, our exploratory study suggests that the sphere of politics and of economic life remains unambiguously marked as masculine. A new generation of male and female teachers about to enter the educational systems in these countries is likely to carry forward an assumption that government and state power remains a male stronghold. In these countries, at the time of the study, women's representation in each national assembly was under 15 per cent, providing little to challenge the association between social contract and civic fraternity. Even though a political discourse of civic duty was found (particularly among male teachers in countries that had experienced dictatorship), it did not appear to have challenged the patriarchal culture of politics, or to have alleviated the negative ways in which women in public life were represented. There was little to suggest that civic brotherhood could be transformed, although a few student teachers admitted that women would be needed to help transform such structures. Both men and women, but particularly women, represented the public realm as remote and in some ways threatening.

The separation and incompatibility of public life and motherhood described by Carole Pateman (1992) was most clearly articulated in the Portuguese and Greek discussion groups, yet in unexpected ways. Transferred into the public realm, the sexual or reproductive power associated with women in the private sphere in these countries was perceived by some men as a threat, with the potential to expose their vulnerability.

Men's anxiety about loss of control in the private, and even the public, domain may explain why men projected their fears onto a polarised femininity. Benton (1991) argued that there is a tendency for men to categorise women as either *mothers/Madonnas* or *whores/sluts*, synonymous with the distinction between reproduction and sexuality. Our findings suggested that the juxtaposition of power and femininity, represented by women in public life, disturbed traditional notions of femininity and was expressed as a kind of corruption in which women, at least in public life, were perceived as overassertive and behaving like men.

In some countries, public women were presented as either using sexuality in non-acceptable ways to retain power or, as if they were rejecting traditional notions of femininity, as a means to success. These representations made it difficult to properly imagine women as legitimately successful and autonomous in public life. Student teachers explored these tensions relating power to femininity by describing public figures who, for them, capture these contradictions.

Underlying these kinds of tension are often unarticulated, culturally specific concepts of 'normal' gender relations. National differences as well as gender differences reveal the ways in which the concept 'woman' was being represented in times of social transition. Female student teachers, in particular, were actively exploring hegemonic representations of public and private life, and forms of femininity associated with each. The way women talked about these issues gave us reason to suggest that there were indications of an emerging feminist consciousness – whether articulated as 'blame' or as the problem of 'womanhood' or through talk of personal 'struggle'. Their comments and observations suggest that what are at stake in the political realm of civic life are personal relations in the home.

Two significant themes were detected. First, women were not represented, either by themselves or by male student teachers, as powerless. Indeed three sources of female power were identified:

- the power of women as mothers and heads of households;
- female sexual power; and,
- feminism as power; that is, feminist challenges to male dominance.

Second, women's struggle for citizenship was clearly being located within the world of private, intimate and domestic relations, rather than in the public sphere. Thus the exclusion of women from public democratic discourses, described herein, should not necessarily imply the failure of women to engage with politics. In some senses, this data retrieves the view that the personal is indeed political. The sexual contract is precisely the focus of women's struggles for citizenship.

Neither male nor female student teachers seemed to need to discuss the source of male power in the public domain which was, to some extent, simply taken for granted. Participants were aware of sex discrimination, although the depth of their concern varied substantially. Male student teachers, although not all, appeared to collude with differentiated gender roles. They expressed little personal commitment to challenging masculine associations surrounding the public realm. The seeming 'naturalness' of male power, and its apparent basis in gender role difference, meant that its continuation appeared to require no further justification, although some men expressed regret about this.

Our study, although limited in scope, suggests that understandings of citizenship remain deeply gendered. One way of interpreting this continuity is to acknowledge, as MacInnes (1998) does, the material and ideological legacy which modernity developed in order to explain and rationalise men's greater power. This legacy involved using gender: as a symbolic structure which distinguishes between masculinity and femininity; and as a means of justifying the sexual division of labour. Such a strategy has meant that boys and girls, men and women, are now considered to be to be socially, rather than naturally, produced into different ways of being. Thus, the same strategy to legitimate patriarchy continues, even whilst the patriarchal basis of modern institutions is being undermined. But it is a strategy that can also be systematically undermined by the key social relations of modernity. In this context, it is interesting that our data illustrate how a small group of European women have confronted social change in their everyday lives. Their insights and concerns, and their ability to articulate tensions underlying the legacies of a historically rooted sexual contract, throw into relief what Pateman calls the 'civic freedom of public life':

> What it means to be an individual or maker of contracts and civilly free is revealed by the subjection of woman within the private sphere. (Pateman, 1988: 12)

Civic education programmes in schools could do worse than bring out into the open, illustrate and discuss these political and gender tensions for a new generation of European youth.

Acknowledgements

The project was funded by the Human Resources, Education and Training Division of the European Commission (Stage 1 in 1994–1995 and Stage 2 in 1995–1996) as one of the projects put forward by its Equal Opportunities Unit. It is being funded under the 3rd Medium-term Community Action Programme. The projects under this programme encouraged the development of measures designed to promote the participation of women in decision-making processes in economic and social life. We are grateful to the Equal Opportunities Unit and the EC for their financial support.

This article was supported by a Leverhulme Research Fellowship grant to Madeleine Arnot for 1996–1997. It was first presented at the Third European Feminist Research Conference, 'Shifting Bonds, Shifting Bounds: Women, Mobility and Citizenship in Europe', Coimbra University, Portugal, July 1997. We would like to thank, in particular, Amanda Coffrey, Pat Mahony, Sneh Shah, Daniella Tilbury, Xavier Ramblas, Xavier Bonal, Roula Ziogou, Christina Athanasiadou and Eleni Mavrogiorgou. I am grateful to all three co-authors – Helen Araújo, Kiki Deliyanni and Gabrielle Ivinson – for allowing me to include this article in the collection.

References

Araújo, H. (1999) 'Em torno da Cidadania a do genero – a produção de discursos de educadres/as e nudança cultural: razoes para um optimism?', in C. Pereira Sousa and D.B. Catani (eds) *Praticas Educativas, culturas escolares profissao docente*. São Paulo.
Arnot, M. and Dillabough, J. (1999) 'Feminist politics and democratic values in Education', *Curriculum Inquiry*, 29(2): 159–90.
Arnot, M., Deliyanni-Kouimtzis, K. and Ziogou R. with Rowe, G. (1995) *Promoting Equality Awareness: women as citizens*, Final Report. Brussels: European Commission.
Arnot, M., Araújo, H., Deliyanni-Kouimtzis, K., Rowe, G. and Tomé, A. (1996) 'Teachers, gender and the discourses of citizenship', *International Studies in Sociology of Education*, 6(1): 3–35.
Benton, S. (1991) 'Gender, sexuality and citizenship', in G. Andrews (ed.) *Citizenship*. London: Lawrence and Wishart, pp. 153–63.
Connell, R.W. (1987) *Gender and Power*. Cambridge: Polity Press.
Deliyanni, K. and Athanassiadis, C. (1997) 'Teachers' representations of gender', in K. Deliyanni and R. Ziogou (eds) *Fylo kai Scholiki Praxi*. Thessaloniki: Vanias, pp. 95–127.
Dench, G. (1997a) 'Introduction', in G. Dench (ed.) *Rewriting the Sexual Contract*. London: Institute of Community Studies, pp. ix–xiii.
Dench, G. (ed.) (1997b) *Rewriting the Sexual Contract*. London: Institute of Community Studies.
Elshtain, J.B. (1981) *Public Man, Private Woman: women in social and political thought*. Princeton, NJ: Princeton University Press.

Hakim, C. (1997) 'Diversity and choice for the 21st century', in G. Dench (ed.) *Rewriting the Sexual Contract*. London: Institute of Community Studies, pp. 165–90.

Ivinson, G. with Arnot, M., Araújo, H., Deliyanni-Kouimtzi, K., Rowe, G. and Tomé, A. (2000) 'Student teachers' representations of citizenship: a comparative perspective', in M. Arnot and J. Dillabough (eds) *Challenging Democracy: feminist perspectives on gender, education and citizenship*. London: RoutledgeFalmer.

MacInnes, J. (1998) *The End of Masculinity: the confusion of sexual genesis and sexual difference in modern society*. Milton Keynes: Open University Press.

Pateman, C. (1988) *The Sexual Contract*. Cambridge: Polity Press.

Pateman, C. (1992) 'Equality, difference, subordination: The politics of motherhood and women's citizenship', in G. Bock and B. James (eds) *Beyond Equality and Difference: citizenship, feminist politics and female subjectivity*. London: Routledge.

Pateman, C. (1997) 'Beyond the sexual contract?', in G. Dench (ed.) *Rewriting the Sexual Contract*. London: Institute of Community Studies, pp. 1–9.

Tomé, A., Bonal, X. and Araújo, H. (1995) *Promoting Equality Awareness: women as citizens*, Final Report. Brussels: European Commission.

Walby, S. (1994) 'Is citizenship gendered?', *Sociology*, 28(2): 379–95.

Wilkinson, H. (1994) *No Turning Back: generations and the genderquake*. London: Demos.

Wilkinson, H. (1997) 'The androgynous generation', in G. Dench (ed.) *Rewriting the Sexual Contract*. London: Institute of Community Studies, pp. 238–47.

Notes

1 Spain, although in the project, is not included in this particular analysis. See Tomé *et al.* (1995).

2 Male student teachers in Wales referred to the 'good citizen' as the 'bowler-hatted gentleman' with the connotations of being male, conforming and part of an elite.

3 We distinguished between political, moral and egalitarian discourses in this analysis: political referred to Graeco-Roman traditions; egalitarian to social citizenship associated with the welfare state; and moral discourses, referred to Judaeo-Christian traditions (Arnot *et al.*, 1996).

4 Questionnaire data were collected from approximately 300 secondary student teachers in Greece, 375 in England and Wales, 103 in Catalonia, Spain and 180 in Portugal. Eight single-sex focus groups were conducted with male and female student teachers in England, five groups in Greece (two male and three female) and two groups in Spain. Each focus group had approximately five student teachers. Female student teachers in most countries were young women aged between 20 and 30, while many of the male teachers (especially science teachers in Greece) were much older (averaging 40). The data analysis was conducted in each country before being translated into English.

5 Student teachers in the UK constructed an image of the sceptical citizen (Arnot *et al.*, 1996).

Part III
Gendered pedagogies and citizenship curricula

5 'England expects every man to do his duty'

The gendering of the citizenship textbook (1940–1966)

with Patrick Brindle

This chapter has two main aims. The first is to explore, in a preliminary way, the nature of the ideological and pedagogic content of citizenship education in the past, as it was expressed in the school texts of citizenship. The second is to investigate how past texts of citizenship education dealt with issues of gender. We shall argue that citizenship education functioned by constructing and defining the nature of political discourse using specific models of the polity; and that past configurations of the legitimate polity are based upon the dualistic and normative distinction between the public (political) and private (apolitical) sphere. In this way, citizenship education was predicated upon the ideal citizen as the active, publicly and professionally defined, male. In effect, the texts of citizenship education echoed Lord Nelson's famous call for 'every *man* to do *his* duty' in terms of political and civic activity. Women's duty (as well as their rights or responsibilities), as we shall argue, either went undiscussed or, commonly, defined that duty as inhering only within the private sphere.

This chapter will not seek to put forward its own definition of education for citizenship. We have taken a socio-historical perspective and we have sought only to highlight the many different definitions of the subject that were present in the texts of school citizenship in the immediate post-war period. Indeed, we might suggest that one of the reasons there is no tradition of teaching citizenship in English state schools is that no group has succeeded in constructing a consensus over the question of what education for citizenship is. Work by Madeleine Arnot *et al.* (1996) and by Ivor Crewe (1996) has detailed a peculiarly English difficulty with forging a popular and formalised discourse of politics and citizenship. Arnot's work with a sample of student teachers revealed that, compared with other European states, the English had what was described as a weak 'political discursive framework' (Arnot, 1997: 20) and did not appear to have access to a formalised set of political and civic languages, other than liberal egalitarianism. A key difficulty facing contemporary English student teachers seemed to be a common inability to construct a model of the polity in comparison with those in, for instance, Greece, Spain and Portugal. As a result, student teachers were normally vague and uncertain in their descriptions of the relationship between the individual's duties, rights and obligations, and the connection between these and the project of creating democratic citizenship.

Arnot *et al.* (1996) also suggested that women may be particularly disadvantaged in terms of access to a discourse of active or formal political participation. This research suggested that the common and contemporary construction of the political as a public and a male sphere served to disenfranchise women as citizens in relation to men. The concept of a 'good citizen' specifically referred to men. Political power was associated with masculinity, thus bringing it into direct conflict with femininity, and making it difficult to associate women with 'public life'. Key to this disassociation of women from the public realm was, first, the separation in political discourse between public and private spheres and, second, their association with masculinity and femininity, respectively. Definitions of the polity as public, as constitutional and as male become critical elements of the social regulation of women, and one of the conditions of their continued marginalisation from social, economic and cultural decision making.

This chapter uses these themes to investigate the 20 years or so following the end of the Second World War. This is not a particularly active period in the history of citizenship education. As we shall discuss, the history of citizenship education is marked by periodic waves of interest followed by disinterest. Unlike the 1910s and 1930s, the 1940s witnessed relatively little pressure-group campaigning on behalf of citizenship education.[1] Yet we have chosen this period because the decades immediately following the Second World War – which encompassed sweeping welfare reform, educational restructuring and a movement to encourage women back to the home – were constitutive of an unprecedented shift in both the actual and the symbolic relationship between the private and public spheres. These changes, grouped around an expanded, social democratic discourse about the role and responsibility of the state in its relationship to individuals and families, served to realign possibilities of, and expectations of, women's role in society and politics. It was our aim to investigate how the texts of citizenship took into account these shifts in the possibilities of the public and private sphere; and the manner in which they were re-presented to children in a pedagogic and discursive form.

This work is based upon a small pilot study carried out with the support of the Leverhulme Trust. Our archive is a selection of the textbooks and method texts for citizenship that were available to educationists, teachers and pupils in the 1940s, 1950s and 1960s. Our goal has been to track the manner in which citizenship education constructed a discourse of the polity in line with the paradigm of social democracy; and how such a process served to manufacture a model of gender relations.

This chapter is divided into three main sections. The first section details the historiographical and historical background to the issue of education for citizenship in England. The second section examines, in broad terms, how our sample of texts adopted certain shared pedagogic approaches in line with the political culture of post-war social democracy. The third section investigates how such texts for citizenship were gendered according to three distinct approaches – exclusionary; inclusionary; and critical engagement – to the question of women's relationship to the political sphere. In our conclusion, we raise what we believe are important questions for more empirical research into the particular nature of English political education.

Historical overview

Research into the history of education for citizenship, and of the repeated failed attempts to establish the subject as part of the syllabus of most English schools, has tended to fall into two strands. The first, articulated in the writings of Tom Brennan (1981), Guy Whitmarsh (1974), Derek Heater (1981, 1990) and Jessie Wong (1991), sets out the political histories of those organisations that have sought, over the last hundred years, to establish education for citizenship in the common school curriculum. The work of these writers revealed that the history of citizenship education in England has been characterised by successive waves of interest and disinterest. However, understanding why the English education system has been so ambivalent in the past about education for citizenship suggests the need for more in-depth study of particular 'episodes' or phases during which activity was greatest. Each different organisation that took up the cause of citizenship education was involved in battles over the nature of citizenship as a philosophical concept, as well as battles over the pedagogic shape of the subject for schools. The history of this ideological and pedagogic set of debates has yet to be written.

Brennan, Whitmarsh and Heater have each described the political struggles of organisations like the Moral Instruction League (MIL), the Association for Education for Citizenship (AEC), and the Politics Association, which have campaigned for the introduction of secular instruction in political and social affairs. Each successive pressure group had great difficulty maintaining a consensus over the nature of the subject. The MIL was established in 1897 to press for the replacement of Religious Instruction with secular training in morality, duty and citizenship, based on the tenets of rationalism and science, but it broke apart after the First World War when it became clear that the organisation could no longer maintain a common goal (Wong, 1991). The AEC was formed in the 1930s by Sir Ernest Simon and Eva Hubback as a response to the threat to democracy posed by continental totalitarianism. Its early radical ambitions for citizenship education were initially shaped by the concerns of inter-war liberalism and Fabianism. In the event, the aims of the AEC became increasingly diluted as the organisation sought to broaden its political alliance by enlisting the support and patronage of prominent conservatives such as Stanley Baldwin and Arthur Bryant (Whitmarsh, 1974). In the early 1970s, the Politics Association, under the leadership of Bernard Crick and Derek Heater, faced a similar problem. Crick and Heater's goal of campaigning for a more critical form of political studies met considerable opposition from members whose concern was the teaching of British Constitution.[2]

Another set of writers, which includes Brian Simon (1994), CCCS (Centre for Contemporary Cultural Studies) (1981), Gary McCulloch (1994) and, indirectly, Andy Green (1990), investigates the history of citizenship education from a different perspective. These writers argue that the education system itself is a social institution which acts to define the sphere of legitimate citizenship. They regard state education as a mechanism for the defence of existing social hierarchies of political and economic power. These are defined explicitly by the larger common curriculum, and implicitly by the hidden curriculum and by the existence of separate, socially stratified structures of schooling. This approach attends to the manner in which political and class identities are inscribed upon children through the very cultures and structures of schooling, regardless of whether or not a discrete subject exists to explicitly teach citizenship.

McCulloch, for example, argues that the 1944 Education Act itself represented a 'civic moment' which not only articulated a new public expectation of egalitarianism and social and welfare reform, but also came to symbolise the failure of the school system to establish the promised egalitarianism. McCulloch's identification of 1944 as a 'civic moment' is a useful one. It draws our attention to how the Second World War itself realigned political discourse in the UK. War, and the welfare reforms that followed in the 1940s, redefined the shape of the British state and its relationship with its citizens. Much contemporary political debate centred on the impact of an interventionist welfare state upon individual and family duties and responsibilities. The state was acting to reconfigure the relationship between the public and private spheres. Importantly, this was also a time when women were conspicuous as active citizens, and when the question of the women's role, both in the home and the workplace, was central to contemporary political debate.[3]

A crucial absence in these histories of citizenship education, whether they deal with a political narrative of pressure-group politics, or whether they seek to explore education as a structural communicator of citizenship, is an understanding of what actually happened in schools. What is required in terms of understanding the English approach to citizenship education is greater attention to the range and type of materials for citizenship education that were available to schools in the post-war period. This is not an easy task. Local authorities and individual schools had responsibility for, and control over, the curriculum. It is difficult, therefore, to ascertain how many schools taught some kind of citizenship education, and it is even more difficult to capture the methods used by those teachers that taught it.

Our preliminary investigations into the early post-war period suggest that education for citizenship played little or no part in the syllabus of most schools. The number of textbooks produced for 'Citizenship', 'Civics', 'British Constitution', and 'Current Affairs' is dwarfed by the number of publications available in more mainstream subjects like geography, history and RE. The records of the examination syndicates also suggest that it was a minority of pupils who were entered for specific named courses on Politics or Citizenship.[4] Records of how many pupils sat public examinations in citizenship subjects provide some indication of how few schools offered the subject at school certificate and higher school certificate level. A sample of records for the London, Cambridge and Northern Examination Boards (1945–1965) suggests a predominance of grammar and independent school candidates. In the 1940s and 1950s, secondary modern schools (which educated the majority of children) did not commonly enter pupils for public examination; most of their pupils took the opportunity to leave school at the age of 15. Little is known about secondary modern schools and what they taught in terms of 'civics', citizenship and social studies. We know even less about how these subjects were negotiated in the classroom (see Lawn, 1996). A full account of secondary modern practice would require extensive use of a number of other methods of inquiry, including oral history.

Given such difficulties, we chose as a strategy a far more limited project – a pilot study of method texts and textbooks of citizenship education produced in this period – whilst recognising that textbooks alone only provide a starting point into understanding how schools and teachers taught citizenship. A bibliography was constructed for the categories of 'citizenship', 'civics' and 'political education' for the period 1940–1966 (Brindle and Arnot, 1998). A collection of 22 texts was identified for in-depth analysis.[5]

Just over half of the texts (12 in total) reviewed in this chapter are school textbooks. Our sample also includes *Current Affairs*; a series of pamphlets produced by the Bureau of Current Affairs (BCA)[6] and made available between 1945 and 1951 to schools as well as to youth and adult education groups. *Citizens Growing Up* (1949) was a discussion document issued by the Ministry of Education and is the only substantial government statement on the issue of the citizenship education of the period. Marjorie Tait's *The Education of Women for Citizenship* is also a discussion document and was issued by UNESCO in 1954. Brimble and May's *Social Studies and World Citizenship* (1943) is an evangelising text for Social Studies, as is Nicholson and Wright's *Social Studies for Future Citizens* (1953). The two AEC books are method texts and discuss the relationship of education for citizenship to the teaching of the other main subjects, its target group being school teachers. Layton and Blanco-White's *The School Looks Around* (1948) was the last major AEC publication and is a guide to teachers on the survey method of teaching.

Education for citizenship in the era of social democratic reconstruction

Our first task of textual analysis was to map the ways in which the concept of citizenship, in relation to the agenda of social democracy, was represented by the authors. Most of the texts in our sample constructed, or suggested, a concentric model of learning. They typically took the localised/immediate character of civic activity and placed it within an idealised community. The majority of textbooks encouraged teachers and pupils to consider an imagined geographical location (most frequently a small market town) and from there to investigate an ever-widening set of political spheres: from town; to county; to Westminster; to Europe; to the Empire/Commonwealth.

The locus of the small town located rural communities and the big cities as marginalised communities, to be visited on special trips during the course of later explorations. The small town became the site of ideal-typical Englishness; they were small enough to act as idealised organic communities in which the investigating writer can introduce each new character in the political map as a familiar addition to the community of belonging. Small towns had other advantages, too. They presented the reader with an image of the modern, and so enabled the author of texts for citizenship education to create an idealised vision of social democracy in action. For the most part, this involved the texts tracking the activities of local individuals (from postmen and dustmen to councillors and MPs) as they passed from the local sphere outwards, and back again. The post-war reconstructed world was to be a modern brave new world. This was best illustrated by descriptions and pictures of shiny new hospitals, schools and other amenities – the icons of a planned, scientific and rational society. In the small towns, the modern could be connected almost physically to a long and ever-improving past. New health centres and fire stations existed alongside medieval guildhalls and Saturday markets. The modern therefore remained connected to the past.

Many of the texts constructed idealised notions of the citizen and larger political communities such as the nation and, rather uncomfortably, the Empire. For all the texts reviewed here, these concepts were filtered through the lens of social democracy. The growth of responsibilities assumed by the state, for example, represented not a burden on state finances, as it might today, but the arrival of a civilised, modern and caring society. The expanding provision of welfare services could be interpreted as both an emblem of progress and the historical fruition of past constitutional and institutional reforms. Pat Thane has described how the coming of the welfare state became a latter-day Whiggism, defining 'progress' through the markers of the state-led battle against poverty, ill-health and inequality (Thane, 1998). This was certainly the case in the post-war texts of citizenship education. Whether conservative or radical in tone, all of the texts we studied placed great faith in the welfare state and the mixed, semi-planned economy as an ideal form of political economic organisation.

What also united the citizenship texts in our sample was a concern for welfare reform. All of the texts reviewed here made it clear that the state's enhanced involvement in people's well-being – manifested in the state's growing involvement in the private sphere – should be matched by a greater interest and participation in democracy on the part of the citizen. In this context, 'civic' participation necessitated the citizen staying informed, interested, active and mindful in all their dealings with society. This was a duty, as much as access to free health care, for instance, was presented as a right.

In summary, in our sample of the texts for citizenship education in the post-war era, the polity was constructed in line with the values and expectations of social democracy. The duty of the state to assume increasing welfare responsibilities was taken as a given. Indeed, statism and welfarism were elements of a new Whiggism (Thane, 1998) and were positioned as the end-point of a long history of social and political reform. The social democratic polity was investigated in many of the texts we analysed through the mechanism of a concentrically defined pedagogy. Each sphere of the polity – from home town to Empire/Commonwealth – represents an additional ring of ever-expanding circles of belonging. An idealised small town provides the locus of real, face-to-face, civic relations and responsibilities, and provides a comforting vision of civic fairness, inclusivity and mass participation. However, such a discourse of democratic fairness and political inclusivity, we found, was not maintained when such texts dealt with the representation of women as citizens and in the civic sphere. In the next section we illustrate this point.

The gendering of texts for citizenship education

Our analysis of the representation of women as citizens in our sample of the texts of education for citizenship identified three different approaches to gender and the private sphere. The first and most common approach – the *exclusionary* – excluded both the private sphere and women from its construction of the political domain. In contrast, a second, small set of texts sought to include women and the private sphere in various different ways. These we identified as *inclusionary* in their approach. Notable exceptions to this stance were some of the BCA pamphlets written for a broader audience, which we have identified as taking a third position of *critical engagement* with contemporary debates about the future nature of gender roles.

It has not been possible to describe in detail the approach taken to gender by all of the 22 texts in our sample. The great majority of citizenship texts, whether radical or conservative in their approach to other issues of democracy and political participation, took an exclusionary approach to the representation of women as citizens. Table 5.1 indicates the categories into which we place our sample of texts; some of which are then used to illustrate the stance adopted by each of the three categories.

Exclusionary texts

In this section, we provide an overview of those texts which typify an *exclusionary* approach to the representation of women as citizens. In exclusionary texts there is a general inattention and lack of interest in the position of women. Indeed, it is not unusual for women to receive no mention at all. Yet that is not to say that such texts do not act to position women in relation to the polity.

C.S.S. Higham's *The Good Citizen* (1931, revised 1952), for example, is typical of civics texts operating within what might be identified as a minimalist political framework.[7] It manufactures a reductionistic model of the civic sphere, reducing the legitimate frame of the political to the institutions of democratic participation and government. District and County Councils, Westminster, the Commonwealth and the United Nations are politically defined, while the 'social' institutions of gender, family, youth and class are constructed as outside the political sphere and thus go unexamined. The political is subsequently stripped not only of gender, but of, amongst other things, historical change, social conflict and ideology. Fundamentally, the political is conflated with the polity (in the traditional sense of the term) not only limiting the rules for political engagement to existing public/institutional mechanisms (voting, standing for election, writing to one's representative and so on) but confirming also the non-political (and implicitly natural/normative) nature of other 'social' institutions – the family, class and gender relations. The examples and illustrations provided of political activity are

Table 5.1 Categorisation of sample texts

Exclusionary texts	Inclusionary texts	Critical engagement
Association For Education For Citizenship (1945) *Education for Citizenship in Secondary Schools.* Borer, M.C. (1962) *Citizenship. Its Rights and Responsibilities.* Brimble, L.F. and May, F.J. (1943) *Social Studies and World Citizenship. A Sociological Approach.* Furth, C. (1949) *You and the State. An Introduction to Civics and Current Affairs.* Higham, C.S.S. (1931) *The Good Citizen. An Introduction to Civics.* Higham, C.S.S. (revised by W.E. Jackson) (1952) *The Good Citizen. An Introduction to Civics.* Howard, B.A. (1948) *Our Own Country.* Jack, M.V. (1946) *The Young Citizen.* Layton, E. and White, J.B. (1948) *The School Looks Around.* Ministry of Education (1949) *Citizens Growing Up: At Home, in School and After.* Murray, J.O. (1952) *State and People. A Handbook of Citizenship for Young People.* Nicholson, F.J. and Wright, V.K. (1953) *Social Studies for Future Citizens.* Palmer, G.B.C. and Armstrong, H.W. (1956) *In the Public Interest. A Book of Civics for Secondary Schools.* Thomas, M.W. (1950) *Citizens All.* Thomas, M.W. (1967) *Citizenship for School Leavers,* Vol. 1: 'The Family'. Wales, P. (1966) *Introduction to Civics.*	Palmer, G.D.M. (1947) *The Chinese Box.* Tait, M. (1954) *The Education of Women for Citizenship. Some Practical Suggestions.*	Bowley, R. (19/02/1949) 'Women in a man's world', *Current Affairs,* 74. London: Bureau of Current Affairs. Hankin, G.T. (26/11/1949) 'Human rights', *Current Affairs,* 94. London: Bureau of Current Affairs. Mead, M. (23/07/1949) 'The family's food', *Current Affairs,* 85. London: Bureau of Current Affairs. Williams, W.E. (11/01/1947) 'Women's Place', *Current Affairs,* 20. London: Bureau of Current Affairs. Williams, G. (18/10/1947) 'Men, women and jobs', *Current Affairs,* 39. London: Bureau of Current Affairs.

of men. Women, as enfranchised individuals, do vote, and as Higham tokenistically points out, some women serve as councillors 'too', but they are overwhelmingly outnumbered by men in the headcount of participation (Higham, 1952: 81). In those few instances where women are represented they are largely limited to traditionally defined caring roles – teachers, nurses and so on.

Similarly, in Mary Jack's *The Young Citizen* (1946) there is no engagement with the domestic sphere. It is the father of two inquisitive boys who is the source of the boys' growing knowledge of the political world around them. Jack writes with the imagined authorial voice of one of the boys. When father brings home the wages, it not only gives him an opportunity to explain to the boys issues of tax and insurance, but also enables the father to talk about 'housekeeping' money (Jack, 1946: 11). During the course of the boys' investigations around their town they encounter only one woman – an assistant librarian – and they are at all times serviced with food and fussing by their mother, who, unlike the boys' father, has no useful knowledge to impart.

J.O. Murray's *State and People: A Handbook of Citizenship for Young People* (1952) presents a broader definition of democracy, which includes examining issues regarded as politically contentious. However, while the conflicting claims to political truth of socialism, liberalism and conservatism are rehearsed, the issue of women's citizenship is reduced to the question of female suffrage (Murray, 1952: 130–2). He asserts that Britain could not be described as a democracy until 1928, when women finally had the vote on the same basis as men. Yet the story of inequality ends with the granting of equality of franchise. There is no consideration of the problems or inequalities faced by women after 1928. Murray also takes the separation of the domestic sphere from the political to extreme lengths. The home, for instance, is considered only if that home is provided by the local authority.

Mary Cathcart Borer's *Citizenship: Its Rights and Responsibilities* (1962) works within a maximalist construction of citizenship. Yet her otherwise wide and inclusive discussion of the political does not include a critical examination of the status of women within politics. Borer confronts some very controversial issues. For instance, she asks her readers to discuss the justification for the possession of nuclear weapons, and the rights and wrongs of selection for secondary school on the basis of the 11-plus. Borer does also examine the issue of gender inequality explicitly. However, her discussion of this issue is centred upon girls' and boys' experiences and expectations of education (Borer, 1962: 34). She observes that, in the past, access to educational and professional opportunity was far greater for boys than for girls.

> For a boy, the whole world lies open to him. He will achieve a position, high or low, according to his ability and application, in the career of his choice and will ultimately marry and have a family ... The pattern is clear cut and universal. Most girls, as they reach school-leaving age, are as much occupied with thoughts of marriage as of a career. Their problem is a difficult one, which each girl must solve for herself, according to her own circumstances, for there is no general answer to it. (Borer, 1962: 50)

Borer encourages her readers to have a new faith, following the war, in British society's meritocratic fairness. She believes that success comes to those who deserve it, and that one's social position is consonant with one's 'ability and application', unhindered by prejudice:

> Women are now emancipated. They have won the vote and are free to take their place in the world alongside men in every sphere of life. (Borer, 1962: 52)

Borer does accept that, in practice, female emancipation has given many women the additional burden of taking on work outside the home without any letting up of their domestic labour:

> She has to do two jobs herself, which is good neither for herself, her family, nor her employer. (Borer, 1962: 52)

The discussion ends on a conservative note with a reference to the problem of 'latch-key' children – children who, she believes, with no home to go to during the day, spend their after-school hours causing trouble while they await the return of their mothers from work. Their working mother's absence:

> deprives them of some of the security on which their happiness depends and many people feel that, except in cases of real need, the mother of young children should stay at home and look after them properly. (Borer, 1962: 52)

The Ministry of Education's pamphlet on citizenship – *Citizens Growing Up* (1949) – similarly engaged with women's role as citizens. Its concern was to make the case for women's emancipation, but at the same time emphasise the essential difference between boys' and girls' future roles. It offered teachers clear guidelines on how citizenship education should be differentiated on the basis of gender. The advice of the Ministry was that 'home-craft' should be regarded as an essential component in any form of education that sought to explore contemporary society. The pamphlet stated:

> Most girls, and to a less extent, most boys also, need some training in the duties and responsibility of owning or renting a house or flat and conducting a home or helping parents to conduct a home. Nearly every girl will need, and most will wish, to understand the arts and skill that furnish and provision a home and clothe its members. (Ministry of Education, 1949: 28–9)

The pamphlet adds:

> the situation has sufficient general truth to call for some systematic domestic training for all but the girl with very exceptional tastes. (Ministry of Education, 1949: 29)

Such texts were remarkable more for their attempts to sustain biological discourses of difference over and above any discussion of women's emancipation.

Inclusionary texts

A small minority of texts sought to include representations of women as citizens. Only one textbook (Grace Palmer's *The Chinese Box* (1947)), one method text (Marjorie Tait's *The Education of Women for Citizenship* (1954)) and the BCA pamphlets explicitly positioned women within the polity as active citizens, and purposively addressed the question of women's rights and the extent of women's access to, or exclusion from, public life and the exercise of power. Palmer and Tait, both writing specifically for and about women, construct what we might identify as a 'liberal rights' discourse of citizenship. The BCA's construction of citizenship in its *Current Affairs* pamphlets is perhaps the most radical of all, and is based upon subjecting every aspect of social and political organisation to critical questioning. These pamphlets will be discussed in the next section.

Palmer and Tait demonstrate not only an awareness of the nature of women's subjection in society, but also a willingness to engage with the causes of that subjection. Neither Palmer nor Tait write with the education of boys in mind – both assume it is girls who must change their ideas more than boys. They are texts *for* women and girls *about* women and girls. These texts defend the rights of women to enjoy equality with men, both in the workplace and in public life, and are conscious also of the prejudice and discrimination suffered by women who seek equality of access, opportunity and participation. Palmer and Tait are nevertheless part of the social democratic tradition. The polity is constructed as a rational and liberal set of institutions, which have within them the potential to facilitate women's active involvement in politics and the world of work. They do not see the system itself as in question; their concern is that the individuals that make up the system are guilty of prejudice; a prejudice which could be overcome given a more enlightened and rational education.

In Palmer's *The Chinese Box*, 'everyday things' are politically defined (Palmer, 1947, Preface). Like many of the other authors in this study, Palmer deploys a concentric pedagogical model. In this case, that model is the eponymous *Chinese Box*, signifying the individual's occupation of a number of different spheres of belonging. What is significant is that the first box is that of the home. The private sphere – the family – is placed as a politically and socially constructed sphere in a similar way to the other 'boxes'/spheres – the local community, the national, and the international. It is the explorations and investigations of an adolescent girl – Edith – that is the pedagogical device by which citizenship is constructed for the reader.

Palmer demonstrates the active role played by women (all women, not just women of 'importance') in the historical construction of the English nation. Women, she argues, should not be written out of the history of England, and even if their role was confined in the past to the rearing of a family, this is nevertheless an essential contribution to the well-being of the race (Palmer, 1947: 7). What is

Figure 5.1 Few texts understood that most working women had to work at home. Unlike most of the texts in our sample, most BCA pamphlets were well illustrated. This is from W.E. Williams's 'Women's Place' (*Current Affairs*, 11 January 1947).

an exclusion from the political in most post-war citizenship texts is regarded by Palmer as an integral and historically important part of the socio-political system. She points out that, following the Second World War, the contribution of women is now even more significant:

> For many hundreds of years girls and women bearing your names have helped to make our homes, our way of life, and our English race. It is your turn now. To-day women help to govern and to defend their country more than they used to do. (Palmer, 1947: 47)

The entry of women into a wider range of occupations in growing numbers marks a break with the past which must be both reflected upon by girls at school and encouraged. She states:

> You will not want to do everything just as your mothers do, for their ways will seem old-fashioned to you. It is good to try new things. (Palmer, 1947: 47)

Palmer asks her readers to consider whether the domestic division of labour ought to change so that women and men share more tasks around the home. The state, she says, may be expanding to take on many of the caring responsibilities once regarded as being women's responsibility; however, she maintains that:

> This does not mean that there could not be more helping and sharing, in the cooking and mending, the care of the children and the sick, than there has been in the past. To meet such new ways homes and towns would have to be adapted. (Palmer, 1947: 18)

It is the growth of the welfare state, alongside developments in household technology, that has, to Palmer, brought about the historical conditions for greater female emancipation (p. 19). This enables her to suggest that gender roles are not a natural given, but are historically and culturally constituted (p. 106). As such they can be reconstituted. This process of reconstitution is primarily what she wants to draw girls' attention to. In so doing, she places and enfranchises young women in an ongoing process of reinvention.

At no point does Palmer question the premise that it remains fundamentally the woman's responsibility to maintain the home and look after the children. It is revealing, also, that the book of civics for girls maintains the centrality of the family and the metaphor of the family in her discussion of all the spheres of belonging. The British Empire, for example, is simply 'a pretty big family' to which all Britons belong.

Palmer presents the reader with a number of positive female role models, both historical and contemporary, not the least of whom is Edith's older sister – the high-flyer of the family, who works as a civil servant – but there are no examples of men which are not traditionally constructed. Edith's father, brother and uncle are all defined by their outside occupations, but Edith's mother remains the central representative of the child-rearer/homemaker.

Marjorie Tait's *The Education of Women for Citizenship* (1954) argues the case for the inclusion of a notion of women's rights and duties at the heart of any conceptualisation of citizenship. In a text sponsored by UNESCO and aimed at teachers throughout the English-speaking world, Tait begins with the premise that social justice for all relies on the defence of equal rights for men and women (Tait, 1954: 12). These, she writes, are basic principles of human rights as defined by the United Nations. Tait then argues that these principles are violated in education systems around the world – anywhere, in fact, where boys enjoy greater access than girls to secondary education and higher education, and where the curriculum is differentiated according to gender (p. 13). For Tait, the assertion that a woman's primary role is that of being a mother and wife (and by extension, teacher) is nothing more than a mechanism to perpetuate the continued inequality of access and opportunity in education, politics and occupation experienced by women (p. 23). Educators, especially women teachers, are asked to confront 'women's questions':

> What are 'women's questions'? Very roughly, at first glance, we can divide them into questions relating to their rights and those relating to their duties. A

Figure 5.2 The seeming modernity of conflicts over women's role is well illustrated by the frontispiece to W.E. Williams's 'Women's Place' (*Current Affairs*, 11 January 1947).

woman may ask what are her rights to education, to the ownership of property, to her children? How do they compare with those of men? Has she the right to practice the profession of her choice? Will she be paid the same rate as a man for the same job? Has she the same rights as her husband in the case of separation or divorce? (Tait, 1954: 72)

However, Tait's vision of enhanced women's participation in politics draws upon essentialist discourses of 'male' and 'female' characteristics:

> Duty as well as inclination in many cases dictates that women in public life should be specially concerned with the care of children, the sick and the aged and the handicapped; with food, health, education, housing and town and country planning. (Tait, 1954: 72)

Tait's model of increased participation for women in politics not only implicitly reproduces the public as the only legitimate political sphere, but also defines a specific grouping of political activities which would be better suited to being administered and legislated by women. Such activities should be kept as a distinct and separate corpus from those political activities defined as 'male'. To Tait, local government, health and education sound like 'pre-eminently a woman's job' (p. 55). Great affairs of state – wars, foreign affairs and so on – remain the natural domain of men:

> National politics may well seem remote and unintelligible to the ordinary woman and, compared with the affairs of local government, much more difficult to relate to her own interests. (Tait, 1954: 67)

Tait's construction of the feminine remains, thus, highly traditional:

> Young girls dream romantic dreams. They gossip with each other about their love affairs. They go over in memory the film they saw last night. They plan their clothes. Older women are mentally in their homes. They plan their work, think about what they will buy with their wages, and exchange stories of their children and neighbours with the women nearby. It is the world outside the workplace which to a very great extent fills their minds. (Tait, 1954: 54)

Critical engagement

The third approach found in our sample of texts was that taken by the *Current Affairs* pamphlets produced by the BCA for schools and adult community groups. *Current Affairs* worked within a *critical engagement* approach which provided readers with a broad range of opinions from which to debate a given topic. In *Current Affairs* the reader was likely to be presented with the most reactionary, as well as the most progressive, of attitudes towards a given topic. The concern of the BCA was to subject every opinion, regardless of how conventional and seemingly axiomatic, to critical questioning through group discussion. The need to provide material for discussion groups generated the need to provide material that was critical and contentious.

Current Affairs, albeit on occasion without design, provided a pedagogic framework which served to undermine the exclusion from the political frame of those spheres of society regarded naturalistically as outside of the sphere of civic debate: women's work; the family and child-rearing; the role of men in the home; the question of equal pay and equal rights for both sexes. It was, ironically, the BCA – an organisation that had emerged from the military propaganda unit, the Army Bureau of Current Affairs (ABCA) after 1945 – that provided the most radical engagement with the social construction of gender in post-war citizenship education.

In 'Women's Place', W.E. Williams, the director of the BCA, sets out some common generalisations about women (Williams, 11/01/47: 3). 'Is,' he asks, 'the woman's place in the home?' If so, 'Who says so? Women themselves? Men? Society as a whole?' And:

> if we say that woman's place is the home, do we mean that is her only province? Do we intend to exclude her from participation in government, public life, social welfare activities? (Williams, 11/01/47: 4)

Williams asks discussion groups to consider whether these statements are true for all women and at all times, and what this might mean for marriage, families, the workplace, politics and for the happiness of women themselves (p. 4). He asks, 'To whom is it "unfair" if a married woman works?' (p. 4).

Williams is not a feminist; he describes as 'preposterous' the 'Ultra-feminist' notion that 'women have the right to do everything that men do', but he does want to give 'the feminist approach' its space (pp. 3–4). He regards feminism as a position held by 'upper-class' women who have access to 'the more elegant professions – novelists, actresses, staff-managers and so on', and he states that most women who work are involved in the most unglamorous and underpaid of factory and shop work (p. 4). He is scathing of the essentialist assertion that women ought not to work at all, pointing out that many women can never marry; that many husbands cannot afford to support a family from their earnings alone and require their wives to contribute to the family wage; and that widows and young unmarried women must support themselves too (p. 7). He states:

> The whole problem of women's work is thus complicated by factors which don't arise for men, and the existence of these factors should check us from making sweeping statements about whether women 'ought' to work or not. (Williams, 11/01/47: 7)

Other problems are posed that also highlight the interconnectedness of seemingly distinct male and female spheres. Williams wonders whether, if women continue to receive a lower wage for the same work as men, then this could serve to make men's employment less secure. Readers are asked to question whether it is only 'custom' that determines that men do one type of job while women do another (Williams, 11/01/47: 8). 'Custom' also dictates, says Williams, higher expectations of sons rather than of daughters, and greater investment and interest in sons' education compared with that of daughters, all of which contribute in some way to the inequality in outcome and attainment between men and women (p. 8). He suggests that the experience of women's service in the war means that there is little the men can do which cannot be done equally well by women (p. 10). He points out that the future is inhabited by women as much as it is by men; and:

> If they [women] are to see created the kind of world in which they would like their children to live, they must share with their menfolk the responsibilities of citizenship. (Williams, 11/01/47: 10)

Williams's own conclusions are similar to Tait's. He writes that 'Woman's place is everywhere' because certain 'feminine' skills and interests – care, welfare, health, and child-rearing – are, or should be, the concerns of all society, and would be best administered if women took a more active role in local and national politics (p. 12). Just as Tait had invoked essentialist distinctions in asserting that the duties of local government are in fact best served under the stewardship of women, so too does Williams, who points out that housing, health, and education are the key political interests of women and should form the starting point for their engagement with politics (p. 12).

Ruth Bowley's 'Women in a man's world?' (1949), another *Current Affairs* pamphlet, puts the case for a greater partnership between men and women at home and in the workplace (Bowley, 19/02/1949). Bowley asks whether this would require the establishment of new work patterns, both in and outside the home. Discussants are reminded that throughout history women have had a dual role, working both in the home and in the workplace 'in a world built by men' and 'planned chiefly for men' (Bowley, 19/02/1949: 2). Women have always been in subjection, she points out, but now, with new laws to protect women and to give them rights, and with the coming of new technologies, women should think about making choices about their future (p. 6). Like Williams, she draws the reader's attention to the question of equal pay between men and women for equal work, and she argues that women will never get rights to equal pay until they have an equal voice and adequate political representation. This means joining unions and women organising themselves to fight for what they want (p. 9). Bowley recognises that if more women with children are to work, new organisations and welfare services will be required to look after children, although she does worry that this might lead to increased family breakdown and an increased burden upon the state (p. 13). She poses the question whether – if women want and have a right to work, and if society is to benefit from this – families should have to reinvent themselves so that the onus of domestic responsibility is shared more fairly between all family members (p. 14). This involves a new partnership between women and men, between workplace and home, and between the family and the state (p. 14).

> In the long run do you think it will be a woman's world where the pubs will serve pots of tea and men will stay at home to do the washing-up? (Bowley, 19/02/1949: 12)

"To whom is it 'unfair' if a married woman works?"

Figure 5.3 The caption read 'To whom is it "unfair" if a married woman works?' (W.E. Williams, 'Women's Place', *Current Affairs*, 11 January 1947).

Other *Current Affairs* pamphlets also did much to problematise the distinction between a public/political sphere and a private/apolitical. Gertrude Williams in 'Men, Women and Jobs' pointed out that the manpower shortage would demand new attitudes to women working, which would subsequently require a new stance towards the family (Williams, 18/10/1947). Margaret Mead's 'The Family's Food' drew attention to the inherently political nature of food production, distribution and transport, and in so doing connected the family as a social unit to a world system of production and consumption (Mead, 23/07/1949). G.T. Hankin's 'Human Rights' re-emphasised the United Nations' commitment to equal rights between men and women, women's right to work and their right to be free from discrimination on the basis of sex (Hankin, 26/11/1949).

Conclusion

We have noted that, while historians and educationists have researched the political history of education for citizenship and the pressure groups that fought for the inclusion of the subject in the common school curriculum, we still know little about how such organisations, and the materials they produced, constructed political and civic discourses. We argued that further research is necessary into the historical existence and negotiation of political and citizenship education in schools and classrooms. This study of the texts of education for citizenship in the 20 years following the end of the Second World War represents a limited start to this project.

We contend that those who write for and about citizenship education are involved in a process of defining and explaining the political. The pedagogue of citizenship education is delimiting a language of politics, and a field of political engagement, within which children will be positioned, and through which they will position other groups and organisations: the government, workers, councils, sub-cultures, families, individuals, and women and men. Texts of citizenship education reflect the range of opinion that is deemed legitimate enough to be provided for children. Each text is involved in a process of configuring the polity, which is used here as a shorthand term signifying the field of legitimate political discourse. The majority of the texts reviewed here constructed the polity in liberal-institutional terms; the arena of contested power relations is strictly confined to constitutional mechanisms of liberal democracy. Actors within this discourse exercise agency through making rational choices within a fair, functioning and facilitating system.

We have argued that citizenship texts were gendered according to three approaches to the representation of women as citizens. By delimiting the political only in terms of the constitutional polity, the great majority of texts in our sample of education for citizenship in the era of social democratic reconstruction acted as *exclusionary* texts, excluding discussions of the private sphere and women from the legitimate frame of political enquiry. Even the most apparently radical citizenship texts worked in such a way as to make women's questions and women's relationship to politics a non-issue. Paradoxically, such approaches were adopted at a time in which the actual reconstitution of social and political relations in

Figure 5.4 According to Williams, 'women's place was everywhere' ('Women's Place', *Current Affairs*, 11 January 1947).

response to the establishment of the welfare state was itself an active process of renegotiating the relationship between the public and the private, and between men and women.

The *inclusionary* texts of Grace Palmer and Marjorie Tait sought to include women and the private sphere within the range of politically defined institutions. In Palmer and Tait's texts, women could make rational choices about their level of participation in a political system which was fair and responsive to those who participated within it. However, Palmer and Tait accepted and reproduced the dominant social assumptions about women and girls' primarily domestic roles and responsibilities in society. They also constructed the public sphere in liberal democratic terms; they regarded both the polity and other social relations as facilitating free and equal access and participation, regardless of gender. Both Palmer and Tait posed their questions for a female readership, and there is no critique of the wider social consequences that would follow, for the organisation of the family as well as the polity, if women did exercise the right to participate equally in the public sphere. The question of what this would mean in terms of social and political reorganisation was posed only by those texts – the BCA *Current Affairs* pamphlets – that adopted a *critical engagement* approach.

The most radical in their approach to gender (as well as to other issues) were the *Current Affairs* pamphlets. The political and social progressivism of *Current Affairs* was a product of its radical pedagogy. The BCA, like the Army Board of Current Affairs before it, idealised the discussion group as the best method of teaching political and civic awareness. The need to stimulate debate about even seemingly axiomatic and straightforward issues directed *Current Affairs* writers in the direction of subjecting all social and cultural assumptions to criticism and contestation. In so doing, *Current Affairs* provided material with the potential to undermine normative and naturalistic assumptions about traditional gender and filial roles.

This work represents only a starting point. By looking at the representations of women in a sample of texts for citizenship, we have begun to highlight some of the inadequacies in social democratic and liberal constructions of the polity and the public sphere. Such accounts have, in the past, acted to exclude women and the private sphere from the frame of what is identified as the political. In effect, such texts kept the private sphere private. We have also drawn attention to some of the gaps in current knowledge of past attempts to establish the teaching of citizenship in English schools. Much work has still to be done into how the curricular materials of citizenship education manufacture and delimit seemingly common sense and normative representations of the polity and the public sphere. Just as the writers for *Current Affairs* established a pedagogy of critical engagement in the 1940s, so we believe that today's researchers must critically engage with modern and historical configurations of notions of citizenship, the ideal citizen, the polity and the public sphere if they want to fully understand the role that education for citizenship can, and does, play in schools.

Acknowledgements

Thanks are due to the Leverhulme Trust, for the Research Fellowship I was granted for my research into Education, Gender and Democratic Citizenship. Thanks also to the Economic and Social Research Council for supporting Patrick Brindle during his period on leave as research associate for the above project. We are indebted also to Jo-Anne Dillabough for her useful comments on an earlier draft of this article and I would like to thank Patrick for permission to reprint the article here, especially since he was the first named author.

References

The Texts of Education for Citizenship

Association For Education For Citizenship (1945) *Education for Citizenship in Secondary Schools*. London: Oxford University Press.

Borer, M.C. (1962) *Citizenship: its rights and responsibilities*. London: Museum Press.

Brimble, L.F. and May, F.J. (1943) *Social Studies and World Citizenship: a sociological approach*. London: Macmillan.

Furth, C. (1949) *You and the State. An Introduction to Civics and Current Affairs*. London: Allen and Unwin.

Higham, C.S.S. (1931) *The Good Citizen. An Introduction to Civics*. London: Longmans, Green and Co.

Higham, C.S.S. (revised by W.E. Jackson) (1952) *The Good Citizen. An Introduction to Civics*. London: Longmans, Green and Co.

Howard, B.A. (1948) *Our Own Country*. London: Pitman.

Jack, M.V. (1946) *The Young Citizen*. London: Collins.

Layton, E. and White, J.B. (1948) *The School Looks Around*. London: Association for Education for Citizenship, Longmans, Green and Co.

Ministry of Education (1949) *Citizens Growing Up. At Home, in School and After.* Ministry of Education, Pamphlet no. 16. London: HMSO.
Murray, J.O. (1952) *State and People. A Handbook of Citizenship for Young People.* London: Harrap.
Nicholson, F.J. and Wright, V.K. (1953) *Social Studies for Future Citizens.* London: Harrap.
Palmer, G.B.C. and Armstrong, H.W. (1956) *In the Public Interest. A Book of Civics for Secondary Schools.* London: Blackie.
Palmer, G.D.M. (1947) *The Chinese Box.* London: Blackie.
Tait, M. (1954) *The Education of Women for Citizenship. Some Practical Suggestions.* Paris, UNESCO.
Thomas, M.W. (1950) *Citizens All.* London: Thomas Nelson.
Thomas, M.W. (1967) *Citizenship for School Leavers. Vol. 1: 'The Family'.* London: Thomas Nelson.
Wales, P. (1966) *Introduction to Civics.* Oxford: Pergamon Press.

Current Affairs Pamphlets

Bowley, R. (19/02/1949) 'Women in a man's world', *Current Affairs*, 74. London: Bureau of Current Affairs.
Hankin, G.T. (26/11/1949) 'Human rights', *Current Affairs*, 94. London: Bureau of Current Affairs.
Mead, M. (23/07/1949) 'The family's food', *Current Affairs*, 85. London: Bureau of Current Affairs.
Williams, G. (18/10/1947) 'Men, women and jobs', *Current Affairs*, 39. London: Bureau of Current Affairs.
Williams, W.E. (11/01/1947) 'Women's Place', *Current Affairs*, 20. London: Bureau of Current Affairs.

Bibliography of Secondary Texts

Advisory Group on Education for Citizenship (1998) *The Teaching of Democracy in Schools. Initial Report.* London: Qualifications and Curriculum Authority.
Arnot, M. (1997) '"Gendered Citizenry": new feminist perspectives on education and citizenship', *British Educational Research Journal*, 23(3): 275–95.
Arnot, M. (1998) 'European citizenship and education', in S. Ormrod (ed.) *Cambridge Thoughts.* Cambridge: Cambridge University Press.
Arnot, M., Araújo, H., Deliyanni-Kouimtzi, K., Rowe, G. and Tomé, A. (1996) 'Teachers, gender and the discourses of citizenship', *International Studies in Sociology of Education*, 6: 3–35.
Association For Education For Citizenship (1939) *Education for Citizenship in Elementary Schools.* London: Oxford University Press.
Bowlby, J. (1952) *Child Care and the Growth of Human Love.* London: Penguin.
Brennan, T. (1981) *Political Education and Democracy.* Cambridge, Cambridge University Press.
Brindle, P. (1998) 'Past histories: history and the elementary school classroom in early 20th century England', Unpublished PhD Thesis, University of Cambridge.
Brindle, P. and Arnot, M. (1998) *The Teaching of Civics and Citizenship. A Pilot Study* (available from the School of Education, University of Cambridge).
Centre For Contemporary Cultural Studies Education Group (1981) *Unpopular Education. Schooling and Social Democracy in England since 1944.* London: Hutchinson.
Crewe, I. (1996) 'Citizenship and civic education', Paper presented at the Royal Society of Arts, published by the Citizenship Foundation.

136 *'England expects every man to do his duty'*

Crick, B. and Heater, D.B. (1977) *Foundations of Citizenship: essays on political education.* Brighton, Falmer Press.
Green, A. (1990) *Education and State Formation: the rise of education systems in England, France and the USA.* London: Macmillan.
Hawkins, T.H. and Brimble, L.J.F. (1947) *Adult Education: the record of the British Army.* London: Macmillan.
Heater, D.B. (1990) *The Civic Ideal in World History, Politics and Education.* London: Everyman.
Heater, D.B. (ed.) (1969) *The Teaching of Politics.* London: Methuen.
Heater, D.B. and Gillespie, J.A. (eds) (1981) *Political Education in Flux.* London: Sage.
Heathorn, S. (1996) 'English elementary education and the construction of national identity, 1880–1914', Unpublished PhD thesis, University of Toronto.
Kelly, E. (1993) 'Gender issues in education for citizenship', in G.K. Verma and P.D. Pumfrey (eds) *Cross-Curricular Contacts.* London: Falmer Press.
Lawn, M. (1996) *Modern Times? Work, Professionalism and Citizenship in Teaching.* London: Falmer Press.
Mackenzie, S.P. (1992) *Current Affairs and Citizenship Education in the British Army 1914–1950.* Oxford, Clarendon Press.
Marshall, C. and Anderson, G.L. (1995) 'Rethinking the public and private spheres: feminist and cultural studies perspectives on the politics of education', in J. Scribner and D. Layton (eds) *The Study of Educational Politics.* London: Falmer Press.
McCulloch, G. (1994) *Educational Reconstruction. The 1944 Education Act and the Twenty-First Century.* London: Woburn Press.
McLaughlin, T.H. (1992) 'Citizenship, diversity and education: a philosophical perspective', *Journal of Moral Education*, 21: 235–50.
Simon, B. (1994) 'Education and citizenship in England', in B. Simon, *The State and Educational Change.* London: Lawrence and Wishart.
Smith, D.C. (1965–66) 'Education for world understanding: an estimate of the impact on secondary schools in England and Wales since 1945', Unpublished PhD Thesis, Institute of Education, University of London.
Thane, P. (1998) 'Histories of the welfare state', in W. Lamont (ed.) *Historical Controversies and Historians.* London: UCL Press.
Thompson, D. (1969) 'The teaching of civics and British constitution', in D. Heater (ed.) *The Teaching of Politics.* London: Methuen.
Whitmarsh, G. (1974) 'The politics of political education: an episode', *Journal of Curriculum Studies*, 6: 133–42.
Whitty, G. (1985) 'Social studies and political education in England since 1945', in I. Goodson (ed.) *Social Histories of the Secondary Curriculum.* London: Falmer Press.
Wong, J.Y.Y. (1991) 'Continuity and change in citizenship education in England in the twentieth century', Unpublished PhD Thesis, University of Liverpool.

Notes

1. It is possible to suggest a number of reasons that the immediate post-war period was not a particularly active time in the see-saw history of campaigns for education for citizenship. We find merit in the observations (see note 2) of Derek Heater and Denis Lawton that the 1940s and 1950s were most unlikely to witness successful calls for more formalised instruction in citizenship and politics because of their association with the curricularised and propagandist methods of Nazi Germany and Stalinist Russia.
2. Our thanks to Derek Heater for this observation. As part of the initial pilot study the authors interviewed a number of key individuals involved in education for citizenship

since the Second World War. We are most grateful to Derek Heater, Denis Lawton and Brian Simon for agreeing to share their observations and experiences in taped interviews.
3 Theories of 'maternal deprivation' as articulated by the work of, for example, John Bowlby (*Child Care and the Growth of Human Love*, 1952), were deployed by the Government to encourage women to return to the home following the end of the war and the demobilisation of the armed forces.
4 The records of the London, Cambridge and Northern examination boards were consulted for the period 1946–1970.
5 The 22 method-texts and textbooks were selected on the basis of a rough estimate of popularity (how many times the catalogue indicated a reprinting) and on availability. As a result some key texts, notably those by Kathleen Gibberd and Alderton Pink, were not studied. It is hoped to rectify these omissions during later investigations.
6 The BCA was the civilian version of the Army Bureau of Current Affairs (ABCA), which provided propaganda pamphlets and guidance in citizenship to soldiers in both the First and the Second World Wars.
7 Terry McLaughlin argued that, in pedagogic and ideological terms, attempts to define the nature of education for citizenship can be identified as occupying varying positions on a continuum between what he calls *minimalist* and *maximalist* definitions (McLaughlin, 1992). A *minimalist* understanding of citizenship education would be based upon a limited conception of the polity, which would be reduced simply to the identifiable institutions of political participation (the courts, parliament, voting, etc.). Such *minimalist* texts tend to deploy a didactic and factual pedagogy that stresses the straightforward communication of knowledge. *Maximalist* texts, on the other hand, have a broader conception of the polity that might include other social institutions and activities (such as questions of ideology and economic organisation) and might deploy a more progressive, child-centred pedagogy.

6 Gender and 'race' equality
Affirmative and transformative pedagogies of citizenship (1970–2000)

In this chapter, I consider the relationship between gender equality, pedagogy and citizenship. Until recently, citizenship studies and the study of gender and education appeared to have little mutual relevance (Dillabough and Arnot, 2001; Dillabough and Arnot, 2003), even though feminist political and educational theorists have addressed similar issues. What unites their interest is the tension between equality and difference. Embedded within the liberal democratic discourse are notions of universalism and undifferentiated abstract notions of citizenship. Feminist political theorists ask how such concepts of citizenship can simultaneously address issues of gender equality and gender difference. At the same time, but often independently, feminist educationalists have considered the same dilemma about how to educate pupils using gender equality as the goal, whilst simultaneously celebrating difference.

The aim of the chapter is to develop an analytic frame with which to explore the connections between gender and race equality, pedagogy and citizenship. Of particular value are Nancy Fraser's (1997b) distinctions between recognition and redistribution justice, and affirmative and transformative remedies. Her analysis identifies the tensions associated with gender as a 'bivalent collectivity' shaped by both cultural and economic structures and injustices. I extend her analysis by tracking the range of political remedies associated with the promotion of gender equality in education in the UK. The pedagogic aspects of these political remedies are contradictory and have their own momentum. My strategy is to consider two different periods in which gender remedies to social injustice were developed: first, the 1970s to 1990s, and second, the 1990s to the 2000s. I revisit these periods in light of the parallel developments around concepts of multiculturalism, anti-racism and the politics of difference which challenged gender approaches within education. The most recent debates around multicultural citizenships and gender have not led to new pedagogical approaches as such, although they appear to suggest that new commitment to a critical pedagogy of difference is required. I conclude by arguing for such a critical pedagogy of difference that is associated with an agenda based on the concept of pedagogic democratic rights.

Equality and difference as civic and pedagogic ideals

In the 1990s, feminist political theorists, especially in the UK and the United States, engaged directly with the political implications of a range of new social movements. These social movements challenged existing liberal democratic and civic republican notions of citizenship, emphasising their inability to address the diverse, complex, shifting terrain of subjectivities, identities and political identifications in the postmodern era. The multiple axes of social class, gender, 'race', ethnicity, disability, sexuality and religion, to name but a few, were understood to contest those definitions of citizenship grounded in Enlightenment categories and relations. Post-structural and postmodern approaches to the relationship between identity, agency and structure signalled the impossibility of locating individuals' identities within tightly bounded categories, hierarchies of power, easily identifiable structural edifices and abstracted ideals. The question which postmodern and post-structuralist feminism posed was whether liberal democratic and civic republican concepts of citizenship could become the foundation for identity politics, or whether such concepts of citizenship should be relegated to the past – especially given their increasingly exposed gendered biases.

There is not the space here to outline the scope, range and contributions to this rich debate (see Chapter 2). Of particular relevance to this discussion of pedagogy and citizenship, however, is the emphasis placed on the dilemmas associated with promoting simultaneously both *equality* and *difference*. In the eighteenth century, Mary Wollstonecraft drew attention to the fact that women could not obtain full citizenship as women, as individuals, because they were seen as sexually different from men (Siim, 2000: 33). The price of equality meant that women would have to become like men. Three centuries later, Anne Phillips (1993: 45) observed: 'When men and women are treated the same, it means women being treated as if they were men; when men and women are treated differently, the man remains the norm, against which the woman is peculiar, lacking, different' (quoted in Lister, 1997: 96).

The usual starting point for a full feminist analysis of the contemporary civic educational project therefore is to consider, first, the embedded gendered basis of modern citizenship. Carol Pateman's (1988, 1989) groundbreaking analysis of the *gender inequalities* associated with liberal democratic philosophy uncovered a range of assumptions about the separation and hierarchisation of male-public over female-private spheres; that the polity was to be governed by a brotherhood which controlled women through the sexual contract of marriage, and the exclusion of motherhood as a civic site (Arnot, 2004a). The role of education in transmitting this public-private distinction and its gendered associations through the curriculum, through teacher expectations and through the transmission of appropriate civic virtues, is pivotal to the reproduction of such forms of liberal democracy (see Chapters 3 and 4).

Equally important for education is the concept of *difference* which lies at the heart of feminist critiques of liberal democratic and civic republican notions of citizenship (Nussbaum, 1999). Shaila Benhabib (1996) argues that there is a deep 'epistemological deficit' in the liberal democratic concept of citizenship, which

Table 6.1 Male and female citizenship characteristics

Public, male, citizen	Private, female, non-citizen
Abstract, disembodied, mind	Particular, embodied, rooted in nature
Rational, able to apply dispassionate reason and standards of justice	Emotional, irrational, subject to desire and passion; unable to apply standards of justice
Impartial, concerned with public interest	Partial, preoccupied with private, domestic concerns
Independent, active, heroic and strong	Dependent, passive, weak
Upholding the realm of freedom, of the human	Maintaining the realm of necessity of the natural and repetitious

Source: Lister (1997: 69)

indicates that it would have to change fundamentally if it is to become valuable to those concerned with difference. Citizenship from an egalitarian perspective would need to accommodate all social cleavages, such as those of religion, social class, ethnicity, 'race' and sexuality, and be inclusive of 'other' social categories such as refugees and asylum seekers, migrants, travellers, etc. At the same time, feminist critics of the concept of citizenship have raised serious concerns about the *institutionalisation of gender difference* through essentialist gender discourses and the promotion of gender dualism (masculine and feminine). Masculinity and femininity are still strongly associated with a range of characteristics, many of which are interpreted as biological. Ruth Lister (1997: 69) characterises these stereotypical differences in Table 6.1 above.

The pervasiveness of these associations and homologies was often masked by a gender-blind/neutral liberal approach which ignored real differences in life experiences of groups of men and women, and the power relations within such groups. As Lister argues, there appeared to be little possibility of celebrating the multitude of identities, the specificity and diversity *within* each gender category and the different styles and experiences of citizenship of men and women. Removing binary divisions and recognising the particularity of different groups of men and women, girls and boys, may mean, however, that the concept of citizenship loses its universalistic elements and the celebration of a community of interest (Lister, 1997; Siim, 2000). The negative consequences of asserting particularity and specificity over and above universalism are thought to be many – the most notable being the fragmentation of the social order, the privileging of individual over collective agency or the creation of arbitrary and somewhat artificial groupings that can also generate essentialist notions of difference. Pluralistic models of citizenship may also leave unchallenged inequalities of power.

A particularly valuable way of conceptualising the problems of equality and difference was provided by Nancy Fraser's (1997b) distinction between two mutually distinct yet intertwined concepts of justice in a 'postsocialist' age. She differentiates between, on the one hand, understandings of socio-economic injustice 'rooted in the political-economic structure of society' (Fraser, 1997b: 13) and, on the other, cultural/symbolic injustice that is 'rooted in social patterns of representation, interpretation and communication' (p. 14). She also differentiates analytically between two different kinds of political remedies for these injustices, which she calls *redistribution* and *recognition*. I have extracted the descriptors of the two remedies below:

> *Redistribution* addresses the ways in which disadvantage is sustained in the socio-economic sphere through exploitation, economic marginalisation and deprivation by advocating a restructuring of the political economy through, for example, 'redistributing income, re-organising the division of labor' and more democratic decision-making.
>
> *Recognition* addresses issues such as cultural domination, non-recognition and disrespect by encouraging cultural or symbolic change. This may involve 'revaluing disrespected identities and the cultural products of maligned groups', 'recognizing and positively valorizing cultural diversity', transforming 'societal patterns of representation, interpretation and communication', thus changing people's 'sense of self'.
>
> (Fraser, 1997b: 15)

According to Fraser, redistribution and recognition strategies in relation to, say, social class and sexuality are relatively unproblematic since both redistribution and recognition have the same goal (i.e. that of removing discrimination). In contrast, the resolutions in relation to gender and 'race' are more complex. Fraser calls these *bivalent collectivities*. 'They are differentiated as collectivities by virtue of both the political-economic structure *and* the cultural valuational structure of society' (Fraser, 1997b: 19). In both these cases, the problem lies in the fact that, although redistributive justice encourages reformers to remove the socio-economic inequalities and disadvantages associated with gender and racial discrimination, the politics of recognition can lead to programmes which celebrate gender or 'race'/ethnic difference. Thus the degendering strategies in the economy are often counterposed to the regendering strategies to be found in the cultural sphere. This contradiction is exposed clearly in the tensions between affirmative-action programmes to redress race inequalities in the economy and affirmative multicultural programmes in schools. Similarly, equal-opportunity policies to remove gender as a segregating and allocatory device in the labour market may be counterposed by a commitment to work *with*, rather than against, gender difference by promoting, for example, either boy-friendly or girl-friendly schooling.

Fraser's discussion of this redistribution-recognition dilemma captures a major contemporary pedagogic challenge – schools today are expected to redistribute educational opportunities in the name of equality at the same time as recognising differences *between* the sexes and *within* each gender group. The overall goal from a liberal perspective is not to legitimate gender essentialisms but to use gender difference as a means of distributing educational opportunities. As we shall see in the next section, responses to these contradictory educational scenarios have developed around what Fraser called *affirmation* and *transformation* – in

142 *Gender and 'race' equality*

other words, different reform strategies used to address social injustice. Where affirmation aims at 'correcting inequitable outcomes of social arrangements without disturbing the underlying framework that generates them', transformative remedies aim at 'correcting inequitable outcomes precisely by restructuring the underlying generative framework' (Fraser, 1997b: 23). Below, I use this framework to illustrate the tensions associated with pedagogic reform in the UK in the late twentieth and early twenty-first centuries. I explore two phases in which very different remedies were offered to gender redistribution and recognition. The first phase focused predominantly on girls, and the second involved a 'boy turn' in education (Weaver-Hightower, 2003b). The dilemmas associated with gender inequality as bivalent collectivity are exposed in this analysis and are suggestive of the difficulties faced by those wishing to employ pedagogic reform to improve the quality and equity of citizenship.

Affirmative and transformative pedagogical approaches in the UK

The history of gender equality pedagogy in the UK is a good example of how the redistribution and recognition dilemma has been affected by the development of officially legitimated affirmative rather than transformative approaches, although the latter (even if marginalised) nevertheless have continued to make their presence felt in the educational arena throughout the last three decades. The first phase of gender equality reform can be summarised by adapting Nancy Fraser's matrix (Fraser, 1997b: 27), shown in Table 6.2.

Gender dualism was built into the framework of post-war English education and was seriously challenged in the 1960s by affirmative redistribution strategies. In the 1970s and 1980s, equal opportunities policies and anti-discrimination tackled economic forms of sex discrimination. Affirmative recognition, however, focused on the shifting of attitudes rather than structures and was reinforced through pedagogic/curricular projects aiming to create 'girl-friendly schooling' (see Arnot *et al.* (1999) for descriptions of projects). This approach was supported and developed in the UK by a quasi-decentralised educational system in which teachers had considerable autonomy in relation to the curriculum. Although both these affirmation remedies highlighted the disadvantages faced by women in the economy, the public sphere and the home, the degendering strategies associated with redistribution conflicted with the use of the category 'gender' for pedagogic and school reform.

Affirmative redistribution remedies (Table 6.2: Cell A1) provided the radical challenge to gender as a factor in gaining access to economic and social capital, whilst affirmative recognition strategies (Table 6.2: Cell B1) offered proactive liberal and radical feminist gendering strategies which emphasised the importance of gender categories (what Connell (1987) called *categoricalism*) and girls' specific educational needs. Single-sex classes in mixed schools and girl-only positive action programmes, especially in vocational and academic courses in sciences and technology, addressed the anxieties and 'special needs' of girls as a group. Schools challenged male sexist language, behaviour and values, and encouraged pupils and staff to value girls' achievements. Girls were offered opportunities to take up leadership positions, widen their horizons and consider a non-traditional range of employment. Teachers asked girls to think critically and reflexively about what it meant to be a woman in society and to consider new ways of 'being feminine'. The use of gender categories within radical feminist pedagogic initiatives, which explored women's ways of knowing, their knowledge, reasoning and values, reinforced the need to focus positive action on improving girls' – as distinct from boys' – chances. In that sense, recognition was of group rights rather than of individual rights. Teachers were encouraged to work with gender in designing anti-sexist projects to value and affirm female experiences and standpoints. Affirmative programmes therefore contained the contradiction of supporting universalism at the same time as privileging traditional particularistic gender dualisms. One result was that some girls (especially white middle-class girls) flourished in the educational system, achieving higher numbers of educational qualifications at 16 and 18 than boys, and even high entry levels to university courses (Arnot *et al.*, 1999).

During this period, alternative transformative resolutions to the equality/difference debate were also put forward. These involved more radical versions of socialist and black feminism, which sought to break down the underlying structures that created gender and racial divisions (Table 6.2: Cell C1). Strong redistributive principles based on socialist/neo-marxist understandings were evoked to challenge capitalist hierarchies, exploitative social relations of production, and labour markets segregated and segmented by sex and race. Social reproduction theory exposed the underlying economic conditions behind gender dualisms which restricted, if not negated, the impact of affirmative redistribution and recognition strategies. The implications for pedagogy were found in the replacement of positive action/equal opportunities initiatives with critical pedagogies, such as anti-sexist and anti-racist programmes that exposed and challenged the principles of social and educational organisation. Although, at that point, the universalist principles of educational equality were still holding, transformative recognition strategies were developed to support white and minority ethnic working-class girls' cultural struggles (Arnot, 2002). Paradoxically, in the UK these transformative gender equality strategies (Table 6.2: Cell D1) were not really practice-oriented, since they tended to focus on the development of a critical feminist sociology rather than on teachers' professional needs (see Arnot *et al.*, 1999). Culley and Portuges (1985) and later Coffey and Delamont (2000) were exceptions to this rule. In

Table 6.2 Gender remedies and pedagogic strategies (1970s to 1980s)

	Affirmation	*Transformation*
Redistribution	Universalism Equal opportunities Positive Action (Cell A1)	Socialist/black materialism Union activism (Cell C1)
Recognition	Particularism Girl-friendly schooling (Cell B1)	Critical pedagogies Deconstructivism (Cell D1)

contrast, North American feminist pedagogues were well represented amongst those developing an appropriate transformative recognition approach (Brookes, 1992; Grumet, 1988; Mayberry and Rose, 1999).

Initially, these transformative redistributive remedies, despite the depth of their critical analysis, did not easily engage with the notion of difference, for which they were strongly criticised by post-structuralists and postmodernists (Dillabough and Arnot, 2001). However, notions of a 'pedagogy of difference' emerged out of the deconstructionist work of feminist post-structuralists such as Madeleine Grumet (1988), Patti Lather (1991), Francis Gore (1993) and Bronwyn Davies (1989, 1997), who worked with, rather than against, the multiplicity of female identities, identifications, subjectivities and multiple agency (Table 6.2: Cell D1). The remedy was transformative recognition strategies, which were very different again from transformative redistribution strategies. Whilst one set (Table 6.2: Cell C1) of strategies privileged class struggles of specific social groups (e.g. marginalised girls), the other set of strategies challenged essentialist notions of social class, gender and ethnicity. Both approaches understood gender categories to be socially constructed, and worked on and with by individuals within the micro-political environments. However, the pedagogic task of post-structuralist deconstructivism (Table 6.2: Cell D1) was to explore the normalising processes, the regulative devices and subject positioning of individuals in relation to such social discourses.

The emphasis was now focused more on the social psychological processes of identity formation than on radical economic restructuring. For example, Valerie Walkerdine (1990) explored the construction of the modern liberal subject through 'schoolgirl fictions' whilst Bronwyn Davies (1989) analysed how gender dualisms shaped the resistances and responses of young children within the pedagogic space. Her research complemented post-structuralist youth cultural research, which exposed the hierarchies and multiplicities within adolescent masculinities and femininities (Mac an Ghaill, 1994). Young men and women, in these later analyses, were shown to be socially positioned through a range of complex pedagogic discourses, only some of which drew upon egalitarian principles. This new research employed a range of deconstructivist methodologies which emphasised the transformative power of narrative, biography, story telling and the eliciting of silenced voices (Arnot, 2006; Lather, 1991). The pedagogic work of deconstruction had begun but, apart from specific feminist-led initiatives, it largely failed to forge strong links with the teaching profession engaged in affirmative strategies (Table 6.2: Cell B1) and with the transformative redistribution politics of the 1980s, which focused on inequalities of wealth, poverty and social exclusion (Table 6.2: Cell C1) (Haywood and Mac an Ghaill, 1997).

In both the affirmative and the transformative remedies of this period, the contradictions between the equality and difference were not resolved. Whilst affirmative approaches were unsure about how to improve girls' chances in life, they promoted a complex range of degendering and regendering strategies. Girls were the problem and their education was the solution. The transformative remedies of the time failed largely to resolve the tensions between materialist and deconstructionist agendas (Haywood and Mac an Ghaill, 1997). Where the former relied on a radical neo-marxist analysis of gendered power relations, the latter relied on a Foucauldian project around gendered discourses, positionings, regulation and normalisation. There was therefore considerable debate about what constituted feminist pedagogies and how they differed from critical pedagogies (Ellsworth, 1989; Gore, 1993).

The 'boy turn' and new affirmations around redemptive equality

The dilemmas that Fraser associated with bivalent collectivities are reconstructed in the most recent phase of pedagogic reform, which was particularly associated with boys' education. In the early 1990s, the UK educational system was massively overhauled in the name of standards and excellence. The neo-liberal agenda employed the language of egalitarianism to legitimate strong competitive performance cultures in schools and marketisation of education. Out of the statistical exposure of gender difference in examination results came the evidence of boys' underachievement and the construction of a new category, 'the failing boy' (Epstein *et al.*, 1998; Raphael Reed, 1999). Gender educational policy and research took a 'boy turn' (Weaver-Hightower, 2003b), colonising the affirmative recognition remedies used to encourage girls in the early 1980s, inverting them in the name of boys. The matrix looks different under the new scenario (see Table 6.3 below).

The redistribution-recognition dilemma in the last two decades is arguably now even more acute in relation to gender equality. Since the 1990s, gender-equality policy was characterised by affirmative redistributive principles relating specifically to women's position in the economy. New Labour used far more intervention into industry in the name of economic flexibility, labour-market neutrality and better family/work balance to address female economic disadvantage (Arnot and Miles, 2005). The government promoted wide-range affirmative strategies (Table 6.3: Cell A2) to encourage industry to improve its record on employing women, reduce sex discrimination at work and encourage women into the knowledge economy through the opening up of science, technology and ICT (Arnot and Miles, 2005). However, this economic rationalism was in sharp contrast to the predominant educational emphasis on male underachievement and the re-assertion of gender dualism in pedagogic thinking (Table 6.3: Cell B2). The dominant redistribution and recognition politics today were both affirmative but arguably even more contradictory in their extensive particularism – where the first focused on women's needs, while the latter focused on boys' educational requirements.

In this new phase, affirmative recognition (Table 6.3: Cell B2) became the 'boys' education debate'. Recognition of diversity came to mean recognition of the needs of male pupils in similar fashion, and sometimes even in similar language, to that used previously to discuss girls' underachievement (cf. Table 6.2, Cell B1). Although little public recognition was given to liberal feminist approaches of the 1980s – indeed, these were even seen as part of the problem and cause of male underachievement (Arnot and Miles, 2005) – many of the same pedagogic strategies were converted to a new use (Martino *et al.*, 2005). Thus single-sex classes, the recruitment of male teachers (Mills *et al.*, 2004), role-modelling, sex-role socialisation and 'therapeutic' pedagogies (Kenway and Fitzclarence, 1997) were called into play to help boys cope with the problems of their (relative) academic failure. The construct of 'boys' underachievement' masked social, economic and cultural differences between boys and failed therefore to challenge the power relations associated with hegemonic masculinities, with working-class male disadvantage and male power over women.

New affirmative recognition remedies to the problem of equating equality and difference in the 1990s have been labelled as 'redemptive equality' (Foster, 1994, quoted in Arnot and Miles, 2005) or 'recuperative masculinity politics' (Lingard, 2003). According to these authors, such strategies represented an attempt to retrieve male educational and social advantage, employing gender essentialisms to do so. In a pressurised performance culture, teachers draw upon their threshold knowledge of gender differences amongst boy and girl learners to adapt their pedagogic styles, classroom strategies, and to set up new gender initiatives. Teachers have been found to have strong convictions about what makes a boy a boy, and how boys are different from girls, in nearly all respects.

In schools and classrooms, these new affirmative recognition remedies (Table 6.3: Cell B2) therefore can reinforce masculine cultures at a time, ironically, when hegemonic masculinity as a gender form has been revealed by sociological research to be one of the major features of male resistance strategies (Weaver-Hightower, 2003a). Traditional (even a macho) masculinity, which was left unchallenged by liberal affirmative politics in the previous decades, is a device which boys use to cope with oppressively competitive managerialist and commodified schooling and the destruction of traditional working-class communities (Arnot *et al.*, 1999; Mac an Ghaill, 1994). Research suggests that, rather than deconstruct this masculinity, teachers often work with preconceived social and/or biological discourses around gender difference, which are fed less by observations about what is essentially 'female' and more now by what is essentially 'male' (i.e. not female). This image can call up notions of, for example, male preferred learning and assessment styles, literacy problems and low levels of emotional and psychological development. Male biological vulnerabilities merge with psychological insecurities

Table 6.3 Gender remedies and pedagogic strategies (1990s to 2000s)

	Affirmation	*Transformation*
Redistribution	Particularism Positive Action for women in the economy (Cell A2)	Universalism Social Inclusion/Exclusion (Cell C2)
Recognition	Particularism Boys' education debate (Cell B2)	Critical pedagogies of difference Pedagogic democratic rights (Cell D2)

and immaturity, and both feed, and are fed, into observed impressions about male learning difficulties, motivations and disaffection.

Affirmative recognition is also often conceptualised around a contrast between 'male' and 'female' learner identities. The research review which my colleagues and I conducted for the inspectorate (OFSTED) (Arnot *et al.*, 1998) suggested that there might be some gender differences in the preferred learning styles of boys and girls. Our summary of the research evidence suggested that 'girls are more attentive in class and more willing to learn. They do better on sustained tasks that are open-ended, process-based, related to realistic situations, and require pupils to think for themselves' (Arnot *et al.*, 1998: 28). Girls were also found to overrate the difficulty of particular subjects, finding timed end-of-course examinations less congenial. Teachers believe that coursework favours girls, but our review suggested that other factors (including syllabus selection) may be more important.

Research has indicated that 'boys show greater adaptability to more traditional approaches to learning which require memorising abstract, unambiguous facts and rules that have to be acquired quickly. They also appear to be more willing to sacrifice deep understanding, which requires sustained effort, for correct answers achieved at speed' (Arnot *et al.*, 1998: 28–9). Boys have been found to do better on multiple-choice papers, whatever the subject. However, without a more thorough analysis of *which* girls and *which* boys employ such learning styles, gender difference can become a self-fulfilling prophecy. In the new ethos of targeting underperformance, gender blindness (gender neutrality) is no longer understood to be helpful (Arnot and Gubb, 2001). Teachers are encouraged to investigate, reflect and work constructively with such assumed or observed learning differences.

In the meantime, research has suggested that any differences in learner identities, in preferred learning styles and behaviour are more likely to be a result of gender identities than pedagogy (Severiens and Ten Dam, 1997). Boys and girls have been found to negotiate their learning identities and preferred learning styles in relation to particular subjects; the social context of their peer group and family culture, and complex relational classroom cultures which define what are appropriate and 'safe' masculine or feminine approaches to learning (Skelton, 2001). Also whilst upper-middle-class girls, for example, have been observed exploiting a range of learning styles and structures to their academic advantage, in sharp contrast, working-class lower-achieving pupils are found struggling to keep control over their learning and trying, with difficulty, to communicate with their teachers about their learning needs (Arnot and Reay, 2006a, 2006b). There is a danger that, as James and Myhill (2004) point out, the two groups become caricatures of the 'successful' female pupil and the 'failing' male student, with the wide range of other learning behaviours being ignored.

As a result of affirmative recognition remedies which are boy-focused (Table 6.3: Cell B2), researchers record pedagogic and curriculum shifts in the UK. Arnot and Gubb (2001), Younger *et al.* (1999) and Younger and Warrington (2005) have identified boy-friendly pedagogic approaches to the teaching of English, modern languages, literacy, etc. There is now greater structuring of learning as seen in, for example, the setting of more targets and competitions, the removal of free revision periods and study breaks, and increased mentoring, monitoring and surveillance. Arnot and Gubb's findings suggest that there is also a shift away from progressive child-centred pedagogies of the 1970s/1980s in mainstream teaching, although there is evidence of increased pastoral provision and more delegation of responsibility to boys in some schools (Arnot and Gubb, 2001). Paradoxically, such affirmative recognition approaches remasculinise schooling, even though there are concerns that this approach will impact negatively on girls and that female students' academic success might be damaged. And the increased masculinisation of schooling, with its tighter surveillance, potentially increases male anxieties in a competitive context in which gender identities are based on being successful (Arnot, 2004b; Skelton, 2001).

Multiculturalism, ethnicity and gender: parallel developments and complexities

It is important to recognise that although these debates about equality and difference in relation to gender equality appear to have a linear and somewhat evolutionary feel, they were frequently disturbed and interrupted by parallel concerns about the schooling of minority ethnic youth in the UK. Over the last four decades, remedies and strategies in relation to race and ethnic inequality have run alongside, in contradiction to gender remedies to social injustice. Indeed, in terms of current transformative agendas, one could argue that the discussions about recognition of difference have gone much further in the field of ethnicity than in that of gender. Fraser reminds us that 'race', like gender, is a bivalent collectivity where there is also a tension between the need to encourage redistributive justice in political and economic spheres and the need to celebrate pluralism and difference in the cultural sphere. There have been attempts to encourage higher educational achievement and economic participation amongst particular minority communities, whilst at the same time reconstructing the nature of British cultural identity and particularly white identities encouraged by schools. These are not easy tensions to resolve, especially in deracialised classrooms where cultures of excellence exclude rather than include (Gillborn and Youdell, 1999).

However, of even greater importance here is the absence in Nancy Fraser's analysis of how two such bivalent collectivities relate to each other. The problems teachers face daily are those of trying to relate two such contradictory equality agendas and remedies within their classrooms (whilst, at the same time, working with universal notions of the normality and 'the pupil'). The interface between gender and race equality strategies within education has always been difficult, not least since the experiences of different groups of girls in schools are diverse, and only some girls experience racial/ethnic disadvantage and the process of 'othering', whilst others achieve considerable success in performance cultures. Indeed the hierarchisation of girls' cultural styles often entails distancing of elite girls from those seen as dirty or dangerous (Kenway, 1990; Arnot *et al.*, 1999). Femininity, like masculinity, is not ethnically neutral – indeed, these gender identities are often at the core of ethnic or racial difference.

Since the late 1970s, gender pedagogies therefore have been challenged by the parallel development of pedagogies which seek to promote sexual and race equality. Whilst concerns about sexual inequalities, particularly discrimination against homosexual and lesbian pupils, were addressed largely and with great commitment by radical feminist pedagogies (Epstein and Johnson, 1998) the relationship between multicultural, anti-racist pedagogies was complicated by the latter's challenge to anti-sexist pedagogies. Black feminism that emerged in the 1980s (cf. Table 6.2, Cell C1) brought to the fore critiques of the whiteness of such gender analysis and its pedagogical concerns around degendering and critiques of male power over and above the need to address institutional racisms. These critiques in the UK made teachers aware that the trilogy of 'race', gender and social class needed to be brought together, even if in most cases there was little pedagogic integration.

In the period between the 1970s and the 1990s, the development of specific affirmative recognition pedagogies around ethnicity and 'race' paralleled mainstream gender pedagogies. Multiculturalism as a curriculum strategy, which was put forward as the means of addressing ethnic and racial inequalities in society, was particularly strong at this time (Arnot, 1985b). Developed by teachers, it made an assumption that the inequalities of ethnic achievement in schools was strongly associated with an assumed negative self-image of black and minority ethnic students. The aim, therefore, was to raise the confidence of such students by teaching elements of their cultures within the curriculum and representing it within school cultures and rituals. This affirmative recognition approach was not dissimilar in style to that of girl-friendly schooling (Table 6.2: Cell B1). Just as teachers tried to teach 'female and gender concerns' in most school subjects, 'other cultures' were taught in multicultural dimensions of subjects such as history, music, religion and even maths and science. However, although attempts were made during this period to link both these affirmative strategies, there was relatively little debate about the practicalities of simultaneously promoting affirmative recognition strategies for the range of different marginalised social groups, and girl-friendly schooling, at one and the same time.

During this period the development of critical anti-racist pedagogies challenged such multicultural approaches not only for being shaped by liberal white concerns but also, even more problematically, for appearing to address structural racial inequalities when not doing so (cf. Arnot (1985a) and (1985b) for a full discussion of this critique). Biting critiques of the deceptions of multiculturalism resonated through the work of, for example, Maureen Stone (1981), David Gillborn (1990) and Barry Troyna (1991). Critical pedagogies around notions of the racialised subject, racism and anti-racism, and critical analyses of government approaches to immigration and racial discrimination, encouraged transformative curricula that exposed the imperial and colonial legacies still shaping society and schooling. The connections with critical gender pedagogies were tentative and often focused particularly on the strategic responses to the added burdens of racial inequality of African-Caribbean, Indian, Pakistani and Bangladeshi girls. Teachers were encouraged to rethink their responses to girls' ethnic cultures (e.g. arranged marriages, separation from boys during adolescence) but it was more likely they assumed that recognition of gender difference (whether affirmative or transformative) would work for all girls who were not achieving in school, whatever their ethnic background.

1990s to 2000s: rethinking difference

In the second period (1990s to 2000s), this relationship between these two 'bivalent collectivities' changed. The 'boy turn' was particularly significant since the majority of failing boys were found to be white working-class boys and/or African-Caribbean or Muslim Pakistani and Bangladeshi boys (cf. Archer (2003); Sewell (1997)). Under New Labour, the realities of social exclusion of black and minority ethnic pupils undermined their agenda of delivering choice, standards and excellence to all. The lack of social cohesion associated with 9/11, the rise of terrorism on home soil, city 'riots' and the high levels of disaffection of male youth all focused attention on the failure of government to create social cohesion at national and community levels. On the whole though, such attention was more likely to be paid to minority ethnic boys rather than minority ethnic girls (whether African-Caribbean or Muslim).

It is an understatement to say that pedagogical implications of the history of multiculturalism, anti-racism and latterly the study of racialised subjectivities of youth are extremely complex. By the 1990s, teachers could be forgiven for being confused about the integration of gender and race equality remedies. The tensions and contradictions between equality and difference *between* – not just *within* – these agendas was especially complicated. The processes of gendering, degendering and then regendering since the 1970s, and the processes in the same period of deracialisation, racialisation and then deracialisation, associated with the New Racism of the 1990s, have never adequately been put together. Whilst academic researchers have encouraged teachers to be aware of the depth of gendered racialised identities within education, on the whole, they did not outline strategic pedagogic processes that would address such identities or find ways of challenging localised 'white' identities of both male and female youth. Official policy also severely curtailed opportunities for both trainee and practising teachers to study such social dynamics and inequalities.

The concern to give all equal rights, yet recognise cultural difference and group rights outside of the framework of liberal freedoms, has been addressed by a number of leading political theorists (less so by educationalists). Zinn and Dill (1996) provided a useful review of feminist responses to such political theorising of difference. Using Fraser's framework, we could argue that the emergence of what Zinn and Dill refer to as 'difference feminism' challenges the universalism of affirmative redistribution strategies and the essentialism of affirmative recognition remedies of the 1970s to 1990s around notions of the 'woman' (Table 6.2: Cells A1 and B1). Zinn and Dill note the ongoing concern of feminists that difference may have replaced equality, on the one hand, and on the other that difference had become commodified (hooks, 1992) – reduced to 'mere pluralism' (hooks, 1992:

20). Feminist theorists have also pointed to the danger that too much recognition of 'exotic' difference can in fact fail to recognise power relations underlying difference, and as a result see the latter as 'the problem'. Zinn and Dill identify what they see as the better way forward, through the notion of a *multiracial feminism* that both draws upon socialist feminist thinking (see Table 6.2: Cell C1) about power relations, and takes account of the diverse voiced experiences of different groups of women of colour.

The work of Iris Marion Young (1990) is a case in point. She argues that the tensions between atomist individualist concepts of justice and the alternative, of collectivist emphasis on group rights and the need to have special treatment for particular groups, should not result in a stalemate. This can only happen if the politics of difference moved outside notions of 'otherness' – what is needed is a *radical democratic pluralism* that is open, flexible, open-ended.

> Difference now comes to mean not otherness, exclusive opposition, but specificity, variation, heterogeneity. Difference names relations of similarity and dissimilarity that can be reduced to neither coextensive identity nor nonoverlapping otherness. (Young, quoted in Dallmayr, 1996: 284)

However, the sheer diversity and plurality of different intellectual and political positions; the shifting conceptions of what 'race' means; the intersectionalities (cross-cutting hierarchies) and the relational nature of domination and subordination; and the complex relationships between structure and agency associated with multiracial feminism, arguably has made it difficult to summarise what sort of pedagogy such multiracial feminism might stand for. The necessity of hearing different voices, finding different notions of truth and different experiences of the world, which academic feminism has made possible through qualitative methodologies, appears to be the main pedagogic device to achieve this goal, although it is not always clear how such voices reach the teaching profession and inform its pedagogic practice.

By the late 1990s, the early research of black feminist educationalists in the UK such as Heidi Mirza (1992), Cecile Wright (1987), and social and political theorists such as Patricia Hill Collins (1990), bell hooks (1992), Shaila Benhabib (2002) and Chandra Talpade Mohanty (1991) had challenged images and stereotyping of 'third world women', uncovered the experiences of minority ethnic girls in schools, and pointed to the discriminatory gender practices based on white middle-class norms. Their deconstruction of gender through the lens of race alerted gender theorists to the ways in which the gender categories that were used in schooling and in social and political definitions of citizenship were deeply racialised. The 'Othering' of female and male black and minority cultures within the political sphere was shown to have shaped the structures and processes of the educational system and its classrooms. Pedagogic processes create young female and male minority ethnic students as marginalised citizens before they have even entered adulthood. Their experiences of social exclusion reflect the ambiguities of a multi-ethnic Britain and their responses to such exclusion. We have been shown the subtle but profound interfaces between ethnic/racial experiences and particular forms of masculinity and femininity (e.g. Mac an Ghaill (1994); Nayak and Kehily (2007), Archer (2003)). Gender identities were demonstrably part of the processes of ethnic civic inclusion and exclusion.

At the same time as such previously silenced voices became part of the educational terrain of the early twenty-first century, gender concerns about the value of multiculturalism have also captured attention. Susan Moller Okin's (1999) attempt to tackle the contradictions between gender and minority rights in her book *Is Multiculturalism Bad for Women?* has been particularly controversial. She argues that multiculturalism and feminism are not easily compatible, especially if the former leads to greater inequality between men and women. Arguably, multiculturalism should address issues of gender and ensure equal rights for women, particularly what she calls the 'realistic rights to exit' their group so as to become 'mistresses of their own destiny' (Okin, 2003). The argument has particular resonance for pedagogy since, as Okin points out, countries with the strongest patriarchal traditions are often those with the largest gap between male and female literacy. Arguably a redistributive strategy that was affirmative would be to allow individuals 'exit rights from a culture of origin' – thus girls would and could be encouraged through education to make the transition out of their cultures of origin in the name of individual rights and freedom. Anne Phillips (2002) describes all the feminist objections to Okin's position, especially the dangers of judging the claims of different cultural groups in terms of pre-ordained notions of universal rights, or monolithic notions of culture that take for granted forms of male dominance. Phillips takes the line that, instead, the three principles of *harm, equality* and *choice* could be used to discriminate between the gender impact of different group practices and cultures – concepts that, like Nussbaum's notion of capability, could in time become new transformative recognition concepts in education.[1]

From the point of view of gender equality, pedagogy and citizenship, the current picture is only just emerging. In the UK, multicultural and anti-racist pedagogies were marginalised by the 1988 Education Reform Act with the latter's emphasis on pupils as consumers/clients, irrespective of their culture and social location (Arnot and Blair, 1993). Concern about ethnicity, this time particularly in relation to liberal and democratic concepts of citizenship, also began to be heard.

The new debate around multiculturalism suggests that social equality and social justice are unlikely to be achieved through a universal notion of citizenship in which difference is hidden, if not neglected. Yet the form of citizenship education in the curriculum of secondary and primary education in the UK does not make clear how difference (particularly ethnic and religious differences) should be recognised and respected. Concern has focused on the ways diversity within the UK was to be linked to the concept of national identity and, in particular, Britishness; to the universal ideas associated with citizenship virtues and moral values; and to issues of social justice and racial/ethnic equality. Archaud (2003) argues that, although the Final Report of the Advisory Group on Citizenship (known as the Crick Report) (1998) was keen to promote a sense of belonging amongst all young people, it put forward a notion of citizenship that relied upon the idea of universal values, such as autonomy and a shared civic identity, as the common ground to be shared by different ethnic and religious groups. Rather than tackle the realities of diversity within the UK and the different values, identities and interpretations of freedom, this Report encouraged a communal identity that could be deeply problematic to such groups. Archaud notes in particular those minority cultures that believed in and practised gender difference and inequality, particularly within domestic and private lives. Such gender inequalities, if recognised in citizenship as part of diversity, would undermine values of commonality, equality and justice.

Various pedagogic solutions to these dilemmas have been proposed. The Parekh Report on *The Future of Multi-Ethnic Britain* (Runnymede Trust, 2000), for example, recognised the ongoing 'conflicting demands of equality and difference as well as those of social cohesion and respect for minority identities' (Runnymede Trust, 2004) and suggested a new transformative recognition strategy based on what it calls a *pluralist human rights agenda* (Runnymede Trust, 2004: 4). In order to promote this agenda in schools, the Runnymede Trust published *Complementing Teachers* (2003), offering teachers guidance on how to promote race equality in schools through the curriculum; apparently some 2000 institutions have used such guidance. Other pedagogic strategies include the setting up of the Real History Directory (www.realhistories.org.uk), which gives teachers online learning resources about cultural diversity in the UK and encourages them to use citizenship lessons 'to provide human rights, opposition to racist beliefs and behaviour and knowledge of global interdependence' (Runnymede Trust, 2004: 6). The new strategy for addressing the tensions between equality and difference is to create community cohesion, a transformative goal which relies upon a critical analysis of the national narrative – the dominant stories in Britain about itself. As part of this rethink, the concept of 'difference' itself has to be rethought:

> Homogeneity in the so-called majority is a myth ... so is the idea that 'minorities' have more in common with each other than they do with people in the so-called majority ... All communities are changing and all are complex, with internal diversity and disagreements. Neither 'minority' communities nor 'majority' communities are static. (Runnymede Trust, 2004: 6)

Difference here is no longer conceptualised as the contrast between static majority and minority cultures, but rather in terms of what could be considered a post-structuralism/postmodern recognition of the 'complexity of identity'.

Exemplars of a new transformative approach, which focuses more on identity and belonging than on educational practice, can be found in the recent report on *Dual Citzenship: British, Islamic or Both?* (Ameli and Merali, 2004) for the Islamic Human Rights Commission[2] that argues that the education of the citizen now needs not just to cover rights and obligations, but also to encourage recognition of religious difference and the emotional elements of belonging. If it does not do so, the report argues, long-term social fragmentation will result. The transformative strategies that engage with these two elements require government-led policies that address the 'common Muslim experience in the UK, which is characterised by

154 Gender and 'race' equality

demonisation, discrimination and aggressive targeting by government, media and policy makers' (Ameli and Merali, 2004: 3). Muslim respondents in this UK study reported that they were still 'outsiders' experiencing a lack of respect. The study recommended a range of transformative redistributive policies which encourage:

- anti-Muslim foreign policy;
- an awareness of Islamophobia, the climate of fear and racism;
- a deeper understanding of Muslims;
- the facilitation of Muslim religious practices/education;
- equal involvement of all in society;
- greater participation of the Muslim community in political processes;
- facilitation of engagement with government. (Ameli and Merali, 2004: 1–2)

Whilst these debates clearly are of great importance to both minority women and men, they might still not resolve the problem of how teachers might address the gender relations *within* minority as well as majority cultures.

These new-century debates about gender, ethnicity and multiculturalism offer important insights into the connections (albeit underdeveloped) between pedagogy and citizenship.[3] Below I have attempted to use Fraser's dual system to map the changing nature of the debates I discussed in this section. Table 6.4 offers at minimum the chance to discriminate between the promotion of liberal rights as the pedagogic terrain of affirmative action (in relation to redistribution and recognition). In contrast the transformative pedagogies emerging in relation to the politics of difference, although often spoken of in terms of the language of rights, engage more with concerns of social solidarity, cohesion, belonging and the need to rethink the concept of 'difference'.

A critical pedagogy of difference

The continued presence, particularly in the academic world, of transformative redistribution and recognition remedies for gender and race equality (Table 6.3: Cells C2 and D2; Table 6.4: Cells C3, C4, D3 and D4) suggests that the debate about transformative pedagogies still sustains a momentum, even if it is confused and confusing. This is not surprising given the economic and political reforms of the late twentieth century and the schizoid agendas (Bernstein, 2000) represented by neo-liberalism. Egalitarian discourses have been used by neo-liberal reforms to mask their unequal social effects (Arnot and Miles, 2005). The re-emergence of social class on the academic agenda retrieves, to some extent, the materialist analysis found in the social democratic era of the 1970s and 1980s in the UK.

Current transformative redistribution approaches towards gender equality (Table 6.4: Cell C2) allow attention to focus again on economic disadvantage and more general social exclusion. This has highlighted, for example, the large numbers of girls excluded from school (Osler and Vincent, 2004) as well as girls who do not fit the normalised model of the good pupil; for example, pregnant schoolgirls (Arnot and Miles, 2005). In the UK each year more than 10,000 pupils, mainly black and white working-class boys, are excluded from schools (Gillborn and Mirza, 2000), with major economic consequences. Despite such evidence however, as Baker *et al.* (2004) point out, there is a denial of class inequality within society and within schools that

> leaves the attitudes of students and teachers in relation to class inequality untouched. There is no non-stigmatised nomenclature for the injustice of class when issues arise ... They lack a vocabulary-of-analysis to name class-based inequalities, thereby allowing them to persist unchallenged over time. (Baker *et al.*, 2004: 156)

As we have seen, contemporary transformative recognition strategies are still developing in relation to the politics of difference that emerged in the late 1990s and which have found new forms of expression in relation to citizenship. Now, the principle of social inclusion requires integrative strategies that can consciously address power as well as difference. Teacher expectations about different boys' abilities have been found to affect their diagnosis of special needs (especially behavioural and emotional difficulties), learning support provision, and disciplining strategies (expulsions, suspensions) (citations in Arnot *et al.*, 1998). The level of bullying reported by pupils in the UK also raises concern about teachers' responses to such incidents, especially when they involve boys. Transformative gender remedies now consider how to challenge the dominance of hegemonic masculinity (Arnot, 2004b) that is associated with male insecurities and vulnerabilities, and can be aggravated by competitive educational environments. The performance of masculinity affects those boys whose masculinity is policed by other boys,

Table 6.4 Minority ethnic remedies and pedagogies strategies (1970s to 2000s)

	Affirmation	*Transformation*
1970s to 1990s		
Redistribution	Universalism Equal Opportunities (Cell A3)	Institutional Racism Race Equality (Cell C3)
Recognition	Multiculturalism Anti-Racist pedagogies (Cell B3)	Deconstructivism/Black feminism Multiracial Feminisms (Cell D3)
1990s to 2000s		
Redistribution	Particularism/Group Rights Multicultural Citizenship (Cell A4)	Inclusion/Exclusion Community cohesion and solidarity (Cell C4)
Recognition	Targetting minority boys 'Right to exit' from culture of origin (Cell B4)	Pluralist Human Rights Critical Interculturalism Differentiated Citizenship (Cell D4)

as well as girls who are used as counterpoints in the construction of aggressive masculinities. The consequences of heterosexual masculinity as a gender form are felt by many groups of pupils and tend to benefit only the few. However, whilst post-structuralist deconstructivism offers superb analyses of all such phenomena, it is not clear that the relay of hegemonic masculinities in schools is being seriously challenged by this tradition.

In the last few years, there has been increasing interest in moving deconstructionist agendas forward by linking them to a reconstructed 'pedagogy of difference'. This concept, although not well defined, can draw upon the range of critical pedagogic traditions (socialist, liberationist pedagogy, post-structuralist feminism, postmodernism) and link to political analyses about the recognition of difference. Many of the current understandings of what this might mean in the 'real world' of the classroom are discussed by Reynolds and Trehan (2001). For example, teachers should avoid irreconcilable fragmentation whilst searching for consensus in the classroom. They should emphasise the value of learning about the significance of differences, avoiding what Ellsworth (1989) described as a failure to confront the dynamics of subordination or to see the significance of silences, the hierarchies of social status already in the classroom or to make any assumption about teachers', as opposed to students', expertise in critical thinking. Key to this notion of a pedagogy of difference is an understanding of the classroom as the real world in which students and teachers employ their everyday strategies of resisting or reinforcing inequalities. These authors link their idea of pedagogy of difference to Giddens's (1994) notion of cosmopolitanism, in which people appreciate one another's integrity and construct mutual intelligent relationships; and to Young's (1986) notion of linking differently identified groups and giving support to their challenges to dominant groups in more public spaces (Young, 1986: 369).

A critical deconstructionist politics of difference can, however, go further. For example, it can encourage transformed understandings of what it means to be 'male', what it means to be 'a good pupil', what it means to be, for example, 'literate'. Bronwyn Davies' (1997) influential notion of *critical literacy* offers pedagogic methods that deconstruct diversity and power in children's books. Here, the goal for educationalists is to identify, create, circulate and legitimate new stories around boys, girls, literacy and schooling. New connections can also be made between traditionally separate masculine and feminine characteristics and spaces, and between familiar elements in boys' worlds – between science, technology, creativity, between humour, assertiveness, reflection and different forms of literacy.

Francis (2000) found in her research that female pupils in English schools no longer appear to associate gender with ability and rely therefore much less heavily on essentialist discourses, even if they recognise the problems boys face in schools. The use of gender difference in pedagogy, which allocates different types of behaviour to either masculinity or femininity, takes us a step backwards. It can lead, in fact, to offering support to those boys who still hold on to strong notions of gender duality in order to distance themselves from those boys whom they consider to be too learning-oriented. By characterising such educationally successful boys as 'effeminate', the lower-achieving boys can affirm their own masculinities. Thus, rather than promote gender strategies for one sex, Francis argues that a critical pedagogy would teach the *discourse of gender* to pupils, encouraging them to engage critically in the allocation of traits and behaviour to one gender, and its consequences (Francis, 1998: 139). This critical deconstruction of difference would become the curriculum topic, not just the pedagogic methodology. Gender difference should not be dismissed, but recognised for the part it plays in the construction of young people's gender identities and performance, and the significance it might have in their social and emotional worlds. Similarly, Baker *et al.* (2004: 154–5) argue that what is needed is a systematic education about social class, and how the forms of cultural non-recognition or misrepresentations of social class, ethnicity and gender can create systematic biases within schooling.

Other critical pedagogies of gender difference have been proposed, and some have been tried. These range from using anti-sexist stories, critical readings and teacher workshops to talking about gender; creating a safe environment for discussions about masculinity; working with resistances; reflections on masculinity, etc. (Francis, 1998, 2000). Kenway and Fitzclarence (1997) offer the prospect of replacing what they call 'poisonous pedagogies' (conventional school cultures which contain and employ forms of violence and forms of violation) with 'narrative therapy' through story telling. Salisbury and Jackson (1996) recommend masculinity workshops for boys. The importance of dialogue – especially in relation to respect and recognition of the emotional elements of difference in transformative pedagogies – is demonstrated in recent projects that support girls' learning and emotional development while at school. In Cruddas and Haddock's (2003) study, girls valued their single-sex developmental group work, which focused on the problematic emotional, affective and relational worlds they inhabited as adolescents. The girls valued opportunities to explore the nature of friendship, confidence, relations with the opposite sex, and their experiences of learning. Like the adolescent girls in Brown and Gilligan's (1992) study, these girls had developed silence as a strategy – which was self-defeating. When given the opportunity to address these personal and intimate domains, they were able to take control of their own educational experience (Cruddas and Haddock, 2003).

A pedagogy which engages critically with the affective domain can also offer male students the opportunity to promote gender equality. The United Nations Expert Panel on the Advancement of Women encouraged discussion of the ways in which men can be taught to help women advance in all spheres in society (Connell, 2003) by, for example, challenging gender-related violence. As Baker *et al.* (2004) point out, the silence, invisibility and devaluation of, for example, the personal and social trauma of gay and lesbian students and teachers in a culture which defines them as 'immoral' or 'deviant' is particularly telling. Gender-sensitive forms of citizenship education courses would focus on the real, but usually hidden, gender and sexual injustices, and alert young men and women to the need to fight against these practices in their communities (Arnot, 2004a).

A critical transformative pedagogy of gender difference repositions such deconstruction work within a more democratised form of schooling in which respect and recognition are given to the many groups who experience status-related inequalities. Baker *et al.* (2004) suggest that what is needed is a *critical interculturalism* (see Table 6.4, Cell D4) that teaches about the inequalities associated with age, sexuality, religious beliefs, disability, language, social class, 'race' or ethnicity as well as gender. The aim is to recreate equality of respect and recognition of difference through teaching about equality within democratised educational institutions. Such democratisation affects the organisation and classroom cultures but, even more critically, it involves student involvement at a much deeper level, not just in cultural deconstruction, but also in decision making. For the most part, schools are undemocratic institutions, restricting political agency of students, albeit in different ways (Gordon *et al.*, 2000). If they were to actively teach equality and democratic citizenship, schools would need to adopt an inclusive, holistic approach.[4] Recognition politics would need to use the lens of dominated groups as common sense to explore peer culture, and to challenge silence, invisibility and devaluation. Students would need to experience difference, develop co-operative practices and support inclusion as a principle and practice. Gendered notions of citizenship could also be replaced by a version of citizenship which encouraged equality of love, care and solidarity, thus challenging the 'false dichotomy between reason and emotion' (Baker *et al.*, 2004: 168).

Equality of power also involves the *democratising of educational relations*, encouraging greater participation in school decision making. By 2007, the concept of a transformative pedagogy (Table 6.3: Cell D2) around social equality suggested that male and female students from diverse cultural and socio-economic groups should have the capacity, motivation and confidence to intervene in the principles which govern their learning experience. One way in which they can do this is by having their voice heard within 'the acoustic of the school' (Bernstein, 2000). Today, student voice is put forward as a new marker in the democratising of pedagogy. However, as Bernstein (2000) argues, a prior condition of this is for *all* pupils to have a stake in society. People must have 'confidence that the political arrangements they create will realise this stake'. These conditions can only be realised in a school if it could ensure what Bernstein called the three *pedagogic democratic rights*. These are the following.

- *Enhancement:* the conditions necessary for 'experiencing boundaries be they social, intellectual or personal, not as prisons, or stereotypes, but as tension points condensing the past and opening possible futures … it is the right to the means of critical understanding and to new possibilities' (Bernstein, 2000: xx). It creates the conditions for *confidence*.
- *Inclusion:* the right of individuals to 'be included, socially, intellectually, culturally and personally' (Bernstein, 2000: xx). This does not mean to be absorbed. Inclusion allows the individual to be part of a community (*communitas*) and at the same time '*to be separate and autonomous*' (Bernstein, 2000: xx). The conditions for achieving these social rights must be the presence of a collective in which individuals have a sense of belonging but are also valued as individuals.

- *Participation:* the right to 'participate in procedures whereby order is constructed, maintained and changed. It is the right to participate in the construction, maintenance and transformation of order' (Bernstein, 2000: xxi). The conditions for such 'civic practice' are political and engagement must have outcomes.

A critical pedagogy of difference which worked with the notion of pedagogic democratic rights would be concerned about the fact that not all pupil voices are elicited, and not all students are heard. Indeed, not all students speak the language of learning – the sorts of pedagogic language being used by teachers in the classroom (whether traditional or progressive in style). As Dwivedi (1996) points out, there are major cultural differences to learning; to talking about learning; and to communicating learning needs that should be addressed. Teachers should consider carefully the implications of the politics of difference for the promotion of pupil voice, especially given the evidence of the discriminatory practices towards black and minority learners, and the negative assessment of their learning abilities and behaviours, found in studies such as Gillborn and Youdell (1999). Being a learner involves considerable skill and familiarity with the expectations of such a communicative setting. Recent research suggests that such pedagogic democratic rights are gendered and racialised and that, rather than reduce difference, they can aggravate social class and ethnic divisions *within* each gender (Arnot, 2006)

Conclusions

Whilst this analysis of pedagogy, gender equality and citizenship is not conclusive, I want to argue that the use of Fraser's dual systems theory has made it possible to trace shifts over time in the different remedies and approaches for different forms of social equality. The analytic distinction and seeming opposition between material processes of political economy (redistribution) and symbolic processes of culture (recognition) reflects an age when 'post-socialist' conflicts and concerns about group cultural identities, with their demands for recognition, appear to have marginalised socio-economic realities. It is important to note Iris Marion Young's (1997) critique of this distinction for exaggerating the degree to which economic struggles have been replaced by cultural struggles. She asks us to be aware of the dangers of seeing cultural recognition struggles as an end in themselves, and that in effect they represent concrete political strategies with which to address economic realities. It is true to say that Fraser's polarising strategy, being abstract, can tend toward misrepresenting cultural and economic resistance to social injustice as separate and even in conflict. Also, there is a danger that such analytic distinctions may be more heuristic rather than corresponding to reality. For example, Fraser did not work through any empirical examples of the contradictions of the two bivalent collectivities of race and gender for institutional practices (such as those of schooling). Yet from an educational perspective, Fraser's dichotomising has been valuable in sifting through some of the pedagogic contradictions associated with gender and race, and thinking about the complex demands made of pedagogy in relation to citizenship and social justice.

160 *Gender and 'race' equality*

Clearly the analysis offered here therefore needs developing. Young's own fourfold categorisation, which combines distributive structures with cultural practices, offers another way in which to judge the justice of social institutions, such as schools and pedagogic practice: (a) the pattern of distribution of resources and goods; (b) division of labour; (c) the organisation of decision-making power; (d) whether cultural meanings enhance self-respect and self-expression of its members. Young also reminds us that the cultural goals of recognition are linked to political economy – for example, Bourdieu and Passeron's (1977) analysis of the role of cultural and economic privilege, and the role of subaltern counter-publics, which help formulate oppositional practices in the public sphere. Recognition politics, of the type I have discussed in relation to the curriculum and pedagogy appear to be ends in themselves. Yet, as Young reminds us, these cultural strategies – even if affirmative rather than transformative – can have radical impacts if they lead to subordinate groups gaining equal respect in society at large. Taken from this perspective, the contradictions within race politics may well have the effect of challenging naturalised essentialisms and universalisms in order to provide the grounds for greater cultural ethnic solidarity in the fight for economic justice. As such, the contradictions between redistribution and recognition in relation to race identity politics may not be as great as Fraser suggests. In contrast, Young accepts that the equality-versus-difference debate 'poses a genuine dilemma for feminist politics', although not, she argues, in terms of redistribution and recognition, but in relation to two different redistributive strategies: one directly addresses economic inequalities, the other challenges the misogyny that encourages violence against women. Again, culture and economic struggles are united.

Fraser (1997a), in her response, agrees that whilst social and cultural politics cannot be separated in reality, her framework is nevertheless valuable in helping analyse 'existing splits' in economic and identity politics. Similarly, I have found her distinctions useful as a starting point from which to explore changing equality agendas in relation to schooling and pedagogy. These distinctions used in an education context do 'give expression in distorted form to genuine tensions among multiple aims that must be pursued simultaneously in struggles for social justice' (Fraser, 1997a: 129). In defence of her polarising strategies, Fraser argues:

> Once we distinguish affirmative approaches from transformative approaches, what looked like an ineluctable contradiction gives way to a plurality of possible strategies from which we must reflectively choose. Some kinds of recognition claims, especially the 'deconstructive' kind, are better suited than others to synergising with claims for socio-economic equality.[5] (Fraser, 1997a: 129)

Fraser's analytic framework has helped offer a new perspective on the complex relationship between gender, ethnicity, pedagogy and citizenship in the UK setting, around issues of equality and difference. The analysis demonstrates the sustained ambitions, over a 30-year period, to break through the historic gender dualism associated with liberal democratic citizenship and its reproduction within schooling. It shows how such goals were addressed by working with and through the difficult binaries of equality and difference found within liberal democracies in the late twentieth century. At stake are universalistic and particularistic notions of citizenship; individual and group rights; various natural, social and political notions of difference; and power relations that are sustained rather than broken down through liberal democratic freedoms and rights.

In conclusion, this chapter indicates that the contradictory relationship between affirmative and transformative educational and pedagogic remedies, using redistribution and recognition agendas, must have been highly confusing to teachers. The teaching profession, more often than not, has been left to resolve such politically confusing cultural and political agendas. Whilst gender theory offers sensitive nuanced deconstructions of gender dualisms and the misrecognition of difference, teachers' professional knowledge has quite often been understood to legitimate and aggravate gender and racial divisions and inequalities. The concept of a 'critical pedagogy of difference' appears to be emerging in embryonic form as a way forward. I have argued, following Bernstein, that this needs to be allied to strong notions of pedagogic democratic rights – pedagogic rights are not simply reflections of individual political rights; rather, they are the rights of all learners (as individuals but also as groups) to take control over the rules which govern their learning. The history of the last 30 years in the UK and the tentative nature of these proposals suggests that the relationship between gender, pedagogy and citizenship – especially in terms of equality and difference – now needs to be debated openly and thoroughly.

Acknowledgements

This paper was originally developed for the Beyond Access project led by Elaine Unterhalter, and presented at the 'Curriculum for Gender Equality and Quality Basic Education in Schools' conference in Nairobi in 2004. I am grateful to Elaine for her comments on earlier drafts of this chapter when submitted to *Theory and Research in Education*.

References

Ameli, S. Reza and Merali, A. (2004) *Dual Citizenship: British, Islamic or Both? – Obligations, Recognition, Respect and Belonging, Vol 1.* British Muslim's Expectations Series, Islamic Human Rights Commission.

Archaud, D. (2003) 'Citizenship education and multiculturalism', in A. Ockyer, B. Crick and J. Annette (eds) *Education for Democratic Citizenship: issues of theory and practice.* Aldershot: Ashgate.

Archer, L. (2003) *Race, Masculinity and Schooling: Muslim boys and education.* Buckingham: Open University Press.

Arnot, M. (ed.) (1985a) *Race and Gender: equal opportunities policies in education.* Oxford, Pergamon.

Arnot, M. (1985b) *Race, Gender and Education Policy-Making.* Stony Strafford, Open University E353 Course Book.

Arnot, M. (2002) *Reproducing Gender? Critical essays on educational theory and feminist politics*. London: RoutledgeFalmer.
Arnot, M. (2004a) 'Gender and citizenship education', in A. Lockyer, B. Crick and J. Annette (eds) *Education for Democratic Citizenship issues of theory and practice*. Aldershot: Ashgate, pp. 103–19.
Arnot, M. (2004b) 'Working class masculinities, schooling and social justice: reconsidering the sociological significance of Paul Willis' "Learning to Labour"', in C. Vincent (ed.) *Social Justice, Identity and Education*. London: RoutledgeFalmer, pp. 97–119.
Arnot, M. (2006) 'Gender voices in the classroom', in C. Skelton and B. Francis (eds) *Gender and Education Handbook*. London: SAGE.
Arnot, M. and Blair, M. (1993) 'Black and anti-racist perspectives on the National Curriculum and government education policy' in A. King and M. Reiss (eds) *The Multicultural Dimension of the National Curriculum*. Barcombe, Falmer Press.
Arnot, M. and Gubb, J. (2001) *Adding Value to Girls' and Boys' Education*. Crawley: West Sussex County Council.
Arnot, M. and Miles, P. (2005) 'A reconstruction of the gender agenda: The contradictory gender dimensions in New Labour's educational and economic policy', *Oxford Review of Education*, 31: 173–89.
Arnot, M. and Reay, D. (2006a) 'Pedagogic voices and pedagogic encounters: The implications for pupil consultation as transformative practice', in R. Moore, M. Arnot, J. Beck and H. Daniels (eds) *Knowledge, Power and Educational Reform: applying the sociology of Basil Bernstein*. London: Routledge, pp. 75–93.
Arnot, M. and Reay, D. (2006b) 'The framing of performance pedagogies: Pupil perspectives on the control of school knowledge and its acquisition', in H. Lauder, P. Brown, J. Dillabough and A.H. Halsey (eds) *Education, Globalisation and Social Change*. Oxford: Oxford University Press.
Arnot, M., David, M. and Weiner, G. (1999) *Closing the Gender Gap: post-war education and social change*. Cambridge: Polity Press.
Arnot, M., Gray, J., James, M. and Rudduck, J. (1998) *Recent Research on Gender and Educational Performance*. London: The Stationery Office/Office for Standards in Education (OFSTED).
Baker, J., Lynch, K., Cantillon, S. and Walsh, J. (2004) *Equality: From Theory to Action*. Basingstoke: Macmillan.
Benhabib, S. (2002) 'Multiculturalism and gendered citizenship', in *The Claims of Culture: equality and diversity in the global era*. Princeton, NJ: Princeton University Press.
Benhabib, S. (ed.) (1996) *Democracy and Difference*. London: Routledge.
Bernstein, B. (2000) *Pedagogy, Symbolic Control and Identity: theory, research, critique Basil Bernstein*, rev. ed. London: Rowman and Littlefield.
Bourdieu, P. and Passeron, J-C. (1977) *Reproduction in Education, Society and Culture*. (Published in association with Theory, Culture & Society) London: Sage.
Brookes, A.L. (1992) *Feminist Pedagogy: an autobiographical approach*. Halifax, Nova Scotia: Fernwood.
Brown, L.M. and Gilligan, C. (1992) *Meeting at the Crossroads: women's psychology and girls' development*. Cambridge: Harvard University Press.
Coffey, A. and Delamont, S. (2000) *Feminism and the Classroom Teacher: Research Praxis, Pedagogy*. London: RoutledgeFalmer.
Connell, R.W. (1987) *Gender and Power*. Cambridge: Polity Press.
Connell, R.W. (2003) 'The role of men and boys in achieving gender equality'. Paper prepared for the United Nations Division for the Advancement of Women Expert Group Meeting, 21–24 October 2003; EGM/Men-Boys-GE/2003/BP.1
Cruddas, L. and Haddock, L. (2003) *Girls' Voices: supporting girls' learning and emotional development*. Stoke-on-Trent: Trentham Books.
Culley, M. and Portuges, C. (1985) *Gendered Subjects: the dynamics of feminist teaching*. London: Routledge Kegan Paul.

Curriculum Review Group (2006) *Diversity and Citizenship.* London: Department of Education and Science (DfES), available at www.dfes.gov.uk/research/data/uploadfiles/RR819.pdf
Dallmayr, F. (1996) 'Democracy and Multiculturalism', in S. Benhabib (ed.) *Democracy and Difference*, London: Routledge.
Davies, B. (1989) 'The discursive production of the male/female dualism in school settings', *Oxford Review of Education, 15*: 229–41.
Davies, B. (1997) 'Constructing and deconstructing masculinities through critical literacy', *Gender and Education, 9*: 9–30.
Dillabough, J. and Arnot, M. (2001) 'Feminist sociology of education: dynamics, debates and directions', in J. Demaine (ed.) *Sociology of Education Today.* London: Palgrave, pp. 30–47.
Dillabough, J. and Arnot, M. (2002) 'Recasting educational debates about female citizenship, agency and identity', *The School Field, 13*(3/4): 81–107.
Dwivedi, K.N. (1996) 'Race and the child's perspective', in R. Davie, G. Upton and V. Varma (eds) *The Voice of the Child: A Handbook for Professionals.* London: Falmer Press, pp. 153–69.
Ellsworth, E. (1989) 'Why doesn't this feel empowering? Working through the repressive myths of critical pedagogy', *Harvard Education Review, 59*: 297–324.
Epstein, D. and Johnson, R. (1998) *Schooling Sexualities.* Buckingham: Open University Press.
Epstein, D., Elwood, J., Hey, V. and Maw, J. (eds) (1998) *Failing Boys?* Buckingham: Open University Press.
Foster, V. (1994) 'What about the boys? Presumptive equality and the obfuscation of concerns about theory, research, resources and curriculum in the education of girls and boys', Paper presented at the AARE Annual Conference, Newcastle, November.
Francis, B. (1998) *Power Plays: primary school children's constructions of gender, power and adult work.* Stoke-on-Trent: Trentham Books.
Francis, B. (2000) *Boys, Girls and Achievement: addressing the classroom issues.* London: RoutledgeFalmer.
Fraser, N. (1997a) 'A rejoinder to Iris Young', *New Left Review, 222*, March–April: 126–9.
Fraser, N. (1997b) *Justice Interruptus: critical reflections on the post-socialist condition.* London: Routledge.
Giddens, A. (1994) *Beyond Left and Right. The Future of Radical Politics.* Cambridge: Polity Press.
Gillborn, D. (1990) *Race, Ethnicity and Education: teaching and learning in multi-ethnic schools.* London: Routledge
Gillborn, D. and Mirza, H.S. (2000) *Educational Inequality: mapping race, class and gender.* London: Ofsted.
Gillborn, D. and Youdell, D. (1999) *Rationing Education: policy, practice, reform and equity.* Buckingham: Open University Press.
Gordon, T., Holland, J. and Lahelma, E. (2000) *Making Spaces: citizenship and difference in school.* London: MacMillan.
Gore, F. (1993) *The Struggle for Pedagogies: critical and feminist discourse and regimes of truth.* New York: Routledge.
Grumet, M. (1988) *Bitter Milk: women and teaching.* Amherst: University of Massachusetts Press.
Haywood, C. and Mac an Ghaill, M. (1997) 'Materialism and deconstructivism: education and the epistemology of identity', *Cambridge Journal of Education 27*: 261–72.
Hill Collins, P. (1990) *Black Feminist Thought: knowledge, consciousness and the politics of empowerment.* Boston: Unwin Hyman.
hooks, b. (1992) *Black Looks: Race and Representation*, Boston: South End Press.
James, S. and Myhill, D. (2004) '"Troublesome boys" and "compliant girls": Gender

identity and perceptions of achievement and underachievement', *British Journal of Sociology of Education*, 25: 547–61.
Kenway, J. (1990) 'Privileged girls, private schools and the culture of success', in J. Kenway and S. Willis (eds) *Hearts and Minds: self-esteem and the schooling of girls*. London: Falmer Press.
Kenway, J. and Fitzclarence, L. (1997) 'Masculinity, violence and schooling: challenging "poisonous pedagogies"', *Gender and Education*, 9: 117–33.
Lather, P. (1991) *Getting Smart: feminist research and pedagogy with/in the postmodern*. New York: Routledge.
Lingard, B. (2003) 'Where to in gender policy in education after recuperative masculinity politics?' *International Journal of Inclusive Education*, 7: 33–56.
Lister, R. (1997) *Feminism and Citizenship*. Basingstoke: Macmillan.
Mac an Ghaill, M. (1994) *The Making of Men: masculinities, sexualities and schooling*. Buckingham: Open University Press.
Martino, W., Mills, M. and Lingard, B. (2005) 'Interrogating single-sex classes for addressing boys' educational and social needs', *Oxford Review of Education*, 31: 237–54.
Mayberry, M. and Rose, E.C. (1999) *Meeting the Challenge: innovative feminist pedagogies in action*. New York: Routledge.
Mills, M., Martino, W. and Lingard, B. (2004) 'Attracting, recruiting and retaining male teachers: policy issues in the male teacher debate', *British Journal of Sociology of Education*, 25: 355–69.
Mirza, H. (1992) *Young, Black and Female*. London: Routledge.
Mohanty, C.T. (1991) 'Cartographies of Struggle: third world women and the politics of feminism', in C.T. Mohanty, A. Russo, L. Torres (eds) *Third World Women and the Politics of Feminism*. Bloomington: Indiana University Press.
Nayak, A. and Kehily, M. (2007) *Youth, Gender and Culture: young masculinities and femininities*. London: Palgrave.
Nussbaum, M.C. (1999) *Sex and Social Justice*. Oxford: Oxford University Press.
Okin, S. Moller (1999) *Is Multiculturalism Bad for Women?* Princeton: Princeton University Press.
Okin, S. Moller (2003) 'Mistresses of their own destiny', in K. McDonough and W. Feinberg (eds) *Education and Citizenship in Liberal Democratic Societies*. New York: Oxford University Press.
Olssen, M. (2004) 'From the Crick Report to the Parekh Report: multiculturalism, cultural difference, and democracy – the re-visioning of citizenship education', *British Journal of Sociology of Education*, 25(2): 179–92.
Osler, A. (2000) *Citizenship and Democracy in Schools: diversity, identity and equality*. Stoke on Trent, Staffordshire: Trentham Books.
Osler, A. and Vincent, K. (2004) *Girls and Exclusion: rethinking the agenda*. London: RoutledgeFalmer.
Parekh, B. (2000) *Rethinking Multiculturalism: cultural diversity and political theory*. Cambridge, MA: Harvard University Press.
Pateman, C. (1988) *The Sexual Contract*. Cambridge: Polity Press.
Pateman, C. (1989) *The Disorder of Women*. Cambridge: Polity Press.
Phillips, A. (1993) *Democracy and Difference*. Cambridge: Polity Press.
Phillips, A. (2002) 'Multiculturalism, universalism and the claims of democracy', in M. Molyneux and S. Razavi (eds) *Gender Justice, Development and Rights*. Oxford: Oxford University Press.
Phillips, A. (2005) *The Politics of Presence*. Oxford: Clarendon Press.
Raphael Reed, L. (1999) 'Troubling boys and disturbing discourses on masculinity and schooling: A feminist exploration of current debates and interventions concerning boys in school', *Gender and Education*, 11: 93–110.
Reynolds, M. and Trehan, K. (2001) 'Classroom as real world: propositions for a pedagogy of difference', *Gender and Education*, 13: 357–72.

Rowan, L., Knobel, M., Bigum, C. and Lankshear, C. (2002) *Boys, Literacies and Schooling.* Buckingham: Open University Press.
Runnymede Trust (2000) *The Report of the Commission on the Future of Multi-Ethnic Britain* (the Parekh Report).
Runnymede Trust (2004) *Realising the Vision*, Briefing Paper, April, available at http://www.runnymedetrust.org/uploads/publications/pdfs/RealisingTheVision.pdf
Salisbury, J. and Jackson, D. (1996) *Challenging Macho Values.* London: Falmer Press.
Severiens, S. and Ten Dam, G. (1997) 'Gender and gender identity differences in learning styles', *Educational Psychology, 17*: 79–93.
Sewell, T. (1997) *Black Masculinities and Schooling.* Stoke on Trent, Trentham Books.
Shain, F. (2003) *The Schooling and Identity of Asian Girls.* Stoke on Trent: Trentham Books.
Siim, B. (2000) *Gender and Citizenship: politics and agency in France, Britain and Denmark.* Cambridge: Cambridge University Press.
Skelton, C. (2001) *Schooling the Boys: masculinities and primary education.* Buckingham: Open University Press.
Stone, M. (1981) *The Education of the Black Child in Britain: the myth of multiracial education.* London: Fontana
Troyna, B. (1991) *Racial Inequality in Education.* London: Routledge
Unterhalter, E. (1999) 'Citizenship, difference and education: reflections inspired by the South African transition', in N. Yuval-Davis and P. Werbner (eds) *Women, Citizenship and Difference.* London: Zed Books.
Walkerdine, V. (1990) *Schoolgirl Fictions.* London: Verso.
Weaver-Hightower, M.B. (2003a) 'Crossing the divide: Bridging the disjunctures between theoretically oriented and practice-oriented literature about masculinity and boys at school', *Gender and Education, 15*: 407–17.
Weaver-Hightower, M.B. (2003b) 'The "boy turn" in research on gender and education', *Review of Educational Research, 73*: 471–98.
Wright, C. (1987) 'The relations between teachers and Afro-Caribbean pupils: observing multiracial classrooms', in G. Weiner and M. Arnot (eds) *Gender Under Scrutiny: new inquiries in education.* London: Hutchinson.
Young, I.M. (1986) 'The ideal of community and the politics of difference', *Social Theory and Practice, 12*: 1–26.
Young, I.M. (1990) *Justice and the Politics of Difference* (version used by Dallymer, p. 282).
Young, I.M. (1997) 'Unruly categories: a critique of Nancy Fraser's dual systems theory', *New Left Review, 222*, March–April: 147–60.
Younger, M. and Warrington, M. (2005) *Raising Boys' Achievement in Secondary Schools: issues, dilemmas and opportunities.* Maidenhead, Berkshire: Open University Press.
Younger, M., Warrington, M. and Williams, J. (1999) 'The gender gap and classroom interactions: reality and rhetoric?' *British Journal of Sociology of Education, 20*: 325–41.
Zinn, M.B. and Dill, B. Thornton (1996) 'Theorizing difference from multiracial feminism', *Feminist Studies*, 22, 2, 321–31, reprinted in Zinn, M.B., Hondagneu-Sotelo, P., and Messner, M.A., (eds) (2005) *Gender through the Prism of Difference.* New York: Oxford University.

Notes

1 *Theory and Research in Education* ran a special issue on discussion of Okin's work in 2003. See *Theory and Research in Education, 1*(1).
2 Available at www.ihrc.org.uk/file/BMEG_VOL1.pdf. (Accessed 02.02.08.)

3 For the curriculum aspects of citizenship education which addresses diversity and citizenship, see Curriculum Review 2006.
4 Baker *et al.* (2004) provide an extensive list of demands that schools would need to meet if they were to become effectively transformative in relation to redistribution and recognition. For example, they argue that schools would need to challenge unequal distributive principles by removing tracking, streaming and grouping that advantage male middle classes.
5 Young's own 'five faces of oppression' – exploitation, marginalisation, powerlessness, cultural imperialism and violence – remove such dichotomies and have been shown to be valuable aids to focus on educational reforms (see Baker *et al.*, 2004).

7 Addressing the gender agenda

The limits and possibilities of national and global citizenship education[1]

with Harriet Marshall

> The transformation of human rights from a feminist perspective is crucial to addressing global challenges to human rights in the twenty-first century. This should be seen in the context of the growth and evolution of women's movements internationally in the past two decades. Women are taking a leading role in redefining social concepts and global policy issues in areas such as development, democracy, human rights, world security and the environment. This means not just looking at what have been called 'women's issues' – a ghetto, or separate sphere that remains on the margins of society – but rather moving women from the margins to the center by questioning the most fundamental concepts of our social order so that they take better account of women's lives. (Bunch, 1995: 11)

Education systems, as we know, play a crucial role in the formation of citizens in a national context and are increasingly being called upon to address global citizenship agendas. As international agencies and world funding agencies are now aware, female access to education is central to the project of social progress. However, the 'rights of access to education' are not sufficient to meet feminist egalitarian goals. Even though gender equality is one of the great democratic principles, we shall argue that the models of democratic citizenship on which educational systems are built often exclude gender concerns. All too often, representations of citizenship are abstracted from real social (gender) relations and little attention is paid to the gendered nature of citizenship ideals. Feminist educationalists, therefore, have sought in many different ways to redefine what is meant by 'democratic', exploring and exposing, in particular, the limitations of liberal democratic educational traditions and its sometimes negative consequences for women. Democratic education from a feminist perspective involves, at a far deeper level, a challenge to the social conditions that have sustained women's second-class citizenship and their experiences of poverty, violence, harassment and economic exploitation.

These debates have moved into new political spaces – significantly they can now be found in the context of discussions about the nature of citizenship education, a subject that appears to have increased importance as a mechanism for sustaining nation-state identities as well as global economic development (Heater, 2004). Many nation states are currently considering the role of education in the creation of citizens in the twenty-first century (Cogan and Derricott, 2000). In response, new centres for civic education have been set up. There is, for example, an Asian network of civic education; Commonwealth countries are being encouraged to consider citizenship education; and the Council of Europe suggests it is time to consider what values and skills individuals will require in the twenty-first century (Cogan and Derricott, 2000). There is also now greater interest in thinking about what would constitute global citizenship education (or cosmopolitan/multiple citizenships), although this is not without its contradictions given the association, within liberal democracy, of citizenship with the nation state (Heater, 2004).

Paradoxically, these curricular initiatives can provide the mechanism for legitimating women's subordination. National concepts of citizenship, by definition, are based on a concept of belonging that is fundamentally exclusionary. Women, minority ethnic groups, refugees and asylum seekers, the disadvantaged and those with disabilities, often find that their needs and concerns are marginalised from state policy but also that they do not have access to the rights of citizenship, either formally because of their status as 'non-citizens' or because of their lack of economic, social and cultural resources, which deny them opportunities to participate in formal political structures (such as voting) and civic associations (e.g. unions, political parties) and state institutions (e.g. educational opportunities). Abstract notions of 'the citizen' can divert attention away from the need to address such social inequalities and forms of social exclusion. If governments are not alert, therefore, citizenship education can become the political device with which to mask social hierarchies and differentiations, and power relations. The establishment of 'mature' democracies is dependent upon educational institutions offering full access and recognition to women, minority ethnic and religious groups and sexual minorities, amongst others. The more such groups claim political and economic territory, the more complex the task of citizenship education becomes. The political spaces it offers are fraught with ambivalence. This chapter can only capture some of those ambivalences.

Here we have joined forces to consider the possibility of national and global citizenship education promoting gender equality. Whilst one of us has focused her research on global education and global citizenship education (Marshall, 2005 and 2007a), the other has been working on the gender dimensions of the English and Welsh citizenship education initiatives in the European context (Arnot *et al.*, 1996 and 2000; and Arnot 2004). We consider whether national or global formulations of citizenship education challenge the economic and political marginalisation of women. Despite the international women's movement, the concept of gender equality within national and global citizenships is highly problematic. We focus on these two very different educational spaces. First, we explore the space represented by a highly conceptualised, somewhat modernist English/Welsh model of citizenship education. We then explore the fluid, amorphous and somewhat disputed field of global citizenship education that offers limited official endorsement of the notion of gender. Ideally these two traditions, whilst both very different and each problematic, could contribute to the promotion of gender equality.

We begin by asking why gender equality was marginalised within the English/ Welsh national citizenship education, and the possible consequences for gender relations of this marginalisation. In the second half of the chapter we discuss whether global citizenship education can instead develop in ways that support gender equality. We consider the extent to which global citizenship education has developed in the UK model and the recognition given the extensive gender issues associated with globalisation. This is the first attempt at combining these two sets of analyses and the connections made are therefore exploratory rather than definitive. If developed, global citizenship could usefully incorporate gender issues identified by feminist challenges to the political conceptualisations of citizenship education, whilst such national programmes will gain greatly from a consideration of the global dimensions of gender equality.

English and Welsh citizenship education

From a gender equality perspective, citizenship is a hotly contested subject. A prime example of the nature of this contestation is the recently introduced English and Welsh citizenship education that represents approximately 5 per cent of the compulsory curriculum. In 2002, all secondary schools in England and Wales were instructed to deliver citizenship education. Not surprisingly, there was a wide national debate about what constitutes the nature of this curriculum. The gender elements of that debate, despite being integral to the teaching of human rights, were nevertheless rather muted. The citizenship education programme itself was also largely silent about issues of gender (Osler and Starkey, 1996), even though 'it identifies "a commitment to equality opportunities and gender equality" as a key value to be acquired by the citizenship education it commends' (Archaud, 2003: 90). The new body of political educators, it seems, has been negligent in not engaging with a major body of Western political thought – feminist policy theory – and feminist educationalists seem to have lost an important opportunity to achieve national recognition for gender equality as one of the guiding principles of this curriculum initiative (Arnot, 2004).

Although – as we shall see – the aim of the new curricular initiative was signalled as 'no less than a change in the political culture of this country both nationally and locally' (Advisory Group on Citizenship (The Crick Report), 1998: 7), from a gender perspective this was far from being the case. In 2000, the Chair of the Advisory Group, Bernard Crick, wrote that he was not unaware of gender issues – indeed he admitted that he was 'irritated' and a 'little ashamed' to discover how casually in the past he himself had used the normative 'he' to represent both men and women (Crick, 2000a). Nevertheless he believed that progress had now been made in not conflating the female with the male as norm. Yet precisely such a conflation characterises the citizenship education programme and guidance offered to English and Welsh schools. These materials fail to address the masculine associations of the concept of citizenship and the different relationships of men and women to citizenship ideals.

The schemes of work produced by the Qualification and Curriculum Authority provide ample evidence of the marginalisation of gender equality for this view. Materials for the study of business and enterprise, the world of work, and even discussion of human rights and global issues, noticeably fail to refer to the impact of structural social inequalities. The Commission for Racial Equality and the Equal Opportunities Commission are not included in the list of relevant and useful contact organisations involved in citizenship issues. There was also no encouragement for teachers to refer to sex or race discrimination policies and legislation other than the Human Rights Act 1998. This is not surprising if we consider that the concept of social 'equality', although initially included in the guidance to schools (QCA, 2000), did not appear to figure in the documentation. Garmarnikov and Green (1999) suggest that the new citizenship education programme reflects the predominance of Third Way politics, with its emphasis on social capital and neo-liberalism. As a result, the social democratic agenda put forward in the post-war period and 'any notion of serious struggle for rights in relation to both the state and other structures of power; citizenship as changing relations of power; and citizenship as fundamentally compromised by systemic, structured inequalities' (Garmarnikov and Green, 1999: 120) were likely to be sidelined, if not replaced altogether. Thus the concepts of the 'empowered' or the 'educated' citizen paradoxically bear little relation, they argue, to any central social justice concerns. There is:

> an almost total absence of concern for structured inequalities, especially economic ones; a misrecognition of the political, social and educational hierarchies embedded in social relationships, networks and associations; and the invisibility of inequalities of power as an issue of social justice.
> (Garmarnikov and Green, 1999: 120)

Citizens, rather than the state, are called upon to take responsibility for economic renewal and for building social cohesion. As a result, this seemingly liberal progressive new curriculum around citizenship sustains rather than challenges globalised and dehumanising economies and 'polarising social inequalities' (Garmarnikov and Green, 1999: 121). Garmarnikov and Green even suggest that, as a result, this citizenship curriculum could lead to authoritarian populism rather than greater democracy. If this critique is valid, then the promotion of gender equality is unlikely to be its main or even its subsidiary goal.

In response to such serious criticisms, Crick (2000c) defended the new citizenship curriculum by pointing to its pedagogic strategy. He argued that the great achievement of the Citizenship Order (the 'gold' as it were) was precisely its success in offering individuals an appropriate form of *political literacy*, a full sense of civic (moral and social) responsibility and duty, and a commitment to become active participants in the society in which they belong. The compromise reached in this Order was that British teachers would teach all viewpoints – they would be balanced and uncontroversial in their pedagogy – but that once young people became active citizens they could then achieve the egalitarian reforms in the name of social justice. One of the key means of achieving this goal in the long run was first to create what he called the 'sceptical' citizen – a citizen with intellectually informed scepticism (Crick 2000c: 71).

Crick's thinking about the most appropriate pedagogy for political education (not all of which was adopted by the Advisory Group) suggested that he had seen the concepts of *equality, democracy, tradition* and *custom* as important. However, he also considered the topics to be too complex for school-based citizenship education. It was essential, he argued, that citizenship education should provide young people with a basic vocabulary so that the politically literate person will be clear about 'what he or she means by "democracy" or "equality"' (Crick, 2000a: 79). Concepts such as 'equality', 'tradition', 'custom' and 'democracy' itself were compounds of the more basic concepts of *liberty, welfare, representation, rights* and *justice* which, from Crick's point of view, could not be delivered *ab initio*. The first stage of educating citizens should involve teaching about *government* (power, force, authority, order and relationship), the concept of *law* (justice, representation and pressure) and the concept of *people* (nationality, individuality, freedom and welfare). Crick argued that it was these three conceptual frameworks that should provide the basis of citizenship education. Equality, and indeed gender equality, would therefore need to be taught at an advanced level of political education.[2]

Crick thought that the new citizenship education, defined by a liberal 'softly, softly but gently' approach to the conduct of government as well as the potentially powerful pedagogy of civic republicanism, might open Pandora's box. The 'irritatingly more unpredictable' free citizens (Crick, 2002a: 114) 'might become more demanding and more knowledgeable about how to achieve their demands' as a result of 'the more disruptive, unpredictable civic republican theory'.[3] One could not preclude the ensuing development of a struggle for greater rights and power. Young citizens would be empowered by scepticism on the one hand, and knowledge and strategic thinking on the other. They would not, in the event, be 'fobbed off' with just 'volunteering' (Crick, 2002a: 115).

When challenged on whether citizenship education implied more democratic schools and greater recognition of the rights of pupils within schools, Crick (2000a) responded that he was proud to be called 'a liberal'. The 'strong bare bones' of the *Citizenship Order*, with its 'light touch order' (Crick, 2000a: 66) from central government to schools was, in his view, fully justified. Minimal government prescriptions, balanced 'non-controversial' teaching and no pressure on schools to deliver social reform of society were the conditions needed to create knowledgeable, skilled and committed citizens. Further, the diversity of school responses to citizenship education would cater for pluralism and social difference.

However, the reasons for the failure to address gender equality as an explicit goal of citizenship education cannot just be attributed to the failure of politics of the time – at heart it was a reflection of the underlying conceptual assumptions of both civic republicanism and liberalism as Anglo-Saxon political philosophies. Unequal gender relations were embedded in both these traditions, marginalised in discussions about governance and the nature of liberty, and institutionalised within gendered notions of the public and the private domains. As Quintin Skinner (1998) describes so well, the contentions between these two philosophies, which were about the relationship of the citizen to the state and, more fundamentally, what constitutes civil liberty, have shaped Anglophone political philosophy over the last three centuries. By the nineteenth and twentieth centuries, civic republicanism – which had been used to attack the English monarchy and defend the American

172 Addressing the gender agenda

colonial revolution – had been replaced by the 'ideological triumph' of liberalism and its claims to hegemonic status. As a result, the concept of an individual's duty to the state came to be dominated by liberalism's focus on the rights of the individual, which were to be guaranteed by the state.

Skinner describes how civil republicanism (i.e. neo-Roman) was largely 'innocent of the modern notion of civil society as a moral space between rulers and ruled' (Skinner, 1998: 17). It had:

> ... little to say about the dimensions of freedom and oppression inherent in such institutions as the family or the labour market. They concern themselves almost exclusively with the relationship between the freedom of subjects and the powers of the state. For them, the central questions is always about the nature of the conditions that need to be fulfilled if the contrasting requirements of civil liberty and political obligation are to be met as harmoniously as possible. (Skinner, 1998: 17)

The failure to engage with the family or the labour market had considerable gender significance. Hannah Arendt (1958: 24) noted the axiomatic distinction in Plato's *The Republic* between man's (sic) private life and a second life (*bio politicos*); between politics and the family/household. The public world symbolised freedom, whilst the social inequalities associated with the private familiar realm were taken for granted. Indeed, civic republicanism saw equality as meaning to be free precisely from being ruled or being a ruler, as in the household. Although modern notions of the distinction between public and private have transformed these classical republican traditions, what appears to have happened is that the private sphere is under closer surveillance by the state. According to Arendt, in response the modern age has constructed a new concept of a private/intimate sphere outside this much extended public realm. However this relocation of the private sphere has not signalled the duty to remove gender equalities found in families and households. The separation between a political realm, where citizens have a duty to be active, responsible and full members of government, and the private sphere in which individuals are rulers or ruled (in which they might yet live in servitude), is arguably still being sustained today.

The failure of civic republicanism to include, in any substantial way, civic society and the quality of life and to engage civic duty in the removal of subordination and dominance within the household meant that it was not likely to encourage recognition of gender inequalities in anything other than the public/political sphere. As Heater (1999: 91–2) points out, this framework models the citizen on the role of men in formal politics, and describes civic virtues in terms of male military valour and political activism. If being a citizen and doing the practice of citizenship has been assumed to be 'a uniquely male function' (Turner, 2001) that is framed by male narratives of nationalism and/or militarism, then women will be excluded from participation in nation building. Also, the tendency to elitism implied by the high level of civic participation required in formal politics is deeply problematic for women.

Such masculine associations of citizenship are also central to democratic liberalism – the other powerful Western European tradition that Crick's group drew upon when constructing their national civic education programme. As Carol Pateman (1989) has so adeptly analysed, the form of social contract, which was defined as the basis of liberal democratic philosophy, was constructed over and above the alleged 'disorder of women' implied by their inferred emotionality, subjectivity and closeness to nature. Associated with the social contract was a second exploitative contract – what she called the sexual contract. Whilst the social contract formed the basis of a 'brotherhood of man' – a political fraternity that controlled the political order – the sexual contract assigned men the right to women through marriage and control over the household. Such a philosophy, whilst signalling the centrality of citizen rights, also constructed marriage and motherhood outside the sphere of such rights and hence of citizenship. Women were allocated second-class citizenship – their entry into the public civic world would only be achieved through the massive disruption of this public-private division. The conditions for women's inclusion in liberal democratic notions of citizenship therefore were their subordination to men in both public and private spheres and their exclusion from the public sphere (see Chapter 4).

With these gendered philosophical underpinnings, the silence about gender equality in the new English/Welsh citizenship curriculum is not surprising. References to gender are well hidden in a text which employs the language of 'discrimination', 'human rights' and 'equal opportunities' without any specific reference to the under-representation of women in public life, the need to encourage female leaders, the importance of women's engagement in civic decision making or the encouragement of men's civic duties in relation to private life and fatherhood. There is a silence about the importance of challenging a historical legacy that has marginalised the sphere of everyday family life (and indeed of motherhood and female virtues) from discussions about rights, duties, justice and freedom. De facto, the main focus of the curriculum subject is the male-centred public sphere. Without specific advice to schools to address such gendered biases, it is likely that women's historic struggle for citizenship will be assumed to have been resolved with female suffrage, and citizenship, with its strong gendered representations of male and female citizens, will be left unchallenged (see Arnot, 2004).

It is significant that in the qualitative data generated by a study of 300 male and female student teachers' conceptualisations of citizenship in Greece, Spain, Portugal and England and Wales, citizenship was found to be strongly gendered (Arnot *et al.*, 1996, 2000).[4] The researchers found a presumed dominance of men in the public sphere. It seemed hard for student teachers to conjure up any positive involvement of women within the public sphere.[5] Men were represented as having most control over policy decisions and public appointments, and an especially strong influence over economic and foreign policy. Women, on the whole, were represented as having a negligible influence on policy and influencing public appointments. Gender and generational differences were also noticeable in the UK, although it seemed that young student teachers were less likely than their college lecturers to see it as important that women should occupy public positions.[6]

This association of public/private with the sexual division of labour was also carried through to the representations of men and women in the private sphere. The images of women in private and domestic life were strong ('caring' and 'efficient') whilst those for men were absent or, if present, rather negative.[7] The lack of a collective representation of women in the public civic sphere and of men in the private sphere, if left unchallenged, could have major implications for the education of girls/boys, especially in relation to their adult lives and their future role as citizens (Arnot *et al.*, 1996, 2000; Ivinson *et al.*, 2000). (See Chapters 3 and 4.)

Particularly relevant to this analysis is that, even in countries with strong civic education programmes, there was little evidence that a new generation of teachers felt that the masculinisation of public life and citizenship could be changed through political action. The source of male power in the public realm was partially taken for granted, despite a strong awareness of sex discrimination. Male student teachers in the different European countries appeared to collude with differentiated gender roles and expressed little personal commitment to challenging masculine associations surrounding the public realm. There was a seeming naturalness of male power based on gender role difference. The juxtaposition of power and femininity represented by women in public life disturbed traditional notions of femininity and was expressed as a kind of corruption in which women, in public life, were either over-assertive (autocrats) or sexually predatory. There also appeared in some instances to be anxiety amongst men about their loss of control over the public sphere, which led to polarised constructs of femininity. In other words, women were not represented as legitimately successful and autonomous in public life.

What really lies at the heart of feminist difficulties with liberal and civic republican concepts of citizenship is that, whilst it represents a socially unifying force, it is deeply ambivalent about the status and role of collective identities and collectivities, and how to address issues of difference (Fraser, 1997). This begs the question about how to discuss the communality of women's experience within citizenship education and whether to frame policy on behalf of women as a social group. As Martha Nussbaum (1999) points out, at issue for feminists, in relation to liberal democratic citizenship, are the assumptions behind the abstract notion of the individual, which cannot easily recognise differences between men and women in terms of life situations and experience. Admittedly, there is always the danger that by recognising gender differences, beliefs about biological/natural sex differences are legitimated. Nevertheless, recognition of the particular circumstances which have shaped women's lives, and the contributions they can and have made to the development of society, is central to the achievement of gender justice.

Feminist political theorists have argued that this absence or marginalisation of women's lives (but particularly also of the private sphere) from definitions of citizenship and citizenship education programmes (whichever the political approach) is linked to deeper associations about the relationship between rationality and citizenship, with the resulting exclusion of 'the affective domain' (Nussbaum and Glover, 1995) – the field of personal/emotional relationships – from civic discourse. The focus on rationality as the basis of civic life can result in the failure to value 'the caring ethos' and maternal values found in the private and familial sphere that might provide alternative models of citizenship and civic virtues (Noddings, 1988). Thus whilst the principle of excluding the private sphere from state control, surveillance and intervention appears beneficial, especially to women within the family, it has the disadvantageous effect of marginalising and discursively subordinating women as non-rational beings, and of reducing the potential impact of other sets of civic virtues from a discussion of citizenship education. Further, the neglect of the affective domain has major consequences for the education of children in their rights in their personal lives.

These points suggest that there is more work to be done to engage with the political aspects of the private sphere in citizenship education. Sue Lees (2000), for example, indicated how the new citizenship education programme, by excluding the 'personal from the political', fails to recognise complex changes in gender relations in the private sphere. Societal shifts in family life, which are relevant to the civic activity and social rights of female citizens, and which have been well documented, should be central to the civic project – for example, the uncoupling of women from traditional family structures; the search for alternative sexualities and lifestyles; the rise in the number of illegitimate children; single parenting and high divorce rates. By the early 1990s, 27 per cent of births in England and Wales were to unmarried mothers; women were marrying later and getting divorced earlier. Divorce has increased sixfold over the last 30 years. Citizenship rights for women as heads of household and single parents, nevertheless, are limited. Indeed, female single parents are now classified as 'an excluded group' (Lees, 2000: 261–2) – in other words, a group which is unable to benefit from citizenship rights such as educational and employment opportunities. *The Citizenship Order* indicates only in passing that young people should be taught 'about the impact of separation, divorce and bereavement on families' (QCA, 2000: 193).

At the same time, the normative stance taken in relation to marriage is problematic, not least because of its confusions and obfuscations. Students at Key Stage 4 (aged 14–16) are expected to know about 'the nature and importance of marriage for family life and bringing up children' and 'the role and responsibilities of a parent and the qualities of good parenting and its value to family life'[8] (QCA, 2000: 193). The Statement of Values reprinted in this initial guidance supported family and marriage on the basis that there was a 'general agreement' in schools about such pro-family values (QCA, 2000: 195). Employing the notion of 'we' to assume such consensus, the document stated:

> We value truth, freedom, justice, human rights, the rule of law and collective effort for the common good. In particular, we value families as sources of love and support for all their members, and as the basis of a society in which people care for others. (QCA, 2000: 196)

On this basis, pupils would be encouraged not just to 'support families in raising children and caring for dependents', but also to 'support the institution of marriage' (QCA, 2000: 196).

176 *Addressing the gender agenda*

This endorsement by the English/Welsh citizenship education programme of the heterosexual (married) nuclear family may reflect the need to ensure national security and social order (Richardson, 1998). However, there are considerable consequences for lesbian and gay youth who already have an uncomfortable relationship with the 'nation' to which they belong, but to which they are considered a threat. The fear (moral panic) of instability puts restraints (such as Section 28 of the 1988 Local Government Act) on teachers, preventing them from promoting alternative lifestyles. Tolerance of gay and lesbian groups is only on the condition that they remain within the boundaries defined by normative society. Lesbian and gay men are 'partial citizens', 'dehumanised' by a 'disembodied' concept of citizenship (Richardson, 1998). As Nancy Fraser (1997) and Baker *et al.* (2004) point out, one of the most common forms of non-recognition, or marginalisation, in society is of those whose sexuality 'is often not named, and if named, is not accepted on equal terms with heterosexuality' (Baker *et al.*, 2004: 155).

The conventional view of citizenship reproduced within this new citizenship education programme tends not to challenge such discriminatory social patterns. Young people in schools have little chance therefore of considering the ways in which lesbians and gay men are excluded from civil, political and social rights, left unprotected from harassment on grounds of sexuality by the law and the police, and experience prejudicial treatment in relation to social rights of welfare. This level of repression of a full discussion about homosexuality, sexual orientation and the civic issues relating to them within the curriculum is extraordinary, in that it:

> denies lesbian, gay and bisexual young people a legitimate social space and language for reflecting upon a defining part of their personal and social identity ... the silence also diminishes the education of heterosexual students by maintaining their ignorance of sexual diversity. (Baker *et al.*, 2004: 155)

Contemporary debates about sexuality, while openly discussed in government, clearly did not frame the conventional political view of citizenship captured in the Crick Report and QCA's *Citizenship Order*. The Advisory Group does not appear to have considered whether citizenship education could challenge conventional models of heterosexuality. Of course, had it done so, this curriculum reform might not have been acceptable to government or to particular constituencies at that time. The compromise that was reached linked citizenship education to personal, social and health education. Key Stage 4 pupils were to be taught to be 'aware of exploitation in relationships' and:

- to challenge offending behaviour, prejudice, bullying, racism and discrimination assertively and take the initiative in giving and receiving support ...
- to be able to talk about relationships and feelings
- to deal with changing relationships in a positive way, showing goodwill to others and using strategies to resolve disagreements peacefully. (QCA, 2000: 193)

Whilst worthy goals, here again we find the failure to engage in questioning gendered power relations. The new citizenship education programme fails to interconnect sexuality education and citizenship education and, as a result, young people are not encourage to develop, in the context of civic rights:

> an understanding of their sexuality, the choices that flow from it and the knowledge, understanding and power to make those choices positive, responsible and informed. (Hanson and Patrick, quoted in Lees, 2000: 262)

It is here that citizenship education in the broad sense could become an invaluable space in which young men and women are taught about the way sexual identities today are constructed and how they shape sexual behaviour/orientation. The right to know about such things should be just as important as the mechanics of contraceptive devices. The institutional and cultural constraints which shape sexual identities and the role of sexual performance in relation to normative notions of compulsory heterosexuality, could be addressed. Then, the 'issues of responsibility and moral choice' could be related not just to political and economic rights, but also to questions of sexual power relations; to the different forms of male and female moral reasoning; and conflicting male and female responsibilities in society.

Another implication of the marginalisation of the private sphere from citizenship education is a lack of discussion about the significance of religious and cultural practices. Archaud (2003) argues that the principles of common values around universal rights, individual autonomy and equal treatment promoted by the Crick Report are potentially threatened by such practices. He asks how the concept of gender equality can provide a guiding principle of citizenship across cultures if the private sphere is structured in ways that promote gender difference and the subordination of women. Of particular concern are the various practices which most frequently lead to intercultural clashes, many of which are to do with gender – Benhabib (2002) quotes Parekh's (2000) list[9] which has twelve such practices.

> Of the (…) practices listed by Parekh, seven concern the status of women in distinct cultural communities; two bear on dress codes (pertaining to both sexes (the wearing of the turban and the *hijab*)); two are about the lines separating private from public jurisdictional authority in the education of children; and one each concerns dietary codes and funeral rights. (Benhabib, 2002: 83)

Most of these practices reflect the status of women, girls, marriage and sexuality. They challenge the notion of a form of liberal citizenship that assumes female autonomy and freedom to access basic rights. For some, these practices are simply described as patriarchal and against the principle of universal citizenship – whilst others, such as Shaila Benhabib, suggest that such different cultures, rather than being seen as 'simply patriarchal', are recognised as containing internal gender contestations, as differentiated, complex and dynamic (see discussion of Okin's theory in Chapter 6). The question of how to educate young people into a more sophisticated view of other cultures, rather than into liberal notions of universality and equality, is one which the citizenship programme has yet to address. It is a crucial question, though, for the gender analysis of citizenship and its connections to multiculturalism, ethnic diversity and pluralism.

Finally, it is not clear from this new citizenship agenda whether there is any sense of an opening up of possibilities for girls and women to achieve any sense of agency, despite its emphasis on the public rather than the private sphere. Research has shown that, although there are some spaces in schools in which agency, negotiation, avoidance, opposition and resistance can be developed, these pedagogic spaces are limited, especially for girls (Gordon *et al.*, 2000). Often the spheres in which female agency can be developed are constrained by conventional definitions of femininity and the regulation of girls' sexuality. The rhetoric of equal and democratic participation that characterises much of citizenship education can place girls in a contradictory relationship to civic activity. If politics were taken not in an instrumental or pragmatic sense, but as a horizon which 'opens up the possibilities of human action and which is a contested symbolic, material and factual terrain', then political education would offer the opportunity to create new social identifications and forms of action (Morrow and Torres, 1998: 22; Dillabough and Arnot, 2002:61–89). Such identifications and forms of action might also be highly relevant to the status and experience of women in the private and intimate spheres, as well as in the public domain.

Our analysis of the English/Welsh citizenship programme suggests that there are now substantial needs in relation to the education of citizens about gender relations, gender equality and gender power. Many of these needs were not met, largely because of the reliance of the Advisory Group on traditional distinctions and separations contained within civic republicanism, liberalism and neo-liberal concepts of the citizen. Reform of the political culture went so far, but was not deep enough in its analysis of civil society and its gendered political cultures to encourage young people to question gender inequalities and oppressions. Schools could be urged to prepare the next generation for social and moral flux, and significant gender changes and gender diversity. In the next section, we consider whether this agenda is more likely to be addressed by educational initiatives which address global citizenship, globalisation and development.

Gender and the global citizenship education agenda: unexplored terrain

Over the last few years, contemporary debates about the value and meaning of a global perspective in citizenship education have also been vibrant (Cogan and Derricott, 2000; Heater, 2004; Osler and Vincent, 2002), and there have been calls for global citizenship education for the twenty-first century from a variety of different sources. However, with the exception of the work of black, Southern and African women's development groups, there has also been only limited recognition of the gender significance of either global citizenship or even the effects of the global dimension on women. Here the tensions between liberalism and civic republicanism are not so clear-cut. They take different form in the debates concerning the meaning of global citizenship education.

It is interesting to note that, although the concept of 'world' or 'global citizenship' has a long history dating back to the Stoics (Heater, 2004; Nussbaum, 2002), the notion of 'global citizenship education' is relatively new in the UK, where current trends can be traced back to the initiative of the Council for Education in World Citizenship (CEWC, 1939–2000). The terms 'education for world citizenship', 'education for international understanding' and 'global education' were used in the second half of the twentieth century when global education teaching was understood to be the means 'to ameliorate the world's troubles by cultivating in the younger generation an understanding ... taken to mean both comprehension and empathy' (Heater, 2001: 246). The discursive framing of 'global citizenship education' is more recent and is, not surprisingly, weak. Moreover, there is persistent concern that the concept of the global citizen is not only disputed, but may also have negligible political meaning (Heater, 2004).

Global citizenship education has been associated with complicated changing global climates and discourses. On the one hand, there are new global policies, such as the UN Millennium Development Goals, requiring increased international collaboration; on the other hand, grassroots counter-movements against economic globalisation call into question the concept of global citizenship. Within the movement for global education, a global citizen has been defined as someone who 'is aware of the wider world and has a sense of their own role as a world citizen; respects and values diversity; is willing to act to make the world a more equitable and sustainable place; takes responsibility for their actions' (Oxfam, 2000: 2). Such discussions are more likely to be framed within a liberal, individualist and often colonial global human rights model, in contrast to the civic republican, active but state-bounded model. This has led some commentators to consider the need for discussion about the existence of multiple citizenships (Delanty, 2000) or cosmopolitan citizenship (Nussbaum, 2002) accompanied by a sense of 'global civic virtue' or 'civic cosmopolitanism' (Delanty, 2000; Heater, 2002) that acknowledges both cosmopolitan or communitarian models of citizenship.

The movement for global citizenship education in schools is somewhat uncertain. It offered only cursory support for the citizenship curriculum for secondary schools in England and Wales discussed earlier. Not surprisingly, reference to 'the global' within the official English and Welsh Citizenship Curriculum is minimal. Fewer than 10 per cent of the issues covered in the programme of study for 12 to 16 year olds (Key Stages 3 and 4) are devoted to the following aims:

> Pupils should be taught about ... the world as a global community, and the political, economic, environmental and social implications of this, and the role of the European Union, the Commonwealth and the United Nations. (QCA and DFEE, 1999: 14)

> Pupils should be taught about ... the United Kingdom's relations in Europe, including the European Union, and relations with the Commonwealth and the

180 *Addressing the gender agenda*

United Nations ... the wider issues and challenges of global interdependence and responsibility, including sustainable development and Local Agenda 21. (QCA and DFEE, 1999: 15)

Recently, the English government and Welsh Assembly have introduced not insignificant recommendations and strategies such as *Putting the World into World Class Education* (DfES, 2004), *Developing a Global Dimension in the Curriculum* (DfES/DFID, 2005) and *Education for Sustainable Development and Global Citizenship* (ACCAC, 2002). These documents are aimed at whole-school, cross- and extra-curricular activity in schools, but ultimately they are little more than recommendations, and global citizenship education currently remains a low priority for the Department for Children, Schools and Families. Two of the documents were also very much designed and facilitated by the NGO sector.

Despite the lack of recognition of gender issues in the statutory mainstream school curriculum, development education centres and national agencies in the UK now promote global citizenship education and the inclusion of global issues in schools. The global dimension features in the cross-curricular theme of education for sustainable development, in the official discourse of Department for International Development (DFID), and in the work of Development Education Centres (DECs) and other global education NGOs (Marshall, 2005). For example, a consortium of organisations including the Development Education Association (DEA), Oxfam, the Commonwealth Institute and the Council for Environmental Education (amongst others) recently published the document *Citizenship Education: the global dimension* (DEA, 2001), alongside the launch of the related website (www.citizenship-global. org.uk) to complement the English Citizenship Curriculum. The consortium used the phrase 'the global dimension to citizenship education' (DEA, 2001: 5) reflecting the controversial nature of global citizenship education. The project emphasises human rights and social justice as key concepts in a global dimension, focusing on poverty reduction. Another key NGO document is the Europe-wide Global Education Congress *European Strategy Framework for improving and increasing global education in Europe to the Year 2015* (2002).[10] Although there is no guarantee that such documents are being widely adopted in schools, their existence recognises the possibilities of global education at a strategic level.

Significantly, NGOs also cannot agree about terminology or meaning. 'Global educators' – NGO workers and teachers promoting global education in schools in England – have been found to be particularly hesitant about using the term 'global citizenship education' until more homogeneity in the movement exists about its meaning and pedagogy (Marshall, 2005, 2007a). Those from development education centres also appear to be concerned about how notions of development were being re-conceptualised in schools. Global citizenship in schools is usually described in terms of the knowledge and understanding, skills and values and attitudes required (Oxfam, 1997, 2000) – terms that are vague but which can also support multi-cultural, anti-racist, development and environment education.

From a gender perspective, global citizenship pedagogies, although problematic, could potentially be an important new vehicle for promoting gender equality at regional, national and international level. Interviews with English global educators, and an analysis of key documents from organisations and commentators within the field, indicate the existence of at least eight fairly distinct but resilient pedagogic traditions of global education (Marshall, 2005, 2007b). Some of these traditions overlap, some have more theoretical than empirical relevance, and together they traverse the spectrum from liberal-individualism to more cosmopolitan notions of global citizenship. The curricular field is therefore heterogeneous and fluid in relation to the different conceptual traditions listed below.

Global education traditions in England

- *World Studies* – now also future studies, with its roots in values education and education for justice and equity (using participatory learning approaches).
- *Human Rights Education* – concerned with citizenship education and different from development education tradition.
- *North/South Linking* – concerned with development education and education for justice, traditionally dominant in Europe.
- *Development Education in the Era of Globalisation* – recent tradition with globalisation theory as the knowledge base.
- *Traditional Development Education* – concerned with sustainable development education with development theory as knowledge base.
- *Global/Global Citizenship Education* – pragmatic tradition working with current official discourse.
- *Environmental and Education for Sustainable Development* – originating from the environmental education movement, prioritising of sustainable development.
- *Christian Global or Development Education* – working overtly in conjunction with Christian morals and values.[11] (Marshall, 2005)

The dominant discourses in the field seem to reflect the conventional development education, human rights and Christian traditions. However, a younger generation of global educators appears to have recognised the importance of globalisation processes as they work through concepts of global citizenship. Not surprisingly, the representation of gender in relation to the content of these pedagogic traditions is erratic and occasional. It is not a systematic theme, nor is gender equality a targeted goal. For example, the Development Education Association documentation on global dimensions of citizenship education (DEA, 2001) fails to include gender as a key issue for exploration, even though it identifies highly relevant ideas for teaching and learning such as trade, faith, school-linking, slavery, Local Agenda 21, health, and so forth. Gender is only sometimes represented in the lists of 'global issues' that NGOs recommend to be taught.

The global education project, run by the British Overseas Aid Group (BOAG), and DFID's 'Get Global' project for Key Stages 3 and 4, address the idea of global citizenship but – significantly, because of its Freirian pedagogic approach – encourages teachers and students to arrive at equality issues themselves. This low-key approach contrasts with the fact that the organisations involved and the suggested resources of information are well known for being actively involved in global gender-related projects of some kind, often in relation to issues concerning poverty and health. Encouragement is to be found in the fact that at the launch of Get Global! (Actionaid, 2003b), gender issues and global citizenship were considered in some workshops and keynote speeches.

These hesitant responses to gender equality fail to reflect the fact that gender has found its place as one of the most important items on the global agenda. Indeed, now high on the international development agenda, women's education exists in a new global context that exposes critical aspects of gendered power relations, shifting boundaries between the public and private spheres and encourages new forms of female agency. Gender inequalities in education since the 1980s have received much attention in international declarations and treaties that put 'flesh on the minimalist bones of existing human rights legislation' (UNESCO, 2003: 27). The Convention on the Elimination of all Forms of Discrimination against Women (CEDAW) was ratified by 173 countries and came into force in 1981. As a result of the Dakar Framework, two of the key Millennium Development Goals supported by the World Bank, UNESCO, UNICEF, etc., are to: achieve universal primary education: ensure that, by 2015, children everywhere, boys and girls alike, will be able to complete a full course of primary schooling (Goal 2: Target 3); promote gender equality and empower women: eliminate gender disparity in primary and secondary education, preferably by 2005, and to all levels of education no later than 2015 (Goal 3: Target 4).

At present the international concern is to bring into line the 28 countries (most of which are in sub-Saharan Africa) that will probably not meet such Millennium Development Goals, although financial assistance is not forthcoming (reflected in recent UN-official calls for the doubling of spending on Millennium Development Goals). Attention is now focused on the extent to which both boys and girls have: (a) the right to an education, (b) the right within education, and (c) the right through education (UNESCO, 2003: 2). As the Director General of UNESCO pointed out, 'the scourge of illiteracy still affects more than 860 million adults, almost two-thirds of whom are women' and, whilst millions of children fail to get access to schooling or drop out of education, the majority of such children are girls (UNESCO, 2003: 2). Women's education as an issue has the potential to expose power relations, shifting boundaries between public and private spheres and new forms of female agency.

Global citizenship education could potentially become an appropriate curricula vehicle to address such global gender inequalities. To do so, it would need to address the ways in which gender relations constantly shift in globalising economies around the world. Globalisation is a destabilising force that exposes the harsh life-realities which women face across the world. At the same time, as Stromquist and Monkman (2000) observe:

> Globalization ... has introduced contradictory ideas in the reproduction of gender ideologies and practices in society: It has provided the space for

critique and alternative social visions and at the same time transfers representations of women and men that are not only highly genderized but also solidify very traditional views of these two sets of actors. (Stromquist and Monkman, 2000: 8)

The multi-faceted and complex concept of globalisation destabilises modernist or state-centred conceptualisations of citizenship – although it 'does not necessarily mean the death of the state or of particular imagined communities' (Blackmore, 2000: 150–1). Instead, Blackmore argues, globalisation is about:

... the changing nature of state relations and relations between different communities (local, regional and global); labour and capital relations; relations between the individual, state and market, and between nation-states; and how education is positioned in these shifting relations. The issue for feminists is to understand better how these new formations and relationships are gendered and to consider how we need to 'develop anti-imperialist curricula and transnational feminist practice. (Blackmore, 2000: 151)

Nira Yuval-Davies (1992) contends that an Orwellian 'doublethink' can be identified in debates about issues of female citizenship (in arenas beyond the nation-state) – a paradox that is not exclusive to totalitarian societies. On the one hand, since the UN naming of the International Year of Women in 1975, women's movements have been 'globalized' (Heater, 2002: 142). The recent Beijing conference was particularly significant because of the explicit inclusion and recognition of female agency. In the West, especially where the advantages of globalisation are more likely to be experienced, social and cultural developments suggest that the woman's movement is experiencing something of a rejuvenation. Commentators have talked about how women of different ethnicities, races and class have differential access to the state in different parts of the world – in other words, questions of national and racist exclusions are gaining a higher profile (Dillabough and Arnot, 2002). Economic globalisation has seen a higher level of participation of women in the labour market with, for example, educated middle-class women having increased opportunities for professional and managerial employment; although many of these feminised jobs in the global arena are low paid, temporary and/or insecure (Acker, 2004: 35).

Whilst the meaning of 'social justice' and 'equity' continues to be disputed, issues of gender and social justice have permeated debates about the effects of cultural and political globalisation, albeit with an emphasis upon individualised notions of choice and rights. However, within this context, an example of globalisation doublethink is illustrated by the existence of obstacles and contradictions for women. For example, whilst 'women feel both the pain and the pleasure associated with seductive notions of choice', Blackmore (2000) poignantly argues that they 'largely bear the responsibility as the competitive state withdraws from its social welfare obligations while reprivatizing women's productive labour' (Blackmore, 2000: 135). Inequality and poverty are said to be the main negative outcomes of globalisa-

184 *Addressing the gender agenda*

tion for women (Acker, 2004; Blackmore, 2000), but entry into the global capitalist arena has also meant 'a restoration or strengthening of traditional, capitalist gender, race and class hierarchies' (Acker, 2004: 37). Inequality and poverty contributes to international trafficking in women and children for prostitution and other forms of labour. However, generalisation about the effects of these global changes (as seen in welfare state systems, employment and migration for example) is highly problematic because effects vary temporally and geographically, and according to gender, race and ethnicity. However, whatever these differences, 'it seems that women may be more negatively affected than men' (Acker, 2004: 36).

Commentators now consider the multi-layers of globalisation, and a dominant way of conceptualising these levels has been in the form of the dualism. A distinction is made between globalisation from 'above' and globalisation from 'below', or the 'upper' and 'lower' circuit of globalisation – referring to the globalising bureaucrats at the upper level and the transnational social justice forces at the lower level. Henry (2001), for example, argues that it is important for feminists to engage with this relationship by thinking about 'how the upper can be made to engage with the lower' (Henry, 2001: 96). However, we must not fall into the trap of simply equating these levels with the bad and the good respectively, nor conclude that any education about globalisation or education for social justice should only focus on the empowerment of those at the 'lower level'. It is more that there is an urgent need to recognise that globalisation can no longer be presented as a solely negative, neutral or straightforward 'economic' term, especially when considered in conjunction with issues of gender, race or ethnicity.

There are clearly aspects of globalisation processes that can be used to strengthen claims for equity and empowerment in education, with one of the key discursive spaces for mounting such a claim existing in global citizenship education. Unfortunately, working against women, in the West particularly, is the claim that 'girls and women are no longer educationally disadvantaged – or more strongly, that boys and men are now the educationally and occupationally disadvantaged groups' (Henry, 2001: 93). This may be one of the reasons that very little has been written at any level about gender and global citizenship education. Education remains a central strategy for competing in the global arena, and as the state becomes much more of a market player than a mediator between civil society and the economy (Henry, 2001: 90).

A gender-sensitive global citizenship education

There have been some attempts to link discussions of gender, globalisation and global education. An exception to the rule can be found in the work of Annette Scheunpflug who, at a recent Global Education Network Europe (GENE) conference, proposed a framework for global education that recognises the complex processes of globalisation, global civil society and global citizenship. Her discussion of the challenges for global learning highlighted the need to deal with knowledge and non-knowledge, certainty and uncertainty, local relationships and spacelessness, and familiarity and strangeness (Scheunpflug, 2004: 40–1). Students would be offered a learning atmosphere where contradictions and 'changes of perspectives' could be explored (Scheunpflug, 2004: 40–2). Scheunpflug's recognition of the factual, temporal, spatial and social dimensions of what she terms global education offers a potential framework for understanding of the relationship between women and globalisation – although the 'economic' dimension of global education is perhaps underplayed in this analysis.

One of the great advantages about global education, over and above the constraints of the type of national citizenship education programme described earlier, is that it allows recognition of the diversity of global cultures, gender formations, relations and identities. It allows children to engage in discussions not just about cultural differentiations in gender – different forms of masculinity and femininity within one culture and across different cultures – but also encourages children to recognise rather than avoid any differences between men and women – whether in terms of their knowledge, experience or identifications. For example, young people have much to learn from an analysis of the functioning of the World Bank initiatives in relation to development and how this affects women and men's lives. They could also consider the post-colonial critique of how women in the developing world are portrayed and the strategies being developed to encourage women's agency and global alliances around development.

Pupils could be introduced to the different meanings attached to women's citizenship globally by a consideration of the texts of recent 'redemptive' declarations. Elaine Unterhalter's (2000) research, for example, demonstrates how international educational policies frame contemporary understandings of the 'female citizen'. Her analysis of the declarations by, for example, the World Bank and UNESCO, reveals the essentialism and passivity ascribed to women's citizenship in the 'developing world' and how an investment in female education is restrained by limited notions of stakeholding and citizenship. Women are seen either as needing to be educated as future mothers of citizens, or as part of economic development – rarely in their own right. In contrast, the Beijing World Conference on Women challenged such redemptive agendas by attempting to put forward a discourse of female agency and human rights that acknowledges 'the diversity of women and their roles and circumstances' (WCW, 1995: 154, quoted in Unterhalter, 2000: 95). The Beijing Declaration stated its commitment to:

> The empowerment and advancement of women, including the right to freedom of thought, conscience, religion and belief, thus contributing to the moral, ethical, spiritual and intellectual needs of women and men, individually or in community with others, and thereby guaranteeing them the possibility of realising their full potential in society and shaping their lives in accordance with their own aspirations. (WCW, 1995: 155, quoted in Unterhalter, 2000: 95)

Noticeable is the refusal of this Declaration, written by women for women, to link the need for women's education to children or the economic growth of society – instead the rationale for women's education is associated with the necessity of women as a social group to be engaged politically through decision making that

186 *Addressing the gender agenda*

is premised upon a social context with others in society. The social actions of women are therefore pivotal to this feminist challenge – not as a straightforward notion of identity politics, but as legitimate social actors inside the public space of social life.

In contrast with the proposals for the national citizenship education curriculum in England and Wales, there are already some examples of interesting practice, albeit in the unofficial field of global citizenship education, which offer young people a choice to engage in gender and development issues in the UK. Some of the most interesting and encouraging resources on gender have come from organisations working within the movement for global citizenship education in the UK. Actionaid, for example, offers a resource for students to explore 'women's rights in relation to HIV/AIDS and education' (Actionaid, 2003a). As part of this online resource, Actionaid provides a fairly comprehensive flow diagram of the reasons for gender differences in education. Students are also offered opportunities to explore issues of gender and identity through the use of photographs and through consideration of the role of the development worker in the less economically developed country. Although this sort of initiative has its limitations, not least the fact that it is an example of what Unterhalter (2003) might call a 'women in development' (WID) approach (rather than a 'gender and development' [GAD] approach) because it neglects to consider the patriarchal nature of the educational and state systems, it goes some way towards considering the multidimensional nature of development and the multiple identities of the female global citizen.

If we are to take up this challenge, a gender-sensitive, global citizenship education programme could usefully address the concerns of the international human rights community that, according to Bunch (1995: 17), has also begun to recognise 'gender-based violations as pervasive and insidious forms of human rights abuse'. The mass violation of women's human rights is not generally considered an appropriate topic for national citizenship education in schools, not least because again it is largely located within the 'private' sphere of intimate relations – but education about the effects of economic globalisation and other global forces could, and arguably should, include issues such as: the battery of women; their physical and psychological imprisonment in the home; the violent entrapment of women in prostitution; violence against women in the home and in places of work; sexual exploitation and pornography; maternal mortality and compulsory pregnancy; rape; female infanticide; the malnutrition of girls; and women, girls and AIDS/HIV.

These are human rights violations that demand urgent attention but they are also issues of relevance to young people. Gendered and sexualised violence are also part of educational environments (Sunnari *et al.*, 2002). There is clearly much work to be done to address such violence, particularly in relation to the education of boys (Breines *et al.*, 2000). Citizenship education itself would require far more extensive, and arguably radical, politicisation in order to address such real, but usually hidden, gender violence in the public and private spheres. Bringing the citizenship agenda into the global arena therefore may go some way to re-examining the gender relations in the public-private sphere and gender power relations described earlier.

The education of the 'global citizen' may also encourage young people to engage in non-exploitative forms of intercultural communication and sharing with countries that might experience economic or humanitarian predicaments on a more significant scale. The goals of global citizenship education encapsulate the key themes of justice, equality, tolerance and peace, ensuring that children are educated about the most important social and economic issues in the world. There are now some attempts to address gender equality and to show how female citizenship issues affect global, national and local communities. Organisations such as the United Nations Development Fund for Women (UNIFEM) have issued mandates recognising that multilateral institutions have a responsibility to understand and respond to the need to 'build women's capacities to advocate their own interests' and to bring 'the women's movement's experience with empowerment into the context of multilateral policy making' (www.unifem.undp.org). Women have made a major contribution to the promotion of global peace and social harmony and have contributed substantially to national development. Arguably, gender-sensitive global citizenship education programmes can provide the political spaces in which their contribution can be valued. Similarly, virtual global communities can offer women opportunities to experience autonomy and independence, and can facilitate active involvement in global alliances (Kenway and Langmead, 2000).

Arguably, global citizenship education offers an important space for thinking through these two ways of strategising and conceptualising gender issues. In this context, it is important to consider the relationship of activists' ideas about gender justice, rights, capabilities and empowerment to patriarchal formations in different nation-states. By considering the problematic nature of universalising notions of the 'third world woman' or 'poor woman as victim', critical questions can be raised about issues of gender and identity.

Conclusions

The UN Assistant Secretary-General's retiring speech in March 2004 highlighted the fact that 'virtually nowhere are women's rights given the priority they deserve'. Nevertheless, it is important to acknowledge advancement in the global status of women.

> Progress has been made in six broad areas: awareness of the importance of gender perspectives in peace support work; development of gender action work plans in disarmament and humanitarian affairs; training in gender sensitivity; deployment of gender advisors; prevention and response to violence against women; work on codes of conduct, including sexual harassment; and support to greater participation of women in post-conflict reconstruction, post-conflict elections and governance. (King, 2004: 3)

Indeed, as this quote indicates, the women's movement has fundamentally changed

188 *Addressing the gender agenda*

the national and global civil society and civic agendas. Citizenship education programmes will need to be far more imaginative if they are to recognise the extent of this change.

Gender relations are changing globally and within many nation-states. They are also changing within social class cultures and ethnic or religious communities (Arnot *et al.*, 1999). A critical feminist politics of citizenship would emphasise the problem of gender inequality, globally and nationally, and work towards its eradication. But it would do so only once questions about particularity and specificity were addressed – not merely as token elements of social life or as mere discourse, but as fundamental to understanding social differentiation in a changing yet unequal world order. Educational institutions, therefore, need to play a major role in reshaping citizenship identities in line with such contemporary changes, but they need to be aware of the models of citizenship they are promoting by considering, for example, how female agency is being recognised. Local, national and global civic education programmes in schools could do worse than bring out into the open, illustrate and discuss these political and gender tensions for a new generation of both male and female youth. Central to any new political agenda in relation to gender equality is, therefore,

- the importance of women's social location in the state, the family and the community in relation to access over power and privilege;
- the need to recognise the opportunities and threats posed by economic restructuring, globalisation, development and the global arena for women;
- the necessity for addressing the re-distribution of resources and the recognition of those women and men who are located outside normative definitions of citizenship;
- the need for the social rights of both women and men to be recognised in the cultural, economic and political decisions which affect the shape and direction of their futures.

This chapter also illustrates how important it is to be cautious in attributing too much hope to a project of citizenship education that is premised upon 'freedoms' that repeatedly recast themselves inside a liberal political or civic republican framework that has failed to offer women full citizenship status. The consequences of this political approach are not only to marginalise issues of social equality (paradoxically), but also to encourage the view that the issues relating to the private sphere, sexuality, and indeed women's contributions to the polity, are insignificant. At the same time, such caution should not prevent us developing alternative visions of citizenship that move away from the oppressive dimensions of liberal democratic or civic republican concepts, to find other, perhaps more cosmopolitan (Nussbaum, 2002), meanings of citizenship and ways of engaging in the political space of social life. If gender equality is to become more than just a silent dimension of national and global citizenship education, then official support must be given to developing an appropriate agenda for schools and the teaching profession. The starting point for this could fall under any or all of the following initiatives:

- the formation or strengthening of appropriate international networks for the development of citizenship education in relation to gender equality;
- the development and cross-fertilisation of comparative research studies on gender and the nature of citizenship education in a global context;
- the promotion of appropriate forms of citizenship education for trainee teachers and educational practitioners as a means of highlighting and addressing contemporary national and global gender concerns and notions of female agency; and
- the development of appropriate citizenship education curricular guidance and material in which gender equality is integral.

As James Donald rightly argued, citizenship has no substantial identity until it is located within an understanding of the organisation of the symbolic, social order. In this respect, the radical potential of the concept is as important as its discriminatory political history (cf. Heater, 1990).

Acknowledgements

This paper was originally presented by Harriet Marshall and me at the University of Glasgow's Global Citizenship Seminar Series in the Faculty of Education and it formed the basis of later presentations at the UKFIET Education and Development conference in Oxford in 2004. I am grateful to Harriet for permission to work on the original version of our article, especially since she was the first named author.

References

ACCAC (2002) *Education for Sustainable Development and Global Citizenship*. Cardiff: Qualifications, Curriculum and Assessment Authority for Wales (ACCAC) for the Welsh Assembly.

Acker, J. (2004) 'Gender capitalism and globalization', *Critical Sociology*, 30(1): 17–41.

Actionaid (2003a) *Citizenship Briefings: Gender*. Available online at www.actionaid.org. (Accessed 30/04/04.)

Actionaid (2003b) *Get Global! A Skills-Based Approach to Active Global Citizenship, Key stages 3 and 4*. London: Actionaid.

Advisory Group on Citizenship (The Crick Report) (1998) *Education for Citizenship and the Teaching of Democracy in Schools. Final Report*. London: Qualifications and Curriculum Authority.

Archaud, D. (2003) 'Citizenship education and multiculturalism', in A. Lockyer, B. Crick and J. Annette (eds) *Education for Democratic Citizenship: issues of theory and practice*. Aldershot: Ashgate.

Arendt, H. (1958) *The Human Condition*. Chicago: Chicago University Press.

Arnot, M. (2004) 'Gender and citizenship education', in A. Lockyer, B. Crick and J. Annette (eds) *Education for Democratic Citizenship: issues of theory and practice*. Aldershot: Ashgate, pp. 103–19.

Arnot, M. (2005) 'Gender equality and citizenship education', *Journal of Social Sciences and their Didactics* (special issues on Gender Issues and Social Studies), www.sowi-onlinejournal.de

Arnot, M. and Dillabough, J.A. (eds) (2000) *Challenging Democracy: international perspectives on gender, education and citizenship*. London: RoutledgeFalmer.

Arnot, M., David, M. and Weiner, G. (1999) *Closing the Gender Gap: post-war education and social change*. Cambridge: Polity Press.

Arnot, M., Araújo, H., Deliyanni, K. and Ivinson, G. (2000) 'Changing Femininity, changing concepts of citizenship in public and private spheres', *The European Journal of Women's Studies*, 7(2): 149–68.

Arnot, M., Araújo, H., Deliyanni-Kouimtzi, K., Rowe, G. and Tomé, A. (1996) 'Teachers, gender and the discourses of citizenship', *International Studies in Sociology of Education*, 6(1): 3–35.

Baker, J., Lynch, K., Cantillon, S. and Walsh, J. (2004) *Equality: From Theory to Action*. London: Palgrave.

Benhabib, S. (2002) 'Multiculturalism and gendered citizenship', in *The Claims of Culture: equality and diversity in the global era*. Princeton, NJ: Princeton University Press.

Blackmore, J. (2000) 'Globalization: A useful concept for feminists rethinking theory and strategies in education', in N. Burbules and C. Torres (eds) *Globalization and Education: Critical Perspectives*. London: Routledge, pp. 133–56.

Bourdieu, P. (1997) 'The forms of capital', in A.H. Halsey, H. Lauder, P. Brown, and A. Stuart Wells (eds) *Education, Culture, Economy, Society*. Oxford: Oxford University Press, pp. 46–58.

Breines, I., Connell, R. and Eide, I. (eds) (2000) *Male Roles, Masculinities and Violence: a culture of peace perspective*. Paris: UNESCO.

Bunch, C. (1995) 'Transforming human rights from a feminist perspective', J. Peters, A. Wolper (eds) *Women Rights, Human Rights: international feminist perspectives*. New York: Routledge, pp. 11–17.

Burbules, N. and Torres, C. (eds) (2000) *Globalization and Education: critical perspectives*. London: Routledge.

Cogan, J.J. and Derricott, R. (2000) *Citizenship for the 21st Century*. London: Kogan Page.

Council of Europe (2000) *A New Social Contract between Women and Men: the role of education, Seminar proceedings*. Strasbourg: Council of Europe, EC/ED(2000)10.

Crick B. (2000a) *Essays on Citizenship*. London: Continuum.

Crick, B. (2000b) 'The Citizenship Order for schools', in N. Pearce and J. Hallgarten (eds) *Tomorrow's Citizens*. London: Institute of Public Policy Research (IPPR), pp. 77–83.

Crick, B. (2000c) 'The English Citizenship Order: a temperate reply to critics', *The School Field*, 9(3–4): 61–72.

Crick, B. (2002) *Democracy*. Oxford: Oxford University Press.

Delanty, G. (ed.) (2000) *Citizenship in a Global Age*. Buckingham: Open University Press.

Department for Education and Skills (DfES) (2004) *Putting the World into World Class Education: and international strategy for education, skills and children's services*. Nottingham: DfES. DfES/1077/2004. Available at http://publications.teachernet.gov.uk/eOrderingDownload/DfES10772004.pdf

Department for Internal Development (DFID) (2005) *Developing a Global Dimension in the Curriculum*. DFID. Available at http://www.globaldimension.org.uk/ResourceDetails.aspx?id=1135

Development Education Association (DEA) (2001) *Citizenship Education: The Global Dimension*. London: Development Education Association.

Dillabough, J. and Arnot, M. (2002) 'Recasting educational debates about female citizenship, agency and identity', *The School Field*, 13(3/4): 61–89.

Fraser, N. (1997) *Justice Interruptus: critical reflections on the post-socialist condition*. London: Routledge.

Garmarnikow, E. and Green, A. (1999) 'Social capital and the educated citizen', *The School Field*, 10(3–4): 103–26.

Gordon, T., Holland, J. and Lahelma, E. (2000) *Making Spaces: citizenship and difference in school*. London: MacMillan.

Hanson, B. and Patrick, P. (1995) 'Towards some understanding of sexuality education', in

S. Inman and S. Buck (eds) *Adding Value? Schools' responsibility for pupils' personal development*. Exeter: Trentham Books.
Heater, D. (1990) *Citizenship: The Civic Ideal in World History, Politics and Education*. Harlow: Longman.
Heater, D. (1999) *What is Citizenship?* Cambridge: Polity Press.
Heater, D. (2001) 'The history of citizenship education in England', *The Curriculum Journal*, 12, 1, 103–23.
Heater, D. (2002) *World Citizenship: Cosmopolitan Thinking and its Opponents*. London: Continuum.
Heater, D. (2004) *A History of Education for Citizenship*. London: RoutledgeFalmer.
Henry, M. (2001) 'Globalisation and the politics of accountability: issues and dilemmas for gender equity in education', *Gender and Education*, *13*(1): 87–100.
Ivinson, G. with Arnot, M., Araújo, H., Deliyanni-Kouimtzi, K., Rowe, G. and Tomé, A. (2000) 'Student teachers' representations of citizenship: a comparative perspective', in M. Arnot and J. Dillabough (eds) *Challenging Democracy: feminist perspectives on gender, education and citizenship*. London: RoutledgeFalmer.
Kenway, J. and Langmead, D. (2000) 'Cyberfeminism and citizenship? Challenging the political imaginary', in M. Arnot and J. Dillabough (eds) *Challenging Democracy: international perspectives on gender, education and citizenship*. London: RoutledgeFalmer, pp. 312–39.
King, A. (2004) *Introductory Statement at the 48th session of the Commission on the Status of Women*. New York 1–12 March, 2004. Available online (accessed 10/05/04) www.un.organisation/womenwatch/daw/csw/csw48.
Lees, S. (2000) 'Sexuality and citizenship', in Arnot, M. and J. Dillabough (eds) *Challenging Democracy: international perspectives on gender, education and citizenship*. London: RoutledgeFalmer, pp. 259–76.
Marshall, H. (2005) 'Constructing Global Education in England'. Unpublished doctoral thesis, University of Cambridge.
Marshall, H. (2007a) 'Global education in perspective: fostering a global dimension in an English secondary school', *The Cambridge Journal of Education*, *37*(3).
Marshall, H. (2007b) 'The global education terminology debate: Exploring some of the issues', in M. Hayden, J. Levy and J. Thomson (eds) *A Handbook of Research in International Education*. London: Sage.
Morrow, R. and Torres, C. (1998) 'Education and the reproduction of class, gender and race: responding to the postmodern challenge', in C. Torres, and T.R. Mitchell (eds) *Sociology of Education: emerging perspectives*. Albany: State University of New York Press.
Morrow, R. and Torres, C. (2000) 'The state, globalization and education policy', in Burbules and Torres (eds) *Globalization and Education: critical perspectives*. London: Routledge, pp. 27–56.
Noddings, N. (1988) 'An ethic of caring and its implications for instructional arrangements', *American Journal of Education*, 96(2): 215–30.
Nussbaum, M. (2002) 'Education for Citizenship in an Era of Global Connection', *Studies in Philosophy and Education*, 21: 289–303.
Nussbaum, M. and Glover, J. (1995) 'Emotions and women's capabilities', in *Women, Culture and Development: a study of human capabilities*. Oxford: Oxford University Press.
Nussbaum, M.C. (1999) *Sex and Social Justice*. Oxford: Oxford University Press.
Osler, A. and Starkey, V. (1996) *Teacher Education and Human Rights*. London: David Fulton.
Osler, A. and Vincent, K. (2002) *Citizenship and the Challenge of Global Education*, Stoke-on-Trent: Trentham Books.
Oxfam (1997; 2000) *A Curriculum for Global Citizenship*. Oxford: Oxfam.
Parekh, B. (2000) *Rethinking Multiculturalism: cultural diversity and political theory*. Cambridge, MA: Harvard University Press.

Pateman, C. (1989) *The Disorder of Women*. Cambridge: Polity Press.
Qualifications and Curriculum Authority (QCA) (2000) *Citizenship at Key Stages 3–4: initial guidance for schools*. Suffolk: QCA Publications.
Qualifications and Curriculum Authority (QCA) (2002) *Citizenship: a scheme of work for Key Stage 4*. Sudbury, Suffolk: QCA Publications.
Qualifications and Curriculum Authority (QCA) and Department for Education and Employment (DFEE) (1999) *Citizenship: The National Curriculum for England, Key Stages 3–4*. Suffolk: QCA Publications.
Richardson, D. (1998) 'Sexuality and Citizenship', *Sociology*, *32*(1): 83–100.
Roland Martin, J. (1994 [1982]) 'Excluding women from the educational realm', in L. Stone (ed.) *The Education Feminism Reader*. New York: Routledge, pp. 105–21.
Scheunpflug, A. (2004) 'Learning and Skills for a Global Society: the education context', in *Learning for a Global Society: Proceedings of the GENE Conference*, London, 23–25 September 2003. Lisbon: North-South Centre of the Council of Europe, pp. 39–46.
Scottish Executive Education Department (2001) *An International Outlook: educating young Scots about the world*. Scotland: SEED.
Sen, A. (1999) *Development as Freedom*. Oxford: Oxford University Press.
Skinner, Q. (1998) *Liberty before Liberalism*. Cambridge: Cambridge University Press.
Stromquist, N. (2004). 'Teacher Intersection of Public Politics and Gender: Understanding State Action in Education', Conference paper presented at the Gender and Policy workshop, CIES annual meeting, Salt Lake City, 11 March.
Stromquist, N. and Monkman, K. (eds) (2000) *Globalization and Education: integration and contestation across cultures*. Langman, MD: Rowman and Littlefield.
Sunnari, V., Kangasvuo, J. and Heikkinen, M. (eds) (2000) *Gendered and Sexualised Violence in Educational Environments*. Oulu, Sweden: Oulu University Press.
Turner, B. (2001) 'The erosion of citizenship', *British Journal of Sociology*, *52*(2): 189–209.
UNESCO (2003) *Gender and Education for All: the leap to equality*. EFA Global Monitoring Report. Paris: UNESCO.
Unterhalter, E. (2000) 'Transnational visions of the 1990s: Contrasting views of women, education and citizenship', in M. Arnot and J. Dillabough (eds) *Challenging Democracy: international perspectives on gender, education and citizenship*. London: RoutledgeFalmer, pp. 87–103.
Unterhalter, E. (2003) 'Gender Basic Education and Development: an overview of literature', Paper given at the introductory seminar at the Institute of Education/Oxfam 'Development and Education: Beyond Access Project'. London, June 2003.
World Conference on Women (WCW) (1995) 'Beijing Declaration', *Women's Studies Quarterly*, *24*(1 and 2): 154–8.
Yuval-Davis, N. (1992) 'Women as Citizens', in A. Ward, J. Gregory and N. Yuval-Davis (eds) *Women and Citizenship in Europe: borders, rights and duties*. Stoke-on-Trent: Trentham and EFSF, pp. 11–16.
Yuval-Davis, N. and Werbner, P. (eds) (1999) *Women, Citizenship and Difference*. London: Zed Books.

Notes

1 This is an amended version of Marshall, H. and Arnot, J. (2006) 'The gender agenda: the limits and possibilities of national and global education', *World Studies in Education*, *7*(1): 81–106. It draws upon some of the analysis of the Crick Report from Arnot (2004) and Arnot (2005).

Addressing the gender agenda 193

2 However, the concept of 'equality', although initially included in the guidance to schools (QCA, 2000), does not appear even to be mentioned in any later documentation, nor, indeed, is the concept encouraged as a more advanced second-order construct.

3 Crick (2002a) revealed that when he chaired the Advisory Group, he found himself cautiously steering a course away from the liberal concept of 'the good citizen' towards the duties of 'the active citizen' required by notions of a civic republic:

> I often wonder how many of my group realised that they were signing up to the radical agenda of civic republicanism rather than the less demanding 'good citizen' and 'rule of law' imperatives of liberal democracy. The 'citizenship order' for schools provides instrumentalities for this more radical agenda: discussion of controversial issues; participation in school and community affairs; learning skills of advocacy; the idea of 'political literacy' as a blending of skills, knowledge, and attitudes; learning awareness of cultural diversities – the different nations, religions, and ethnic groups within the United Kingdom; all this and more where there was no national curriculum for citizenship before. (Crick, 2002a: 114)

4 In these countries, student teachers were found to support notions of a citizen's duty to encourage democracy over and above the action of the state. However, the strong discourse of duty tended to be used mainly by male teachers in the sample. Women appeared neither to use the discourses of civic republicanism, nor to find a position for themselves in it. Female teachers in all national samples were more likely to employ the *Judaeo-Christian* discourses of morality, emphasising the ethics of care and community involvement, or contemporary egalitarian discourses around state-provided social rights and social justice. That is, the 'good citizen' as presented by the grandmother, the mother, or the carer in the private sphere rather than the civic leader, representative or voter (see Chapters 3 and 4).

5 For example, more than 62 per cent of these student teachers in the English/Welsh sample selected the word 'competitive' and 51 per cent chose the image of 'powerful' to represent men in public life, whilst 34 per cent of student teachers described women as 'efficient', 27 per cent described them as 'competitive' and 25 per cent as 'independent' rather than powerful.

6 See Ivinson *et al.* (2000) for further details.

7 Forty-three per cent of the sample of English and Welsh student teachers described men in private life as 'disorganised', 'hesitant' (31 per cent) and 'dependent' (18 per cent) in domestic life.

8 Teachers are encouraged to discuss such relationships in single- and mixed-sex groups.

9 'These include: female circumcision; polygamy; Muslim and Jewish methods of animal slaughter; arranged marriages; marriages within prohibited degrees of relationships; scarring children's cheeks or other parts of the body; Muslim withdrawal of girls from co-educational practices such as sports and swimming lessons; Muslim insistence on wearing or taking off traditional turbans; Gypsy and Amish refusal to send their children to public schools either altogether or after a certain age; Hindu requests to be allowed to cremate their deceased; the subordinate status of women and all that entails' (Parekh, 2000: 264–65; quoted in Benhabib, 2002, 83–4).

10 Available online at www.globaleducationeurope.net (Accessed 30/03/04.)
11 For a full discussion of these different traditions see Marshall (2005).
12 Whether Kabeer's (discussed in Unterhalter 2003: 5–6) three dimensions of empowerment or Sen's (1999) 'capabilities approach', a concern with material inequality or a more postmodern concern with societal representations of inequality are employed, it will be necessary to take their underlying values and ethics into account.

Part IV
Individualised learning and global citizenship education

8 'Freedom's children'?

Gender, individualisation and the neo-liberal learner citizen

This chapter considers the contemporary role of educational systems in creating an individualised citizen and the implications for democracy. The aim here is to focus particularly on the processes of individualisation, since this concept is increasingly being used to explain young people's attitudes to their futures. Youth cultural researchers have found that young people today employ the language of individualisation and the concepts of freedom and choice, to justify their lifestyles and decisions. There is, therefore, great interest in the ways in which individualisation is being worked on by the younger generation (cf. Furlong and Carmel, 1997; Lagree, 2002). In contrast, there appears to be relatively little sociological analysis of how individualisation has shaped the education of the male and female learner citizen, especially in relation to contemporary pedagogy.[1] In this chapter, I consider the formation of new personalised learners and individualised youth cultures in the UK in light of the social theories of reflexive individualisation in late modernity, questioning whether such an individualisation process contributes to the alleviation or aggravation of social injustice.

In an earlier version of this chapter, I employed John Beck's (1998) distinction between the education of the citizen and the education for citizenship, in order to consider separately the notion of the *citizen as learner* and *the learner as citizen* (Arnot, 2005). This heuristic distinction is valuable in differentiating between the development of the pupil into citizen through the organisational aspects of schooling, and the specific curriculum tasks of designing citizenship education. It focuses attention on both the pedagogic and curricular aspects of schooling. Together, however, these aspects have even greater significance, as I shall try to show in this chapter. The education of the learner citizen is, as Rose (1990) argued, 'the citizen *in potentia*', but the learner citizen also represents 'society in the making'. The rise of the *individualised learner citizen* within the so-called 'risk society' is of direct relevance to the promotion of democracy and social justice. Educationalists are currently being challenged to think about what sort of citizen schooling is now being asked to create, and in preparation for what sort of society.

I begin by describing how contemporary processes of individualisation have been understood as a constraint or as a freedom, drawing particularly on the early work of Ulrich Beck and Elizabeth Beck-Gernsheim. I then consider how the notion of individualisation has started to reshape school pedagogies in the UK, encouraging notions of personalised learning and an independent learner, and promoting the use of pupil voice and consultation as part of the new democratised (and hence, seemingly more equitable) processes of schooling. Research has already begun to suggest that such notions of personalised/individualised learner citizens may hide the ways in which this construct is shaped by gender and other social inequalities, and even contributes to them. Youth cultural theorists, however, have provided contradictory evidence about how far individualisation, as a process within neo-liberalism, characterises contemporary youth – pointing to the contrasting male and female displays of such postmodern identities. Bauman's insights provide some thought-provoking conclusions to this contemporary debate.

Individualisation as constraint or as freedom?

Leif Moos, a Danish educationalist writing in a new anthology on *Democratic Learning* (MacBeath and Moos, 2004) draws to our attention Habermas', (2001) four defining characteristics of neo-liberal globalising societies – all of which do not bode well for democratic education or for those committed to using education to alleviate social inequalities and promoting social justice. The four characteristics are:

- an anthropological view of human beings as rational instruments, willing and able to make informed decisions and to offer their labour freely in the marketplace;
- an image of a post-egalitarian society that tolerates social marginalisation, expulsion and exclusion;
- an image of a democracy where citizens are reduced to consumers in a market society, and where the role of the state is redefined to that of a service agency for clients and consumers;
- a view that policy should be aimed at dismantling state regulation (Moos, 2004: 2).

In such globalising societies, governance is about market efficiency, not about promoting the sort of civil society which is regulated by 'communication and community, orality and ethics, and trust and reciprocity between subjects' (Moos, 2004: 2). As Moos points out, in this scenario, governance shifts from the state down to the classroom and to the individual. Governance is through the promotion of self-managing individuals:

> No longer are citizens presumed to be members of a political community, which it is the business of a particular form of governance to express. The old and presumed shared political process of the social contract disappears in favour of a disaggregated and individualised relationship to governance. (Peters *et al.*, 2000: 118, quoted in Moos, 2004: 3)

'Freedom's children'? 199

In direct contrast to this view, the concept of individualisation and the self-managing individual has been associated with greater democratic freedom. Ulrich Beck and Elizabeth Gernsheim-Beck (2002), for example, initially took a rather optimistic tone when they argued that two 'epochal forces of modernity:

> ... individualisation and globalisation, are changing the foundations of living together in all spheres of social action. Both only superficially appear to be threats: they force but they also permit society to prepare and reshape itself for a second modernity ... [C]ultural individualisation and globalisation create precisely that historical orientation and those preconditions for an adaptation of institutions to a coming second modernity. (Beck and Beck-Gernsheim, 2002: 169)

Countering those who see the negative destructive effects of globalised economies and a risk society, Beck and Beck-Gernsheim (2002) and Beck (1992) perceive the rise of what they call *'Freedom's Children'* – children who have been brought up, unlike their parents, to become choosers, or consumers of what life has to offer. Their new culture is described as *a self-culture* which combines the 'indeterminacy of self and of the ensuing conflicts, crises and developmental opportunities and a binding or bonding of self-oriented individuals to, with and against one another' (Beck and Beck-Gernsheim, 2002: 42). Central to this self-culture are the processes of reflexive individualisation, in which individuals come to see themselves as centres of their own life world. People's lives become an art form – something to be created. In the first stage of modernity, the ethos was of *'being individual'* and reflective – in contrast, in the second stage of modernity, the new generation of youth are now *'becoming individual'* through reflexivity. The new credo is not, 'I think, therefore I am' but rather, 'I am I' (Lasch, 2002: ix).

Beck and Beck-Gernsheim argue that, as a result, in this new 'second' stage of modernity, the 'quality of the social and the political' will be changed so that individuals no longer locate themselves in traditional communities, with traditional identities of class, gender and ethnicity. They argue that ascribed statuses, such as class, gender, ethnicity and regionality (which traditionally have been associated with social inequality) will all pale into significance – *normative* biographies will be replaced by *choice* biographies, and new alliances will be formed by individuals on the basis of shared common risks rather than any restrictive notion of social contract (Beck, 1992).

The political implications are likely to be major. In this century, *'Freedom's Children'* will experience difficulty in being directed from above or being forced into particular identities or types of commitment, preferring their own self-organisation and political action that is focused on different activities rather than on participation in a given democratic order. Young people will move outside the left–right spectrum, their identifications becoming more fluid. The form of civic participation for young people involves the right to take charge of matters that are thought to be important – a process of 'complaining, campaigning and acting about all things possible and impossible', developing through the centrifugal dynamic of a 'life of one's own'. The new self-culture thus represents what Beck and Beck-Gernsheim call a *third sphere* or sector – outside the money economy and political ballot box.

According to Beck and Beck-Gernsheim, evidence of the development of this self-culture is already visible in a variety of social changes: the new forms of social movement that act as forms of 'resistance within civil society'; 'the many kinds of moral and aesthetic experimentation' by people on how they live their lives, with their emotions, their personal relationships, 'parenthood, sex and love'; the 'great unfinished experiment' with healthy eating shifting people's relationship to nature and their bodies; 'the new forms of active empathy' with animal rights, asylum seekers, AIDS victims, drug addicts; the new forms of vigilantes protecting 'niches of prosperity'; the conflicts, great and small, between men and women in all spheres (Beck and Beck-Gernsheim, 2002: 44).

What characterises this culture is an *'internationalised practising consciousness of freedom'* (Beck and Beck-Gernsheim, 2002: 43). This increase in freedom, Beck and Beck-Gernsheim argue, is not a crisis – it is only a crisis if such freedom is understood as a threat to the traditional authority structures and forms of social privilege which sustained the first stage of modernity. Changing values (especially those of self-development) and acceptance of democracy arguably can go hand in hand. There is no necessary connection between this legally sanctioned individualism and either an inflation of material demands or a breaking down of altruism and community. Indeed, such individualisation might even lead to a rejection of the domination of a work-focused 'growth-oriented labour society' (Beck and Beck-Gernsheim, 2002: 162); a questioning of the custodians of public interest, and a great desire for more personal fulfilment, time and pleasure. Reflexive individualisation could also, if focused, ensure that there are more co-operative or altruistic individualists who are able to think for themselves and live for others at the same time. Beck argues that if we are fortunate, in the new world, traditional certainty will perish and be replaced by *'legally sanctioned individualism for everyone'* (Beck and Beck-Gernsheim, 2002: 157). The new forms of society will provide the conditions for an *internalised democracy* that is an extension of the Western heritage – another stage in the pursuit of individual development and social fulfilment. In this context, Western European democracy reaches its zenith. Beck (2001) later called this the 'democratisation of democracy' itself.

Clearly, educating *Freedom's Children* with new sets of values and a sense of belonging represents quite a challenge. Crude moral codes or simple national identities already look very dated and inappropriate, but then so do the forms of educational knowledge in current curricula. Critical thinking would be needed to address major cross-generational chasms about what forms of knowledge are valued. In the new social order, educational institutions would need to provide basic social and political rights and offer opportunities to develop an informational base; and to acquire the skills of preparedness for conflict, capacity for compromise, civic courage, curiosity, tolerance of ambiguity and the making of alliances. These forms of education would also have to stress the malleability of knowledge, the uncertainty of explanations and the relativity of perspective

(Arnot, 2004). Knowledge would be non-linear, as would institutions. There would not necessarily be an interlocking system of institutions, since strong connections would be established between individuals and the socio-technical world (Bauman, 2002). In such a future it may make little sense to talk about knowledge as property or subject positions – rather, reflexive modern individuals could be offered knowledge that was 'possibilistic, probabilistic and uncertain' (Lasch, 2002). In the future, learning is likely to be intense, at speed, with ranges of choice and opportunities for immediate decision making. The individual would be nomadic; finding the rules and roles him- or herself – there would be *a de-normalisation of roles*.

This transformation of the learner citizen is to some extent now underway, but not necessarily in the utopian fashion described by these theorists. The individualisation of the learner citizen is a rather complex affair, often masking – through its languages of choice, rights and voice – the social inequalities within contemporary Western economies. As Bernstein (2000) observes, contemporary educational agendas represent 'schizoid' or 'schizophrenic', often pathological, scenarios.[2] Today we have a unique coupling – what Bernstein called a 'pedagogical Janus' (Bernstein, 1990: 87) combining market-oriented modes with political discourses which exploit the language developed by egalitarian critiques of such markets. Thus neo-liberal agendas can be found clustered around the complex and often contradictory notions of possessive individualism, which allies itself with moral agendas, worrying about social exclusion and creating new citizenship identities to hold society together, whilst tearing apart the social fabric. The complexity of this discursive coupling, which I discuss below, can be found in the UK educational system today.

The individualising of the learner citizen

In the UK, as in other Western European countries, individualisation has already affected schooling, and particularly classroom learning, in a diverse range of ways – from the idea of a flexible school, the introduction of ICT learning, which can be highly individualised, to the flexibility of the curriculum and the discursive construction of the independent learner – all in their different ways imply the individualisation of learning and learners. Children are encouraged to see themselves as choosers making their own decisions about school, about work and about their life plans. However, the process of reflexive individualisation, when recontextualised within essentially modernist institutional settings and regimes, looks rather different from that described by Beck and Beck-Gernsheim. Rather than generate counter-narratives and alternative 'mindsets' (Rowan *et al.*, 2002) exploring the 'kindness and beauty' of the citizen (Beck and Beck-Gernsheim, 2002:165), the processes of individualisation are associated with high-performance cultures and expectations and, as we shall see, new modalities of social exclusion. Below I unravel the ways in which individualisation is brought into school pedagogies in the UK and the implications of this new political initiative for gender relations and the male and female learner citizen.

Personalisation, independent learning and pupil voice

By 2004, the Labour government in the UK used an egalitarian ethos to extol the virtues of the consumer in education and the connections between notions of voice and choice, yet always within a commitment to neo-liberal reforms of the educational system. Two models of so-called *personalised learning* were put forward – one by the then Prime Minister, Tony Blair, and the other by the then Minister for State for School Standards, David Miliband (Johnson, 2004b). Whilst the former encouraged the notion of personalised learning as a means of reorganising public educational provision in line with marketisation, Milliband represented personalised learning as a new means of opening up access to educational achievement by emphasising new types of pupil-based assessment for learning.

Tony Blair, as Prime Minister, hailed the egalitarianism of personalised learning. Using the rhetorical device of referring to giving 'power to the people', Blair masked his intention to streamline central government and hence produce a 'leaner' and 'fitter' welfare state, operating to minimum standards in line with New Labour political purposes. Although there was no evidence that parents or pupils as consumers had requested 'personalised learning', nevertheless it was, and still is, assumed to be the means by which the 'needs, interests and aptitudes' of individual pupils are addressed. This new discourse of civic engagement derives from Albert Hirschman's (1970) influential *Exit, Voice and Loyalty: Responses to decline in firms, organizations and states* (a text originally about rail transportation in Nigeria). Hirschman developed a theory that the performance of a firm or organisation in open markets was affected by two sorts of strategies open to consumers: the first is what he called the *exit option* – an economic strategy whereby the customer chooses to stop buying the product, or leaves the organisation (Hirschman, 1970: 4). The alternative is the so-called *voice option* whereby customers or members 'express their dissatisfaction directly to management or to some other authority ... or to anyone who cares to listen' (Hirschman, 1970: 4). Exit and voice are described as 'impersonations of economics and politics', respectively, since exit belongs to the former and voice to the latter. Exit encourages market forces to induce recovery (Hirschman, 1970: 15). Thus when parents move their children to different schools, they are trying to make schools more responsive to their members. The alternative is to open channels of communication between members and management. Hirschman argued that the political strategies relating to voice had far more potential for improving economic performance than neo-liberal economists realised. However, as Johnson (2004a) notes, it was not clear whether this commitment to personalised educational service had any real meaning at all, nor whether the implications for pedagogy had been thought through. What was implied was a change in the pedagogic relationship, with more attention being placed on the pedagogical style rather than on content (Johnson, 2004a: 6).[3]

This tension between personalisation of learning and individualised learning was felt by Miliband, who was anxious to reassure the public that such allegedly progressive/emancipatory approaches would not lead to the breakdown of the social activity of learning and collective social/moral orders created through schooling (see, for example: Johnson (2004a, 2004b); Fielding (2006); Whitty and Wisby (2007)). In a major speech to the North of England Education Conference on 8 January 2004, entitled 'Personalising Education: the future of public sector reform', Miliband (2004: 1) argued that the new social democratic settlement would now be designed to 'make universal the life chances of the most fortunate'. Three great challenges were identified: that of equity and excellence; that of flexibility and accountability; and that of universality and personalisation. Successful modern economies required flexible specialisation of individuals, not just of products and services:

> This leads straight to the promise of personalised learning. It means building the organization of schooling around the needs, interests and aptitudes of individual pupils: it means shaping teaching around the way different youngsters learn; it means taking the care to nurture the unique talents of every pupil. I believe it is *the* debate in education today. (Miliband, 2004: 3)

Pupils were now officially recognised as the driving force in 'whole-school improvement' – the 'whole-school team has to now take time to find out the needs and interests of students' (Miliband, 2004: 5). Miliband argued that *choice* and *voice* are understood to be 'strengthened by the presence of the other: ... the ability to make your voice heard provides a vital tool to the consumer who does not want to change shops, political parties every time they are unhappy' (Miliband, 2004: 7). He declared:

> The challenge is to ally choice with voice. Voice for the pupil. Voice for the parent. That is the new frontier for education. Personalised learning aims to engage every parent and every child in the educational experience. (Miliband, 2004: 7)

The voices here of pupils and parents are not the critical, deconstructivist voices of critical pedagogues (cf. Arnot, 2006). Nor is it that 'individualised learning where pupils sit alone at a computer. Nor is it pupils left to their own devices – which too often reinforces low aspirations' (Miliband, 2004: 7).

This new concept of personalised learning in schools was defined in a series of publications developed by a Demos working group,[4] a quasi-independent think-tank that was asked to find a working vocabulary that would clarify the concept of 'learning to learn' and to 'advise on the implications for the policy and practice of personalised learning'. Its first publication, *About Learning: Report of the Learning Working Group* (Demos, 2004) laid the terrain which Charles Leadbeater (a member of Demos) developed in *Personalisation through Participation: a new script for public services* (Leadbeater, 2004a). Leadbeater argued that the concept of personalisation was a 'very potent but highly contested and ambiguous idea that could be as influential as privatisation was in the 1980s and 1990s in reshaping public provision' (Leadbeater, 2004a: 18). He distinguished between *shallow* and *deep* personalisation, the latter offering opportunities to have a far greater role in designing solutions, and greater responsibilities. Choice on its own was understood to be 'a disruptive form of governance' (Leadbeater, 2004a: 46) – it was not sufficient as a social organising principle for reform (Leadbeater, 2004a: 50). Equally, citizenship (i.e. formal democratic participation) was not enough to improve public services. What was needed in a performance culture was 'direct voice'. If handled properly, deep personalisation could be the 'harbinger of an entirely new organisational logic'. The concept of 'personalisation through participation' would, according to Leadbeater, define a new form of civic participation associated with the language of 'freedom' and the 'public good':

> A state that is committed to protecting private freedom must also continuously shape how people use their freedom in the name of the wider public good. Personalisation through participation is part of the solution to this dilemma of how to rule through freedom, to allow the public good to be created within society rather than relying on the state to deliver it. (Leadbeater, 2004a: 90)

'Personalisation through participation' was taken up by the DFES, which supported the co-publication by Demos and the National College of School Leadership of Leadbeater's *Learning about Personalisation: how can we put the learner at the heart of the education system?* (Leadbeater, 2004b) that was sent out to all schools and made available on web. It also produced a spate of new publications and web sites for teachers: for example, *A National Conversation about Personalised Learning* (DFES, 2004a).[5]

The discursive framing of 'personalisation through participation' symbolically positioned it within the neo-liberal innovation agenda, in the construction of a 'new technological world with high information levels, informed requests, individual choice, professional flexibility, and giving citizens voice'. The organisation of the educational system would be premised on helping young people achieve these skills – Charles Clarke, as Secretary of State for Education, described the new system thus:

> The central characteristic of such a new system will be personalisation – so that the system fits to the individual rather than the individual having to fit the system. This is not a vague liberal notion about letting people have what they want. It is about having a system which will genuinely give high standards for all – the best possible quality of children's services, which recognise individual needs and circumstances; the cost effective teaching at school, which builds a detailed picture of what each child already knows, and how they learn, to help them go further, and as young people begin to train for work, a system that recognises individual aptitudes and provides as many tailored paths to employment as there are people and jobs. And the corollary of this is that the system must be both freer and more diverse – with more flexibility to help meet individual needs: and more choices between courses and types of provider so that there really are different and personalised opportunities available. (Clarke, 2004)

This revived focus on student-centred learning implied a school ethos that *listens* – a concept that was also not new. It had already been advocated by Maud Blair *et al.* (1999) as essential for engaging with the needs of minority ethnic pupils. The privileging of such a 'listening to learn' culture (DfES, 2002) this time led to the establishment of an action plan to involve children and young people in educational policy-making through surveys, focus groups and integration into the decision-making processes. A Children's Commissioner for England was established in the Children Act 2004, and Children's Trusts were set up, with strong involvement of children, young people and their families in local planning of integrated services for children and young people (www.everychildmatters.gov.uk).[6]

The key to this policy shift lies in the concept of an independent, self-managing learner citizen (Arnot and Reay, 2004a) – a concept whose emancipatory elements was reinforced by repeated references to the United Nations Declaration of the Rights of the Child (1989) (cf. Rudduck and Flutter (2004: 125)). Article 12 is seen to have especial relevance since it declares the right of children to participate in their own lives – in accordance with age and maturity. Children should be heard and taken seriously in all matters affecting them, including judicial and administrative matters. This declaration implies that pupils should not just have a voice in relation to their own learning but should also have the capacity and confidence to intervene in the principles which govern their learning experience. Yet the emancipatory approach symbolised by pupil voice, it turns out, may have little to do with such democratic declarations, and more to with what Fielding (2006) called a 'new authoritarianism', or even 'totalitarianism', (Fielding, 2006) when situated within strong performance-led school cultures. What is clear from the critiques I discuss below is that the introduction of personalised learning is understood by most critical commentators to cause considerable confusion, not only because of its vagueness, but also because of its assumed historical associations with critical pedagogies. These commentators seem to agree that personalised learning does indeed represent a process of individualisation that ties in with post-Fordism and the use of more micro-levels of power within education. Below I explore some evidence that points in this direction.

Social inequalities and the individualised neo-liberal learner citizen

Although the new notions of voice, choice and, ultimately, what politicians represent as the 'co-production of public services', offer a vision of a new egalitarianism (Giddens and Diamond, 2005), yet the introduction of personalised learning could equally have much to do with what Basil Bernstein (1977), in a prescient article on invisible and visible pedagogies, called a shift away from individual property to one which he called 'radical personalising'. Bernstein saw such notions of personalising as part of a new social contract/order (or in Durkheimian terms, a new form of organic solidarity). He observed that the strong classifications of what he called 'the collection code' between subjects, specialist teachers, and between students gaining specialised knowledge as a form of property, had started to weaken. New integrated codes were emerging in the late 1970s which were strongly associated with the new middle classes (especially those involved in symbolic forms of knowledge production and communication). The emergent new middle classes required forms of communication more suitable for the new forms of knowledge-based occupations. These forms of education would reproduce the ideologies of class, creating new social types and new forms of personalised organic solidarity within the middle classes. The result was likely to lead to ambiguous personal identities and flexible role performances. Bernstein argued that the more knowledge boundaries and modern grand narratives were weakened, the more likely it was that socialisation would be deeply penetrating, reflecting the fact that more of the personality of the child was more visible (hence more accessible to intimate surveillance).

The class assumptions of this new 'invisible' pedagogy would be of a middle-class conception of educational time and space, an elaborated mode of communication (taught by the middle-class mother) and small classes. At that time, Bernstein did not envisage the extension of such modes of socialisation and control as moving into secondary schools, especially since the middle classes required the certification of specialised knowledge in order to sustain economic privilege. In his later writings however, Bernstein (2000) recognised that such competence-based performance pedagogies now dominated secondary and higher education. Life-long learning for him signified a shift to what he called a totally 'pedagogised' society. Radical personalising was no longer contained within progressive primary schools.

Critiques of this discursive shift from progressive quasi-democratic to neo-liberal notions of child-centred policies, involving the increasing involvement of children in school effectiveness and improvement and 'customer satisfaction', have begun to emerge. There is concern for the inegalitarian impacts of using both voice and choice as policy devices. Individualisation, from this point of view, becomes a mechanism of surveillance and social control, overriding any notion of democratic freedom that might be associated with the concept. Individual learner citizens are now expected to assess their own learning and have been given the responsibility of improving their own performance – they are expected to act as clients in charge of their own treatment. At the same time, they are not expected to take control of the nature of their learning and its processes. Such individualisation, therefore, is not necessarily coupled with strong notions of civic agency in relation to learning and the learning experience. Indeed, the transition from pupil to citizenship may involve a loss of agency. The abstract notion of the learner citizen inscribed in schooling, as argued by the Finnish sociologists Tuula Gordon and Elina Lahelma, and Janet Holland, a British sociologist, implies a process of normalisation:

> Education prepares children to take up their place as future citizens. A process of normalisation takes place in schools, which is based on conceptions of proper adulthood and the rights and duties of citizens. In this process, children and young people are seen as abstract 'pupils', abstracted from diverse social and cultural contexts, and trained equally to become the future citizens.
> (Gordon *et al.*, 2000: 188–9)

However, these authors found that there were few spaces in schools where pupils can achieve what they call *agentic embodiment* – opportunities to enact their agency. In the English and Finnish secondary schools they researched, young people followed the route from pupil to citizen within the official school, the informal school and the physical school, without being able to control the forms of educational knowledge taught to them, or the curriculum of the body which organised them through varied time-space paths. Spaces for agency, negotiation, avoidance, opposition and resistance were limited. When exercised, such spaces were significant in the context of tensions between emancipation and regulation, control and agency (Gordon *et al.*, 2000: 187–8). Within the strongly externally controlled pedagogies of marketised economies, the route to citizenship is also socially differentiated. Boys, for example, were provided with more space to exercise agency, whilst far less physical and emotional space was offered to girls. 'Patterns of student agency are thus prefigured by existing gender inequalities' (Gordon *et al.*, 2000: 200).[7]

Such research reveals that social differences from the 'external environment' (Jorgensen, 2004) – such as those of gender, ethnicity and class – enter into the learning process and deeply distort the 'inner environment' of learning outcomes, perhaps in increasingly subtle ways. Traditional social inequalities appear not only to have shaped such prescribed processes of individualisation, but also to be 'masked' in the pedagogic relationships of individualised learning. However, we are not necessarily able to see or recognise such social constructions. Learning styles, assessment modes, even the seemingly democratic process of student consultation on which contemporary notions about 'the independent learner' are based, encourage us to misrecognise learning as socially neutral cognitive processes. They redirect attention away from the fundamentally unequal processes associated with any communication system, such as schooling (Bernstein, 2000).

Recent research on student voice, such as that by Roger Holdsworth and Pat Thomson (2002) in their analysis of South Australia *Student Voice Indicator Tools*, points to the encouragement of a centrally controlled sample of student opinion rather than a commitment to 'enable and enhance a diversity of views and voices'. Student voice here becomes an 'accountability tool' within individualising and coercive discourses and top-down management cultures. The danger is that only those students who are successful in the curriculum and school will have a voice:

> There is an ideal student in the text ... who likes school, negotiates, resolves conflicts, manages their own learning and constructs knowledge. Students who have 'a voice' are well behaved. Calling out, yelling, or walking out ... does not constitute 'voice'. (Holdsworth and Thomson, 2002: 6)

There is little recognition in such student consultation that the child being consulted brings to the dialogue a range of social identities and experiences constructed within social hierarchies and power relations. Holdsworth and Thomson (2002) argue, therefore, that there are serious difficulties with student consultation mechanisms:

> In the Australian context, the notion of student voice is one that is highly problematic. In some locations it does support democratic activity, but more often than not, it is a thin conservative version of democracy in which already advantaged students are selected to erect the façade of participation and consultation. (Holdsworth and Thomson, 2002: 12)

This ideal student has certain qualities which dovetail into successful management:

> Students are expected to speak with one voice and to have one youth culture, neither of which challenge the status quo. At the same time there is a strong appeal to democratic principles of action with the agreed processes of vision, mission, planning and review – with no recognition of the potential conflicts and tensions between the mandated implementation of systemic policy and procedure and democratic 'voiced' school decision making. (Holdsworth and Thomson, 2002: 7)

The use of student voice in relation to school reform has tended to centre on organisational aspects – but as Silva (2001) points out:

> If schools intend to embrace student voice as a tenet of the decision-making and reform process, it is critical not only to examine the role of the school but also to explore how students negotiate and define their positions as participants or non-participants in the school change efforts. Particularly with respect to disturbing race- and class-based inequities in American public schools and a growing movement of related equity based reforms, it is vital to consider how and why some students choose to participate while others opt out of the school change process. (Silva, 2001: 95)

Silva's own three-year ethnographic research discovered the 'powerful influence of racial, class and gender identity on student participation, particularly in the context of a school struggling to overcome a culture of inequality and division' (Silva, 2001: 95). The more formal the connection between school management and a consultation outreach group, the more it seemed to encourage the participation of white, high-achieving girls. It was important for them that the consultative group was an official, legitimate part of the school. These girls had already experienced success within school rules and policies and felt it appropriate to continue that way. For other students, any formal connection to the school was unsettling. Many of the experiences of students of colour, and those with the lowest level of achievement, were 'harsh' and contentious. Such students were only incited to participate if they thought they could disturb traditional decision-making and reform processes rather than be part of them. Significantly, many of these students were boys. Rather than promoting higher levels of reflexive subjectivity, participation and self-direction, pupils can therefore become incorporated in the project of social control.

In this context it becomes extremely important to consider, as did Bernstein (2000: xxi), whose voice is heard and whose voice is listened to in what he called the 'acoustic of the school'. Findings from a recent study that Diane Reay and I conducted, on pupil consultation, address some of these questions from the perspective of gender, social class and ethnicity (see Arnot and Reay (2004a; 2004b; 2006)). In our project we conducted group discussions with 14- and 15-year-old male and female, higher- and lower-achieving pupils from different ethnic and class backgrounds.[8] We asked pupils to comment on the degree to which they felt able to describe their own abilities and learning progress. Our discussions focused on whether they were ever consulted about how they learnt; about whether they could communicate their needs (in terms particularly of the pace of learning) to teachers; about whether they were consulted about what they learnt, and why. What we were tapping was whether they were really self-managing pupils – or independent learners.

Our research findings highlight the fact that independent/individualised learners, and the forms of pedagogic communication typical of today's competitive classrooms, are heavily class and gender nuanced. Many pupils in our study were aware that neither they nor teachers had control over the content of lessons, and this affected the motivation of working-class pupils who wanted what they saw as 'useful' knowledge. If any pupils were likely to gain some limited (discretionary) control over the choice of activity, the pace of classroom learning or even their seating, it was the higher-achieving upper-middle-class pupils (especially the girls). Irrespective of the perceived relevance or irrelevance of the curricula, the highest-achieving (often professional middle-class) girls were found to be able to exploit the pedagogic agendas of the individualised learner and at the same time uncouple themselves from constraining and stereotypical models of femininity. These girls seemed to have an appropriate pedagogic language and emotional competence when relating to teachers. They were rather nonchalant about consultation, possibly because they felt that, unlike less successful pupils, they had a voice and were more in tune with the school's purposes. Since they were able to manage informal dialogue between themselves and their teachers, they were asked, listened to and heard. These pupils thought themselves to be in control of their learning, even within the constraints of the compulsory curriculum. They worked with notions of individual choice in terms of when to co-operate, when to slow down, speed up (or zoom through) their work. They worked independently, but they also made considerable demands on the teacher to deal with their needs for extension work. The threat to these girls' control of their learning were teachers who failed to cope with their needs, especially in a mixed-ability, mixed-sex environment where they had to cope with the demands especially of working-class lower-attaining boys. Perceiving these boys' manipulation using disaffection, endless demands for attention, disruption of the rules, requests to repeat work from earlier stages and teachers' acquiescence, all these girls proposed segregation by ability. In contrast, black working-class girls suggested a change in their own attitudes to try to understand the boys, and the rest of the girls expressed frustration. Lower-achieving white working-class girls were left to negotiate personal relationships with teachers and relied on inter-personal skills to acquire some modicum of control in the classroom setting. Both these latter groups had little real sense of independent control over their school learning.

The issue for working-class boys of whether to gain control over the pace and level of work appeared to be deeply affected by the image of the curriculum as irrelevant to their interests and needs (Arnot and Reay, 2004a and b). They attempted to be independent, but they were, in effect, deeply dependent learners – assuming, on the one hand, that intelligence was the key to achievement (not hard work) and that it was the teachers' responsibility to help them get it right. Learning was a risky business, since these boys might not be able to perform well publicly and could be ridiculed by the teacher and other boys. There were only negative academic and social consequences if they said the work was too easy or too difficult, the pace too fast or too slow. Despite girls' view of boys' power within the classroom setting, these working-class boys experienced strong regulation by teachers who intervened on their seating and their learning patterns, and largely failed to meet their demands – they appeared to be the least able to communicate with teachers and received the least help. *Thus, those who most needed to have control over their learning had the least control* (Arnot and Reay, 2004a and b). As a result, they used physical disruption of the classroom, breaching behaviour rules in an attempt to regain control over their learning. Thus, whilst teachers struggled to maintain control, these lower-achieving boys were trapped in a dynamic that was hard to break. Their lack of power was expressed in dysfunctional attention seeking and classroom dominance.

The discussions we held with lower-achieving pupils, particularly boys, often from working-class backgrounds, revealed just how tense and vulnerable they felt in the classroom, and how they tried to find ways of learning but had difficulty with so many aspects of classroom life. They did not feel trusted by teachers and were therefore not confident about their learning. The notion of independent learning represented for them a form of regulation rather than an aid to learning. Once pedagogic communication had broken down, the main sources of support in learning were their friendships and peer-group cultures. Paradoxically therefore, the assumption of the independent learner, with its expectations of communicative competence, appeared to reinforce strong male peer-group cultures and male dominance in the classroom (Arnot and Reay, 2004a).

The model of the independent/individualised learner we observed implied that all students can speak the language of learning – the sorts of pedagogic language being used by teachers in the classroom (whether traditional or progressive in style). As Bernstein (2000) argued, a common communication code was essential for any radical personalising pedagogy. Being such a learner citizen involves considerable skill and familiarity with the expectations of such a communicative setting. It does not just entail having the appropriate vocabulary that a teacher can recognise, but also having an appropriate relationship with the teacher in order to be able to communicate effectively. Paradoxically, the most dependent learner citizens needed to have great maturity in handling their relationships with teachers, since their work and classroom behaviour was often not in line with teacher expectations.

Pupils, when consulted, recognised that a number of elements would be needed to ensure successful communication about learning; for example, communicative competence; emotional maturity; a high level of trust in the teacher; patience; a motivation to learn; and appropriate family support (Arnot and Reay, 2004a, 2004b, 2006).

The data from two different secondary schools suggest that we need to examine the extent to which a positive pedagogic identity of the new learner citizen is achievable for, in particular, working-class boys and girls in the current learning environment. Bernstein writes about how socialisation within schooling can be 'deeply wounding' either for those who wish for, but do not achieve, a pedagogic identity; or for the majority for whom the pursuit of such an identity is even made irrelevant (Bernstein, 1975: 250). An increase in individualisation and personalisation through participation means that the images, voices and practices that the school provides may make it even more difficult for working-class children to recognise themselves in schooling. It may be particularly problematic for white and minority ethnic working-class boys who already experience daily the strong regulative culture of the classroom and confrontational relations with teachers. This clearly has profound consequences for the production of positive pedagogic identities so desired by the new goals of life-long learning within a risk society. The implication is that the individualised learner citizen as a pedagogic ambition is one which hides the inequities built into the social structure, and by doing so, potentially aggravates such inequalities just as easily as it provides opportunities for the exploration of voice and choice amongst the most privileged. As Fielding (2004) points out, 'so long as an undifferentiated notion of student voice is assumed or valorized' and unless power differentials are taken into account when consulting pupils, there is a significant danger that 'issues of race, gender and class are sidelined and in that process of presumed homogeneity the middle class, white view of the world conveniently emerges as the norm' (Fielding, 2004: 302).

By differentiating between the means and ends adopted for different modes of personalisation, Michael Fielding (2006) argues that when personalisation occurs within instrumentalist high-performance learning cultures, it is used in what he calls the *totalitarian* and *manipulative* modes. In both cases, personalisation encourages a breakdown in social solidarity and collectivity. In contrast, person-centred learning communities can offer *expressive* and *intentional* modes of personalisation that take as their central purpose the value of the personal (in the case of the former) and the promotion of collective identities and a humane social and moral order (in the case of the latter). What Fielding also notes is the anxiety that such personalisation of learning can create – a theme found in many critical accounts of personalised learning. Such anxiety is associated with, on the one hand, the commodification of education and the engagement of youth as consumers and allegedly co-producers of education; and second, with so-called 'responsibilisation', which leaves the individual responsible for the risks, choices and chances they take, and for protecting themselves (Whitty and Wisby, 2007). Such anxiety, as we shall see, can take different gendered forms.

Individualised young citizens

> Pupils as citizens should be autonomous, knowing, responsible and aware of their culture, but the emphasis is on future citizenship. (Gordon *et al.*, 2000: 199)

At the macro level, the impact of globalised risk society has entailed more than the transformation of the learner citizen in the classroom. Arguably it has also been linked to the transformation of gender relations in the twentieth century and predicted changes in the twenty-first century. The education of girls over the last century is often seen as symbolic of the struggle for greater individualisation and freedom (Beck, 1992; Sen, 1999). Women have fought for the opportunity to become full autonomous citizens in their own right, precisely to become the *I am I*, identified by Beck and Beck-Gernsheim (2002). Evidence of the impact of individualisation on women can be found in the range of youth cultural studies that identify the individualistic, hedonistic life-values amongst young women today. We talk now in the UK about the *Can Do* girls; girls who think that the world is at their feet – at least in their teenage years. The extraordinary transformation of white working-class girls' discourse to one of possibility and the language of choice is mapped in *Closing the Gender Gap*, which I wrote with Gaby Weiner and Miriam David (Arnot *et al.*, 1999). Here we see the key role which education has come to play in so many young women's lives, with many now achieving higher-level qualifications and higher education. The shift in gender values, about whether women have a right to work, to be independent earners and to share childcare with their partners, has been found to be one of the strongest generational gaps in modern society (Wilkinson 1994). Significantly, grandparents and grandchildren have been found to disagree most over gender issues – over and above politics, environment, and health.

Drawing on the German experience, Ulrich Beck and Elizabeth Beck-Gernsheim argue that these 'irreversible shifts' in gender relations internationally mark precisely the beginning of a liberation of a new generation from the feudally ascribed roles for the sexes, with all their associated antagonisms. Young women, they argue, are uncoupling themselves from 'the clutches of family life', and a life of caring service, to take control over their own lives. Men, in contrast, have appeared to be deeply committed to traditional identities in work and domestic spheres – a strategy that might well, in itself, be a response to turbulent social change. These authors perceive a widening gender gulf in the future:

> All the factors which dislodge women from their traditional role are missing on the male side. In the context of male life, fatherhood and career, economic independence and familial life are not contradictions that have to be fought for and held together against the conditions in the family and society: instead their compatibility with the traditional male role is prescribed and protected. But this meant that individualisation ... strengthens masculine role behaviour. (Beck, 1992: 112)

If this continues, Beck argues, it is likely that the position of men and women will become 'increasingly unequal, more conscious and less legitimated' (Beck, 1992: 104).

In the world of education, there is now a good deal of discussion about whether these processes of individualisation are gendered in the way suggested. Are '*Freedom's Children*' largely female? As a result, Mairtin Mac an Ghaill and I found that educational researchers are now going behind the discourses of individualisation to investigate and reveal the multiplicities, fluidities and hybridities of gender identity formation and identifications of both male and female young people; and of differences, discontinuities and tensions *within* each gender category, giving support in some respects to the individualisation thesis (Arnot and Mac an Ghaill, 2006). Relational worlds are, as suggested, no longer portrayed as merely proscribed by strong structural determinants derived from economic and state formations. Instead, gender relations are portrayed as the product of substantial identity work; constructed, policed and challenged on and in and through various discursive positionings, such as those pertaining to sexuality, ethnicity and religion, as well as through time, space and locality. The epistemological and political shifts associated with post-structuralism, and in particular, the use of Foucauldian theories of power and knowledge and psychoanalytic concepts of identity and subjectivity, rupture the original modernist political agendas. They create new theoretical spaces in which to study the social-psychological domains of regulation, disciplining and surveillance; the discursive positionings of subjects, and the framing of fantasy, desire, engagement and reaction to gender orderings. Gender identity is conceptualised now as individualised embodiments of social, cultural and historical constructions. As a result, contemporary research explores the physical embodiment and socio-psychological anxieties around gender identities – the expression, if you like, of individualisation and reflexivity in society.

The findings of such socio-psychological studies of the transitions to adulthood, of social mobility and educational achievement of youth, also challenge the extent to which individualisation has in reality shifted the material bases of gender power, and whether there are simple gender divisions in relation to individualisation. As Walkerdine (2003) has demonstrated in her research on middle- and working-class girls, although initially it seemed that women were the '*reflexivity winners*', the working through of the discourses of individualisation and the realities of unstable social environments has many different outcomes. The task of the neo-liberal citizen is to 'become somebody' – somebody who is commodified and made 'Other' through the experiences of an upward social mobile trajectory. Female agency (for example, that of the 'new' educated working-class woman) is understood as freedom from the inherited ascriptions of institutional structures. However in Walkerdine's research, the narratives of upward mobility associated with the individualised 'neo-liberal' subject are not just accepted by young working-class women, but are also the result of a complex process of negotiation using the lens of hope, despair, success and failure, and the desire to belong to a new place as well as not wanting to give up belonging to the old. The reality is that 'the autonomous liberal subject [is] made in the image of the middle class' (Walkerdine, 2003: 239), and therefore 'upward mobility becomes a central trope of class/ification in which women and the qualities ascribed to femininity have a central place' (Walkerdine, 2003: 242). The qualities associated with femininity are those associated with middle-class individuality. For the working-class girl then, individualisation and its associated personalising represents a form of *embourgeoisement*,[9] succumbing to the middle-class agenda associated with self-reflexivity, self-made and motivated. Thus, individualisation and upward mobility create strong destructive emotions amongst working-class women – it has 'a deeply defensive aspect' moving away from pain, silence and the lack of material means of becoming middle class (Walkerdine, 2003: 243). If successful, they are always the *parvenu* (Bauman, 2001a) – since the rational, unitary and autonomous subject is at heart a fiction, it is therefore delusionary. The 'fiction' of individualisation (Walkerdine, 2003) within performance cultures could well confirm notions of new middle-class femininity, making them 'producers of themselves as objects of the gaze' (Walkerdine, 2003: 242).

When Skelton (2005) explored Beck's thesis of the individualised individual by comparing two generations of female academics in the UK, she found that shifts in identity were more likely to take place at the level of individual than of groups; that the process of individualisation might represent a much more complex articulation with gender identity; that social class was far more salient in shaping individualising processes than Beck's theory initially allowed. Choice and self-interest were bound up with social class, but also with personal concerns about equity issues and lack of opportunities. In McLeod and Yates' research on contemporary Australian youth's sense of intimacy and friendship, they found that gender relations were being transformed. In some senses, femininity was being detraditionalised, and in the case of middle-class professional boys, so too was masculinity. However, significantly femininity seems now to be rearticulated to include and embody conventional feminine aspirations, with girls trying to sustain notions of connectedness, service, affectiveness and sensitivity alongside masculine aspirations (McLeod, 2002). Tamboukou and Ball (2006) go further in their exploration of young black women's attempts to 'take control of and remake their identities'. They employ the concept of the nomad to understand the social movements, performance and experimentation associated with acquiring female agency in a shifting world – space, place and location play a pivotal role in framing the girls' responses to these dominant discourses of choice.

McLeod describes examples of middle-class boys employing the language of choice and individualisation, rearticulating masculinity through relational narratives, whilst working-class boys reasserted 'an emphasised and intransigent form of white provincial, working-class masculinity'. These different masculine modalities are well documented by, for example, Connell (1995), Mac an Ghaill (1994), Sewell (1997) and Archer (2003) amongst others, although it is not yet clear whether and how the individualisation of learning will affect male social class and ethnic identities. One study by Miles (2004), for example, found that the young men he studied in South Wales achieved what he calls a 'mezzanine' condition

– of wanting to acquire some of the accoutrements of a middle-class status without rejecting a working-class collective culture. Male educational underachievement contrasts with men's success in civic and economic spheres and dominance of different forms of privilege (Arnot *et al.*, 1999).

The evidence from youth cultural research suggests that Beck and Beck-Gernsheim's thesis on reflexive individualisation overstates the process of detraditionalisation, particularly from social class conditions. At the same time, it draws attention to the shifting discursive world of what constitutes successful upward mobility and performance within an educational system focused on individual learners and their choices. If the process of creating a learner citizen is getting that much more individualised, and young people themselves are constantly shifting and contesting individualising processes, then schools will need to think carefully about the various ways in which such messages are negotiated and responded to.

Educational ethics and the threat of freedom

The reconstruction of the learner citizen in a risk society is one fraught with danger for those concerned about social inequality and injustice. Despite its egalitarian rhetoric, the individualisation of learners, and of youth as a process associated with globalised postmodernity, can create greater, rather than less, polarisation. Within pedagogy, as Edwards and Usher (2000) point out, the new learner-centredness, whilst appearing to relocate itself 'into a discourse of abstract liberal humanism', denies the particular effects of (dis)location of teachers, learners and knowledge. Here, bodies of knowledge become disembedded from the practices which created them, the pedagogic engagement with learning creates not an educated person but an individualised reflexive project. At the same time, in the most optimistic of scenarios, such an individualised learner-centred pedagogy could create new forms of solidarity, shifting coalitions, a reduction in the exclusiveness associated with traditional categories and collective endeavours. It could have, according to these authors, 'a kaleidoscopic impact', which allows for new forms of meaning-making to emerge (Edwards and Usher, 2000: 134).

This contradictory scenario, on a societal scale, is one which frames contemporary theorists trying to capture the nature of the emergent social order. Beck (2001: 57) himself realised that there is always the 'possibility of the self destruction of freedom'[10] – individualisation can mean the loss of obligation and option maximisation. The new learner citizens, in such an environment, could become what Beck called 'the ugly citizen' (Beck, 2001; Beck and Beck-Gernsheim, 2002: 165) where the civic virtues and values can become ugly and aggressive. What Beck calls the 'democratisation of democracy' (Beck, 2001: 57) can make possible 'the perversions of society' when 'the paradoxes of freedom break through'. In fact, such paradoxes may be proof of the 'advancing democratisation and secularisation of power' (Beck, 2001: 57). One example of such a paradox is that in Germany where, despite its wealth, one in seven children live on income support. There is an 'infantilism of poverty, a growing poverty of women, particularly single parent mothers' (Beck, 2001: 58).

Table 8.1 Reduction of social rights and the radicalisation of social differences

Radical social differences	Fundamental social rights	Fundamental political rights	Form of reaction
+	−	−	Class society
−	+	+	Welfare society
+	−	+	Ugly citizen

Source: Beck (2001: 3) (translated by D. Faas)

Another aspect of this contradiction is that today's citizens are worried by both *insecurities and unsafeties*. Insecurities increase as a result of 'cultural uncertainties and confusion' – a result of the '*heteronomy of freedom*' and the new globalised ways of life that encourage rivalries, catastrophes, cultural diversity and otherness as part of life. These insecurities are the other side of freedom. Insecurities are different from unsafeties, which are life threatening. The changing 'weekly poison' associated with nuclear power, the ozone hole, extinction of species, drugs, criminality and violence in inner cities can create what Beck (2001: 57) called a *'fabricated insecurity and the radicalisation of social injustice'* where there is a spread and rapid increase of, amongst other things, unemployment and poverty in a cross-section of life cycles; the indirect exclusion from rights, such as individuals and groups being cut off from legal subsistence and the ability to be self-sufficient through the loss of social benefits; the reduction of legal and social rights through, for example, tampering with mail, tapping into telephone secrets and breaking into homes; and challenges to the freedom of the press. Hence, the development of modernity comes not from the evolutionary development of legal, political and social rights but from a reduction of incompleteness of such rights ('incomplete citizenship', 'precarious poverty', 'incomplete family'). If social rights are reduced when there are greater social differences and when more political rights are supported, then we are likely to see the rise of the ugly citizen. Beck summarises this thesis graphically in Table 8.1 above.

So-called 'second modernity', therefore, is a complex 'intersection between internalised rights of freedom and the reduction of basic social rights and securities' (Beck, 2001: 56–7). The real world contrasts sharply with the notion of 'accepted rights of freedom'. Significantly, gender conflict is listed by Beck as one of the dangers of this new social milieu. These are:

- a (hectic) chaos of diverse, often antagonistic ideologies and ideological combinations, mixtures and mélanges;
- a steady source of economic irritations due to enormous restructuring of resources, and the accompanying 'struggles for survival' of all against all;
- a breeding ground for militarism, with regard to the pushing through of national and public interests and the militancy regarding growing interpersonal propensity to violence;

- a model of ecological sensibility of the ordinary subject, and bureaucratic ignorance of ecological dangers; and
- *an untidy arena of ongoing conflict between the sexes and (still) increasing (and more and more intolerant) lifestyle conflicts of all sorts.* (Beck, 2001: 60 – my emphasis)

Similarly, Zigmund Bauman in *The Individivualised Society* (2001b) points to the dangerous consequences of the succumbing of the moral project of the state to the demands of the market and 'universal deregulation'. This leads, in his view, to the dominance of

> ... irrationality and moral blindness of market competition, the unbound freedom given to capital and finance at the expense of all other freedoms, the tearing up of societally maintained safety nets and ... the neglect of all security but economic considerations ... the increased polarisation within and between societies. (Bauman, 2006: 96)

Such uncertainty, unpredictability and instability of itself creates greater social marginalisation, particularly of the poor.[11]

> The ever more explicit surrender of their traditional duties by nation states, switching from the project of national community as the guardian of the universal right to a decent and dignified life, and endorsing instead the promotion of the market as a sufficient guarantee of a universal chance for self-enrichment, deepens further the suffering of the new poor – adding insult to their injury, glossing poverty with humiliation and with a denial of consumer freedom, not identified with humanity. (Bauman, 2001b: 85)

Bauman, like Beck, also argues that the sort of society produced by individualisation is one which is characterised by 'uncertainty, hesitation, lack of control' and hence considerable anxiety:

> This anxiety is the price paid for new individual freedoms and new responsibility. However enjoyable such freedoms may be in other respects, many people find the price too high to be paid gladly ... They would rather opt for a world less complex and so less frightening; for a world in which choices are simple, rewards for good choices assured and the signs of a good choice clear and unmistakable. For a world in which one knows what to do to be in the right. A world which hides no mysteries and does not take one by surprise. For many people cast into freedom without being asked, the offer of a 'great simplification' is one they find tempting and difficult to refuse. (Bauman, 2001: 88)

Here identities and identifications (the 'I' of citizenship and civic agency (Gordon; 2006)) are likely to be 'split into collections like snapshots' (Bauman, 2001: 87).

Instead of constructing one's identity gradually and patiently as one builds a house – through the slow accretion of ceilings, floors, rooms, connecting passages – a series of 'new beginnings', one experiments with instantly assembled yet easily dismantled shapes, painted one over the other; this is a truly *palimpsest identity*. The kind of identity which fits a world in which the art of forgetting is an asset no less, if no more, important than the art of memorizing, in which forgetting rather than learning is the condition of continuous fitness, in which ever new things and people enter and exit the field of vision of the stationary camera of attention, and here the memory itself is like video-tape, always ready to be wiped clean in order to admit new images. (Bauman, 2001: 87, his emphasis)

In this postmodern world, the education system may encourage such palimpsest identities through its pedagogies based on prospective reflexive individualised learning, student voice and choice. Or it could make a major attempt to achieve some sort of civic public form of 'coordination' between two incompatible goals – on the one hand 'the effort to "rationalise" the world' and on the other hand, 'the effort to groom rational beings fit to inhabit it' (Bauman, 2001: 138). Bauman is pessimistic. He argues that the latter goal, which is the 'underlying assumption of the modern educational project, seems no longer credible' (Bauman, 2001: 138).

In the new scenario, Bauman argues, it is not clear who acts as teacher, who as pupil; nor who owns knowledge, receives it, decides that it is worth teaching. Democratic society itself becomes the teacher, a 'huge pedagogical institution'. Bauman believes that in this new world, tertiary learning outside inherited educational institutions and educational philosophies is what postmodern men and women will need in order to survive. The cluster of skills; their ability to live daily with uncertainty and ambivalence; their capacity to 'change the frames'; is a type of learning that is unfamiliar for education institutions and very demanding of their capacity to deliver. The task for schooling in relation to individualisation could be reduced to just showing that 'meaningful and effective interventions can be made into the way our collective life is lived'.

At heart, social theorists such as Bauman, Beck and Bernstein view the right to choose an identity as 'the sole universality of the citizen/human' as fundamentally dangerous since the right to individuality is increasingly being polarised. The new individualism promises but does not deliver 'the genuine and radical freedom of self-constitution and self-assertion' (Bauman, 2001: 96). *In reality, the right to individuality is being increasingly polarised.* If it is to encourage a genuine democratic society, a new ethos – a redefined humanism – is needed, which will promote, for example, the full distribution of individual freedom, critical and self-critical faculties, the co-habitation with, and tolerance of, other identities, and the rights of the stranger, the poor and dispossessed. Bauman (2001: 93) therefore calls for a 'new ethics for the new age':

Contemporary humanity speaks in many voices and we know now that it will continue to do so for a very long time to come. The central issue of our times is how to reforge that polyphony into harmony and prevent it from degenerating into cacophony. Harmony is not uniformity; it is always an interplay of a number of different motifs, each retaining its separate identity and sustaining the resulting melody through, and thanks to, that identity. (Bauman, 2001: 93–4)

As Fielding (2006) argued, at the heart of the individualisation debate is a challenge to education to retrieve its social and moral/humanistic mission in the name not of the individual but of society.

Acknowledgements

This paper was first presented as a keynote address at the 'Critical Thinking and Learning' Conference, University of West Indies, St Augustine, Trinidad. Later it was presented as a plenary address for the Nordic Educational Research Association's 32nd Annual Congress, 'The Positioning of Education in Contemporary Knowledge Society', Reykjavik, March 2004, and for the 12th World Congress of Comparative Education Societies, 'Education and Social Justice' in Havana, Cuba, October 2004. I am grateful to Fazal Ali, Elina Lahelma and Rosemary Preston for making such presentations possible.

References

Archer, L. (2003) *Race, Masculinity and Schooling: Muslim boys and education*. Buckingham: Open University Press.

Arnot, M. (2002) *Reproducing Gender? Critical essays on educational theory and feminist politics*. London: RoutledgeFalmer.

Arnot, M. (2004) 'Gender categories and the learner citizen', paper presented at the Critical Thinking and Learning Conference, University of West Indies, St Augustine, Trinidad.

Arnot, M. (2005) 'Freedom's children: a gender perspective on the education of the learner citizen', *Review of Education*, 52(1): 67–87.

Arnot, M. (2006) 'Gender voices in the classroom', in B. Francis, C. Skelton and L. Smulyan (eds) *Handbook on Gender and Education*. London: Sage.

Arnot, M. and Dillabough, J.A. (eds) (2000) *Challenging Democracy: International Perspectives on Gender, Education and Citizenship*. London: RoutledgeFalmer.

Arnot, M. and Mac an Ghaill, M. (2006) '(Re)contextualising gender studies in education: schooling in late modernity', in M. Arnot and M. Mac an Ghaill (eds) *The RoutledgeFalmer Reader in Gender and Education*. London: RoutledgeFalmer.

Arnot, M. and Reay, D. (2004a) 'The framing of pedagogic encounters: regulating the social order in classroom learning', in J. Muller, B. Davies and A. Morais (eds) *Reading Bernstein, Researching Bernstein*. London: RoutledgeFalmer, pp. 137–52.

Arnot M. and Reay, D. (2004b) 'The social dynamics of classroom learning', in M. Arnot, D. Peddar, D. McIntyre and D. Reay (eds) (2004) *Consultation in the Classroom: Developing Dialogue about Teaching and Learning*. Cambridge: Pearson Books.

Arnot, M. and Reay, D. (2006) 'The framing of performance pedagogies: pupil perspectives on the control of school knowledge and its acquisition', in H. Lauder, P. Brown, J. Dillabough and A.H. Halsey (eds) *Education, Globalisation and Social Change*. Oxford: Oxford University Press.

Arnot, M., David, M. and Weiner, G. (1999) *Closing the Gender Gap: Post-war Education and Social Change.* Cambridge: Polity Press.
Bauman, Z (2001a) 'Pariahs and parvenus', in P. Beilharz (ed.) *The Bauman Reader.* Oxford: Blackwell.
Bauman, Z. (2001b) *The Individualised Society.* Cambridge, Polity Press,.
Bauman, Z. (2002) 'Individually, Together', foreword in U. Beck and E. Beck-Gernsheim (eds) *Individualisation: Institutionalised Individualism and its Social and Political Consequences.* London: Sage, pp xiv–xix.
Beck, J. (1998) *Morality and Citizenship in Education.* London: Cassell.
Beck, U. (1992) *Risk Society: Towards a New Modernity.* London: Sage.
Beck, U. (2001) 'Der hässliche Bürger', in A. Brosziewski, T.S. Eberle, C. Maeder (eds) *Moderne, Lonstanz: UVK Verlagsgesellschaft* (translated by D. Faas), pp. 57–68.
Beck, U. and Beck-Gernsheim, E. (2002) *Individualisation: Institutionalised Individualism and Its Social and Political Consequences.* London: Sage.
Bernstein, B. (1975) *Class, Codes and Control, Vol. 2,* 2nd ed. London: Routledge and Kegan Paul.
Bernstein, B. (1977) *Class, Codes and Control, Vol. 3.* London: Routledge and Kegan Paul.
Bernstein, B. (1990) *The Structuring of Pedagogic Discourse. Volume IV, Class. Codes and Control.* London: Routledge.
Bernstein, B. (2000) *Pedagogy, Symbolic Control and Identity: Theory, Research and Critique,* rev. ed. Lanham: Rowman and Littlefield.
Blair, M., Kenner, C., Bourne, J., Coffin, C. and Creese, A. (1999) *Making the Difference: teaching and learning strategies in successful multi-ethnic schools (Research Report).* London: Prentice Hall/Harvester Wheatsheaf.
Clarke, C. (2004) 'Foreword', in *Five Year Strategy for Children and Learners.* Department of Education and Skills, CM6272.
Connell, R.W. (1995) *Masculinities.* Cambridge, Polity Press.
Demos (2004) *About Learning: Report of Learning Working Group.* London: Demos.
Department for Education and Skills (DfES) (2002) *Listening to Learn.* http://www.dfes.gov.uk/listening to learn (Accessed 12/08/2004.)
Department for Education and Skills (DfES) (2004a) *A National Conversation about Personalised Learning, Learning about Personalisation.* Nottingham: DfES.
Department for Education and Skills (DfES) (2004b) *Five Year Strategy for Children and Learners.* Nottingham: DfES, CM6272.
Dillabough, J.A. and Arnot, M. (2002) 'Recasting educational debates about female citizenship, agency and identity.' *The School Field,* XIII, 3/4, 61–89.
Edwards, R. and Usher, R. (2000) *Globalisation and Pedagogy: space, place and identity.* London: RoutledgeFalmer.
Fielding, M. (2001) 'Beyond the Rhetoric of Student Voice: New Departures or New Constraints in the Transformation of 21st Century Schooling?' *Forum:* 100–109.
Fielding, M. (2004) 'Transformative approaches to student voice: theoretical underpinnings, recalcitrant realities', *British Educational Research Journal,* 30(2): 295–311.
Fielding, M. (2006) 'Leadership, personalisation and high performance schooling: naming the new totalitarianism', *School Leadership and Management,* 26(4): 347–69.
Furlong, A. and Carmel, F. (1997) *Young People and Social Change. Individualisation and Risk in Late Modernity.* London: Open University Press.
Giddens, A. and Diamond, P. (eds) (2005) *The New Egalitarianism.* Cambridge, Polity Press.
Gordon, T. (2006) 'Gender and Citizenship', in B. Francis, C. Skelton and L. Smulyan (eds) *Handbook on Gender and Education.* London: Sage.
Gordon, T., Holland, J. and Lahelma, E. (2000) *Making Spaces: Citizenship and Difference in School.* London: MacMillan.
Habermas, J. (2001) 'Warum braucht Europa eine Verfassung?' ('Why does Europe need a constitution?'), lecture given at the University of Hamburg, 26 June; published in *Die Zeit,* 27 June. (http://www.zeit.de/2001/27/Politik/200127_verfassung_lang.html)

Harris, A. (2006) 'Citizenship and the self-made girl', in M. Arnot and M. Mac an Ghaill (eds) *The RoutledgeFalmer Gender and Education Reader*. London: RoutledgeFalmer.

Hirschman, A.O. (1970) *Exit, Voice, and Loyalty: Responses to decline in firms, organisations and states*, Cambridge, MA: Harvard University Press.

Holdsworth, R. and Thomson, P. (2002) 'Options with the regulation and containment of "student voice" and/or students research and acting for change: Australian experiences', Paper presented at the AERA symposium.

Johnson, M. (2004a) 'Personalised learning – an emperor's outfit?' Unpublished paper for Institute for Public Policy Research (IPPR), March.

Johnson, M. (2004b) 'Personalised learning: new directions for schools', *New Economy*, 224–8.

Jorgensen. P. Schultz (2004) 'Children's Participation in a Democratic Learning Environment', in J. MacBeath and L. Moos (eds) *Democratic Learning: The Challenge to School Effectiveness*. London: RoutledgeFalmer, pp. 113–31.

Lagree, J-C. (ed.) (2002) *Rolling Youth, Rocking Society: youth take part in the post-modern debate on globalization.* Paris, UNESCO.

Lasch, S. (2002) 'Individualisation in a Non-linear Mode', introduction, in U. Beck and E. Beck-Gernsheim (eds) *Individualisation: Institutionalised Individualism and Its Social and Political Consequences.* London: Sage, pp. vii–xii.

Leadbeater, C. (2004a) *Personalisation through Participation: a new script for public services.*

Leadbeater, C. (2004b) *Learning about Personalisation: how can we put the learner at the heart of the educational system?* Nottingham: National College of School Leadership, and Demos.

Mac an Ghaill, M. (1994) *The Making of Men: Masculinities, Sexualities and Schooling*. Buckingham: Open University Press.

MacBeath, J. and Moos, L. (eds) (2004) *Democratic Learning: The Challenge to School Effectiveness*. London: RoutledgeFalmer.

McLeod, J. (2002) 'Working out intimacy: young people and friendship in an age of reflexivity', *Discourse*, 23(2): 211–26, reprinted in M. Arnot and M. Mac an Ghaill (eds) *The RoutledgeFalmer Reader in Gender and Education* (2006). London: RoutledgeFalmer.

Miles, P. (2004) 'Educational Transitions and Late-modern Anxiety: The Impact of Credentialism and Individualisation on Working Class Youth'. Unpublished PhD thesis, University of Cambridge.

Miliband, D. (2004) 'Choice and Voice in Personalised Learning', Speech at a DfES Innovation Unit, Demos, OECD Conference: 'Personalising Education: the Future of the Public Sector Reform'. London, 18 May. /www.dfes.gov.uk/speeches/search_detail.cfm?ID=118 (Accessed 15/03/05.)

Moos, L. (2004) 'Introduction', in J. MacBeath and L. Moos (eds) *Democratic Learning: the challenge to school effectiveness.* London: RoutledgeFalmer.

Peters, M., Marshall, J. and Fitzsimons, P. (2000) 'Managerialism and Educational Policy in a Global Context: Foucault, Neo-liberalism and the Doctrine of Self Management', in N.C. Burbules and C.A. Torres (eds) *Globalisation and Education: Critical Perspectives.* New York: Routledge.

Rose, N. (1990) *Governing the Soul: The shaping of the private self*. London: Routledge.

Rowan, L., Knobel, M., Bigum, C. and Lankshear, C. (2002) *Boys, Literacies and Schooling*. Buckingham: Open University Press.

Rudduck, J. and Flutter, J. (2004) *How to Improve your School.* London: Continuum.

Sen, A. (1999) *Development as Freedom*. Oxford: Oxford University Press.

Sewell, T. (1997) *Black Masculinities and Schooling*. Stoke-on-Trent: Trentham Books.

Silva, E. (2001) 'Squeaky wheels and flat tires: a case study of students as reform participants', *Forum*, *43*(2): 95–9.

Skelton, C. (2005) 'The "self-interested" woman academic: a consideration of Beck's model of the "individualised individual." *British Journal of Sociology and Education*, 26(1): 5–16.

Tamboukou, M. and Ball, S. (2006) 'Nomadic subjects: young black women in Britain', in M. Arnot and M. Mac an Ghaill (eds) *The RoutledgeFamer Reader in Gender and Education*. London: RoutledgeFalmer.

UNESCO (2003) *Gender and Education for All: The Leap to Equality*. EFA Global Monitoring Report. Paris: UNESCO.

United Nations Convention of the Rights of the Child (1989) UN General Assembly Resolution 44, 25.

Walkerdine, V. (2003) 'Reclassifying upward mobility: femininity and the neo-liberal subject', *Gender and Education*, 15(3): 237–48.

Walkerdine, V., Lucey, H. and Melody, J. (2001) *Growing up Girl: psychosocial explorations of gender and class*. Houndsmill, Basingstoke: Palgrave.

Whitty, G. and Wisby, E. (2007) 'Whose voice? An exploration of the current policy interest in pupil involvement in school decision making', *International Studies in Sociology of Education*, 17(3): 303–19.

Wilkinson, H. (1994) *No Turning Back: Generations and the Genderquake*. London: Demos.

Notes

1 Edwards and Usher (2000) are an exception.
2 Bauman (2001b) also makes this point.
3 See also Johnson (2004b).
4 This group consisted of three head teachers and three cognitive scientists under the chairmanship of David Hargreaves.
5 Leadbeater (2004a: 58) describes four steps including intimate consultation, expanded choice, enhanced voice and partnership provision advocacy, co-production, funding.
6 The *Five Year Strategy for Children and Learners* (DfES, 2004b) has a section on personalisation and choice in the secondary years. See also Whitty and Wisby (2007) for related documents.
7 For further discussion of gender and agency, see Dillabough and Arnot (2002).
8 We focused on all pupils in one tutor group in each of the two secondary and two primary schools. In all, 62 children were involved in a total of 24 discussion groups. Five lower-achieving pupils were observed in Maths and English classes and were interviewed individually. Later, we asked the form tutors and Maths and English teachers to build strategies of pupil consultation into their lessons and we evaluated these initiatives (Arnot and Reay (2004a; 2004b; 2006)).
9 For a discussion of embourgeoisement see Arnot *et al.* (1999) and Arnot (2002).
10 The ugly citizen can also exist in an affluent milieu (as we can see with the violent outbreaks of young people today).
11 Rich Europe counts amongst its citizens about 3 million homeless, 20 million people evicted from the labour market and 30 million living below the poverty line.

9 Educating the global citizen

The gender challenges of the twenty-first century

> As a woman, I have no country. As a woman, I want no country. As a woman, my country is the whole world. (Virginia Woolf, 1938)

Sociology as a discipline could be considered a modernist project par excellence. The initial disciplinary sociological project in education was rather grand – it aimed to uncover the generic relationship between education and society. It drew out of the density of social life and its complexity the principles which governed the structures, processes and the multiplicities of cultures and cultural identities. In so doing, sociologists also had emancipatory ambitions. Critical sociology of education has tried to promote social justice by informing governments of the impact of their policies on people's lives. It has also attempted to support diverse forms of political resistance and action by working – although, it must be said, not that often – with particular groups engaged in struggle.

The tensions between these two projects – the *disciplinary* and the *emancipatory* – have resulted from a very close marriage between sociology of education and the liberal democratic welfare state with its offer of social as well as political and economic rights. The sociological discipline has allied itself largely with this social democratic project and worked, albeit largely through critique, to reshape the welfare state so that it could and would deliver on these promises. As a result, sociological research on education has focused particularly on the relationship of schooling to *national* social structures – on specific cultural formations and political processes and policies within the nation state. Beck (2000) describes such a conflation of society and the state as 'methodological nationalism' (Beck, 2000: 64). The consequence is a narrowing focus to a territorial state that 'contained' society. The educational questions as a result tended to privilege the local, the particularistic and the specific. Sociological research has often, therefore, been used to unpack the ways schooling has affected the life chances of each generation of children, within national territorial boundaries.

But now we are in a different time frame. National boundaries are challenged by international organisations and agendas. In the twenty-first century, post-national and post-colonial scenarios frame discussions about what education is and what it should be. Sociologists of education are now expected to broaden their national horizons, to release themselves from the politics of the nation-state and address what are highly complex and largely ill-defined or contested sets of global economic, political, social and cultural processes. Thus, whilst we continue to analyse schools as socialising institutions, the role of such institutions is rapidly being transformed – indeed, some would argue, being replaced (cf. Bauman (2000), quoted in Chapter 8).

Globalisation (albeit a fuzzy concept) breaks the boundaries of macro and micro, the global and local, the categories of time and space, and challenges existing social classifications and stratifications whilst generating new ones. In the new global context, sociologists of education experience a loss of audience and focus. The link between education and society has been reframed into the so-called North–South axis, linking each society to a new network of countries and hemispheres. Thus, sociologists of education have had to shift from the *ethnographic* to the *global graphic*. Suddenly the concept of the ethnographic has become almost untenable in its size and scale. The local is now seen as both a reflection and a response to global social orders as well as national social orders.

Today, some sociologists of education, especially within the UK, US and Australia have offered strong critical narratives of globalisation and neo-liberal educational reform (part of the disciplinary project); see, for example, Torres (1998); Stromquist and Monkman (2000); Burbules and Torres (2000); and Lauder *et al.* (2006). There is also a range of sophisticated analyses of the impact of globalisation on gender equality and the gendering of education (see Henry (2001); Stromquist (2005); and Blackmore (2000). However, for the most part, sociological studies in the UK have not engaged with some of the other more contentious and contradictory educational demands that are likely to be made (or have already been made) of state education in the name of globalisation.

Reading contemporary sociological theories of change throws light on the new socialisation demands that globalised economies make of institutionalised schooling systems. Two contrasting narratives stand out – one which reports *globalisation* as destructive of the social fabric, extending and aggravating social inequalities; the other which offers possibilities of *democratisation* of individuals in a global society. The tensions between these critical narratives are problematic for social scientists seeking, on the one hand, to sustain their disciplinary project at the same time as contributing to an emancipatory role for educational systems.

The tension between these two narratives is to be found affecting most directly the concept of global citizenship education – the education of the *global learner citizen*. As we saw in Chapter 7, global citizenship education has emerged to fill the space between the destruction of democratic values and structures, and the possibilities of global democratic transformation. Not surprisingly, global citizenship education is a highly contested concept, not least by those committed to promoting gender equality. It contains within it all the contradictions of the global era.

In this chapter, I extend the preliminary analysis of the possibility of promoting gender equality through global citizenship education that Harriet Marshall and I developed (c.f. Marshall and Arnot 2007 a and b). We identified some of the tensions associated with globalisation, but also the possibilities for the promotion of gender equality developed by NGOs working within the fields of global education, global citizenship education and development education. Although neither consistent nor comprehensive, such themes as poverty, difference, conflict, sexuality and others were already highlighted by such activists, often outside mainstream schooling. In this chapter, I return to some of those themes to consider, from the perspective of feminist social and political theory, what the implications are for developing a more rigorous form of citizenship education – one that addresses not the normative values of society, but engages young people in the global controversies of this new century. If educational systems are to create politically aware, informed and active global learner citizens, then a 'global gaze' is essential. But so too is what Yuval-Davis and Stoetzler (2002) called the 'gender gaze'. Gender is not an add-on to our disciplinary and emancipatory project, it is fundamental to it. As I hope to show, the women's movement and gender theorists offer important insights into the workings of global society. If anything, they are at a considerable advantage in tracing the probable effects and possibilities of global transformation, not least because they have now spent some 30 to 40 years promoting gender equality as a key goal of the new millennium.

The ways in which I approach this debate reflect the fact that I am located within the UK, a country that has a particular political approach to social justice. The Anglophone world, with its own global interventions, has a particular slant on debates about contemporary democratic values in a global era – it has yet to be reshaped in its thinking by Southern theory (Fennell and Arnot, 2008). My starting point is to consider the implications associated with globalisation for education, before moving on to a set of major themes that are now being identified by gender theorists in light of globalisation. I consider the implications for the nature and teaching of global citizenship education of these different controversial agendas.

The democratisation of the learner citizen?

Paradoxically, associated with this reconstruction of the role of the state as a result of the global economy is the alleged strengthening of democratic values. We are told by neo-liberal governments that the transmission of democratic values will result from the processes of marketisation and commodification of schooling, offering all consumers choice. We have also been promised a fairer and freer educational system through the process of individualisation and personalisation. New pedagogical approaches will apparently draw upon notions of voice, exit and choice for young people who increasingly will be defined as the new stakeholders of public and private educational provision (see Chapter 8). The individualisation of the learner citizen this century is represented as enormously important for the development of democratic societies.

The model here is one of market-oriented pedagogies where the global learner has to acquire a range of competences such as the ability to acquire quick knowledge, to take risks and to work with uncertainties. The individualising processes encourage flexible social identities, fluid pathways and social and physical mobility. In the future, democratisation, according to Beck and Beck-Gernsheim (2002), would be extended to the personal level, removing the restrictions of institutional structures, knowledges and processes. The consequence apparently would be the 'democratization of democracy itself', an internalisation of democratic consciousness (see Chapter 8).

Preliminary evidence from a wide variety of countries, published in the UNESCO report *Rolling Youth, Rocking Society* (edited by Lagree, 2002), suggests that young people have already been deeply affected by this individualising ethos. Individualisation is found to be one of the main factors that is transforming different societies – along with the knowledge and information society, the transformation and the weakening of regulatory and socialising institutions and frameworks. Individualising processes were found in the 'growing exacerbation of the sense of the individual and the acceptance of or demand for personal responsibility for one's own trajectory and destiny, (Lagree, 2002: 25). As a result, schools, along with family, army and the church, are 'being eroded, cracking, splintering and being recomposed'. Lagree argues that the result:

> ... is an ever more vociferous questioning of the ways in which citizenship is exercised, or the type of democracy used in our modern societies and last but not least, of the content of today's concepts of civil society and social cohesion. (Lagree, 2002: 9)

However, the evidence suggests that such questioning by youth does not necessarily lead to less inequality – existing social divisions do not necessarily lose their influence.[1] In effect, the normative life course of young citizens is being replaced by a diversity of routes. Spiralling individualisation appears to be releasing some people from conventional structures, but trapping others in even greater dependencies and greater social inequalities. In this new scenario, it is unclear how social order will be sustained, or what moral ethos could provide the basis of social cohesion.

A global conscience collective – global citizenship education?

In the early twenty-first century it seems that the revitalisation of the human rights discourse is beginning to fill this space – providing what Durkheim (1997 [1893]) might have called *a global conscience collective*. Human rights discourses have been swept up into public diplomacy, become a key element, a new 'buzz word' in international relations and part of the condition for economic aid. In a world which is politically fraught, the imaginary of global democracy is said to offer a new world of global welfare and world 'domestic' politics. Education is now called up to help construct the conditions for a new sort of global civil society, a form of *global democratic governance* that will, according to Zigmund Bauman (2000), scramble 'the categories of national citizenship'. The promise of this global democracy is that the new forms of global governance will be based on the principles of human rights. The new democracy will cope with multiplicity, multiculturalism and multiple diverse identities. Rather than base entitlements, rights and duties on nation-states, everyone will be entitled to the *right to have rights* (cf. Demaine (2005: 6)).

In this re-conceptualisation, global citizens would be entitled to protection against violence, entitled to free expression about how the world society should be run, entitled to a cultural identity and a livelihood through employment. The implications of such global citizenship are that, according to Galtung (2004: 1076), in such a post-national world, global citizens would need to focus on transactional, transversal politics. The new global citizens would have to move outside the national political framework and engage with global governance and responsibilities. They would have the duty to serve in mediation and peacekeeping forces, to pay global taxes, to be represented and participate in global political life and to show respect when engaged in dialogues with others, globally. They may, in fact, have to become almost *anti-national* because of the role of the state in failing to challenge ethnic exclusions, racism, and the separations of public and private spheres. The new global learner citizen will worry about the role of the state in relation to global warming, genetic engineering, peace, and ethnic and religious diversity.

In the context of democratic global governance, global citizenship education acquires strong moral connotations – it represents a moral response to the internationalisation of human rights; an attempt at a remoralisation of young people that would counter the destructive effects of individualisation. If successful, global citizenship education could create a new form of solidarity across national divisions and difference – a communality based less on individualised identities and more on common global values. The education system would need to transmit a new moral code in shaping a global community based on a universal notion of humanity. Martha Nussbaum (2002) expresses this goal well. Global education for citizenship in an era of global connection would extend rather than restrict our humanity:

> Citizens who cultivate their humanity need an ability to see themselves as not simply citizens of some local region or group but also, and above all, as human beings bound to all other human beings by ties of recognition and concern.
> (Nussbaum, 2002: 295)

The global learner needs above all to acquire a critical perspective on global poverty and violence, world communications and cultures, world migrations and their consequences, and the extraordinary pluralism, diversity and difference within and across nation-states. Nel Noddings (2005) adds global warming; genetic engineering; ways of life; moral relativism; conflict with national citizenship; patriotism; peace education; economic justice; social and political justice; caring; ethnic and religious diversity; gender; and religion to this knowledge base.

If this were not sufficient, Nussbaum and Noddings both see the new global learner as someone who also recognises the universal validity of rights, who can respond to the legitimate claims of the oppressed, and ultimately become a human being capable of love and imagination (Noddings, 2005: 301). Griffiths's (1998) description of an ethical and humane global learner captures this goal well:

A picture then of the global citizen: not merely aware of her rights but able and desirous to act upon them: of an autonomous and inquiring critical disposition: but her decisions and actions tempered by an ethical concern for social justice and the dignity of human kind: therefore able, through her actions, to control and enhance 'the trajectory of the self' through life while contributing to the commonweal, the public welfare, with a sense of civic duty to replenish society. (Griffiths, 1998: 40, quoted in Davies *et al.*, 2005: 4)

At its most moral, global citizenship education should encourage future global citizens to learn 'outrage' – a global citizen is someone who 'knows how the world works, is outraged by injustice and who is both willing and enabled to take action to meet this global challenge' (Oxfam, 1997: 1, quoted in Davies *et al.*, 2005: 4).

At its most political, this new emancipatory critical pedagogy can help focus resistance to the destructive unequal effects of globalisation whether in advanced or less advanced nations.

> We should raise our children to find it intolerable that we who sit behind desks and punch keyboards are paid ten times as much as the people who get their hands dirty, cleaning our toilets, and 100 times as much as those who fabricate our keyboards in the third world. (Bauman, 2001, quoted in Demaine, 2005: 105)

And it can help to encourage different global worlds through what Doreen Massey (2000), as cited in Vargas (2003), called a 'global interconnectedness', by linking global learners to the emergent ideas of international networks and radical protest movements. However, one has to be aware, as Demaine (2005) argues, that new politics around global injustice could also make young people feel even more powerless. Even though global citizens can expose 'the inequalities between citizens' rights and resources both within and between nation states' – globalised rich and localised poor (Beck, 2000: 55) – developing a sense of outrage could be a goal that is meaningless in income-rich countries.

The political ramifications of human rights for gender equality is now discussed in a variety of academic quarters. On the whole, there is support for global human rights discourses as the means by which women can achieve their rights of citizenship. However, it would be wrong to assume that there is agreement amongst feminist and gender writers about the value of the human rights agenda. The social neutrality of human rights education is clearly a matter of great concern. The ambiguity of global declarations of human rights in relation to gender is already evident in the new international equity goals. Even though two of the Millennium Development Goals are devoted to the need to ensure that boys and girls alike will be able to complete a full course of primary schooling and that by 2015 gender disparities should be removed from education, it is not clear that this can be achieved through targeting and global monitoring.[2] Gender equality in education refers, in effect, to the access of women to the full economic, social and political rights of national and global citizenship. The educational systems are most likely to have embedded within them the conventional gender boundaries and hierarchies, producing and reproducing the hierarchies and power of masculinity that are associated with women's oppression as well as traditional forms of femininity. In order to achieve these egalitarian goals, international agencies and governments would need to challenge gender power relations embedded in the state and in societies that sustain such educational inequalities. This would mean challenging the very premises on which national educational systems are based.

The agenda set by feminist and gender theorists for global citizenship education, therefore, is a challenging one. What gender theorists argue for is not increased individualisation of women or of men, but rather a form of education that engages young people in the gender issues associated with globalisation. If gender equality is to be promoted through such a curriculum, then the issues which it needs to face are the gender controversies of the twenty-first century. These controversies are likely to affect discussions about citizenship for a good while yet. The question we need to ask is whether schools are the places where such themes and issues can ever be addressed. Below I discuss in more depth five key themes. These are:

1 Recognition of diversity
2 Sustainable development and poverty reduction
3 Sexual and reproductive citizenships
4 Gendered violence, conflict and peace education
5 Women's global agency and activism

1 Recognition of diversity

Global citizenship education offers a unique opportunity to make sense of gender as a sub-category of ethnic, cultural, religious diasporic communities. Global citizenship as a concept implies an awareness of this tension between unity and difference, globally and nationally. It can focus attention not only on gender difference and gender diversity within nations, but also on gender diversity *across* nations. Urry (1999: 323) reminds us that citizenships are exclusionary, discriminating between those inside and those outside, between citizens and non-citizens, between those who are recognised as global citizens (e.g. white, skilled workers) and others, the enemy. Recognition of the diversity of global cultures could mean greater understanding of the internal inequalities as well as the different ways masculinity and femininity are defined by majority and minority cultures within national citizenship.

Similarly, Silvia Walby (2000, 2005) emphasises the importance of becoming aware of the different gender projects and different gender regimes in each country. These different types of social inequality and patriarchal formation affect different groups of women in diverse ways. Recognition of such cultural diversity is not to say that the continuing dominance of men within economic and political power structures does not cross national territories, bonding women in a common experience.

230 *Educating the global citizen*

The goal of linking gender and cultural diversity within citizenship education can be found in the description the European Union's research programme *Citizens and Governance in a Knowledge-based Society* (2004–6):

> Gender relations influence and at the same time are affected by different notions and practices shaped by diverse cultures. The object is to develop significant new perspectives on how different and changing notions and practices of citizenship relate to gender issues in Europe's multicultural context and the implications for policies. (EU, 2005: 16)

The EU sought to attract research on how the 'current notions of citizenship and multiculturalism incorporate a gender perspective, with a focus on the European context and the relations between gender, race, ethnicity, class and different notions and practices of citizenship'. The EU accepted that linking of gender, multiculturalism and citizenship raises important questions about the different perceptions of nationality, cosmopolitanism and European citizenship, the extent to which specific groups of men and women are affected by differential access to political, social, economic and social rights, and the differences and similarities found in multicultural and more homogeneous settings.

In the 1990s Lynch (1992) and Banks (1997) addressed the ways in which citizenship could engage with a multicultural diverse society but unfortunately not the gendered aspects of it. Banks, for example, argued that the national ideals of democracy should link to cultural values, communities and global world society. This involves moving into the social psychological levels of citizenship, understanding community cultures and reflecting on one's own culture through the eyes of others. Liberal models not only masked diversity, but could not easily address either group rights or traditionalism. In contrast, global education promises notions of cultural democracy that might address such issues more positively (although it is unclear how the gendered aspects of traditionalism were to be encountered). Similarly, Lynch argued that the internationalisation of national citizenship to a multiple-level global citizenship is required. However,

> [e]ducation for global citizenship will require a radical change in values, epistemologies, structures and mechanisms whereby we regulate our interactions as members of local communities, nation state and international society. (Lynch, 1992: 20–1)

New organic modes of human association, and new social, economic and environmental self-restraint would need to replace what Lynch saw as instrumental, competitive, materialistic, atomised and exploitative relationships.

At the heart of this theme also lies a need to address the ways in which global economic forces affect the lives of men and women in different social classes, ethnic groups and cultures, globally. The diversity of men's and women's experience is now a reflection not just of national citizenship, but also of the rolling back of the nation-state, and second, the use of male and female labour within a global, not just a national, economy. If young people are to engage with global arenas and debates about rights, then they need to understand what the transfer of power to global economic forces means for men and women, both in income-rich and in income-poor nations.

One theme that emerges from the literature is that the repositioning of the state is deeply problematic for working-class women and women living in poverty. Much has been written about the ways in which women and the women's movement, particularly in welfare nation states, have called upon the state to act on behalf of women. Although the patriarchal nature of the state has been criticised, the power of national citizenship rights for women cannot be underestimated. The women's movement historically has sought justice through the nation-state by pressurising it to respond to demands for equal citizenship, the redistribution of economic/fiscal opportunities, recognition of women's experiences and life course in policy and gender equality of access, treatment, participation for all women, irrespective of social background, colour, ethnicity, sexuality or religion. As such, the culture and focus of women's politics has been nationally conceived and delivered.

However, as Jan Jindy Pettman (1999) argues, the state has always been 'a difficult construction' for women, since it was ambiguous about women's political demands. State policies frequently enforce masculinist power. As Western nation-states respond to globalisation and global markets, they cut back on unproductive social expenditures, thus reducing the political space of citizenship and at the same time reducing the social rights of women. This rolling back of the state welfare alone is profoundly gendered in its consequences reducing social support, health and education. Women 'largely bear the responsibility as the competitive state withdraws from its social welfare obligations while reprivatizing women's productive labor' (Blackmore, 2000: 135). Arguably, active female citizenship requires state support. Yet hard-won feminist gains are now under attack from neo-liberal state ideologies. Not surprisingly women have tried to 'reclaim the state and citizenship which arguably is more accessible than global power' (Pettman 1999).

Generalisation about the effects of these global changes in the economy and the state is problematic because these effects vary temporally and geographically and according to gender, race and ethnicity. There is what Pettman called a 'global prowl' for cheap labour, which recruits young women who are employed in flexibilised low-paid, risky conditions, in factories and sweatshops and outwork. They become part of the global feminised working class. Inequality and poverty contribute to international trafficking in women and children for prostitution. The changing global division of labour is marked by a predominantly male core of skilled workers and a vast global assembly line of casualised feminised labour.

In this global economy, there is little sense of women workers having political agency – access to citizenship is becoming even more gender differentiated. Women participate directly in globalisation flows and are often 'out of place'. Pettman documents that well over 1200 million people live outside their country of birth, many of whom are women. They are 'non-citizens', strangers, migrants, moving across national boundaries in search of work. Often they are beyond state legal reach, lacking formal citizenship or legal rights. The international service class of female employees loses its rights in its own country as well. Barbara Ehrenreich and Arlie Hochschild (2005), writing about 'the global woman' reminds us that the 'care deficit' in wealthier countries pulls women from poverty-stricken countries into the domestic labour force, away from their own families and children. This 'female underside' of globalisation reflects what they call 'a world-wide gender revolution'. Such migrant women workers are often denied both rights and agency both in their own country and in the country in which they are employed. The concept of global citizenship therefore has little meaning in a context where the effect of global power is increasing such poverty, racialisation, migrantisation and lack of support of citizens. Nation-states police their boundaries by policing women's mobility, relations and bodies.

One of the ways suggested as a means of tackling female poverty and exploitation globally is to provide an education in the concept of a global democracy that bases global governance on the universal principles of human rights. This ideal could open up the conditions, for some, of a global feminist sisterhood. However, as some feminists are more than aware, there are powerful contradictions associated with teaching about global democracy. There is a great 'desire for innocence' – performing what Heald calls the 'colonialist trick' (Heald, 2004) of 'assuming that we in the North are in charge of the identities and experiences of people in the South' (what we can do for them) rather than recognising the complex interdependencies and power relations. In contrast, as the University of Glasgow Global Citizenship Project (2003) points out, the relationship between women in income-rich and those in income-poor countries might be better taught rather than ignored.

> The global citizen is someone who is aware of the ways in which her life is interconnected with those of others across the world. These interconnections can be a cause of poverty and injustice: the consumerist lifestyles of rich Western countries form part of a global pattern of poverty and debt. But the interconnections also give us an opportunity: to challenge these injustices, simply through looking again at the way we live. (Global Citizenship Project, 2003, 6)

2 Sustainable development and poverty reduction

This notion of global sisterhood that crosses the divide between rich and poor nations brings us to our second theme. Although global discourses tend to refer to 'free markets', there have been more deliberate interventions by international organisations that try to sustain the gender concerns within the overarching development project. It is now widely recognised that gender inequality, female illiteracy and the lack of girls' education is a serious hindrance to economic development and the reduction of poverty. As the Director General of UNESCO pointed out, 'the scourge of illiteracy still affects more than 860 million adults, almost two-thirds of whom are women' (UNESCO, 2003) and, whilst millions of children fail to get access to schooling or drop out of education, the majority of such children are girls.

However, as Fiona Leach (2000) states, development policy usually fails to recognise the gendered effects of such global development processes, and it does not consider effectively the gendered nature of societies that are encouraged to adopt international values and indicators. There are major dilemmas associated with current methods of 'measuring' development strategies in relation to education and gender (for example closing the gender gap in education) where indicators merely relate to the quantity and longevity of female students and teachers in schools rather than the nature of gender equality itself (Leach, 2000; Stromquist, 2004). As Connell (2005) points out, when the UN Development Program, in its 2003 annual report on world human development, constructed a gender-related development index and a gender empowerment measure, it was able to publish a league table in which most countries were shown to be far from gender equal. Yet whilst offering useful statistical measures, these indices, as Connell points out, nevertheless conceal the substructures of gender that work to sustain economic and human development, and male power and privilege.

> It is clear that, globally, men have a lot to lose from pursuing gender equality because men, collectively, continue to receive a patriarchal dividend. (Connell, 2005: 1808)

If global citizenship education takes up this theme, then it needs to consider alternative ways of linking gender and development. Those working with gender and development will want young people to consider what it means to universalise notions of gender equality. How can gender equality and economic development be measured? Even more fundamentally, what gender values lie underneath such declarations and agendas?

Elaine Unterhalter's (2000, 2007, 2008) extensive analysis of international agendas and transnational declarations that have attempted to promote economic development and poverty reduction highlights the struggle the women's movement had to get women's rights recognised as human rights. Global citizenship education could usefully begin with the Beijing Declaration (WCW, 1995) which saw the necessity of women as a social group to be engaged politically in a society. Since then there have been various phases in which the notion of social justice internationally has been defined and redefined. Over the last 40 years, Unterhalter argues, there were *inter-national* gender values that drew on liberal notions of needs, rights and capabilities as terms of value. In the second phase (dating from the 1990s) what she called the *in/ternational approach* still drew on this language, but shifted attention to national and individual notions of agency, solidarity, equality, freedom, negotiation and the calibration of global institutions. Gender equality refers not just to equal amounts, but to a 'more substantive idea associated with solidarities and confronting injustice'.

Gender concerns are now part of global poverty reduction strategies internationally and nationally – for example, the World Bank and IMF's attempt to reduce poverty mainstreamed gender (Sen, 2006). However, as Pyle and Ward (2003: 465) point out, these interventions are ironic given that global restructuring has 'decimated countries' physical and social infrastructures and their capabilities to meet such goals'. Arguably, if we are to develop gender selective courses on global citizenship for young people, then a critical analysis of the connections between gender and postcolonial development agendas is essential. Wright (2001) also warns us to notice the complexity of human rights goals in relation to Euro-American and colonial roots. 'Global history is a history of colonialism.'

> Those individuals who cannot recognize their own position within colonialism are often the most vociferous in their demands that human rights are the representation of universal values of freedom, equality and justice. (Wright, 2001: 224–5, quoted in Marshall and Arnot, 2007a: 170)

A global citizenship curriculum that is not thought through could represent unrestrained Westernisation, Rizvi (2000) argues, but it could also provide the space for the production of the 'global imagination' through the use of more radical educational approaches that developed new 'epistemic virtues of historicity, reflexivity, criticality and relationship in global citizenship education related topics'. Sen's (1999) concept of 'development as freedom' and his notion of capabilities has reshaped debates about gender equality, offering a different framework for understanding citizenship outside traditional liberal democratic concepts. The shift in thinking is away from materialist concerns to identifying what is valued – and how what is valued can be achieved. The question now is whether individuals have the freedom to achieve what they personally value (Jelin, 2000). Nussbaum and Glover (1995), for example, list a whole range of universal human capabilities that could be used to define sustainable economic and human development and to assess the impact of education on individuals and communities. Their conceptualisation of human development and freedom asks, 'What do human beings need in order to survive, to feel, to achieve a sense of belonging?' Here the inequalities of access are replaced by notions of identity building, self-reflection and an equal chance to develop capabilities.

3 Sexual and reproductive citizenships

One of the most important ways in which patriarchal relations are sustained and economic development held back is through the sexual oppression of women. Taking gender equality seriously involves global citizenship education in a consideration of the concept of sexual and reproductive citizenship. The separation of public and private spheres that was endemic to liberal democratic thought and civic republicanism had major implications for female citizenship. The sexual contract that underlies the social contract developed by Western European philosophers, according to Carol Pateman (1989) and others, implies the ownership of women's reproductive capacity by men (see Chapters 3 and 4). This assumed control of women's bodies by men within liberal democratic citizenship is now challenged by gender theory.

Today, there is not only an awareness of the different ways the state has intervened into the private and intimate spheres of parenthood, childcare, reproduction, sexuality and even intimacy. Paralleling these developments are the new social movements of the 1980s and 1990s in which, increasingly, the women's movement and the gay movement have demanded new rights of protection from discrimination and violence, and new levels of tolerance and freedom in relation to private sexual lives. In this context, the concepts of *sexual citizenship* and *reproductive citizenship* have come into the political and academic arenas. These notions bridge the public and private domains; they are transgressive and therefore controversial, but they are also seen as the natural extension of Marshall's notions of social rights.

As Weeks explains, the sexual citizen is a hybrid being. Its presence reflects the primacy given to sexual subjectivity, the pace and scale of cultural transformation and the new possibilities of the self and identity (Weeks, 1998: 35). To some extent the concept of a sexual citizen is a 'sensitising' concept (Plummer, 2003) since it draws attention to the need for citizenship to address what Giddens (1992: 330) called the globalised 'transformation of intimacy' – the desire to allow freedom of sexual expression and association, to tolerate a diversity of sexual lifestyles, to recognise the importance of emotions and also to understand the political exclusions of sexual minority groups from their rights as citizens, nationally and globally.

Social currents around detraditionalisation, egalitarianism, the quest for personal autonomy and sense of self, and concern about social exclusion associated with citizenship, have encouraged an interest in this notion of sexual citizenship. The concept of sexual citizenship creates a new political space in which the 'would-be sexual citizen' can claim a hearing (Weeks, 1998: 49). It is now recognised that the sexual citizen is framed by a whole range of controls: criminal laws (such as the age of consent, certain sexual practices, public indecency, pornography); medical discourses which define normality and perversions, and deny medical or reproductive treatments to certain groups; religious discourses that can lead to 'hate speeches'; and institutional exclusions (such as the army, marriage, etc.).[3] The concept of a sexual citizen encourages discussion about an individual's (a) right in participate in sexual activity; (b) right to pleasure; (c) the right to sexual and reproductive self-determination.[4]

Global citizenship education, in breaking through the boundaries of contemporary thought, would engage then with a recognition of social-sexual diversity, the right of individuals to choose sexual partners, and the right to sexual relations that are valued in the public domain. The concept of sexual obligations; sexual consent; care and respect; tolerance of sexual association; and expression are also implicated in this concept (Richardson and Turner, 2001). Since young people are directly affected by the law referring to the age of sexual consent and have already discussed homophobia in the context of bullying, discussion about the global diversity of sexual citizenship would be challenging and informative.

Patriarchy, religion and state control are deeply embedded in the notion of sexual freedoms and the transgressive notions of sexual citizenship raise important questions about the extent to which the state should, and can, intervene in the intimate world.

The concept of *reproductive citizenship* highlights the fact that only some people have the right to reproduce whilst others are denied this right; that the social and legal conditions under which people may reproduce, and with whom, discriminate against particular groups (e.g. the disabled, gay and lesbian couples). Richardson and Turner (2001) links reproductive citizenship to Nussbaum and Glover's (1995: 78) theory of human development since it involves the capability to be in control of one's own body and bodily functions. This right was taken up by the 1994 International Conference on Population and Development when it recognised that all women have the right to a satisfactory and safe sexual life and the right to choose when to reproduce and how. The neglect of these elements in political theory, but also in society, according to Diane Richardson, means that, 'heterosexuality has been constructed as a necessary condition for citizenship' – the British post-war welfare state, for example, made major assumptions about the link between citizenship and the stable nuclear family, working husband and working wife (Richardson and Turner, 2001: 331).

In Western societies, the state promotes the desirability of fertility and reproduction as 'a foundation of social participation': whilst parenthood is normal, heterosexuality is 'the defining characteristic of the average citizen and the basis of social entitlement':

> Reproducing the next generation of citizens through marriage and household formation has been a central means of acquiring effective parental entitlements of citizenship and fulfilling its corresponding obligations. (Richardson and Turner, 2001: 336–7)

As Richardson and Turner point out, the interest of the state in sexuality and sexual identity is actually 'secondary and subordinate to its demographic objective of securing and sustaining the connection between reproduction and citizenship' (Richardson and Turner, 2001: 337).[5] Many citizenship rights are about reproductive rights, for example, access to in-vitro fertilisation, compulsory sterilisation and the right to an abortion. There are many questions that could be asked therefore about the involvement of the state in new reproductive technologies and the rights of the citizen. With this sort of education, the 'issues of responsibility and moral choice' could be related to questions of reproductive relations, and conflicting male and female responsibilities in society as well as to issues of discriminatory access to such reproductive technologies.

Heterosexualisation can also be endorsed by a range of global forces. There is now much more awareness of the global sex trade, internet pornography, and how male and female bodies and health are portrayed on the web. Moore and Clarke (2001), for example, suggest that images of the male and the female body, and men's and women's relationship to their bodies (what the authors call *cyberanatomies*) are shown through the lens of heterosexuality. The female body is represented as reproductive, not sexual. Body politics arguably is now being reshaped by such global practices. Ligouri and Lamas (2003) argue that a critical engagement in the ways in which gender and heterosexuality are linked would help with one of the most powerful aspects of HIV/AIDS:

> Today, democratic demands for a new sexual citizenship based on respect for human rights, are at one with cultural strategies indispensable to combating HIV/AIDS. For the good of everyone, a new cultural discourse that questions double standards, accepts feminine sexuality and recognises the sexual practices and love among people who do not follow heterosexual norms must gain legitimacy. Heterosexism and homophobia, which are intrinsically linked to dominant gender roles, make it difficult for people with homosexual desires to be accepted. They carry great risks for women who are unable to be sexually assertive for fear of earning a bad reputation and for men who have sex with other men who have not openly accepted their practices. The magnitude of the consequences of what people will do to avoid being assigned stigmatised identities can be seen in the growing number of HIV-positive men and women.
> (Liguori and Lamas, 2003: 89)

These heteronormativities could be part of a global citizenship education, although they are highly controversial. National educational systems teaching national cultural heritages and notions of nationhood often help reinforce the normalisation of heterosexual gender identities (Petersen, 2000). Yet global citizenship education could explore the connection between nationalism and heterosexuality, especially the portrayal of women's bodies through analyses of visual imagery and cultural artefacts.

Finally, there are other consequences signalled by an absence of concern about sexuality and reproduction as central citizenship rights. The absence or marginalisation of the private sphere from definitions of citizenship reflects deep associations about the relationship between rationality and citizenship (Nussbaum and Glover, 1995). The citizen is excluded, by definition, from 'the affective domain' – the field of personal/emotional relationships – of civic discourse. This can result in the failure to value 'the caring ethos' and maternal values (Noddings, 1998) found in the private and familial sphere that might provide alternative models of citizenship and civic virtues (cf. discussion of maternal feminism in Chapter 2). This begs the question whether global citizenship virtues should be based on abstract principles or the forms of *connectedness* and moral reasoning found amongst women (cf. Gilligan, 1982). Thus whilst the principle of excluding the private sphere from state control, from surveillance and from intervention appears beneficial, especially to women within the family, it has the disadvantageous effect of marginalising and discursively subordinating women as non-rational beings and of reducing the potential impact of other sets of civic virtues from a discussion of global citizenship.

Lynch, Lyons and Cantillon (2007) argue that the self-sufficient rational economic actor (REA) citizen promoted by neo-liberalism effectively excludes the dependent citizen and the person who is responsible for dependents. The only interdependencies that are recognised are those which relate to the competition for resources: 'the world of care is left outside the global frame of economic and political understanding: it is a private world' (Lynch *et al.*, 2007a and b).

> The citizen carer only seriously enters the educational frame when professionals are being trained to manage or service her or his needs, as social workers, nurses, therapists, psychologists, social care workers or counselors/therapists. ... In programmes of civil, social and political education, caring may be included but it is not focused on the personal; where care is named, care for the environment is prioritised increasingly. (Lynch *et al.*, 2007a: 3)

The reconstruction of global citizenship education from a feminist perspective would need to 'break the silence' that surrounds emotional labour of 'care, love and solidarity' – validating the role of emotion and feelings within society.[6] Fennell and Arnot (2007) point to African feminists' view that Northern feminism has sidelined, if not denigrated, mothering as one of the main sources of woman's identity and power within developing countries.

4 Gendered violence, conflict and peace education

Sexual and reproductive citizenships are strongly linked to the extent of gender violence in society. It is hard to separate violence from gender, yet generally it is probably true to say that citizenship education rarely connects to the development of peace education, anti-violence education or even anti-bullying school policies. Teachers of global citizenship education, on the other hand, would find it hard to avoid discussing the realities of global violence and, in particular, the violence against women globally. Yet gender violence between men, or against women, cannot be divorced from arguments about sustainable development and good governance. Also, 'violence against women and girls', as Charlotte Bunch (1997) argued, is 'the most pervasive violation of human rights in the world today':

> Its forms are both subtle and blatant and its impact on development profound. But it is so deeply embedded in cultures around the world that it is almost invisible. Yet this brutality is not inevitable. Once recognised for what it is – a construct of power and a means of maintaining the status quo – it can be dismantled. (Bunch, 1997: 1)

Bunch points out that half of humanity is faced with assault, rape, sexual slavery, arbitrary imprisonment, torture, verbal abuse, mutilation, even murder, because they were born a member of a particular sex. Women face gross violations of their human rights. It is impossible, Bunch argues, to talk about human security ('peace, peace at home, peace at large' (Bunch, 1997: 1)), without looking at the continued murder and violation of young girls and women. More than one million children, overwhelming female, are forced into prostitution each year – with younger children sought in the wake of AIDS epidemic. The statistics are overwhelming; the growing emancipation of women globally has not reduced; violence – some suggest it is on the increase globally.

The prevalence of family violence globally means that in many contexts, girls learn a lesson early on about what is possible in the face of male aggression, and about their notions of male honour, religious duty and patriotism (Bunch, 1997; Davies, 2004). The international human rights community has taken up the issue of 'gender-based violations as pervasive and insidious forms of human rights abuse'. For example, the Global Tribunal on Violations of Women's Human Rights[7] confirmed the view that women's rights and girls' rights were an inalienable, integral and indivisible part of universal human rights' (Bunch, 1997: 4). In 1993, the UN adopted the Declaration on the Elimination of Violence against Women and, in the same year, the Convention on the Elimination of All Forms of Discrimination against Women (CEDAW), which had been drafted as early as 1979, was ratified by 160 countries. The Convention of the Rights of the Child (ratified by 191 countries in June 1997) also attempted to find ways of stopping or preventing violence (Bunch, 1997). In 1994, the UN appointed a Special Rapporteur on Violence against Women.

It is not clear, as Bunch argues, that government officials have staked their careers on removing gender violence. Can we say the same of educationalists? The mass violation of women's human rights and gender violence is not generally considered an appropriate topic for national citizenship education in schools, not least because, again, it is largely located with the 'private' sphere of intimate relations; and indeed there is the likelihood that some girls at school will have already experienced violence in their lives. This argument sustains the view that schools should see as their task the protection of children's innocence from the adult world. There is also the view that teaching about violence will lead to violence. Of course, this argument denies the ways in which schools as institutions teach what Kenway and Fitzclarence (2006) called 'poisonous pedagogies', which can violate the child and also tolerate or ignore forms of sexualised and racialised violence within educational environments (Sunnari *et al.*, 2002).[8] However, even when gender violence is researched and curricular guidance given, it can be marginalised by the political priorities of citizenship education.

Recent work has now brought gender violence into the heart of discussion about constructing a 'violence free' or 'peaceful culture'. On the initiative of a well-known Swedish writer, Eva Moberg, a group of committed individuals (mainly men) mobilised public support and placed the need for a new male gender role on the agenda of the United Nations. In 1997, UNESCO set up an Expert Group Meeting to explore the relationship between masculinity, conflict resolution and peace. It published a text on *Male Roles, Masculinities and Violence: a culture of peace perspective* (Breines *et al.*, 2000), which closely linked patriarchy and masculinity in relation to global levels of violence. There is clearly much work to be done to address male violence. Although not all men are violent and not all violent people are men, violence has been associated with men (Davies, 2007). By bringing together researchers and activists in the areas of peace and conflict resolution and gender studies, with experience of anti-violence work among men, the UNESCO expert group was able to explore

> the development of new more egalitarian and partnership-oriented types of masculinities as opposed to traditional and stereotyped expectations of masculinity that might lead to undue acceptance of the use of authority, dominance, control, force, aggressiveness and violence. (cf. Breines *et al.*, 2000: 271)

Recognition of the role of male and female movements for peace in this context becomes important, as does recognition of the variety of men's movements which have attempted to address these issues. Davies (2004) and Yuval-Davis and Stoetzler (2002) provide excellent discussions on how the role of women in many internationally famous peace movements is taken for granted. As Yuval-Davis and Stoetzler argue, women are 'constructed as symbolic border guards for the collectivity and representing the collectivity's 'honour'', but at the same time they can be excluded from military, public and political spheres. Women's peace movements therefore are often about gender as well as nation, about cross-ethnic and national boundaries – demonstrating a 'transversal politics'. But Davies (2004) also quotes a number of contemporary studies showing how women are also implicated in violence, conflict and wars – one cannot therefore assume that femininity is inherently peaceful.

Central to discussions about violence are the ways in which conflict is associated with hegemonic masculinity (with men becoming perpetrators or victims). There has been an upsurge of masculinity politics in recent years and several distinct forms of movement with competing political agendas around masculinity have emerged. Arguably, global citizenship education could explore the varying agendas of contemporary men's movements. Some encourage, as we know from Scandinavian initiatives, men's roles as husbands and fathers, whilst others attempt to reinstall men as heads of families. In contrast, there are men's movements that defend masculine fundamentalism, which encourages the bodily superiority of men, their mastery of technology and violence. Often such movements 'offer no criticism of the institutional power of the military or the symbolic violence of sport' (Connell, 2002). There are also movements, largely American that encourage a greater acceptance of emotional bonds between men, and even the 'inner warrior' exploring emotions and relationships that would undermine conventional patterns of male violence. These focus on the therapeutic/healing of men's wounds. Since the 1960s, the Men's Liberation Movement and queer politics have also shown how transformative politics can reshape gender relations usually emphasising peaceableness, sharing and an anti-sexist stance (Connell, 2002).

Democratic gender relations, according to Connell, if pursued by education, would aim to promote 'equality, non-violence and mutual respect between people'.

Traditional qualities associated with masculinity (courage, steadfastness, ambition) would be associated with the cause of peace. The global task would be not to abolish gender but to reshape it. For boys this would have to:

> disconnect courage from violence, steadfastness from prejudice, ambition from exploitation. (Connell, 2000: 30)

Global citizenship education could usefully teach about the history of global masculinities and their interconnections – it could encourage young people to consider the various ways of being men in the public, community and private domains, to acknowledge the diversity, complexity and hierarchies of masculinities, their institutional and social forms, their associations with power, with violence and their involvement historically in peace movements.

Lyn Davies's ground-breaking book *Education and Social Conflict* (2004) takes us even deeper into the relationship between schooling and gender conflict – the history of gender violence in war, the role of men and women in conflict and resistance movements; all of which are directly relevant to global citizenship education. This history suggests that more thought needs to be given to the rather complex nature of social conflict as a theme in the school curriculum, linking it, for example, with the gendering of emotional literacy, heroism and the problem of showing fear. In her recent work, Davies (2007) argues that another role for schooling is the promotion of national and personal security. A politicised education would need to confront the recruitment of young men and women into extreme organisations and how schools might counter this by, she suggests, encouraging an acceptance of ambiguity rather than absolutism and single truths; a secular basis to human rights; the breaking down of 'Otherness' in society; encouraging reconciliation rather than revenge and honour; and promoting the value of free speech and humour.

The current fear of terrorism also has gendered dimensions. Iris Marion Young (2003) makes some telling comments about the new anxieties created by the American governmental responses after the events of 11 September 2001. The new language of security encourages the view that the nation is under threat and that abnormal protocols are needed. Masculinist bellicose approaches can hide a new form of authoritarianism, whilst the concept of global security may represent a militaristic and undemocratic position. Both construct 'good citizens' (those in need of protection; everything is done in their name – including war, terror, and suspicion of citizens within the state) and 'bad citizens' (who are either seen as the enemy or as a threat). In this context, public criticism of government policy is considered unpatriotic. But also women as citizens are being asked to be complicit in an argument that implies that the country had gone to war to 'save women' from barbaric customs.

Schools increasingly find themselves needing to engage with this global agenda around war and violence, and security, although probably not from a gender perspective. The implications of the focus of this international educational agenda around a 'culture of peace' is that young women as well as young men could simultaneously consider what they could to assist in the creation of gender equality, while at the same time ending gender-based violence.

5 Women's global agency and activism

The education of the 'global citizen' can encourage young people to engage in non-exploitative forms of intercultural communication and sharing with countries that might experience economic or humanitarian predicaments on a more significant scale. Having said that, the notion of global political agency has to avoid what could be a major danger – the image of men as global actors and women as the victims of globalisation. The international women's movement of the last 30 years is a major global force, forging change in many countries and now seeing its impact in the new Millennium Goals for the twenty-first century. Organisations such as the United Nations Development Fund for Women (UNIFEM) have issued mandates recognising that multilateral institutions now have a responsibility to understand and respond to the need to 'build women's capacities to advocate their own interests' and to bring 'the women's movement's experience with empowerment into the context of multilateral policy making' (www.unifem.undp.org). But in some ways, this taking up of gender equality by global agencies almost seems to deny the extraordinary role of feminist and women's activism within and across continents and countries.

If global citizenship education is to serve the needs of gender justice, then it has to challenge actively the image of women standing outside of politics and political action. As Jane Roland Martin (1994) argued, women are usually located in the ontological political basement as far as politics are concerned. Global citizenship education, with its emphasis on interconnectedness and alliance, could do well to recognise the strong role women's activism has played in changing global agendas (Yuval-Davis and M. Stoetzler, 2002). The autobiographies of women's activists demonstrate the crossing of boundaries and borders – representing, as Jaggar (2005) argues, their situated imaginings and new forms of transversal politics and political projects. For some, the creation of 'a third sphere' (that of community and communitarian traditions) offers women a chance to develop new civic engagements, often around education (Jaggar, 2005; Reay and Mirza, 2000). The rise of international and national NGOs, often run by women, involving women, and often about women, exemplifies this grassroots political approach. There are many examples of how new models of citizenship have been developed by women (for example, Oxfam's (Sweetman, 2004) *Gender, Development and Citizenship* documents some fascinating examples). The intersection of the national and global means that women's activism is becoming even more important since it now involves holding the nation-state to account both for its policies in relation to women and also for the impact of its policies on women the world over.

Arguably, global citizenship education could play a role in challenging stereotypical views of gender and women's lives in Southern cultures. As Shaila Fennell and I argued, it is likely that representations of women from developing contexts have probably been left largely unchanged by gender equality initiatives in income-rich countries. All too often, so-called 'women in the third world' (Mohanty, 1988; Yuval-Davis, 1997) are represented universally as oppressed, without any capacity or history of activism (Fennell and Arnot, 2007). Representations of such 'Southern' women include the image of barbaric customs, the lack of personal autonomy and an assumed political immaturity. Such women, according to Mohanty (1988), are frozen in history in feminist writings. They are archetypal victims, with no agency. Euro-American (what Connell (2008) calls 'metropolitan') feminism is in danger of assuming that it brings agency to women in developing countries. Post-structuralism has reminded us that feminism is not a 'specifically Western phenomenon' and that a sensitivity to difference and multipositionality is of growing importance. Nevertheless, there are concerns that non-European national cultures and traditions are seen as patriarchal and anti-feminist. Euro-American feminism becomes a hegemonic form of cultural imperialism. As Yuval-Davis and Werbner (1999) pointed out, there is still little dialogue between feminists from these two worlds – it is largely 'the dialogue of the deaf' (Yuval-Davis and Werbner, 1999: 134).

Global gender theory needs to be reworked by learning from the Southern feminists if the intellectual traffic is to be two-way (cf. Fennell and Arnot, 2007). Global citizenship education could usefully discuss the issue of whether a global feminist sisterhood is possible (taking it out of time and location) or whether women's liberation is the primary goal in the context of the need for global poverty alleviation. It would also need to consider the growth of new associations for 'development alternatives for women', and the role of women and men in the World Social Forum and working with global agencies such as the United Nations, in bringing together global social movements against neo-liberal globalisation. These initiatives show the challenge and opportunity that the 'global space' brings for different feminisms and gender politics (cf. Vargas, 2003; Harcourt, 2006). Stromquist (2008) and Sen (2006) indicate the value of exploring different forms of feminist organisational strategy and structure in empowering women through NGOs and different models of international policy advocacy and social activism employed by the international women's movement.[9]

One of the major strands of women's activism has been women's own struggle for the right to have an education, and the ways in which that struggle has been responded to. Davies (2007) points to the levels of violence that can occur in trying to prevent girls from being educated in some societies. The struggle for female citizenship through the school system raises important questions for citizenship education. Stromquist (2005) points to, for example, the use of schooling itself as the emancipatory project; the 'romancing of the state' to act in the name of women, and 'dissolving' of the 'space for ethics and social improvement' by the spread of market-centred society and its consequences for schooling as one of the few spaces in which solidarity could be fostered and agency in the name of social justice be encouraged. 'Understanding gender', she argues, means engaging with politics and the state in the public sphere. Campaigning for women's rights, social justice, environmental rights and sustainable economic development, and preventing destructive conflicts and the HIV/AIDS epidemic from spreading, encourage young people's commitment, activity and agency within global civil society. In this way, they *become* rather than *being assumed to be* citizens of the world (Carter, 2001).

An ethical pedagogy for educating the global learner citizen

In the last century, as we know, the school system in Western Europe was the modernist project *par excellence*. It represented both the best of liberal ideals as well as the most extensive experiment in training for obedience, conformity and social control. Modernity's ambitions, as Durkheim listed, contained extraordinarily contradictory goals of educating for individuality whilst preparing for a highly stratified and unequal social order, sustained through the dominance of economic forces as well as political notions of contract (the conditions for what he called 'organic solidarity'). Modern state schooling prepared children, therefore, for one of the greatest contradictions of the twentieth century, a training for democracy as well as capitalism (Heater, 2004).

Educating the global learner is a very different affair today. The forms of solidarity that lie at the heart of the social order have evolved into something that much more individualised; the social bonds are less easily described the more complex the social formation becomes. The economic conditions of schooling are far less immediate, and social stratifications now stretch across the world. In this context, discussion about the role of schooling and the learner citizen has shifted dramatically. There is a desire now to extend the notion of citizenship far into the heart of childhood. Instead of using the nineteenth-century concept of the child as 'innocent', in need of protection from the adult world, there is the concept of the young would-be citizen who needs to start learning the principles of democratic citizenship as soon as possible – even as early as the first years of primary schooling. It is almost as if it is too dangerous to wait for citizenship to be acquired at the age of 18, along with economic and political rights. Today we need to think about preparing young people more actively for democracy, through pupil consultation, pupil councils, engagements in the control over their own learning, and even an assessment of their own learning. The rights of the child, endorsed by the United Nations as early as 1989, are only now beginning to be taken up internationally – interestingly, in a period of great international interest in neo-liberal models of school governance and performance monitoring in the name of excellence.

There is already so much talk in the early twenty-first century about global citizenship as the way forward, over and above nationally forged notions of citizenship virtues, values and practices. Much of the discussion about global citizenship and global citizenship education is confused, contradictory and complex for an educational community that is already struggling to cope with the new performance demands of unstable national economies, massive migrations of people and destabilised local communities. What actually should constitute the education of the learner citizen in this context is one of the great challenges of this new century.

This chapter suggests that even the most critical models of liberal citizenship education are simply not sufficient to address the range of gendered global issues outlined here. The education of the global citizen requires far more extensive, and arguably radical, politicisation in order to give young people the knowledge, awareness and understanding to engage with global cultures, practices and conflicts, to help them feel that they can engage politically, whether through a sense of 'moral outrage' or through a desire to participate in a global civil society merely as members of it. The range of issues associated with globalisation, globalism, the international–national interface or just the reconstruction of the nation is vast. Bringing the citizenship agenda into the global arena therefore will open up critical discussions about what is meant by 'democracy', 'democratic values' and 'democratic governance'. This chapter suggests that, as part of this education, young people should also be encouraged to think through these debates using a variety of different yardsticks. One of those criteria, I have argued, must be that of gender; not only, not exclusively, but nevertheless present. Gender relations are embedded in the construction of the 'global citizen' just as much as the liberal democratic notions of the 'good citizen' or the citizen worker.

The sorts of issue raised in this chapter suggest that, rather than shy away from controversial issues relating in this case to gender, children could be offered a '*controversial education*'. It is significant that globally women suffer some of the worst effects of exploitation, oppression and violence. It is even more significant that the global citizen, like the learner citizen back in the classroom, is a gendered citizen. The more we discuss global citizenship education, particularly from a gender perspective, the greater the need for young people not to receive a normative education, one which implies consensus. Rather, they deserve an education, particularly in adolescence, that addresses some of the great debates of the twenty-first century around citizenship – its practices, ethos, problems and possibilities, nationally and globally. The powerfully controversial issues which gender theory has raised about the economic and political structures and processes, about the positioning of women and men within these, and the implications for political agency, resistance and activism in creating new 'other worlds' (Vargas, 2003) are important ones, not just for educationalists to debate, but also for young people to discuss. As Marianne Talbot advised:

> Controversial issues are important in themselves and to omit informing about and discussing them is to leave a wide and significant gap in the educational experience of young people, as is to fail to prepare them for adult life. Many controversial topics are major issues of the day: moral, economic, political and religious issues which young people ought to know about either because the issue could directly affect them or because they will in some way in a democratic society have opportunities to take a part in influencing the outcome … Social issues concerning war and peace, concerning relationships between peoples of different colour, ethnicity and creed, concerning oppression and justice, and religious issues concerning the value of human life … etc. are all of this order. (Advisory Group on Citizenship (The Crick Report), 1998: 56, para 10.4)

Global citizenship would also need to replace a normative stance with a new ethical base, arguably one that addresses the issues which feminists have highlighted. Davies (2004) suggests that this ethical base is the outrage mentioned earlier about global injustice, but with the addition of a 'disposition to challenge'. She calls this 'interruptive democracy'. Challenging involves taking control of global agendas rather than becoming the victim of them. Other feminist writers have stressed the need to move away from victimisation of women and to explore the contribution of women to alternative global ethics. Reflecting the discussion about maternalism in Chapter 2, it is interesting to learn that Ruddick (1990) argues for a maternalist ethic of care that would offer non-violent strategies for peace. It would create a new moral orientation to international relations emphasising the essence of human life, the particularities of individual needs, the practicalities of life and caring within relational worlds (cf. Hutchings (2002)). When Mohanty (2003) asks how feminist theorising and the teaching of women's studies could address antiglobalisation struggles, she takes a more political approach, arguing for the value of feminist solidarity that neither explores women's lives globally like 'tourists', nor uses the 'feminist as explorer' who moves outside national settings to become absorbed in women's lives far from home without recognising the importance of the political interconnections between the global and their own local/national positionings. The comparative feminist model, she argued, would focus on the 'effects of global restructuring on the "real" raced, classed, national, sexual bodies of women in the academy, streets, households, cyberspaces, neighborhoods, prisons and in social movements' (Mohanty, 2003: 60). The emphasis here is on mutuality and communality across borders, cultures and nations.

The education of the citizen in the name of democracy is now probably at the most controversial point in its history. Global transformations are creating the demand for *two contradictory types of learner citizen* – the individualised learner citizen and the global learner citizen. On the one hand, the educational system is addressing the process of globalisation through the transformation of knowledge and the learner's relationship to knowledge. The individualised learner citizen is promoted as the educational system's response to the post-national state, to the breaking of borders, territories, time and space. It is creating a new form of organic solidarity in which interdependences and alliances are the means of creating a new social order. On the other hand, global citizenship education encourages an engagement with the immoralities of the global world, highlighting social injustices and attempting to establish the moral parameters of universal human rights. This is a form of mechanical solidarity, the global glue which underlies individualising processes and global disruptions. One model of the global citizen encourages spiralling differences between men and women, and between socio-economic groups; another encourages global outrage at social inequalities. Whilst neo-liberalism, with its individualisation of citizens, creates greater social polarisations and difference, human rights call into play universal concepts of global citizenship.

Democratic education, we now know, involves at a far deeper level a challenge to the social conditions that have sustained women's and men's experiences of poverty, violence, harassment and economic exploitation. Feminism and gender theorists have not avoided the debate about what constitutes democracy in the global climate of the twenty-first century. The gender gaze ensures that the global will be seen in a different light.

Acknowledgements

The first version of this paper was presented at the 'Education in Conflicted Societies' conference at the Von Leer Jerusalem Institute and Centre for Jewish Education, Haifa University, Israel, in 2006. It was later presented in the Vice Chancellor's Public Lecture series, University of Delhi and in the Presidential Session for the Sociology of Education Research Committee in the XVI International Sociological Association World Congress in Durban, South Africa. The chapter also formed the basis of the talk 'Democracy, Gender and the Learner Citizen: The Challenges of the Twenty-First Century' I gave when receiving an honorary doctorate at the University of Uppsala, on 23 January 2007. I am grateful to Halleli Pinson and Hanan Alexander, Poonam Batra, Carlos Alberto Torres and Karin Hjalmeskog for these opportunities to develop my ideas.

References

Advisory Group on Citizenship (The Crick Report) (1998) *Education for Citizenship and the Teaching of Democracy in Schools. Final Report.* London: Qualifications and Curriculum Authority.
Banks, J.A. (1997) *Educating Citizens in a Multicultural Society.* New York: Teachers College Press.
Bauman, Z. (2000) *Globalisation: the human consequences.* Cambridge, Polity Press.
Bauman, Z. (2001) 'Whatever happened to compassion?' in T. Bentley and D. Stedman Jones (ed), *The Moral Universe.* London: Demos.
Beck, U. (2000) *What is Globalisation?* Cambridge, Polity Press.
Beck, U. and Beck-Gernsheim, E. (2002) *Individualisation: institutionalised individualism and its social and political consequences.* London: Sage.
Bernstein, B. (1977) *Class, Codes and Control, Vol 3*, 3rd ed. London: Routledge and Kegan Paul.
Bernstein, B. (2000) *Pedagogy, Symbolic Control and Identity: theory, research, critique Basil Bernstein*, rev. ed. London: Rowman and Littlefield.
Blackmore, J. (2000) 'Globalization: A useful concept for feminists rethinking theory and strategies in education', in N. Burbules and C. Torres (eds) *Globalization and Education: critical perspectives.* London: Routledge, pp. 133–56.
Breines, I., Connell, R. and Eide, I. (eds) (2000) *Male Roles, Masculinities and Violence: a culture of peace perspective.* Paris: UNESCO.
Bunch, C. (1997) 'The intolerable status quo: violence against women and girls', http://www.unicef.org/pon97/women1.htm (Accessed 09/06/05.)
Burbules, N. and Torres, C. (eds) (2000) *Globalization and Education: critical perspectives.* London: Routledge.
Carter, A. (2001) *The Politics of Global Citizenship.* London: Routledge.
Colclough, C. (2007) 'Global gender goals and the construction of equality: conceptual dilemmas and policy practice', in S. Fennell and M. Arnot (eds) *Gender Education and Equality in a Global Context: conceptual frameworks and policy perspectives.* London: Routledge.

Connell, R.W. (2002) 'Arms and the man: using the new reseach on masculinity to understand violence and provide peace in the contemporary world', in I. Breines, R. Connell and R. Eide (eds) (2000) *Male Roles, Masculinities and Violence: a culture of peace perspective.* Paris: UNESCO.

Connell, R.W. (2005) 'Change among the gatekeepers: men, masculinities and gender equality in the global arena', *Signs: Journal of Women in Culture and Society*, 30(3): 1801–25.

Connell, R. (2008) *Southern Theory: the global dynamics of knowledge in social science.* Cambridge, Polity Press.

Davies, L. (2004) *Education and Social Conflict.* London: RoutledgeFalmer.

Davies, L. (2007) 'Gender, education, extremism and security', Paper presented to UKFIET conference. September.

Davies, L., Harber, C. and Yamashita, H. (2005) 'Global Citizenship Education: the needs of teachers and learners', unpublished report. University of Birmingham,.

Demaine, J. (2005) 'Education and global citizenship', *The Journal of Diversity in Organisations, Communities and Nations*, 5(3): 103–9.

Durkheim, E. (1997 [1893]) *The Social Division of Labour.* New York: Free Press.

Edwards, R. and Usher, R. (2000) *Globalisation and Pedagogy: space, place and identity.* London: RoutledgeFalmer.

Ehrenreich, B. and Hochschild, A.R. (2005) 'Global woman', in M.B. Zinn et al. (eds) *Gender through the Prism of Difference.* New York: Oxford University Press.

European Union (2005) *Citizens and Governance in a Knowledge-based Society*, FP6 programme, 2004–6.

Fennell, S. and Arnot, M. (eds) (2007a) *Gender Education and Equality in a Global Context.* London: Routledge.

Fennell, S. and Arnot, M. (2009 in press) 'Decentring hegemonic gender theory: the implications for educational research', *Compare*, 2008, special issue on *Gender, Education, Community and Nation*, vol 39, 1.

Galtung, J. (2004) 'Imagining global democracy' *Development and Change*, 35(5): 1073–9.

Giddens, A. (1992) *The Transformation of Intimacy: sexuality, love and eroticism in modern societies.* Cambridge: Polity Press.

Gilligan, C. (1982) *In a Different Voice: psychological theory and women's development.* Cambridge, MA: Harvard University Press.

Global Citizenship Project (2003) 'Global Citizenship: The newsletter of the Global Citizenship Project,' Winter. Global Citizenship Project, Faculty of Education, University of Glasgow. Available on http://www.global-citizenship.org

Griffiths, R. (1998) *Education Citizenship and Independent Learning.* London: Jessica Kingsley.

Harcourt, W. (2006) *The Global Rights Movement: power politics around the United Nations and the World Social Forum*, Civil Society and Social Movements Programme Paper 23. UN Research Institute for Social Development.

Heald, S. (2004) 'Feminism and teaching about globalization: contradictions and insights', *Globalisation, Societies and Education*, 2(1): 117–25.

Heater, D. (1990) *Citizenship: a civic ideal in world history, politics and education.* London: Longman.

Heater, D. (2004) *A History of Education for Citizenship.* London: RoutledgeFalmer.

Henry, M. (2001) 'Globalisation and the politics of accountability: issues and dilemmas for gender equity in education', *Gender and Education*, 13(1): 87–100.

Hutchings, K. (2002) 'Feminism and global citizenship', in N. Dower and J. Williams (eds) *Global Challenges: a critical reader.* Edinburgh: Edinburgh University Press.

Jaggar, A (2005) 'Arenas of Citizenship: civil society, state and the global order', *International Feminist Journal of Politics*, 7(1): 3–25, March.

Jelin, E. (2000) 'Towards a global environmental citizenship?' *Citizenship Studies*, 4(1): 47–63.

Kenway, J. and Fitzclarence, L. (2006) 'Masculinity, violence and schooling: challenging "poisonous pedagogies"', in M. Arnot and M. Mac an Ghaill (eds) *The RoutledgeFalmer Gender and Education Reader*. Abingdon: RoutledgeFalmer.

Lagree, J-C. (ed) (2002) *Rolling Youth, Rocking Society: youth take part in the post-modern debate on globalization*. Paris, UNESCO.

Lauder, H., Brown, P., Dillabough, J-A., Halsey, A.H. (eds) (2006) *Education, Globalisation and Social Change*. Oxford: Oxford University Press.

Leach, F. (2000) 'Gender Implications of Development Agency Policies on Education and Training', *International Journal of Educational Development*, 20: 333–47.

Liguori, A. and Lamas, M. (2003) 'Gender, sexual citizenship and HIV/AIDS', *Culture, Health and Sexuality*, 5(1): 87–90.

Lynch, J. (1992) *Education for Citizenship in a Multi-cultural Society*. London: Cassell.

Lynch, K., Lyons, K. and Cantillon, S. (2007a) 'Breaking the silence: educating for love, care and solidarity', Paper presented to the International Sociology of Education Conference. London, 3–5 January.

Lynch, K., Lynos, H and Cantillan, S. (2007b) Breaking Silence: educating citizens for love, care and solidarity, *International Studies in Sociology of Education*, 17, 1/2: 1–19.

Marshall, H. and Arnot, M. (2007a) 'Globalising the school curriculum: gender, EFA and global citizenship education', in Fennell, S. and Arnot, M. (eds) *Gender Education and Equality in a Global Context: conceptual frameworks and policy perspectives*. London: Routledge.

Marshall, H. and Arnot, M. (2007b) 'The gender agenda: the limits and possibilities of global and national citizenship education', *World Studies in Education*, 7(2): 81–106.

Massey, D. (2000) 'The geography of power', *Red Pepper*, July.

McIntosh, P. (2005) 'Gender perspectives on educating for global citizenship', in N. Noddings (ed.) *Educating Citizens for Global Awareness*. New York: Teachers College Press.

Mohanty, C.T. (1988) 'Under Western Eyes: feminist scholarship and colonial discourses', *Feminist Review*, 30, Autumn: 61–88.

Mohanty, C.T. (2003) 'Antiglobalisation pedagogies and feminism', in M.B. Zinn, P. Hondagneu-Sotelo and M.A. Messner (eds) (2005) *Gender through the Prism of Difference*. New York: Oxford University Press.

Moore, L.J. and Clarke, A.E. (2001) 'The Traffic in cyberanatomies: sex/gender/sexualities in local and global formations', *Body and Society*, 7(1): 57–96.

Noddings, N. (1998) 'An ethic of caring and its implications for instructional arrangements', *American Journal of Education*, 96(2): 215–30.

Noddings, N. (2005) 'Global citizenship: promises and problems', in N. Noddings (ed.) *Educating Citizens for Global Awareness*: New York: Teachers College Press.

Nussbaum, M. (2002) 'Education for Citizenship in an Era of Global Connection', *Studies in Philosophy and Education*, 21: 289–303.

Nussbaum, M. and Glover, J. (1995) 'Emotions and women's capabilities', in *Women, Culture and Development: a study of human capabilities*. Oxford: Oxford University Press.

Oxfam (1997; 2000) *A Curriculum for Global Citizenship*. Oxford: Oxfam.

Pateman, C. (1989) *The Disorder of Women*. Cambridge: Polity Press.

Peterson, V. Spike (2000) 'Sexing political identities/nationalism as heterosexism', in S. Ranchod-Nilsson and M.A. Tetreault (eds) *Women, States and Nationalism*. London: Routledge.

Pettman, J.J. (1999) 'Globalisation and the gendered politics of citizenship', in N. Yuval-Davis and P. Werbner (eds) *Women, Citizenship and Difference*. London, Zed Books.

Plummer, K. (2003) *Intimate Citizenship*. Montreal: McGill and Queen's University Press.

Pyle, J.L. and Ward, K.B. (2003) 'Recasting our understanding of gender and work during global restructuring', *International Sociology*, 18(3), September: 461–89.

Reay, D. and Mirza, H. (2000) in M. Arnot and J. Dillabough (eds) *Challenging Democracy: international perspectives on gender, education and citizenship*. London: RoutledgeFalmer.
Richardson, D. (1998) 'Sexuality and Citizenship', *Sociology*, 32(1): 83–100.
Richardson, D. (2000) *Rethinking Sexuality*. London, Sage.
Richardson, E.H. and Turner, B.S. (2001) 'Sexual, intimate or reproductive citizenship?' Review article, *Citizenship Studies*, 5(3): 329–38.
Rizvi, F. (2000) 'International education and the production of the global imagination', in N. Burbules and C.A. Torres (eds) *Globalisation and Education: critical perspectives*. London: Routledge.
Roberts, K. (1996) 'Individualisation and risk in Eastern and Western Europe', in H. Helve and J. Bynner (eds) *Youth and Life Management Research Perspectives*. Helsinki: Helsinki University Press.
Roland Martin, J. (1994 [1982]) 'Excluding women from the educational realm', in L. Stone (ed.) *The Education Feminism Reader*. New York: Routledge, pp. 105–21.
Rose, N. (1990) *Governing the Soul: the shaping of the private self*. London: Routledge.
Ruddick, S. (1990) *Maternal Thinking: towards a politics of peace*. London: Women's Press.
Schweisfurth, M., Davies, L. and Harber, C. (eds) (2002) *Learning Democracy and Citizenship: international perspectives*. Oxford: Symposium Books.
Sen, A. (1999) *Development as Freedom*. Oxford: Oxford University Press.
Sen, G. (2006) 'The quest for gender equality', in P. Utting (ed.) *Reclaiming Development agendas: knowledge, power and international policy-making*. Basingstoke: Palgrave MacMillan.
Stromquist, N.P. (2004) 'Teacher Intersection of Public Politics and Gender: Understanding State Action in Education', Conference paper presented at the Gender and Policy workshop, CIES annual meeting, Salt Lake City, 11 March.
Stromquist, N.P. (2005) 'A social cartography of gender education: reflections on an uncertain emancipatory project', Eggerton Lecture, Comparative and International Education Society, Stanford University.
Stromquist, N.P. (2008) 'Adult learning and the politic of change: feminist organization and educational action in Latin America', in Fennell, S. and Arnot, M. (eds) *Gender Equality and Education in a Global context*. London: Routledge.
Stromquist, N.P. and Monkman, K. (eds) (2000). *Globalization and Education: integration and contestation across cultures*. Langman, MD: Rowman and Littlefield.
Sunnari, V., Kangasvuo, J. and Heikkinen, M. (eds) (2000) *Gendered and Sexualised Violence in Educational Environments*. Oulu, Sweden: Oulu University Press.
Sweetman, C. (ed.) (2004) *Gender, Development and Citizenship*. Oxford: Oxfam.
Torres, C.A. (1998) *Democracy, Education and Multiculturalism: dilemmas of citizenship in a global world*. Maryland: Rowman and Littlefield.
UNESCO (2003) *Gender and Education for All: the leap to equality*, EFA Global Monitoring Report 2003/4. Paris: UNESCO.
Unterhalter, E. (2000) 'Transnational visions of the 1990s: Contrasting views of women, education and citizenship', in M. Arnot and J. Dillabough (eds) *Challenging Democracy: international perspectives on gender, education and citizenship*. London: RoutledgeFalmer, pp. 87–103.
Unterhalter, E. (2007) *Gender, Schooling and Global Social Justice*. London: Routledge.
Unterhalter, E. (2008) 'Global values and gender equality in education: needs, rights and capabilities'. in Fennell, S. and Arnot, M. (eds) *Gender Equality and Education in a Global Context*. London: Routledge.
Urry, J. (1999) 'Globalisation and citizenship', *Journal of World Systems Research*, V(2), Summer: 311–24.
Vargas, V. (2003) 'Feminism, globalization and the global justice and solidarity movement', *Cultural Studies*, 1(6): 905–20.

Walby, S. (2000) 'Gender, nations and states in a global era', *Nations and Nationalism*, 6(4): 523–40.
Walby, S. (2005) 'Introduction: comparative gender mainstreaming in a global era', *International Feminist Journal of Politics*, 7(4): 453–70.
Weeks, J. (1998) 'The sexual citizen', *Theory, Culture and Society*, 15(304): 35–52.
Woolf, V. (1938) *Three Guineas*. San Diego, CA: Harcourt Brace.
World Conference on Women (WCW) (1995) 'Beijing Declaration', *Women's Studies Quarterly*, 24(1 and 2): 154–8.
Wright, S. (2001) *International Human Rights, Decolonisation and Globalisation: becoming human*. London: Routledge.
Young, I.M. (2003) 'Feminist reactions to the contemporary security regime', *Hypatia*, 18(1): 223–31.
Yuval-Davis, N. (1997) *Women and Nation*. London: Sage.
Yuval-Davis, N. and Stoetzler, M (2002) 'Imagined boundaries and borders: a gendered gaze', *The European Journal of Women's Studies*, 9(3): 329–44.
Yuval-Davis, N. and Werbner, P. (eds) (1999) *Women, Citizenship and Difference*. London: Zed Books.

Notes

1 Roberts (1996), quoted in Lagree (2002: 26).
2 See Marshall and Arnot (2007a) for a full discussion of the EFA initiative and MDGs and their implications for the school curriculum. For more discussion of the measures, see Colclough (2007).
3 Free Gay Realtor Directory www.glbtq.com (Accessed 02/02/08.)
4 For more discussion of this issue, see Richardson (1998, 2000).
5 As a result, lesbian and gay youth are likely to be negatively affected and young people in schools have little chance of considering the ways in which lesbians and gay men are often excluded from civil, political and social rights, left unprotected from discrimination and harassment on grounds of sexuality by the law and the police, and experience prejudicial treatment in relation to social rights of welfare (see Chapter 8).
6 This resonates with the discussion of good citizenship in Chapter 3.
7 During the 1993 World Conference on Human Rights.
8 This text was funded by the European Commission, the Nordic Council of Ministry and the Academy of Finland, and was supported by the Women's Studies Department at Umea University in Sweden.
9 See also Schweisfurth *et al.* (2002) for a discussion of gender and global governance.

Index

Acker, J. 183–4
Actionaid 182, 186
Advisory Group on Citizenship report see Crick Report (1998)
affective domain 18, 157, 174–5, 237
    and gender equality 157
affirmative pedagogic approaches (Fraser) 142–5
    and education for boys 145–7
Ameli, S. Reza and Merali, A. 153–4
Archaud, D. 152
Archer, L. 214
Arendt, H. 172
Arnot, M. and Gubb, J. 147–8
Arnot, M. and Mac an Ghaill, M. 213
Arnot, M. and Reay, D. 205, 209–11
Arnot, M. *et al.* 96, 98–9, 102, 106, 115–16, 139, 142–4, 147, 155, 157–8, 168, 188, 201, 212
Association for Education for Citizenship (AEC) 117
autonomy 23, 31, 37, 39, 46, 65–6, 235
    attitudes towards 101, 103, 105
    threats to 177
    through globalisation 187

Baker, J. 155
Baker, J. *et al.* 157–8, 176
Baldwin, Stanley 117
Banks, J.A. 230
Bauman, Z. 201, 214, 217–19, 226
BCA *see* Bureau of Current Affairs (BCA)
beauty and female influence 103
Beck, J. 197
Beck, U. 212–13, 215–16, 223, 225–6
Beck, U. and Beck-Gernsheim, E. 20–1, 199–201, 212–13, 215
Beijing World Conference on Women (1995) 183, 185, 233

Benhabib, S. 139–40, 151, 177
Benton, S. 92, 108
Bernstein, B. 17, 42, 51, 154, 158–9, 161, 201, 205–7, 209–11, 218
'bimbo' effect 15, 101
'bivalent collectivities' (Fraser) 141
black feminism 11, 42–4, 143, 149, 151, 155
Blackmore, J. 47, 183–4, 224, 231
Blair, M. *et al.* 205
Blair, Tony 202
Borer, M.C. 122, 123–4
Bourdieu, P. and Passeron, J.–C. 43, 71, 160
Bowley, R. 122, 130–1
'boy turn' 145–8
boys 109, 123–4, 125, 127, 140
    ethnicity and education 150
    teacher expectations 146–7, 154–5
    see also masculinity
boys' education 123–4, 125, 127
    affirmative and redemptive strategies 145–8
    cf. girls academic achievements 143
    critiques 154–5
Breines, I. *et al.* 186, 239–40
Brennan, T. 117
Brimble, L.F. and May, F.J. 119, 122
Bryant, Arthur 117
Brysk, A. 6, 22
bullying 155
Bulmer, M. and Rees, A.M. 23
Bunch, C. 167, 186, 238–9
Bureau of Current Affairs (BCA 1947–9) 119, 121, 122, 125, 129–32
Butler, J. 42

'can do' girls 212
caring discourses, and citizenship 78–81

Carter, A. 244
'categoricalism' (Connell) 142
Challenging Democracy (Arnot and Dillabough) 4, 15–16
child custody issues 107
Children's Commissioner 205
children's rights 205
The Chinese Box (Palmer) 122, 125–7
Citizens Growing Up (Ministry of Education) 124–5
Citizenship: It's Rights and Responsibilities (Borer) 122, 123–4
citizenship
   key debates 5–9
   equality and difference discourses 139–61, 168–9
   gendered discourses 13–14, 223–47
      male and female characteristics (Lister) 140
      moral and rights-based education 226–9
   liberal feminist critiques 39
   moral discourses 78–84
      and the caring citizen 78–81
      'goodness' and social class 82–3
   political discourses 73–8
      and the critical citizen 74–6
      and the sceptical citizen 76–8
   relevancy concerns 66–7
   spatial dimensions 70
   studies from student teacher discourses 63–92, 95–110
      key discursive frameworks 73–88
      ascribed and achieved notions 71
      as inclusive/exclusive 70–1
      spatial dimensions 70
      and the state 71–3
      transformative role of women 90–2
citizenship education 17–20, 51–2
   attitudes to gender discourses 19, 168–9, 178–81, 184–7
   development of an ethical pedagogy 244–7
   feminist studies 9–10
      levels of analysis 51–2
   global strategies 167–9, 178–87
      in England 181–4
      gender-sensitive approaches 184–7
   historical overview 4–7, 117–21
      concurrent social welfare education 119–21
      and the gendering of texts 121–32
   impact of new global democracies 226–9
   individualisation processes 197–219
   introduction of *Curriculum Guidance 8* (NCC 1990) 17–18

key political doctrines 65
key sociological debates 5–9
key themes
   diversity recognition 229–32
   gendered violence, conflict and peace education 238–42
   poverty reduction and sustainable development 232–4
   reproductive and sexual citizenship 234–8
   women's global agency and activism 242–4
      as a modern male narrative 64–9
      rationality and social justice 64–7
      unity and difference 67–9
      personal and private spheres 175–7
      UK national strategies 167–89
      and gender-sensitive strategies 178–81
'citizenship gap' 6, 22
Citizenship Orders 18, 171–8
Citizenship and Social Class (Marshall) 6–7
civic communities 67
   see also public and private domains; public spheres
'civil republicanism' (Skinner) 172
Clarke, Charles 204
Closing the Gender Gap (Arnot *et al.*) 212
Cogan, J.J. and Derricott, R. 178
collective rights 20
collectivity and identity 67–8
colonialism 234
community construction, boundaries and exclusions 68
Connell, R.W. 14, 88, 100, 214, 233, 240–1, 243
Convention on the Elimination of all Forms of Discrimination against Women (CEDAW) 182
cosmopolitanism (Giddens) 156
Crewe, I. 115
Crick Report (1998) 18, 152–3, 169–71, 245
   and Citizenship Orders 171–8

Crick, Bernard 18, 117, 152–3, 169–71, 245
'critical literacy' (Davies) 156
critical pedagogy
    and the democratic school 46–7
    making alliances 47–8
Cruddas, L. and Haddock, L. 157
Culley, M. and Portuges, C. 143–4
cultural diversity
    and global citizenship education 229–32
    see also multiculturalism
Current Affairs (BCA 1947–9) 119, 121, 122, 125, 129–32, 133–4
Curriculum Guidance 8 (NCC 1990) 17–18
curriculum in schools
    gender essentialisms and sexism 38–9
    and hegemonic masculinity 43
    historical perspectives 118–19
    national education of the citizen 51–2
    see also citizenship education

Davies, B. 144, 156
Davies, L. 240–1, 243, 246
Davies, L. *et al.* 228
'degender' goals 37
Demaine, J. 20, 228
democracy 4, 200, 215, 226, 230–2
    and citizenship education 244–7
    and feminist politics 29–54
    and difference 42–4
    and globalisation 5–9
Democracy in the Kitchen (Walkerdine and Lucey) 45–6
Democratic Learning (MacBeath and Moos) 198
democratic pedagogic rights (Bernstein) 17, 138, 146, 158–9, 161
'democratisation of democracy' (Beck) 200, 215
Demos working group 203
Dench, G. 98
Development Education Association (DEA) 181
Dietz, M.G. 40, 92
difference
    and citizenship 67–9
    and democracy 42–4
    and equality, civic and pedagogic ideals 139–42
    policy revisions and critiques 150–60
disenfranchisement from political life 99
The Disorder of Women (Pateman) 30–1

diversity and global citizenship education 229–32
    see also multiculturalism
domestic labour, equality discourses 43
Donald, J. 12, 189
Dual Citizenship: British, Islamic or Both? (Ameli and Merali) 153
Durkheim, E. 226
Dwivedi, K.N. 159

economic domains, women's influence 98–9
education
    balancing 'equality of opportunity' and cultural 'difference' 141–2
    critical pedagogy critiques 46–7
    democratization processes 225–44
    and feminism
        and the 'fraternal pact' (Pateman) 10–12
        liberal feminist critiques 38
    gender differences
        affirmative and transformative strategies 142–50
    individualisation processes 197–219
        emergence of the student 'voice' 202–5, 207–11
        personalisation and independent learning 202–5
        potential threats 215–19
        and social inequalities 205–11
    official curriculum
        gender essentialisms and sexism 38–9
        and hegemonic masculinity 43
        historical perspectives 117–19
    pedagogic democratic rights 158–9
    performance-led cultures 205, 206
    technological transitions 65–6
    transformative pedagogic approaches 142–61
        cf. affirmative strategies 160–1
    universal and compulsory 24
    and women-centred practice 41
    see also citizenship education
Education Act-1944 118
Education and Social Conflict (Davies) 241
The Education of Women for Citizenship (Tait) 119, 122, 125, 127–9
Edwards, R. and Usher, R. 215
egalitarian discourses 14, 18–19, 84–8
    affirmative and transformative approaches 142–5

as civic and pedagogic ideal 139–42
the protesting citizen 83–8
Ehrenreich, B. and Hochschild, A. 232
Ellis, C. 92
Ellsworth, E. 156
Elshtain, J.B. 40, 96
Enlightenment 66
Equal Opportunities Unit (EC) 63, 92, 110, 170
ethnicity, and gender 149–50
European agendas on citizenship and gender 4–5, 8, 11, 13–14, 22, 63, 66, 95, 168, 179–80, 230
   see also 'Fortress Europe'
EU funding initiatives 13, 63, 92, 110, 230
European Commission 63, 92, 110
Exit, Voice and Loyalty (Hirschman) 202

family life
   changing gender roles 95, 102–7
   sexual division of labour 95, 97, 102–7
   and violence 239
The Family's Food (Mead) 132
female autonomy 23, 31, 37, 39, 46, 65–6, 235
   attitudes towards 101, 103, 105, 207
   threats to 177, 186
   through globalisation processes 187
female cultures 177–8
female learning 146–7, 207–11
   individualised citizens 212–15
female politicians 100–1
female sexuality 15, 46, 47–8, 101
   attitudes towards 100–2
   and power 100, 108
   regulation and control 39, 51, 105
female teachers 12, 27, 46, 80, 84–6, 108, 193
femininity
   changing concepts 95–110
   women in public life 100–1, 116
   and power 174
   qualities and characteristics 46, 140, 209, 214
      and ethnic difference 148–52
Feminisms and Critical Pedagogy (Luke and Gore) 47
feminist political theory 10–12, 30–6
   the gendering of nationhood and nation-states 32–4
   levels of analysis 48–53
      by civic spheres 49–51
      by education and the national narrative 51–2
      by political identities, differences and subjectivities 52–3
   order and disorder 30–2
   'women as a political category' 34–6
feminist studies
   and citizenship education 9–10
      key problems 10
   development fragmentation concerns 49
   equality vs. complementarity principles 35
   gender analysis and democracy in education 36–48
   new post-structural discourse 44–6
   political theory and gender 10–12, 30–6
      levels of analysis 48–53
Fennell, S. and Arnot, M. 238, 242–3
fertility issues 236
   see also 'reproductive citizenship'
Fielding, M. 203, 205, 211, 219
'Fortress Europe' 68
Foucalt, M. 12, 45, 50
Francis, B. 156–7
Fraser, N. 138, 140–2, 148, 150, 154, 159–61, 176
Fraser, N. and Nicholson, L. 49
'fraternal pact' (Pateman) 10–12, 31, 68
freedom discourses 66
Freedom's Children (Beck and Beck-Gernsheim) 20–1, 199–201
funding for gender and citizenship education studies 13, 63, 92, 110, 187

Galtung, J. 227
Garmarnikow, E. and Green, A. 170
gay and lesbian groups 176
gender analysis and democracy
   critical pedagogy and the democratic school 46–7
   democracy and difference 42–4
   feminist theory and liberal democratic education 37–9
   making alliances 47–8
   'new' feminism and the deconstruction of democracy 44
   poststructural feminism 44–6
   women, materialism and democratic education 3s7–42
gender 'cathexis' (Connell) 100–1
gender and citizenship 12–15
   feminist political theory 10–12

historical perspectives 16–17, 115–34
    background and overview 117–19
    citizenship education and social welfare education 119–21
    the gendering of educational texts 121–32
    key discourses 13–15
    language and gender change 12–15
    see also gender analysis and democracy
gender conflict 216–17
gender difference 39–40
gender education 3, 10–12, 63, 142–50
    curriculum reforms 38–9, 142–50
gender-equality 96, 138–61, 167–9
    limits and possibilities through education 167–89
    redistribution and recognition strategies 141–54
        critical pedagogy of difference 154–9
        Fraser's matrix 142–3
    see also feminist political theory; feminist studies
'gender gaze' 3, 225, 247
gender identity formulation 33, 51, 208, 213–14
    role of gender difference constructs 157
gendered pedagogies
    overview 15–17, 46–8
    see also gender and citizenship
'genderquake' (Wilkinson) 98
gender relations 3, 9, 12, 16, 19, 20, 23, 27, 41–5, 48, 50–2, 63–4, 88, 92, 95–6, 102, 108, 116, 121, 154, 167–71, 175, 178, 182, 187–8, 201, 212–14, 230, 240–1, 245
Get Global projects 181–2
Giddens, A. 156, 235
Giddens, A. and Diamond, P. 205
Gilbert, R. 64–6
Gillborn, D. and Youdell, D. 159
Gilligan, C. 40
girl citizenship characteristics 140
girls-only schooling 142–3, 157
Giroux, H. 8–9, 15, 48, 65–6, 91–2
global citizenship education strategies 167–9, 178–87
    in England 181–4
    gender-sensitive approaches 1847
    key themes 229–44
        gendered violence, conflict and peace education 238–42

recognition of diversity 229–32
reproductive and sexual citizenships 234–8
sustainable development and poverty reduction 232–4
women's global agency and activism 242–4
Global Citizenship Project (2003) 232
global civil society 21–2
global conscience collective 226–29
    key themes 229–44
Global Education Network Europe (GENE) conference 184–5
'global gaze' 225
'global interconnectedness' (Massey) 228
global learner citizen 224–7, 244–6
globalisation
    and democratisation 5–9
    and human rights 6
    and individualisation 20–2
    multilayered conceptualisations 184
    and a new global order 20
    and the welfare state 20
The Good Citizen (Higham) 121–3
Gordon, T. *et al.* 16–17, 206–7
Gore, F. 144
Greece
    male dominance and matriarchy 102–4
    masculinity and citizenship 14–15
    student teacher studies
    on citizenship 63–92
    gender portrayals 99–102
    on the separation of the public and private life 98–102
Green, A. 117–18
Griffiths, R. 228
Grumet, M. 144

Habermas, J. 198
habitus (Bourdieu and Passeron) 71
Hakim, C. 95, 107–8
Hankin, G.T. 122, 132
Hanson, B. and Patrick, P. 177
Haywood, C. and Mac an Ghaill, M. 144–5
Heald, S. 232
Heater, D. 64–5, 117, 167–8, 172, 178–9, 183, 244
Henry, M. 184
Higham, C.S.S. 121–3
Hill Collins, P. 151
Hirschman, A.O. 202
historical perspectives of gendered citizenship 16–17, 115–34

background and overview 117–19
citizenship education and social welfare education 119–21
the gendering of educational texts 121–32
    critical engagement approaches 129–32
    exclusionary texts 121–5
    inclusionary texts 125–9
HIV/AIDS 237
Holdsworth, R. and Thomson, P. 207–8
hooks, b. 151
human rights
    and citizenship 6–7
    and the 'protesting citizen' 85–8, 228
    and citizenship education 227–9
    and global migration 6
    and globalisation 6

identity and citizenship 18–19
    women's position within the nation state 32–3
    see also gender identity formulation
'individual/society' vs. 'no individual/no society' discourses 66–7
individualisation processes 197–219
    and civic engagement 206–7, 212–15
    and globalisation 20–2, 198–201
    of the learner citizen 5, 20, 197–8, 201–11
    personalisation, independent learning and the pupil voice 202–5
    potential threats 215–19
        loss of social rights 215–16
        and *palimpsest* identity (Bauman) 217–19
        radicalisation of social differences 216
    and social inequalities 205–11, 216
    and youth citizenship 206–7, 212–15
individualised learner citizen 5, 20, 197–8, 201–11, 246
The Individualised Society (Bauman) 217–19
information society 66
institutional racism 18
Islamic Human Rights Commission 153–4
Ivinson, G. *et al.* 96, 99–102

Jack, M.V. 122, 123
Jaggar, A. 43, 242
Johnson, M. 202–3
Jorgensen, P. 207

Kenway, J. and Fitzclarence, L. 157, 239
Kenway, J. and Langmead, D. 187
King, A. 187

Lagree, J.-C. 226
Lasch, S. 199
'latch-key' children 124
Lather, P. 144
Layton, E. and White, B.J. 119, 122
Leach, F. 233
Leadbeater, C. 203–4
learner citizen
    democratisation processes 225–44
    individualisation processes 5, 20, 197–8, 201–11, 246
    student-centred learning 204–5
Lees, S. 175, 177
lesbian feminist critiques 44
Leverhulme Trust 116
liberal democracy 4, 9, 30, 37, 45–8, 51, 65, 96–7, 139, 193
    alternative political frameworks 40–1
    feminist critiques 4, 10–2, 20 29–32, 34
liberal feminism 10–12
    key assumptions 37
liberalism 6, 7–8, 29, 37, 117, 171–3, 178–9
life-long learning 8
Ligouri, A. and Lamas, M. 237
Lister, R. 140
Luke, C. and Gore, J. 47
Lynch, J. 230
Lynch, K. *et al.* 237–8
Lyotard, J.F. 66

Mac an Ghaill, M. 144–5, 152, 214
McCarthy, C. and Apple, M.W. 47–8
McCulloch, G. 117–18
MacInnes, J. 109
McLaughlin, T.H. 16–17, 72
McLeod, J. 214
male culture 155–7
    and sexual identity 177
    see also masculinity
male learning styles 156–7
male teachers 71–6, 79–83, 86–92, 94, 98–109, 111
    on 'duty' 193
    on female roles in society 15
    on male public role models 14
    recruitment 146
marriage
    and the educational curriculum 175–6
    and the sexual contract 97

Marshall, C. and Anderson, G.L. 68
Marshall, H. 168, 178–81, 224–5
Marshall, H. and Arnot, M. 234
Marshall, T.H. 6–7, 67, 84
Martin, R. 34
masculinity 14, 31, 43, 88, 107, 109, 116, 140, 146, 152, 155–7, 229, 239–41
    and the 'fraternal pact' (Pateman) 31
    and individualisation 214–15
    and the public sphere 98–102
    relationship with violence and conflict 239–40
    traditional qualities 241
masculinity workshops 157
Massey, D. 228
maternal feminist analysis 40–2, 50
matriarchy, challenges, Greece 102–4
'maximal models of citizenship' (McLaughlin) 16
Mead, M. 122, 132
Miles, P. 214–15
Miliband, David 202–3
Millenium Developmsent Goals 179, 182, 228
Mirza, H. 151
Mirza, H. and Reay, D. 43
Moberg, E. 239
Mohanty, C.T. 151, 243, 246
Moore, L.J. and Clarke, A.E. 236
Moos, L. 196
moral discourses 14, 78–84, 89
    and the caring citizen 78–81
    'goodness' and social class 82–3
    'mother as reformer' 83–4
Moral Instruction League (MIL) 117
morrow, R. and Torres, C. 178
'mother as reformer' 83–4
motherhood and citizenship 68
    feminist analysis 40–2, 50
'mothers or Madonnas' 15, 108
Mouffe, C. 12, 53
multicultural feminism 151
multiculturalism
    and gender 149–50
    'rethinking' difference 150–60
Murray, J.O. 122, 123

national citizenship education strategies 167–89
    background 167–9
    England and Wales 169–78
nationhood and nation states
    gendering practices 32–4, 51–2
    and citizenship 18, 65
    see also the state and citizenship

neo-conservatism 8
neoliberalism 8, 21, 51, 53, 154, 170, 198, 238, 246
    defining characteristics 198
New Labour, personalised learning and 'choice with voice' 202–5
NGO documents 180
Nicholson, F.J. and Wright, V.K. 119
Noddings, N. 40–1, 175, 227
non-synchronous model of schooling (McCarthy) 47–8
Nussbaum, M.C. 139, 152, 174–5, 179, 188, 227
Nussbaum, M.C. and Glover, J. 174, 234, 236

Okin, S. Moller 152
opportunity discourses, and liberal feminism 37–8
Osler, A. and Starkey, H. 18
Oxfam 179–80, 228, 242

palimpsest identity (Bauman) 217–19
Palmer, G.D.M. 122, 125–7
Parekh Report (Runnymede Trust 2000) 153, 177
Pateman, C. 10, 11, 30–1, 38, 68, 95–8, 107–9, 139, 173, 234
patriarchy 95, 97, 105
    relationship with violence and conflict 239–40
peace education 238–42
pedagogic democratic rights (Bernstein) 17, 138, 146, 158–9, 161
Petersen, V. 237
Peters, M. *et al.* 198
Pettman, J.J. 231
Phillips, A. 29, 32, 40, 90, 139, 152
Pieterse, J.N. and Parekh, B. 32–3
Plummer, K. 235
political discourses on citizenship 73–8, 173–4
    and the critical citizen 74–6
    and the sceptical citizen 76–8
'political neutrality' 37
political power
    and gender 14, 31–2, 90–2, 99–102, 116
    discourses on motherhood 40–2
    equality strategies 37
    key requirements 188
    perceptions of female politicians 100–1
Politics Association 117

Portugal 15
    family life and sexual freedom 104–6
    student teacher studies
        on citizenship 63–92
        gender portrayals 99–102
        on the separation of the public and private life 98–102
post-Enlightenment feminism 12
Post-modernism, Feminism and Cultural Politics (Giroux) 48
post-structural feminism 44–6
    critical pedagogy and the democratic school 46–7
    and the non-synchronous model of schooling 47–8
poverty reduction initiatives, education strategies 232–4
privacy, social constructs 68
private domains
    changing gender roles and egalitarianism 95, 102–7
    and citizenship education 175–7
    women's sexual and reproductive 'power' 102–3, 107, 108–9
    see also family life
Promoting Quality Awareness: women as citizens (Arnot *et al.*) 63–92
    aims and outline 63–4
Public Man, Private Women (Elshtain) 96
public and private domains 15, 67–9
    gender differences
        separation of the public sphere 98–102
        and the 'sexual contract' 96–8
        stereotypical characteristics 140
public spheres
    and gender separation 98–102
        historical perspectives 121–3, 128–9
    and patriarchy 97–8

Qualification and Curriculum Authority (QCA) 169–78

racial equality, as civic and pedagogic ideal 139–42
racism 18
    gendered education discourses 43–4
Reay, D. and Mirza, H. 242
redistribution and recognition strategies (Fraser), described 141–2
relational ethics 40–1
'reproductive citizenship', education strategies 234–8

reproductive 'power' 107
Rewriting the Sexual Contract (Dench) 98
Reynolds, M. and Trehan, K. 156
Richardson, D. 176
Richardson, E.H. and Turner, B. 235–6
rights *see* human rights; women's rights
Rizvi, F. 234
Roland Martin, J. 242
Rolling Youth, Rocking Society (UNESCO/Lagre) 226
Rose, N. 23–4
Rowan, L. *et al.* 201
Ruddick, S. 246
Runnymede Trust 153

Salisbury, J. and Jackson, D. 157
Scheunpflug, A. 184–5
The School Looks Around (Layton and Wright) 119, 122
school syllabuses *see* curriculum in schools
schooling *see* education
'self-culture' 199–200
Sen, A. 212, 234
Sewell, T. 214
'sexual citizenship', education strategies 234–8
'sexual contract' theory (Pateman) 10, 14–15, 30–1, 96–8
    challenges 102–7
    separation of the public sphere 98–102
sexual exploitation 186
sexuality 101, 234–8
Siim, B. 14
Silva, E. 208
Simon, B. 117
single-sex education 142–3
Skelton, C. 214
Skinner, Q. 171–2
social class
    and educational opportunity 155, 157–8
    impact of school-based individualisation processes 205–11
    and notions of citizenship 82–3
    as taught subject 157
social contract 6
social order 31, 44
Social Studies for Future Citizens (Nicholson and Wright) 119, 122
Social Studies and World Citizenship (Brimble and May) 119, 122

Index

social welfare education, historical perspectives 119–21
Southern Theory 225, 243
Spain, student teacher studies on citizenship 63–92
Starkey, H. *et al.* 19–20
  the state and citizenship 71–3
  see also citizenship; nationhood and nation states
State and People. A Handbook of Citizenship for Young People (Murray) 122, 123
Stromquist, N. 243
Stromquist, N. and Monkman, K. 182–3
student-centred learning 204–5
Sultana, R.G. 68
Sunnari, V. *et al.* 186, 239
sustainable development initiatives, education strategies 232–4
Sweetman, C. 242

Tait, M. 119, 122, 125, 127–9
Talbot, M. 245
Tamboukou, M. and Ball, S. 214
teacher training 51–2
  levels of gender literacy 63
  understanding of citizenship and gender discourses 63–92, 95–110
teachers
  on construction of citizenship and changing concepts 63–91, 95–111
  on gender violence 238
technological educational perspectives 65–6
terrorism fears 241
Thane, P. 120
Thatcher, Margaret 15, 66, 90, 100
'third space' (Mirza and Reay) 43
transformative pedagogic approaches 142–61
  cf. affirmative strategies 160–1
'the ugly citizen' (Beck) 21, 215
UN Declaration of the Rights of the Child (1989) 205
UN Development Fund for Women (UNIFEM) 187, 242
UN Millenium Development Goals 179, 182, 228
UNESCO 182, 185, 226, 232–3
United Kingdom
  student teacher studies, on negotiating equality in family life 106–7
  student teacher studies on citizenship 63–92

United States, state education system 65
Unterhalter, E. 185–6, 233
Urry, J. 229

Vargas, V. 228, 245
violence and gender, education strategies 157, 186–7, 238–42

Walby, S. 91, 95, 229
Walkerdine, V. 144, 213–14
Walkerdine, V. and Lucey, H. 45–6
Weeks, J. 235
Weiler, K. 54
welfare state, threats from globalisation 20
Wexler, P. 64–7
Whitmarsh, G. 117
Whitty, G. and Wisby, E. 203, 211
Whitty, G. *et al.* 18
Wilkinson, H. 98, 212
Williams, G. 122, 132
Williams, W.E. 122, 129–30
Wilson, E. 35
'Wollstonecraft's dilemma' 68
women-centred democratic practice 41
women's activism, education strategies 242–4
women's identity
  as a political category 34–6
  as transformative agents in political life 90–1
  within the nation state 32–3
women's movements 231
  globalisation trends 183
Women's Place (Williams) 122, 129–30
women's rights 18, 177, 184–7, 227–8, 242–4
Wong, J. 117
Woolf, V. 223
World Bank initiatives 185
Wright, C. 151
Wright, S. 234

The Young Citizen (Jack) 122, 123
young women, and pregnancy 154
Young, I.M. 34–5, 151, 156, 159–60, 241
Younger, M. 147
Younger, M. and Warrington, M. 147
Yuval-Davis, N. 32–3, 67–8, 183
Yuval-Davis, N. and Stoetzler, M. 225, 240, 242–3
Yuval-Davis, N. and Werbner, P. 243

Zinn, M.B. and Dill, B. 150–1